SCHICK

ON FIL

SCHICKEL
ON FILM

Encounters—Critical and Personal—with Movie Immortals

RICHARD SCHICKEL

WILLIAM MORROW AND COMPANY, INC. *NEW YORK*

Library of Congress Catalog Card Number: 88-64105

ISBN: 0-688-05001-8

Printed in the United States of America

First Edition

1 2 3 4 5 6 7 8 9 10

BOOK DESIGN BY JAYE ZIMET

ACKNOWLEDGMENTS

*T*he essays on John Ford, Preston Sturges, Humphrey Bogart, and Ronald Reagan appeared originally, in slightly different form, in *Film Comment,* and the piece on the Hollywood Ten was published there in a much shorter version. I appreciate the hospitality of its editors, Richard Corliss and Harlan Jacobson— and the tact and care with which they conduct their business, which is publication of the only American film magazine that intelligently addresses the interests of the common reader who cares about this subject. The piece on Charles Chaplin originally appeared, in a much shorter form, in *The New York Times Magazine,* as did a portion of the Hitchcock piece. Some of the new Chaplin material is drawn from reviews of his work that I did for *Time,* and I have recast the Hitchcock material very extensively, conflating it with some material I used in a piece I wrote about him for the now defunct *On Cable* magazine. The piece on Douglas Fairbanks appeared originally in *American Heritage,* became the basis for my little book, *His Picture in the Papers,* and appears here in its more or less original form, but with some additional material borrowed from that book. The essays on James Cagney and Harold Lloyd are taken from the introductory chapters of my books on those two actors; the essay on Gary Cooper introduced a collection of photographs of him that appeared in the regrettably short-lived *Legends* series, which was published by my best editorial friend, Colin Webb, of Pavilion Books in London. (The Bogart article, incidentally, was originally intended for that series as well.) The Stanley Kubrick article appeared first in *Omni's Screen Flights/Screen Fantasies,* edited by Danny Peary and published by Doubleday & Co. The piece on Woody Allen contains a few quotations and ideas originally expressed in an

ACKNOWLEDGMENTS

article I did for the London *Sunday Times Magazine,* but as it appears here it is essentially a new work, though I thank my friend George Perry for the assignment that inspired this much longer effort to come to grips with its subject. The Marlon Brando essay had the most checkered career of any of the work contained herein. It began many years ago as an unpublished article, saw partial light as a contribution to a part work called *The Movie,* published by Orbis Publishing Ltd. in London, was recast again as a section of my book *Intimate Strangers,* and has been revised and expanded yet again for this publication. I thank all the copyright holders for permission to reprint material.

—R.S.

CONTENTS

INTRODUCTION
MOVIES AND THE COMMON READER

*H*owever they may strike the reader, the essays gathered in this book represent for me some of the most pleasurable passages in my life as a writer. There are both personal and general reasons for that assertion.

The former are quite easy to state. Almost every week for over two decades I have written a review of a new movie for a magazine (for *Life* at first; for *Time* since 1972). It is interesting work, but it has its exactions. The largest of these is that your subject is imposed upon you: This movie is coming out now; it is news; something must be said about it. Sometimes you are writing about a picture about which you really have nothing much to say—certainly nothing very deeply felt. Sometimes—less often, alas—you are trying to compress a complex response to a complex work into a rigidly unyielding space. Always you are writing in haste, against a deadline. This is not entirely a bad thing; a clock is a powerful inspirational tool. And since my most profound impulse is to drift out of the present into the past or some other equally imaginary realm, I need something to keep me involved with contemporary reality, weird as the movies' refraction of that reality often is. But still, the need to write at length and at leisure about matters that suggest themselves in less coercive, more insinuating tones abides—nags, actually. And since the subjects that either propose themselves to me or are successfully proposed to me by editors are generally of a historical nature, these assignments offer me legitimizing excuses for absenting myself intellectually from contemporary life and escaping into the past, which is not always more congenial but is generally speaking more emotionally manageable for me.

There are, of course, other reasons for making these time trips. The most down-to-earth distinction between a reviewer and a critic that I know was drawn by Walter Kerr, who observed that the former writes for those who do not know the work under discussion, the latter for those who are familiar with it. It follows that it is liberating for the reviewer to try to be a critic for a day (or, in the case of these pieces, for a week or two—not counting the revisions). The critic's obligation to purely journalistic functions—the who, what, when, and where of plot summary, for example—is less, his obligation to historical perspective—fitting particular movies, or perhaps just a moment or two from them, into the overall pattern of a career or into the spirit of the time in which they were created—is larger than that of the reviewer. The critic is also freer to be less opinionated, or anyway less pointedly so. Indeed, the largest assertion of value in a critical essay may be an implicit one, the choice of its topic. One would scarcely reach backward in time to pluck from the infinite number of available subjects figures the writer regards as minor or contemptible or about whom his response is dim or inchoate. And though time may or may not lend enchantment to a body of work, looking back on it after the intervention of at least a few years, a writer finds a range of intellectual and emotional responses opening up to him that the contemplation of a single work at the moment of its appearance rarely stimulates.

I have enjoyed discovering these connections, which are often quite surprising. And I have enjoyed trying to make, to the best of my abilities, other kinds of connections. All the pieces I have included in this book are what I think of as critical profiles of men (and in one case a group of men) whose contribution to the history of American movies, and to our larger social history, seems to me indisputable, whatever their critical standing at this moment. Though I have known a few of them personally, in every case I have tried to respond analytically to their work, rather than journalistically to their personalities. This is not to say that I have attempted some variation on what used to be known as the "new" criticism. Especially in the case of actors, whose instruments are themselves, it is obvious that personal history powerfully influences public performance. But even so, my primary concern has been with working lives, not private lives, with creations, not re-creations. And with matters one so rarely has the opportunity to take up when reviewing discrete works at the moment of their initial appearance—namely, the interaction between personality, movie history, and social history.

Doubtless the opportunities these pieces presented to indulge myself in more speculative critical writing than I am usually able to practice was their largest lure. But it was not their only one. For the writer is also, of course, a common reader, whose favorite reading matter happens to be the essay. For reasons I find it impossible to explain fully or to justify completely, this form has always struck me as the most civilized and attractive kind of written discourse. Perhaps this is because its formal demands are less stringent than those of the poetic and fictional forms or of the long, scholarly forms like biography and historical narrative, so that one feels oneself to be more directly in touch with the author. Perhaps, too, the brevity and freedom of the form put the writer into a more relaxed frame of mind, so that he is freer to be himself—to be at once more tentative and more daring—than he can permit himself to be on grander occasions. In any event, the form that so easily seduces me as a reader was bound to seduce me as a writer.

Especially as a writer about movies. For I do not believe the other side of me, the common reader side, has so far been very well served by the literature of the movies.

To some degree the literary community is to blame for this situation. What was once an openly acknowledged prejudice against the movies as a medium hopelessly tainted by commercial calculation and distressing popularity has become an unacknowledged one. Magazines and book publishers simply do not as a rule apply the same standards to writing in this field that they apply to work in the more traditional fields, and the reviewing media are similarly casual, not to say condescending, in the application of rigorous standards to writing about the movies.

There is no logic in all this. The common reader is, commonly, a moviegoer. The same people I talk with about books I talk with about films. We share most of the same affections and disaffections on all sorts of subjects, from presidential politics to psychoanalysis. We constitute, I think, an audience in search of literate performance in every realm of experience, and as both the writer and the first reader of the pieces assembled here I have tried to keep our shared standards in mind. These essays assume, for example, that classic work in the movies has the same intrinsic interest and continuing relevance to the civilized man or woman that a great piece of writing does—and that when one refers to such a work, the reader will have some familiarity with it and interest in it. They also assume that the movies have existed long enough—almost a century now—to have forged a tradition (maybe even a great tradition) and that examining this or that aspect of it can be rewarding for its own sake as well as for what it may tell us, by inference and comparison, about the state of that tradition in a changing world. Finally, at a moment when the discussion of movies, such a promising topic just a couple of decades ago, when I first tentatively joined in it, has come to seem so debased, not only by the poor literary performances I have mentioned, but, at another level, by the television clown acts, I do immodestly hope to assert here the possibilities of addressing the subject in somewhat different tones.

All these essays had their beginnings elsewhere—mostly as magazine pieces or as introductory sections to books either by myself or by someone else. One of them was originally commissioned as a contribution to an anthology, and another, which began as a magazine piece, found its penultimate form as a section in the middle of another of my books before I recast it yet again for inclusion here. Yet another conflates two approaches to the same subject. All the pieces, however, have been very extensively revised, and most have been greatly expanded for this publication—so much so that at least half of them should be regarded as fresh work.

This is not because I am ashamed of the originals I reworked. I really did not intend to do so much with them when I started preparing them for this book. But the fact is that all these essays are about people whom, like anyone greatly interested in the movies, I have long since internalized. By that I mean that one goes on thinking about figures of this stature long after you think you have finished writing about them. And of course, you keep reencountering them on television, in the revival houses, in the videocassette stores, and, naturally, in books, articles, and conversations. So the desire to add to, occasionally to subtract from, writing you once confidently believed you had completed constantly stirs. And I consider it a stroke of good fortune that I have had this chance to assuage that desire.

Finally, a few words about some omissions and an inclusion. There are obviously many more movie figures that I would as happily contemplate as the ones I have taken up here. It is the luck of various occasions, not any coherent plan, that dictated my initial choice of subjects. I am particularly and painfully aware that no women are represented in this volume. For reasons unclear to me I have not often been asked to write at length about women in the movies, and for reasons equally unclear I myself have not proposed to write about them very often either. If this be sexism, I would argue that it is not mine, but Hollywood's, that is largely at fault. No woman has, as yet, been permitted a directorial career as long or as influential as any of those I have taken up here. And indeed, few of them have been permitted star careers in which they could present themselves as forcefully and as coherently over a long run of the years as the men I have written about have. The victims among them—the Marilyn Monroes and the Rita Hayworths—do not elude my sympathy. Those who at least for a time asserted themselves successfully against the industry's masculine insensitivity—the Davises and the Hepburns—do not elude my awed admiration. The ones whose spirits have delighted me—the Irene

Dunnes and the Jean Arthurs—can never elude my undying affection. But perhaps because they all elicit responses in me that are somewhat inchoate, they have, up to now, eluded me critically. If, for the moment, I have to admit to a certain frustration in regard to this subject, I refuse to abandon the possibility of engaging with it in the future.

I am also aware that one of the essays that will loom large for many readers, that on the Hollywood Ten and their career in history, is unlike the others I have included. It is a group portrait, not an individual one, and the arguments it pursues are primarily ideological rather than aesthetic. But since this is—obviously, deliberately—the most controversial subject I have ever taken up, it would seem pusillanimous to ignore it now. And anyway, if not by their work, then by their deeds, the Ten have surely become consequential historical figures—perhaps more certainly so than most of the other figures I have written about here. I wish history could have avoided them, and vice versa. Certainly I wish I could have avoided them since my view of their activities is not the conventional one. But there they are—troubled and troubling, inconvenient and inescapable. My "revisionist" view of them is not, to my mind, more radical than some of the other revisions I have attempted here. But it is in the nature of political metaphors to elicit response more passionate than the aesthetic ones. I leave it to the common sense of the common reader to see that my treatment of this topic is neither more nor less "liberal" than my treatment of the other subjects I have taken up in these pages.

—RICHARD SCHICKEL *Los Angeles June 12, 1988*

I
BENIGHTED ARTIST

CHARLES CHAPLIN
AN UNEXAMINED PREMISE

*P*raise, at a certain point, became superfluous. Chaplin received it, in fullest measure from his peers ("the greatest artist that was ever on the screen"—Stan Laurel; "the greatest comedian who ever lived"—Buster Keaton; "the greatest artist that ever lived"—Mack Sennett; "the best ballet dancer that ever lived, and if I get a chance I'll kill him with my bare hands"—W. C. Fields); from the critics ("It seems unlikely that any dancer or actor can ever have excelled him in eloquence, variety and poignancy of motion"—James Agee; "one of the few great comic geniuses who have appeared so far in history"—Robert Warshow; "Chaplin's career is a cinematic biography on the highest level of artistic expression"—Andrew Sarris); and from the upper echelons of the literary world ("the only genius developed in motion pictures"—George Bernard Shaw; "among his age's first artists"—Edmund Wilson).

One could fill an essay with such quotations and still have plenty left over. Moreover, one would in the end have a sentence or two from almost every critic and every artist one admires. Or so it sometimes seems. It is a measure not merely of the impact of Chaplin's art but of the force of his astonishing ego that one simply cannot find an article written while he was alive that presumes to criticize him, or even to view his life and work with decent objectivity, which does not begin with some sort of apology and end in humility, with the writer bowing his way backward out of the throne room, murmuring assurances of his fealty to the great man and his works.

It was understandable, even to those of us born after, say, 1930, whose feelings for the "Little Fellow" (Chaplin's own term of choice for his great Tramp creation) were rather abstract. We may not have experienced the excitement of discovery, that sense of possessing (and being possessed by) the Little Fellow that earlier generations felt. But we knew who he was, of course, and our elders endlessly guaranteed his greatness to us, so if we found it impossible to love him as he was loved by those who had been present at the creation, we felt honor-bound to appreciate him. This was especially so in the 1940's and 1950's, when it was vitally important not to seem to be making common cause with Chaplin's enemies, those right-wing crazies hounding him about his admittedly Stalinist, but really quite innocently motivated, politics and about a personal morality that, with the passing decades, begins to seem equally unworthy of extensive, let alone outraged, comment. (*People* magazine today would spare no more than an indifferent page or two for the adventures that once created scandalized headlines the world over.) One made allowances for him, for the blowhard conclusions of *The Great Dictator* and *Monsieur Verdoux,* the self-sentimentalizing egotism of *Limelight,* the arid longueurs of *A Countess from Hong Kong*—and was secretly relieved that he withheld *A King in New York* from the American market, so (correctly, as it turned out) dismal were the reports of it. One said: Well, he is old. One said: Well, he is understandably bitter at the way people turned on him. One also thought: He is isolated from the world in his Swiss exile and, perhaps, isolated from his best self by his wealth and by the belated but obvious happiness he found in his last marriage and in the vast family he and Oona O'Neill created. Anyway, time enough—an eternity—to test his claims *on* eternity after he was gone and the burden of his self-regard, at once so oppressive and so delicate, was lifted from us.

This last assumption, however, contained an unspoken assumption, which was that the world after he left it would remain pretty much as it had been when he departed. But it has not. Consider quite a minor matter, the decline of serious film criticism over the last decade or so. There was never much of it to begin with; but it now lacks even the few public forums it could once command, and even the best of them is—shall we say, putting it mildly?—uninterested in historical issues like the Chaplin question. Indeed, film history (as opposed to movie nostalgia) now ends about two months ago. Movie reviewing has become a form of performance art when it is not merely a minor adjunct of the publicity machinery. And the young film scholars, though they may well be film school-trained, have not been brought up to care very deeply about the formative masters of their medium. At best they seem to be able to muster only a sort of distant patronization for the likes of Griffith, Eisenstein, and everyone else who had the misfortune to labor in daunting, distancing silence. Can't blame them, really. The witnesses to these great lives have mostly disappeared; the issues raised by their art grow more distant; the stylizations within which they operated grow more and more remote. For better or worse, the world has moved on. Like the rest of his contemporaries, Chaplin has become the wrong sort of Mr. October—someone to be hurried appreciatively but dispassionately past in Survey of World Cinema's first boring weeks, someone whose importance is now, alas, merely historical.

Where once the reality of the man was shrouded in heedless praise, now it is wrapped in undiscerning indifference. Perhaps he would not care. Alive, he seemed to seek, above all, the status of unexamined premise, so perhaps passing into posterity that way would have pleased him: a great man, known by name to everyone, known as a troublesome, problematic reality only to an ever-dwindling, ever-aging band of specialists.

Somehow, though, one does not see him content with this role. Nor should we be. For there was always more here than met the eye at first, more here than a "universal" figure, the Little Fellow, who seemed to encompass in his brilliant pantomime routines the common lot of the common man. That was, for Chaplin, just the beginning, and he lived to see that if he had stopped there, his career would have had no more historical resonance than those of his major rivals, Harold Lloyd and Buster Keaton. He might have been rich but unhappy like the former, lonesomely rattling around in a great empty mansion, or poor but unhappy like the latter, sadly rattling around in nightclubs and TV commercials.

It was almost as if Chaplin could discern the possibility of such a fate and, from the beginning, worked to avoid it by involving himself and his audience in a far larger drama—a drama, as it turned out, in one of the classic twentieth-century molds, that of the artist-visionary in endless conflict with his age. It was, and is, infinitely more fascinating than any of the Little Fellow's adventures—with its author engaged, right to the end, in creating for us an aesthetically satisfying climax for it. This was the urtext for all the great celebrity dramas that have followed, and as such it has a significance that far transcends any of the individual works that were finally best understood merely as incidents in this larger creation.

The drama was divided, as all epic works used to be, into five crowded acts, which might be subtitled "Self-discovery," "Success," "Struggle," "Tragedy," and—when the audience at the 1972 Academy Awards ceremony rose in cheering, tearing ovation to welcome him back to the industry and the community he as much as any single individual created, and everybody forgave everybody—the last act, "Triumph." If there was high novelty in this scenario, it consisted largely of his reversing the usual order of Acts Two and Three, placing "Struggle" after "Success." But in that, too, he was prescient, for as time has worn on, that is the way things have tended to be ordered in the other great celebrity tales of our century.

Like his greatest routines, the Chaplin drama has a simplicity, an inevitability (and a self-consciousness) that are awesome. Of course, fate helped him out a little bit, especially with his opening scenes, for he was born into poverty, the son of a drunken father and a mother who went mad. A Dickensian childhood ensued, but one which turned out to have its uses as the source of his art, which he began to perfect at an early age, becoming, at age twenty-one, the leading man in one of the Fred Karno comedy troupes, where he learned the classic English music hall style. As everyone knows, it was at that age that Chaplin came to the United States with a Karno company. It was while working with it that he was discovered by Mack Sennett, for whom he began working in 1914.

The English comic style was not Sennett's; Chaplin's relationship with his new, roughneck colleagues was edgy. A lot of his best bits were cut out of his early Keystones, Chaplin claimed. As the world would soon know, however, Chaplin always had what any unique artist must have to survive: utter confidence in the correctness of his own judgment. He fought out the stylistic issue with the Keystone crowd, finally finding a way to demonstrate what he had been trying to tell them. It happened one day when Sennett was observed glumly studying a hotel lobby set, chewing on his cigar. "We need some gags here," he muttered, then turned to Chaplin and told him, "Put on a comedy make-up. Anything will do."

At that point, if life were as well managed as a movie, the clouds should have broken and beams of sunlight should have lit Chaplin's way to wardrobe. For his time had come. "I thought I would dress in baggy pants, big shoes, a cane and a derby hat. I wanted everything in contradiction: the pants baggy, the coat tight, the hat small, and the shoes large." The mustache was added, he said, because Sennett had expected him to be much older and Chaplin thought it would age him without hiding his expression.

He continues: "I had no idea of the character. But the moment I was dressed, the clothes and make-up made me feel the person he was. I began to know him, and by the time I walked onto the stage he was fully born." He claims—and one is a trifle dubious about this —that he was able instantly to describe his creation to Sennett in rather poetic terms *before* a foot of film had been shot: "You know this fellow is many-sided, a tramp, a gentleman, a poet, a dreamer, a lonely fellow, always hopeful of romance and adventure. He would have you believe he is a scientist, a musician, a duke, a polo player. However, he is not above picking up cigarette butts or robbing a baby of its candy. And, of course, if the occasion warrants it, he will kick a lady in the rear— but only in extreme anger."

Perhaps he really was that knowing (and that articulate) that quickly. Perhaps not. No doubt, however, he was inspired, sensed there was something more here than just another role, something through which he could express more of his feelings and visions than he ever had before. Most critics, however, believe it required most of the rest of the year with Sennett, plus a good bit of the following year (with the Essanay company), before the Tramp began to demonstrate all the dimensions Chaplin ascribed to him on, as it were, their first meeting. In particular, the undercurrent of pathos, which in time was to become a veritable torrent, was not visible for another year.

Still, the public almost immediately observed that something wonderful had been wrought. The demand for films featuring the Little Fellow was immediate and huge. The 1915 Essanay contract called for $1,250 a week and a $10,000 bonus on signing. A year later he was to receive $675,000 for a year's work with Mutual, and a little more than a year after that, in 1917, Chaplin finished building his own studio and signed his famous $1 million contract with First National. Close with his money, and determined never to suffer again the kind of poverty he had so recently escaped, Chaplin began accumulating one of the great show business fortunes.

He was entitled to it. For in an age when forty or fifty prints of a movie comedy could satisfy the demand for other actors' work, distributors had to make up close to two hundred prints of Chaplin's films—for which they could charge well above the going rates. It was a golden time. It required only a simple poster of the Tramp bearing the legend "I AM HERE TODAY" to bring the people in. And the two-reel length of these early comedies was perfectly suited to his gifts. Agee wrote: "Before Chaplin came to pictures people were content with a couple of gags per comedy; he got some kind of laugh every second," mainly "through his genius for what might be called *inflection*—the perfect, changeful shading of his physical and emotional attitudes toward the gag." Every writer has his favorite moments in these two-reelers. Agee, for example, loved Chaplin's drunken bout with a malevolent Murphy bed in *One A.M.;* Gilbert Seldes cites *The Pawnshop,* where Chaplin includes business with a feather duster, then a sequence in which he tries to dry dishes by passing them through a clothes wringer, and then some nonsense with a clock, where a simple inspection leads to disaster, as all the clockworks litter the screen. Both men mention, as the quintessential Chaplin moment, a sequence in *A Night Out* where Ben Turpin, himself far gone in booze, is dragging a stiffened Chaplin through the streets after the bars have closed. Chaplin awakens, sees how splendidly his friend is serving him, and reaches out to pluck and delicately sniff a flower.

There are lots of ways to put it: He found poetry in the ordinary; he transcended reality; he extended the range of pantomime to previously unimagined dimensions. Yet none of them quite explains his phenomenal appeal. Chaplin was never generous in acknowledging influences, but some critics have noticed a correlation between his work and that of Max Linder, who had earlier brought something of the European comic tradition to the screen through his Pathé shorts. Edmund Wilson emphasized how much Chaplin owed to the classic turns of the English music halls. And despite his protests, it is clear that Chaplin learned a great deal from Sennett, especially about pacing and the use of the chase as a climax.

In short, he summarized much that had gone before, linking the art of screen comedy to much older traditions. This was very significant to the development of the movies. He was, when he came to them, precisely what they most needed, a common-consent great artist, a man who, by his work, proposed the possibility that they might be something more than a fad on their way to becoming an industry, that they might be a great art form as well. He was equally an invaluable figure to those populist intellectuals who began to take the movies seriously in the teens and twenties of this century, someone on whom they could pin their hopes for this new expressive form, so vulgarly "commercial" in its origins and development.

In turn, their writing proved extremely valuable to Chaplin, ensuring his reputation as an artist against both direct assault and the more insidious danger of neglect during the long periods when he was absent from the screen. In effect, their enthusiasm committed all of us to him irrevocably. Through all the long years when most of the literary community, most of the bourgeoisie for that matter, were exercising their contempt for movies in general, Chaplin was always cited as the medium's one unquestioned, unquestionable artist, the individualist amid the corporate herd, a man clinging to his peculiar vision while everyone else went hooting off in pursuit of momentary excitements. Or submitted to degrading manipulation by the studios. Or simply faded away as his great contemporaries (and sometime United Artists partners) did—Griffith, Fairbanks, Pickford.

Yet this fact remains: Chaplin never again achieved the perfection of those first years. The best of the little films of the Little Fellow were, in effect, solo ballets. As such they had no more need of plot, of subsidiary characterizations, of great themes than one of Nijinsky's variations did. Despite the reams of appreciative analysis written about the early films, the pleasure we derived from them was essentially kinesthetic and therefore non- (and even perhaps anti-) intellectual. One could go on watching them for a lifetime. Indeed, one has.

Perhaps the cruelest demand of criticism is the one that insists on endless innovation by major artists. No matter what they *thought* they thought they were doing, there was in the endless concern of his commentators over where Chaplin was heading an implicit insistence on "development," a hint that if he was going to reach his full potential, he must reach for big ideas, big statements. Perhaps Chaplin, who was nothing if not ambitious, would have made the same demands on himself eventually. But perhaps not.

The finest Chaplin scholarship of recent years has been done not in print but on film, in the form of the three-part television series *Unknown Chaplin,* produced, written, and directed in England by Kevin Brownlow and David Gill in the early eighties. They were granted access to Chaplin's film vaults by his widow and to material he created during his Mutual year, which had passed into the hands of the late Raymond Rohauer, the silent-film collector-impresario. Here were hundreds of hours of outtakes, from which they created an unprecedented portrait of the artist in his studio, sketching, refining, and often rejecting ideas. The films they made from Chaplin's films form a portrait not merely of his working methods but of that most invisible of human endeavors, the creative process.

Above all, the Brownlow-Gill films reveal an innocent, unpretentious, and thoroughly likable side to Chaplin in his early days. He had no choice but to be an improviser. His kind of comedy could not be mentally envisioned in advance or worked out on paper. It depended on kinesthetic specifics, which had to be arrived at practically—on the set, with props in hand, supporting players at hand, and the master toying with his animate and inanimate foils, seeing what effects he might achieve and how richly they might be orchestrated. It was only by studying what Chaplin the comedian had done that Chaplin the director could judge the work in progress.

His starting point was generally a set or an elaborate mechanical prop, like the escalator in *The Floorwalker,* which at first suggested only vague potentials to him, but which, as he worked with it, retake after retake, day after day, becomes the basis for a long and marvelously intricate sequence. Perhaps the most memorable example of Chaplin's working methods that Brownlow and Gill turned up occurred during the making of *The Cure.* He starts work on a sequence in a spa, pushing a large, gouty man in a wheelchair. Nothing very funny about that. But as time passes, that single chair multiplies into a half dozen of them, and Chaplin himself metamorphizes into a bellboy functioning as a policeman trying to straighten out the splendidly lunatic traffic jam they inevitably create. But dozens upon dozens of takes later, Chaplin abandons this sequence entirely—it does not appear in the finished film —and turns himself into a spiflicated patient entangled with a revolving door, a piece that is yet more painstakingly worked out and still more brilliantly timed.

How attractive he is demonstrating his comic grace under self-generated pressure (his Mutual deal required him to turn out a film per month, but such was his popularity at the time, and the primitive state of his competition, that all of them did not have to be master-pieces). How certain we are, studying the results, that this was a mind infinitely better suited to creating elegant complications of simple human situations than it was to propagating simple solutions to insufferably complicated intellectual issues.

One has to think as well that Chaplin himself treasured the relief from the importunings of celebrity life that focused concentration on the endless and highly detailed problems of making a movie presented him. For the Brownlow-Gill films show that at least in the early days he was at his best—that is to say, his least pretentious and most generous—when he was on the stage shooting. At these times this normally tightfisted man was capable of wild profligacy in pursuit of his comic visions. On *The Gold Rush,* for example, he took a huge cast and crew into the high country near Truckee, California, built a complete mining town set, labored in the deep snow for weeks—and then used only a couple of shots from the location in the finished film. He preferred to rebuild the town on his Hollywood backlot, where his caprices were not subject to nature's as he toiled to perfect what was undoubtedly his greatest feature-length film. Later, to shoot what seems a simple sequence, the meeting of his Tramp character with Virginia Cherrill's blind flower girl in *City Lights,* he spent eighty-three days, sixty-two of which were devoted to thinking the scene over while his company idled—on salary. Sometimes, as with *The Professor,* he would start a film, complete entire sequences as masterful (on the evidence of the material Brownlow and Gill discovered) as any he ever made, and then junk the entire work (though a flea circus routine he first experimented with in this film does show up in refined and expanded form in *Limelight*).

The fact that even his weakest films, excepting perhaps *A King in New York* and *A Countess from Hong Kong,* all contain sublime sequences of the kind we are discussing leads one inescapably to the belief that Chaplin's was not a mind that took naturally to narrative or to the exploration of abstract ideas. So does the fact that in what seems to me his most fully satisfying feature-length movies, *The Gold Rush* and *The Circus,* there is no real attempt at plotting; they are each essentially compilations of marvelously developed routines, held together more by unity of setting than by story.

Perhaps, indeed, his insecurity about these matters is what led to the long gaps between films after the marketplace, as well as his own ambitions, forced him to expand his pictures to feature length. Perhaps his heavy reliance on simple, generalized, and rather cloying sentimentality, beginning with *The Kid* in 1921, as the principal thematic binding for his films—so at odds with the subtle intensity of his comic inventiveness—may be seen as a rather desperate cover for this deficiency. And, possibly, for a larger one as well.

This was a kind of schizophrenia. Whatever else he was, Chaplin was unquestionably the greatest narcissist in screen history—obviously a prize for which there have been virtually as many contenders as there have been names above the title. He wished nothing to distract us from our pleasure in contemplating what he regarded as the world's supreme object of contemplation—his dear self. (His movies are among the most underpopulated in the history of the medium, perhaps most notably so in *The Great Dictator,* a film that has epic ambitions, but that even in battlefield and mob scenes offers only a thin straggle of extras, nothing that could seriously divert our attention from the star.)

It was the narcissist who resisted not just technological innovation but advances in the art of screen storytelling. As early as 1925 Edmund Wilson accurately noticed and, in the kindliest possible terms, described, this failing: "His gift is primarily the actor's, not the director's or the artist's. All the photographic, the plastic development of the movies, which is at present making such remarkable advances, seems not to interest Chaplin. His pictures are still in this respect nearly as raw as *Tillie's Punctured Romance* or any other primitive comedy."

This is an extremely perceptive comment, coming as early as it did in Chaplin's career. For it now seems evident that he perceived every stylistic and technical change that came to the movies after the end of World War I as something with the implicit power to interfere with his (and our) contemplation of his screen self. Length, of course, implied the necessity for subplots and the presence of other actors in significant roles. Very distracting. The growth in movie "plasticity" that Wilson spoke of similarly threatened to disrupt our concentration on the nuances of his art. Very upsetting. And talk, when it came to the screen, had the potential to be fatally interruptive.

Wilson added that he saw small likelihood of Chaplin, so jealous of his independence, allowing himself to be written for, directed, or even advised by others. In this he was far nearer the mark than he knew. For it was not merely that Chaplin was resistant to industrial production methods, or that he was a radically self-sufficient artist in the traditional sense of the term. It was that he was a truly—often quite literally—a raving egomaniac. Thanks to Brian Taves's "Charlie Dearest" (*Film Comment,* March–April, 1988), we now have the reminiscences of Robert Florey, an accomplished commercial director and friend of Chaplin's, who was invited by the great auteur to co-direct *Monsieur Verdoux* with him. It was a nightmare, largely because Florey discovered that Chaplin, because he was so exclusively focused on himself, had never bothered to discover anything about movie technique. To be sure, he would deny his fellow players their close-ups for the mean-spirited reasons that are customary with some stars—because he did not want to be challenged by them, or let them share in his glory. But the truly shocking thing was that he did not know he needed them in order for a scene to cut properly. Nor did he seem to understand that when he ordered a close-up of himself it was technically impossible, no matter what focal length the cameraman employed, to keep the rest of his body, or some portion of the background he wanted to show, in frame at the same time. The blitheness of his ignorance—especially at this late date (1947, when the picture was shot)—is shocking. The basic grammar of film, the film school ABCs, he dismissed as "Hollywood chi-chi." And anyone trying to instruct him in these matters was subject to outraged denunciation. How bad was it? A cat who scratched him in a scene he was playing with the creature was killed and stuffed and returned to the set in that more pliable condition for the rest of their work together.

In other words, his much-praised independence and the technical deficiencies that critics and fans indulged, even took as earnests of his artistic purity, were, in fact, expressions of self-regard raised, finally, to near-psychopathic heights. Wilson's worry that he would never learn to take "advice" states the issue rather too mildly. What use is "advice" to a sensibility riveted by the search for new evidence of his own perfection? That was certainly the case with Chaplin. He was a secretive man, unable to confront, let alone openly draw upon, autobiography for material. Hence, of course, the resort to his highly stylized makeup, costume, and manner as the Tramp. Hence, also, the resort to unexceptionable sentiment and gaseous platitude when, backed into a corner by the requirements of one of his primitive stories, he had to seem to speak personally, "from the heart." He could not face himself nakedly or speak of himself intimately—and he certainly could not present the strangers in the audience with the opportunity to do so.

But there was an alternative, and it was one he bravely explored in 1923's *A Woman of Paris,* though Wilson was rather dismissive of the effort ("flat light and putty make-up"). It was a film in which he appeared only briefly and, for the first time, not in the Tramp's disguise. It was also a film rather more elaborately (and conventionally) plotted than any of his previous works. A provincial boy and girl fall in love despite their parents' objections and plan to elope to Paris. His father dies as they are about to leave, and the girl, not knowing why he missed the train, goes on without him—to become Adolphe Menjou's elaborately kept woman in the capital. Later the young lovers meet, there is the promise of love's renewal, but circumstances and the young man's priggishness intervene. Tragedy and then a coda, at once ironic and uplifting, end the picture.

It has been said that *A Woman of Paris* was made as a vehicle to express Chaplin's gratitude and love for its leading lady, Edna Purviance, who had played opposite him in thirty-five of his early comedies and who was apparently the first grand passion of his life—after his mother, of course. It was handsomely tailored to her talents, for she makes the transition from naive country girl to worldly courtesan (and back again) with wonderful ease. Better still, the woman she becomes has a way of flashing glimpses of the girl she once was that is unselfconscious and very touching.

But it is as a disguised autobiographical work that it exerts its continuing fascination. For we can see that the two male figures in the film represent aspects of Chaplin's own personality, especially in his attitudes toward women, sex, family. The young artist is, like Chaplin, at heart rather bourgeois in his values. His mother actually shares his garret with him, and his paintings, like his dress and manner, are formal and staid. He sentimentalizes virtue just as Chaplin did in the soppier passages of his work, and a side of his nature, like a side of Chaplin's, aspires to the kind of upper-class Victorian family stability that Chaplin, the heavily buffeted lower-class Victorian waif, never knew. On the other hand, as decades of scandalized headlines made clear, Chaplin was also a boulevardier as dandified and as dangerous to youthful virtue as Menjou is in this picture. Chaplin obviously saw to it that the actor invested this character with genuine charm, style, and worldly understanding. In other words, he shone the best possible light on his own dark side.

Ernst Lubitsch frequently said that *A Woman of Paris* was the film that most influenced him, and one can readily see why. It is, like Lubitsch's ruefully funny romances, knowing, acceptant, but never cynical about what we will do for love. It is, perhaps, all right to die for it, as the young artist finally does in Chaplin's picture, but, the film implies, that is not necessarily nobler than expressing your devotion by carefully creasing your trouser legs, the Menjou character's way of putting the matter.

Be that as it may, this is a lovely film, wonderfully controlled in its wit, far more stylish, in its insinuating way, than Wilson allowed. Above all, Chaplin, hidden safely behind the camera, found in it a way of expressing intimate emotions and some highly personal (and not necessarily universally agreeable) ideas about the world that he could not state in the Little Fellow's persona. Unfortunately, though extremely well received by the critics, it was not a popular success, and so it became a signpost on a road not taken by Chaplin. He might be restive with the Tramp and the inherent expressive limits the character imposed on him, but the public assuredly was not. In any event, as we have observed, Chaplin's art and his production pace grew hesitant. From the time *A Woman of Paris* was completed to 1940, when *The Great Dictator* appeared, Chaplin made just five films, the last of which, of course, contained his final appearance as the Tramp—but in a role that was quite overwhelmed by Chaplin's impersonation of Hynkel, the dictator.

I agree with Otis Ferguson, the first great populist critic of movies since Vachel Lindsay, who, echoing Wilson, wrote that *Modern Times* was "about the last thing they should have called the Chaplin picture. . . . Its times were modern when the movies were younger and screen motion was a little faster and more jerky than life, and sequences came in forty-foot spurts." Ferguson called it "a feature picture made up of several one- or two-reel shorts" and proposed for them titles like *The Shop, The Jailbird, The Watchman, The Singing Waiter*. Like everyone else, he could see the momentary beauties of these sequences, but they did not, he thought, make Chaplin "a first-class picturemaker. He may personally surmount his period, but as director-producer he can't carry his whole show with him, and I'll take bets that if he keeps on refusing to learn any more than he learned when the movies themselves were just learning, each successive picture he makes will seem, on release, to fall short of what went before."

Very prescient. For what Ferguson said of this film could be applied to almost all of Chaplin's later work. But it was not just his failure to "keep up" that was responsible for the discomfort his sound features induce. As I implied earlier, I do not believe sound's advent was a major contributor to his hesitations and wrong turns of this period. As a matter of fact, Chaplin counterattacked sound with a boldness that can be read as near-reckless bravery. In *City Lights* and *Modern Times* he simply dismissed the microphone from his stages and filled the sound track with music, effects, and an occasional burst of gibberish. No, what we see in the sound films are imperfect attempts to solve the same problems that were beginning to afflict him in the silent pictures, which were, I believe, projections of unresolved issues in his own personality. Indeed, each of the major sound films represents a radical and no more than partially successful attempt to evade these issues.

City Lights, with its mawkish romance between the blind girl and the tramp she thinks of as a swell because she cannot see how he is dressed but can hear (and otherwise sense) the elegance of his manners, the kindness of his spirit, represents the height of Chaplin's self-sentimentalization. In no picture before or after did he so thoroughly blanch out the impetuous cruelty that had, early on, been his saving gracelessness, the truest source of his humor and humanity. *Modern Times,* of course, is his most overtly Marxist film, the first and only time the Tramp is consciously invested with class consciousness, openly a victim of corporate industrialism.

The Great Dictator is, obviously, anti-Fascist in intent, with its endless concluding speech a not-so-small anthology of the Popular Front rhetoric of the time, presaging the similar, blessedly shorter (but no less banal) speechifying that was such an unedifying convention of American films made during the war. *Monsieur Verdoux,* which may be the most interesting of these films, at last vents the misogyny that, according to some psychological theory and most feminist theory, always motivates womanizers of the kind Chaplin surely was until his marriage to Oona O'Neill. As such, of course, it presents the comedian with the most difficult problem he ever faced: how to retain sympathy for his character, and get laughs, while playing a serial murderer. That he gets at least a little of both is a tribute, of course, to Chaplin's skills as a performer. But it, too, concludes with an awful speech. Like the desperate love-as-panacea preachment that brings the previous film to its limp conclusion, this oratorical outburst is embarrassing because the speech is not truly felt, remains merely empty words, though one imagines Chaplin thought he meant them at the time. But *Verdoux*'s climactic speech is much more bitter in tone: How is Verdoux, the murderer of a handful of lonely women—and for the justifiable end of supporting his dear family—worse than all the munitions manufacturers, etc., etc.? Once again we are embarrassed by the intellectual bankruptcy we are forced to endure, this time deepened by the staleness of the paradox he was working. Moreover, Chaplin is not enough of an actor, in the traditional sense of the word, to bring it off. He had an unfortunate, off-putting voice, that of a prissy schoolmaster, the sort of person to whom the Tramp might have given a hotfoot, but whom it was impossible to imagine his becoming.

Finally, thank heavens, Chaplin set politics aside. But in favor of self-pity. *Limelight* is about a clown who has lost his hold on his audience, as surely Chaplin had by that time. It was, as Andrew Sarris pointed out, "an imagining [of] his own death, a conception of sublime egotism unparalleled in the world cinema," since "to imagine one's own death, one must imagine the death of the world." One could not help being touched by this implication of the work. But the manifest object, the movie taken on its own terms, is chilly and almost contemptuously manipulative in the obviousness of its assault on our feelings not for the character Chaplin played but for the performer himself. He was suggesting that we might finally resolve them by simply feeling sorry for him—poor little rich man.

It is probably true that some of the difficulties Chaplin faced in mounting these films are explicable in megapolitical terms. He was an artist universally beloved because he had created a great symbol of the common man's indomitable spunk, a man who had helped create a great new populist medium, and a man whose devotion to the highest standards and aspirations had given the medium respectability as an art form. Yet as the century wore on, the common man increasingly showed himself to be capable of the most terrible crimes and indifferences; to be the dupe of such evil mass movements as fascism and Stalinism. And the medium itself increasingly demonstrated its capacity to mislead, to corrupt its audience. Indeed, David Thomson has asked if Chaplin's common man "was so far from Hitler? He spoke to disappointment, brutalized feelings and failure and saw that through movies he could concoct a daydream world in which the tramp thrives and in which his whole ethos of self-pity is vindicated."

This is admirably daring criticism, but one does not have to go quite that far to identify the bind in which Chaplin found himself as this century exposed more and more of its true face. One can content oneself by agreeing with Robert Warshow's less formidable contention: that the Tramp was done in because the essentially innocent relationship between him and his society could no longer be sustained. "The satiric point of the relationship lay precisely in [the] element of fortuitousness ... it *happened* that the Tramp and the society were in constant collision, but neither side was impelled to draw any conclusions from this. The absurdity in the Tramp's behavior consisted in its irrelevance to the preoccupations of the society; the viciousness of the society consisted in its failure to make any provision for the Tramp, its complete indifference to his fate."

But in truly modern times this kind of relationship was impossible. "Now the two were compelled to become conscious of each other, openly and continuously, and the quality of innocence ... could no longer be preserved between them." As Warshow observes, the factory in *Modern Times* is "a living, malevolent organism," as is the state in *The Great Dictator*. There is no longer even a thin margin on which the Tramp could survive.

As with the Tramp, so with Chaplin himself. His embrace of dismal leftist ideology must be read as a fairly desperate attempt to find a solvent powerful enough to melt this malevolence, to restore the world to that state of grace in which the Little Fellow could go on his merry, politically unconscientious way. When it turned out not to live up to the claims that had been made for it in the advertisements, and when the acid dripped onto his own hands, painfully burning him, he was left bitter and bereft. If *Limelight* is a convalescent's whimper—"How could this happen to me?"—then his next films represent a still deeper, almost senile withdrawal into a totally private world, a world of self-absorption, but not of self-examination.

When in 1976 we were finally permitted to see *A King in New York,* almost two decades after he had made it, the flaccidity of its comic invention, the languor of its pace, the unrelenting chill of its language, the dullness of its imagery, the sense that Chaplin himself was now as distanced from his instinctive self as he was from the world the rest of us inhabited were astonishing.

Chaplin had the temerity to cast himself as what he obviously felt himself to be, a deposed king. Coming to America to promote an Atoms for Peace plan, he discovers a country where the movies are drenched in sex and violence, the jazz is too loud, and—worst of all, from his point of view—the treatment of the famous is crass and importunate. All right, he had been away for a decade when he made the film (in England) and could perhaps be excused his lack of current knowledge of American manners and morals. But there was no passion, no bite to his satire. He was like an old man muttering to himself in the chimney corner about the dang fool younger generation. Even on a matter about which he had reason to feel strongly, congressional witch-hunting, his commentary was pallid. He breaks up a committee meeting with a fire hose that unfunnily goes out of control. To be sure, when his royal alter ego becomes an unwitting participant in a *Candid Camera* type of TV show or when, needing some money, he endorses a cheap whiskey, and Chaplin shows how an isolated and unworldly fellow can fall victim to the prying and exploitation of the press, the movie fitfully stirs to life. This was a matter about which Chaplin obviously had powerful opinions. But these did not call forth resounding comic responses, even if they are marginally more humorous than anything he managed to invent for his last film, *A Countess from Hong Kong,* a film so dim it is impossible either to recall or to sit through again.

One would, indeed, gratefully skip extended comment on *A King in New York* were it not for two interesting points it raises. The first is that Chaplin obviously still hoped to reingratiate himself with his old American audience, therefore pulled his satirical punches. The other and more important one is that because it has nothing else to offer, no distractions, no evidence however minor or brief of his comic genius, it presents us with the purest imaginable example of his besetting flaws, his self-regard and his rejection of common reality. He can live, on the screen, only in settings that are purely his own invention —that is to say, a projection of his own inward-turned sensibility. If the horror of old age is that it reduces us to our essence, strips away the disguises energetically inventive youth finds to wrap around its motivational mainsprings, then this terrible movie becomes— ironically—the most brutally truthful of Chaplin's works. It is not the

31

serenely forgiving work of a great artist in autumn, it is more like an émigré political tract, something an old revolutionist, alone and far from home but obliged to pretend he is still a movement, a force, would crank out on his dim mimeograph machine.

Was he in fact what David Thomson claimed him to be in another of his breathtaking critical leaps: "the looming mad politician of the century, the daemon tramp"? Or was he what I, less boldly, think him to be: the first great product of the modern celebrity system, appropriately enough turned into that system's first great victim? That is to say, the man on whom unprecedented fame and wealth were lavished, thereby alienating himself from his youthful self, that self from which all great art derives.

His life in his late years seems to bear out this supposition. He was seen abroad only occasionally and then largely in the company of those few world-class celebrities who were his peers. When he addressed the rest of us, he was distant, abstract, patronizing. He preached love of mankind in general but appeared incapable of affectionate gestures toward anyone outside his family circle, that ever-expanding extension of himself. *My Autobiography,* published in 1964, reinforced this dire suspicion. The first third is wonderful, one of the great portraits of turn-of-the-century life, rich in color, anecdote, feeling. But the last two thirds? They are cold, simplistic, a dreary listing of the great man's encounters with other great men, none of whom is as interesting as he. And he is too interesting, too complex to be discussed.

In that book's last lines Chaplin wrote: "I sometimes sit out on our terrace at sunset and look over a vast green lawn to the lake in the distance, and beyond the lake to the reassuring mountains, and in this mood think of nothing and enjoy their magnificent serenity." So was the great humanist finally lost to humanity, smugly contemplating the best view money could buy, looking back on the life of wealth and privilege he had acquired through the development and exploitation of a great natural resource—his own native talent. He had strip-mined its most obvious veins, coolly fobbed off some ideological fool's gold as the genuine article, and missed the richest ore of all, that which lay far down the deepest, darkest tunnels of the quaking self. But such unseemly toil was long since beyond him, if it had ever truly been within his strength.

The bitterest irony he could not see from his twilit terrace, the posthumous transformation of his great creation, the Tramp, the Little Fellow, into a cute marketing tool for a vast corporation's line of computers. What would the old leftist have made of that? More important, what would the Old Egoist have made of it—this final detachment of creation from creator, which implied, as well, its detachment from his personal history and from the history of the art and the society, in which he had once been such a dominant figure. He had surely not meant to become a premise this unexamined, or this trivial to posterity. And yet one feels, looking back on this life, a certain inevitability about this fate.

II
FOUR DIRECTORS

JOHN FORD
THE ROAD NOT TAKEN

*H*ard to think of an odder coupling than this one: John Ford and Lindsay Anderson. The social and political conservative; the social and political radical. The insider always looking longingly out; the outsider always looking longingly in. Unschooled instincts and schooled ones. Unreconstructed Irishman and reconstructed Englishman. If they have anything at all in common as directors, and perhaps as men, it is a powerful desire not to be understood too quickly or pegged too easily, which is no guarantee that two such prickly individualists will ever acknowledge their underlying affinity.

But strange are the ways of fandom. Returning vocationless from service in World War II, Anderson one day chanced upon Ford's western *My Darling Clementine*. His socks, formerly neatly gartered by prim, middle-class notions of what art should be, were knocked off by it. "Lyrical populism" is perhaps as good a phrase as any to describe the quality he identified in it and responded to as quite foreign to anything in his previous moviegoing. Possibly it is too much to say that the path leading from that accidental encounter to Anderson's later career as a maker of such bold cinematic gestures as *This Sporting Life, If . . . , O Lucky Man!* became clear to him at that moment, but certainly the possibility—not at all obvious to respectably raised youths at that time—that the movies might be an art form worthy of a rebellious spirit's attention did begin to occur to him as he left that great picture palace the Leicester Square Odeon. At Oxford he began writing critical essays for the undergraduate magazines and took up Ford's work as his new films appeared. Anderson was attempting, it would seem, to rationalize what was, in essence, a blind passion. Subsequently he exerted himself to correspond with and then to meet with Ford, volunteering himself for that alteration of abuse and affection (both often inexplicable and very likely the product of alcoholism) with which the director treated all acquaintances, whether distant or intimate. They were in touch, intermittently, until Ford died in 1973.

Eight years thereafter Anderson pulled together and expanded, without quite binding together, his several efforts to come to terms with Ford and his work and published them under the title *About John Ford.* It is a disarming volume, very much in the film buff manner which so often passes for scholarship in the movie world. Personal reminiscences jostle against highfalutin critical assertions and cosmic mediations on the nature of screen poetry, while in the appendices undigested interviews with some of Ford's actors nestle against correspondence from some of his screenwriters, the latter at least implicitly asserting their claim to a greater share of Ford's auteurship than he (or his most devoted apologists) might care to admit. It is all a little slapdash. But there is an emotional forthrightness in Anderson's approach, an openness in his enthusiasms and in his dislikes, that is very engaging—even moving in a curious way.

For it is clear that his encounters with Ford's work were archetypal. More than one young man of his generation, and of the generations on either side of it, had his eyes opened to the notion that movies might be something more than an instrument for fantastic escape from childhood's constraints, picked up his first hints of film's larger possibilities as an expressive form, and made his first inchoate emotional commitments to that form—commitments that led eventually to professional engagement with the movies—because of John Ford's pictures.

I was certainly one of those young men. In my personal history Ford's movies of the thirties and forties were consequential events. Everyone's entry point into his world was different (my first Ford film was a re-release of what is now generally regarded as a lesser work, *Drums Along the Mohawk*), though it is also a highly characteristic one. But everyone's commitment points were different, depending on the moment in the director's career that coincided with one's most impressionable moviegoing years (for me that occurred in the period between 1946 and 1950, beginning where Anderson began, with *My Darling Clementine,* deepening as the cavalry "trilogy" came along).

In that period, and later, precisely because the American film industry, having bestowed a half dozen Oscars on him, made Ford its official Great Director, and because the cinéastes who ran our college film societies took Hollywood at its word, it was possible to see in revival most of the earlier sound movies on which his reputation largely rested. He was, in fact, the only common-consent world-class director whose work was readily accessible to us. In those days in middle western America Eisenstein, Murnau, Renoir, the rest of the great Europeans were mainly rumors to us, and just then Ford's Hollywood peers were not really competitive with him either. An old master and a younger one, Griffith and Lubitsch, both died in that period, while the reputations of Hitchcock, Sturges, Capra, Chaplin, and Fritz Lang were all, for various reasons, in actual or perceived decline. And the world in general had not yet recognized the worth of Hawks and the other great American genre directors. (The only film history commonly available, Paul Rotha's *The Film till Now,* identified Hawks as "a good all-rounder" and let it go at that.)

But even if a longer, broader view of film as art had pertained in those days, I'm not certain the younger generation would have been able to appreciate fully the felicities of a Lubitsch or a Lang, for example. Perhaps it is only because I came to them later in life, but still, it seems to me that the pleasures they offer us are mostly mature ones. Ford's virtues, on the other hand, are much more innocent and self-evident. They are correctly identified by Anderson as a talent for narrative and for "poetic" expressiveness with the camera.

As Anderson sees it, it is Ford's narrative gift that is the first, and most basic, of his abilities, the one from which his second, equally large talent in fact derives. He was "from the start, and all his life, a teller of tales," Anderson writes, a traditionalist working for "an audience who wanted only to be entertained, were not looking for originality or enlightenment...." This skill was always a simplifying one. At his best Ford told stories in a marvelously straightforward and wonderfully paced manner, neither too rushed nor too languorous—very much that of the tale spinner at the fireside, with a practiced instinct for the moment at which to linger over a detail, the time to hurry on to the next turning point in the story.

The tales Ford most often and most successfully told were historical in setting and epic in scale—mainly, but by no means exclusively, westerns. The major theme in these works Anderson correctly identifies as the defense of what can be summarized as communitarian values when they are threatened by outlawry, otherness (mainly, of course, represented by Indians), the anarchy of great historical forces unleashed. Whether we are dealing with a real family, like the Joads of *The Grapes of Wrath,* or a hierarchical pseudofamily like a military unit, or one that is temporarily patched together for mutual protection (the travelers in a stagecoach or in a wagon train heading west), most of Ford's best beloved and best-remembered films from, say, *Stagecoach* through, say, *The Searchers* set up situations in which the strength of familial ties were in some way tested.

At the time these works of what we might now term his middle period were coming into release I was no more aware of their thematic content than I was of their thematic unity—or that there were such things as middle periods in artists' lives. Indeed, I was not entirely aware that movie directors were artists. All I was aware of—quite inarticulately at the time, of course—was that somehow these films were different from other films that employed similar settings, characters, generic conventions. They had a distinctive look, a singular tone—yes, a "poetry" about them—that one rarely encountered in American movies at that time and scarcely dared speak of for fear of the hooting of one's peers.

This visual style—Ford's second great strength—was acutely attuned to his substance. Those lonely Monument Valley vistas that he offered in such handsomely composed, formal images suited his purposes perfectly. Ford had a great, instinctive sense of scale, and the images one most vividly retains from his best work are of men in a landscape. The former tend to be American archetypes, and they are always under threat of domination by the harsh and untamed land, yet somehow the braver for their seeming puniness and for the obvious tenuousness of their efforts to impose the fragile structures of a primitive civilization on this apparently unyielding earth. This imagery, serene and classical in composition, does have, as Anderson puts it, the ability to "transcend narrative," enabling Ford to transform his simple stories "into poems for those who have eyes to see and ears to hear."

In the end it is this gift for transformation that is the main reason Ford meant so much to Anderson, to me, to everyone for whom learning to take the movies seriously was a significant part of coming of age. No other American director so consistently or so generously proposed the poetic possibility in the context of easily apprehended genre films.

Moreover, Ford's legend was as romantic and adventurous as his movies—and almost equally available to us. For he was one of the few directors written about quite regularly in the popular press, and one gained an impression from places like the *Saturday Evening Post* of a sort of lovable grouchy bear, fiercely protective of his stock company of actors, writers, technicians, despite his often heavy-handed tests of their loyalty (and manliness), ferociously independent of front-office opinion about his work, and, of course, heroic in his own person, whether as a naval officer producing documentaries during the war or standing up to Cecil B. De Mille and his reactionary band when they attempted to impose a loyalty oath on Directors Guild members during the McCarthy era.

In 1970, three years before his death, I spent a lovely twilight hour with him, interviewing him for a book I was doing, and it remains one of the unforgettable experiences of my life. With nothing better to do, he was playing his legend full-time, full out by that time. He lived in a dark, comfortable house just off Sunset on Copa del Oro in Bel Air.

He was a semi-invalid by then, and he received me in his bedroom, where a hospital bed had been installed. He was wearing a nightshirt, out of which poked gray chest hair, which he frequently scratched. His famous eyepatch was pushed up on his forehead. His doctor had told him to cut down on his cigars, and he was taking the order with comic literalness. He would carefully cut a stogie in half, puff it down to a stub, and then light the remaining half from the glowing end of that stub. He apologized for his house being "teetotal." He asked me if I was a director, and I replied, "No, of course not."

He glared at me. "Why, 'Of course not'? Everybody else is." And so it must have seemed to him, so many young men having crawled out from under his overcoat, having taken their places behind the camera, and then having found, as I had, some excuse to drop around and pay their respects.

We talked mainly about D. W. Griffith, for whom Ford had worked as a rider in *The Birth of a Nation*. He described the Los Angeles premiere of that film, at the end of which "I actually strained my voice yelling." He said "we copied from him outright," and there is more truth in that statement than most of Ford's admirers know. His sense of landscape and his ability to place a small, telling bit of behavior against a grand background were similar to Griffith's, as were his essential simplicity and conservatism of sentiment. As I left Ford's house, I noticed what I had not as I entered. By the front door stood a canvas director's chair, on the back of which, as if ready for the master to scoop up as he departed for the set, was draped a short outdoorsman's jacket, made of some water-repellent material. Above it, on pegs, hung a selection of hats—western, naval, workman's—also ready for him to grab in haste. There was something brave, touching, and showy about this display. It was like an image in a John Ford movie, seemingly casual but carefully calculated to create an impression—in this case that the sick old man upstairs was not ready to be counted out just yet.

And yet I think we *were* beginning to count him out by that time. Yes, official honors like the American Film Institute's Life Achievement Award continued to come to him. And yes, people continued to refer to him routinely, unthinkingly, as "America's greatest director." But these references had begun to lose their former resonance, and for most people, I suspect, his name evoked only a vaguely reverential emotion, a bit like their feeling for his sometime subject, A. Lincoln. To me, he had begun to seem like the author of a favorite series of boys' books, for which one felt a pleasing nostalgia not just for the works themselves but for the time one had discovered them and for the self one had been at that time.

But I cannot say that I was any longer truly engaged with his work. There was no powerful impulse to reexamine it. And when one chanced upon it, one's response tended to be either dutiful or idly indulgent. This was not just a question of out of sight, out of mind. Some of the other directors whose names I previously evoked—Lubitsch, Sturges, Hitchcock, Hawks—remained lively, controversial figures to me, and I actively sought out their works not only to renew my pleasure in them, but because I found that as I matured, many of their films seemed to speak to me with new voices, kindling new responses that may not have been better than my first ones but were at least different and thus kept my inner dialogue with their creators refreshed. I did not feel that we were repeating ourselves as the fire burned low and our glasses emptied.

In time, frankly, I began to avoid Ford's work, for fear that his films would not hold up in adulthood, that second sight, second thought would spoil sweet memories. I also feared that investigation of those noncanonical works that I had missed would further distress the good opinion of Ford's work to which I preferred to cling. If nothing else, I owe to Anderson, and the infectious contentiousness with which he writes about Ford, a revived involvement in his films. The trouble is that it has turned out to be an involvement every bit as contentious as Anderson's but one that, on the whole, comes to a much more dubious conclusion.

Before raising these doubts, however, I must pause to record an epiphany. A couple of years after his encounter with *My Darling Clementine,* Anderson found an obscure suburban theater playing *They Were Expendable,* betook himself to it at some inconvenience, and encountered what he quite correctly describes as a great film. It is an adaptation of a wartime best seller by William L. White, recounting the adventures of John Bulkeley, skipper of the PT boat squadron that, among its other duties, ferried General Douglas MacArthur out of Manila, just before its fall, bringing them all to a point on Mindanao, where they could be airlifted to Australia, where the general assumed supreme command of the Allied war effort in the Pacific. The picture had been put into work by MGM not long after the book's publication in 1942, and Ford had been the first choice to direct it. But he was busy with his own military duties, and it was not until he met Bulkeley in London, where the sailor had been transferred, and rode on his PT boat for several days in the English Channel, that Ford became enthusiastic enough about the project to seek detached duty to film it. It was not released until the war was over and, worse, was not about its later days of triumph but about its early months of defeat. It was greeted by critical distraction and commercial failure. And since, as Anderson says, the subject of the film is "the ethos and dedication of men at war," it has remained "distinctly unfashionable (and therefore underestimated) as a work of mid-twentieth century art." But art it indeed is, and, to borrow another phrase from Anderson, "a masterpiece."

It would be easy to describe *They Were Expendable* as an epic of loss. But "loss" is too mild a word to describe what happens to the men of Motor Torpedo Boat Squadron Three in the months immediately following Pearl Harbor. Devastation, decimation—these would be better words. In part they have themselves, their own sense of mission, to blame for this. For their superiors do not believe their little plywood craft can be used offensively; they keep insisting the boats be used for picket duty and messenger service, and some are lost in the process of proving that their craft have aggressive potential. But the issues of the film are, in fact, much larger than that. It is, finally, an evocation of, and an ode to, self-sacrificing duty. These men are professionals, career navy officers and ratings, trained to do what they must in whatever circumstances they find themselves serving. In this case their business is to conduct a rearguard action, to buy as much time as they can for their inadequately provisioned and prepared comrades facing the surprise attack by the Japanese in the Philippines, as well as for their country, desperately trying to come to grips with the fact that war has finally come to the United States, desperately trying to organize itself for a victory everyone knows will be years in the making.

Throughout they conduct themselves uncomplainingly, quietly accepting the blows fate continuously rains down upon them. There are two or three moments in the film where they get to strike back at their enemies, but mostly Bulkeley (renamed Brickley in the film and played with marvelous restraint by Robert Montgomery, who was himself a PT boat commander in the war), his number two, Ryan (John Wayne, playing, as he often did in wartime movies, a man impatiently fuming over the dilatory ways of the brass and the system), and their command can do nothing but mourn as, one by one, their boats are knocked out of action, as day by day their comrades are struck down. Often, in the later part of the picture, they are forced to leave them behind, to make their way as best they can in the growing chaos of defeat.

There are wonderful moments throughout the film: a formal dinner at which the officers gravely gather to meet the army nurse (Donna Reed) with whom Ryan falls in love when he is briefly hospitalized; another scene in which they visit a wounded comrade and all parties bravely bicker away their knowledge that he is dying; a sequence in which something like half their number, rendered redundant by the loss of their boats, march off to fight with the army and only the most taciturn and manly farewells are exchanged; a scene in which they must desert a civilian dry dock manager who has helped them repair the last of their boats and he is glimpsed, dry-eyed, almost expressionless, with "Red River Valley" playing over him as they sail away. Best of all is the long concluding sequence in which, their last boat having been rendered inoperable, Brickley and Ryan join a shambling retreat toward some kind of last stand. They are, however, rescued and ordered out of the Philippines on the last plane for Australia. On board, awaiting takeoff, two other officers are ordered off to make room for men with higher priorities, and the poignancy of their uncomplaining departure, their descent back into hell, as it were, is a brilliant summary of the film's theme.

Besides its reluctance to force up the heroism of its protagonists, there are other admirable refusals in *They Were Expendable*. Almost alone of American combat movies made during the war, it avoids speech making. At no time does anyone lecture anyone about why we are fighting or about the brave new world that will surely be built on the rubble of war. Nor is there any dialogue about the vileness of the enemy, no discussion of his atrocities, or his less than human morals or mores. Indeed, though we see Japanese ships and planes, we never see a Japanese face or hear a Japanese voice. Moreover, Ford avoids his own besetting sins as a filmmaker. There is no roistering in the ranks, no patronization of women and children (Reed's character is treated with the full dignity to which her rank and profession entitle her), no unconscious racism, relatively few quotations from military airs and banal folk songs on the music track. The composition of his shots, the elegant traditionalism of his editing, and, finally, a narrative pace that is much less propulsive than is usual with Ford—his elegy has a truly elegiac rhythm—combine to grant the film a distinction shared by very few American films of its time or, for that matter, any other. It is, in short, as close to perfection as John Ford ever came in his work, and of all his films, it is the one that most deserves the accolade Anderson bestows on it: "a heroic poem."

They Were Expendable is, for Anderson, the apex of Ford's career, and my eyes having been opened to it by him, I agree. He is also quite correct, I think, to locate the beginning of Ford's upward ascent as some kind of screen artist in 1936, with *The Prisoner of Shark Island,* which recounts the story of Dr. Samuel Mudd, the doctor who, in all innocence, set John Wilkes Booth's broken leg as he fled from the assassination of Abraham Lincoln and was, in the ensuing hysteria, suspected of being part of the plot to kill the President and sentenced to life imprisonment in the eponymous jail in the Dry Tortugas. He is pressed into medical service when an epidemic fells the prison doctor, and his humanitarian activities earn him a pardon. He is, as Anderson observes, the first entirely typical Ford hero: a modest, dutiful man whose heroism consists largely in doing his job, whatever misfortunes befall him. As Anderson also says, the picture has yet a certain awkwardness about it in its domestic scenes and, as he does not say, a certain genial and discomfiting racism in its treatment of the faithful black servant who is Mudd's prison companion.

Ford's progress immediately thereafter was erratic. But in the three-year period just before the outbreak of World War II he made a succession of movies that, taken as a group, exhibit the full range of his talent, ambition—and faults. In order they are: *Stagecoach,* his first exploration of Monument Valley, John Wayne's advent in the A's, but a film in which our intense memories of smashing imagery tend to block out our recollection of excessive chat among its stock characters; *Young Mr. Lincoln,* which aspires to the Sandburgian in its treatment of its hero but mostly alternates rowdiness with rube comedy and broad sentimentality (its ending, with Lincoln mounting his mule, his long legs almost touching the ground, and announcing that after his first country lawyer successes he must go on to the next hill, while "The Battle Hymn of the Republic" swells up and light breaks through the clouds, is among the most boldly corny—and crudely felt—conclusions in movie history); the aforementioned *Drums Along the Mohawk,* Ford's first color film, which upon reseeing, I have to believe worked so powerfully on me as a boy because of the spooky combination of ghostliness and childlike cruelty with which Ford's Indians menaced the domesticity of his settlers in this eastern western. *The Grapes of Wrath,* which imparts a possibly falsifying heroic stature to John Steinbeck's victims of agrarian dislocation and a beauty to the land which perhaps should be visioned as a torment but is still powerfully affecting in its highly simplified way; *The Long Voyage Home,* an O'Neill adaptation where self-conscious beautification of imagery really betrays Ford's theme; *Tobacco Road,* which is a little too tidy but gives Ford his fullest and most appropriate opportunity for the kind of lojinks he often misemployed for comic relief in more sober enterprises; and *How Green Was My Valley,* a tony, teary, exotic exploration of poor people—Welsh coal miners—grappling with poverty and its threat to their community—*The Grapes of Wrath* without movement but with chorales.

These films have energy, a mature mastery of the medium, and great stylistic confidence, however disparate their narratives, whatever failures of unity in emotional tone mark them. The majority of them, to some degree or other, show communities and families attempting to preserve themselves under pressure, and if the dutiful man humbly, anonymously doing a job that turns out to be heroic does not emerge as forcefully in these films as he does in the postwar westerns, he is still certainly a presence in them.

I do not think I misrepresent Anderson by suggesting that he sees this group of films as (unconscious) preparation for *They Were Ex-*

pendable, representing, as it does, a refinement of technique and of emotional control over his material that Ford did not fully achieve earlier—and would not achieve again. For though Anderson finds felicities in much of Ford's postwar work, he does not find the perfect balance of manner and means in them that this film demonstrates. Kindly, he puts the matter this way: "The lyric gift rarely survives for a long lifetime: energy wanes and experiences blunt aspiration." And so, without abandoning his allegiance to *My Darling Clementine* and without entirely casting out the cavalry westerns or *The Quiet Man,* he makes of Ford's fifties and sixties films a long, dying fall, not even excepting from his criticism, however reluctant, everybody's late favorite, *The Searchers.*

In general, I agree with him, but not so kindly. Before I pass on to that matter, however, it is only fair to make room for someone who dissents from both of us. Andrew Sarris has been Ford's doughtiest critical defender even in the director's worst moments. If in his little book *The John Ford Movie Mystery* he agrees with Anderson that Ford was least effectively poetic when he was at his most self-consciously poetic (in works like *The Informer* and *The Fugitive*), and if he shares with Anderson a general admiration for the middle period (though, of course, disagreeing in the ranking of specific films, with Sarris liking, for instance, *Fort Apache* a little more, *The Grapes of Wrath* somewhat less, than Anderson does), all this is but a preparation for a much larger disagreement.

For Sarris argues that the prewar and the immediate postwar years were all prologue. It was only in deepening twilight that Ford finally found the material that was perfectly appropriate to his poetic gift, which was all along to be a "rememberer of things past." Never mind that the pictorial gift seems to shrink, that most of the later movies have about them a cramped and careless air. Never mind Anderson's good point: that the last films cannot be seen as "a confident, close-knit" group and that there is no "personal stamp" on Ford's choice of subject matter in his last years. Sarris, working hard, manages to identify a theme that binds them together and permits them, in his view, to achieve greatness. They are for the most part, he says, "legends of honorable failure, of otherwise forgotten men and women who rode from glory towards self-sacrifice." In this period *The Searchers* becomes a crucial turning point, not just in the argument between Sarris and Anderson but, finally, in everyone's attempt to come to terms with John Ford.

The picture has had a curious history. Not particularly well received when it was released in 1956, it has become, over the years, a touchstone movie for younger critics, those whose impressionable years coincided with Ford's declining ones. They write about it constantly, and largely thanks to their ballots, it turns up regularly now on those international polls in which critics are asked to list their all-time favorite films. It excites them, as *Stagecoach* and *The Grapes of Wrath* excited an earlier generation of cinéastes. For it is the one truly aspiring movie of his later years, the only one that has something of Ford's old sweep and spaciousness about it, the only one that raises substantial moral and aesthetic issues worth grappling with critically. Indeed, since it is about a man who rode away, if not from glory then from comfort and for-getfulness, into obsession and madness, it could be argued that in it Ford sent John Wayne riding for the first and last time into modernism—or a precinct as close to it as either dared to come.

At its simplest level *The Searchers* is a revenge western. Wayne's character, Ethan Edwards, returns from the Civil War to the only family he has, that of his brother, his wife, and children. Shortly thereafter a renegade Indian band goes on the warpath and while Ethan is with a party pursuing them, they attack his relatives' cabin, slaughtering the parents and their boy, abducting the two daughters. Ethan, accompa-nied by Martin, the family's adopted son (Jeffrey Hunter), who is sup-posed to be one-eighth Cherokee), and a small party set out to track the marauders. The older girl is raped and murdered (off-camera), but Debbie, the younger, is carried deep into the wilderness, where (after she grows to the young womanhood portrayed by Natalie Wood) she becomes the captive bride of Scar, the chief who has led the raid. Ethan and Martin obsessively pursue Scar, Debbie, and their band for some-thing like a decade, in which time it becomes clear that Ethan intends to kill her since she has been "ruined" by her savage captor. In the film's climactic sequence, however, he has a change of heart and, instead of riding her down, sweeps her up into the safety of his avun-cular arms and turns for home and a final restoration of conventional order.

The film's deepest interest derives not from plot but from subtext. In the beginning, we understand, mainly through looks and gestures, that Ethan and his brother's wife have been, and still are, in love and that it is his unwillingness to confront this unspoken fact that has delayed Ethan's return from the war for several years. Later we will begin to sense that Ethan unconsciously analogizes Scar's abduction of his lover's daughter with his brother's abduction of the woman he loved. If he were to kill the aptly named Scar and the girl, he would, symbolically, heal the hidden wound that has for many years tormented him.

Obviously we are in the realm of the revisionist western, that cu-rious 1950's hybrid, intended to be revivifying, but more often stupe-fying, in which this most stylized of movie forms was freighted with current social and psychosexual concerns. Equally obviously, Ford knew he was entering this alien territory when he undertook *The Searchers,* for his feelings—and Wayne's—about what he was doing are manifestly ambivalent. The latter does not sustain the obsessed side of Ethan's nature consistently, and this is not from the lack of ability to do so; he is very effective when he chooses to play Ethan's growing lunacy openly. But much of the time Wayne reverts to his more customary screen character—impatient, short-tempered, but essentially good-natured. And Ford lets him get away it. He probably even encouraged him to do so. For Ford himself is desperately eager to navigate around his tale's dark currents.

This is particularly evident in his attitudes toward the Indians. In the brilliantly staged attack on the Edwards cabin, as darkly menacing as any such sequence in film history, they are at least granted the dignity of their otherness. They are presented as strange beings moved by forces quite beyond the white man's understanding. If this be disguised or unconscious racism, it could also be argued that it is an improvement on the too-ready "tolerance," the too-hasty "understanding" of alien races and cultures that have been so much a part of postwar popular culture. Thereafter, however, the Indians become much more conventionalized savages, mere rapacious brutes. Worse, however, is a witless comic passage in which Martin accidentally acquires a fat and stupid Indian wife, who trails after them for a time, much to the guffawing amusement of Ethan. It is patronizing, discomfiting, and entirely out of keeping with what should be the through-line of the film.

But that is not its only unconsidered digression. There is also a good deal of witless domestic comedy in *The Searchers,* most of it motivated by the blight Martin's long absence imposes on his romance with a neighbor girl (Vera Miles). While he is away, she is courted by an overcivilized youth, and his attentions culminate in a typical Ford brawl between Martin and the interloper. Though handsomely lit and well staged, it, like this whole subplot as Ford states it, is an absurd imposition on the story. If he intended to contrast the brave efforts of the settlers to impose civilized order on the anarchical wilderness (and certainly Ford's beautifully composed shots of the Edwards ranch and later, the neighboring Jorgensen ranch, which becomes the searchers' substitute home place, both looking impermanent, fragile, against his rugged Monument Valley backgrounds suggest this), then this comedy works against his intent. For these petty, blabbering citizens (among them a moron, Old Mose, played by Hank Worden, whom Ford seems to think is quite funny) are unworthy of the land they seek to master. If *The Searchers* were true to its own symbolic logic, these people would be defeated by the land and its native inhabitants. As it is, what is defeated are our sympathies for them.

Not Sarris's, though. He argues that all this "rugged frontier slapstick" is "a necessary relaxation of the frightful tensions within the characters." Even the highly dubious Anderson invokes Shakespeare, observing the comic relief he inserted into his tragic and epic works, though he very sensibly observes that in this instance Ford scarcely achieved bardic heights with his comedy. But Sarris's obliviousness to this failure, and Anderson's patience with it, understate its effect on a film that had the potential for greatness. Very simply, it represents a reversion to Ford's worst habit, which was to avoid the deepest issues of his story by telling a joke, singing a song, introducing a colorful bit of extraneous action, and, when he was not wooing us away from those issues by these means, wowing us away from them with a breathtaking scenic composition.

In his interview with Henry Fonda, Anderson records the actor's recollection that his first quarrel with Ford was over a jokey bit the director wanted to insert into the sequence leading up to his priest character's execution in *The Fugitive*. He also alludes to their fistfight on the *Mr. Roberts* location, which Fonda—who had fully internalized his role over the years he had played it onstage—recounted more fully in his autobiography. It was over Ford's attempts to insert more slapstick into a drama in which the controlling mood was wistfulness. But we really don't need Fonda's memoirs to remind us that this was Ford's weakness; the evidence is present in almost all his films. For the fact was that Ford was born and raised an Irish Catholic of the most old-fashioned kind, taught to repress his most subtle emotions and to relax his "frightful" inner tensions through booze, brawling, and vulgar sentiment. In films on the epic scale, like the cavalry westerns, these impulses could, indeed, be effectively deployed in something like the manner of Shakespeare's historical plays. But of course, *The Searchers*, despite its great vistas and despite its several action sequences, is not really an epic. It is a psychological drama about a man trying to resolve deep, dark questions about sex and race; if humor can be employed at all in such a tale, it must be of quite a different character from that which Ford placed on the screen.

If, finally, *The Searchers* is at best a spoiled masterpiece, then what claims can be made on behalf of the rest of Ford's work in this period? Fewer than Sarris makes for them, clearly. For that matter, fewer than the hesitant Anderson makes for them. The films immediately preceding it were, by any standards, dreadful. *What Price Glory?* is a farcical travesty of a play that was, by 1952, no more than a historical curiosity, though, when Raoul Walsh made it as a silent, it had its touching moments, which Ford in his turn utterly failed to realize. *The Quiet Man* was, of course, much liked at the time, but to see it now is almost unbearable. It is full of the worst kind of stage Irish stereotypes, and its attempt to extract humor from a situation in which a bride withholds sexual favors from her husband until he straightens out the matter of her dowry with her overweening brother is painful. The film is one long cliché—and patronizing toward women and the Irish peasantry, toward its audience. And the rest? A return to the Judge Priest stories (which Ford had used before, in his ghastly Will Rogers phase in 1934) in *The Sun Shines Bright,* perhaps the most heavy-handed exercise in nostalgia ever filmed; an unfelt remake of *Mogambo;* military sentimentality in *The Long Gray Line;* the *Mr. Roberts* fiasco (finished by many other hands).

After *The Searchers* the record does not greatly improve. Sarris considers *The Wings of Eagles* "sublime," and possibly underneath its masculine ruckus it has a little more authentic feeling than some of Ford's other late work, since it is a tribute to his sometime screenwriting collaborator Frank "Spig" Wead. Like *They Were Expendable,* which Wead wrote, it is a record of loss, with its protagonist bravely bearing the death of a child, the loss of his wife, even finally his inability to serve in his beloved Navy as a result of a crippling flying accident, but the film is rambling, unshaped, and bleary-eyed. *The Last Hurrah,* an adaptation of a best-selling novel about a Boston Irish politician is muted and dim, with a hasty and superficial air about it. Edwin O'Connor had some rather intelligent things to say about the passing of old-time ward politics and their replacement by celebrity politics in the age of television; but Ford was not up to realizing these ideas on film, and the picture as a whole is rather congealed. *The Horse Soldiers* is a straightforward story of a Union cavalry raid behind Confederate lines during the Civil War. It has one quite moving sequence, in which the young cadets of a military school attempt to engage the raiders, but basically it is pictorially handsome genre filmmaking of no great distinction. A dozen directors might have done it as well as Ford did. *Two Rode Together* takes Ford back into *Searchers* country: A bounty-hunting sheriff and a decently dutiful cavalry officer ride bickering into Indian country in search of white women captives, and again a potentially large theme is muddled by misplaced humor and, in this instance, sentimental romantic strivings. Out of affection for favors past one might join Sarris in indulging *Donovan's Reef,* but to say that it is Ford's *"Picnic on the Grass* just as *Picnic on the Grass* is Jean Renoir's *The Tempest"* (as Sarris does) rather overstates the case for a film centered on a relationship between two men who meet annually to have a fight. Still, there is a certain farfetched eccentricity to the comedy, which is set in the South Seas—fresh territory for Ford—and a certain energy in Ford's realization of yet another story of contentious masculine friendship. *Seven Women,* Ford's last movie, is, in Sarris's estimation "a genuinely great film." But this story of a group of women gathered in a Protestant mission in China, their lives and virtue threatened by invading Mongol hordes—Anne Bancroft's character ultimately sacrifices herself sexually to Mike Mazurki, playing the barbaric chieftain—is a ludicrous melodrama. It feels almost like a bad silent movie, so visibly quaint are its dramaturgy and its morality.

I have omitted from this not very distinguished list a couple of very minor works and two films that are, perhaps, a little more defensible. One is *Sergeant Rutledge,* Ford's interesting movie about a black cavalryman, serving on the frontier, who is falsely accused of murderous assault on a daughter of the regiment and her father, the colonel. His story is told in flashbacks from the court-martial where he is on trial for his life, and the first flashback from testimony there, about his rescue of another young woman from marauding Indians, is as fine and suspenseful a piece of work as Ford has ever done; frontier noir might be a fair description of its tonalities. And again, Ford's exploration of the themes of loyalty and duty is quite moving, especially with the element of race added in. The massive, quietly authoritative presence of Woody Strode in the title role gives the picture a powerful center. On the other hand, Jeffrey Hunter, as his defense attorney, is not a strong actor, and there is a good deal of ill-considered badinage among the members of the tribunal (its presiding officer is always trying to get back to his bottle and his poker game) and a good deal of aimless twittering among female spectators in the courtroom. Finally, the revelation of who actually committed the crime for which the sergeant is on trial is strained and gimmicky. Still, Ford's feeling for the horse soldiers and their lonely, thankless duty on the outposts of the nineteenth-century American empire remains what it was in the cavalry trilogy, decently romantic, and intermittently it shines through. These soldiers, like their Indian adversaries, had a unique capacity to awaken an authentic response in him, and it was one that he was able to express clearly and simply, without large discomfort. Indeed, the analogy between these films and *They Were Expendable,* which is after all about men doing a lonely, thankless job on the outposts of the twentieth-century American empire, grows more striking with the passage of time.

Finally, there is *The Man Who Shot Liberty Valance* to consider. In Sarris's scheme of things, it not only "achieves greatness" but becomes a summarizing statement of nostalgia for "the legends of honorable failure" and "one of the enduring masterpieces of that cinema which has chosen to focus on the mystical processes of time." Claims this large, and critical writing this deeply felt, cannot be lightly dismissed. But still I cannot help finding Sarris's close reading of *The Man Who Shot Liberty Valance* altogether richer, more resonant than the film itself, though I suspect that here the stripped-down quality of this most problematical of Ford's final works may really be a product of his failing health rather than a conscious effort at an autumnal simplification of major themes. Be that as it may, the film plays better in memory, and on the critic's printed page, than it does on the screen.

The basic story line is quite marvelously ironic. A tenderfoot, Ransom Stoddard (James Stewart), comes west to settle in the small town of Shinbone, there to hang out his shingle as a lawyer and bearer of the civilized virtues. On his way, however, he is set upon by the psychotic bandit whose name gives the film its title (he is played by Lee Marvin) and is rescued by a rancher-gunfighter, Tom Doniphon (John Wayne), who is the only man with the courage to stand up to Valance. He becomes the priggish Stoddard's protector, and at the film's turning point he kills the outlaw, but in circumstances that make it appear that it was Stoddard who did so. On that incident the latter builds a political career that eventually takes him to the U.S. Senate. Doniphon's skills —and character—are of less use as the frontier passes, and he falls into poverty and anonymity. It is his pauper's funeral that brings Stoddard back to Shinbone at the opening of the picture, and it is the inquiries of a young newspaper reporter about why he has returned that launch him into recollection and the film into the succession of flashbacks through which its main narrative is told. When the reporter recounts this tale to his editor, it is the latter who speaks the film's now-famous epigraph: "When the truth becomes legend, print the legend." As a result, Stoddard's lie is preserved, and so is Ford's great theme: that our true heroes are generally unacknowledged.

In outline, as Anderson says, this tale has the quality of a ballad, but on the screen this quality is not realized. Visually the picture is sound stage-bound; it lacks the openness the form requires, and the crudity of the film's playing, and the perfunctory staging of what should be its strongest scenes, vitiate the film's implicit power. As a result, the story's obligation to large, elegiac emotions is never quite discharged. Instead of rising to them, it falls back toward a more humble heritage, that of the town street western. As such it is, perhaps, more complex than most, more interesting to contemplate critically, but also, precisely because of its unrealized ambitions, less satisfying than some of the more modest films of its type. It is less satisfying, indeed, than Ford's other film of this type, *My Darling Clementine,* with its heroic up-angles on Wyatt Earp (Henry Fonda) as he dutifully, modestly goes about his Fordian duty of pacifying a primitive community. It is marred by banal romantic subplotting, and it is morally far less complex, but its visual "poetry" is transforming where the visual flatness of *Liberty Valance* is ultimately deadening.

The Man Who Shot Liberty Valance is the last of Ford's best case scenarios. If it, like *The Searchers* and *Sergeant Rutledge,* must be judged a failure, then Sarris's case for the work of these years must be judged a failure, too—a triumph of emotional commitment over common sense and the plain view. But I cannot let that matter go quite so dismissively. There are, I think, mitigating circumstances to be introduced on Sarris's behalf. All of us who follow the critic's trade are desperate for coherence, and the discovery of it in apparently messy artistic lives is not only a joy for the critic but a significant aspect of his function. If he is not about this business, what is his business? The trouble is that our schemata, especially when they have the pleasing symmetry of Sarris's, permitting a man of generous spirit to round off his consideration of an admired career in a dramatically and emotionally persuasive way, must be honored. Contrary to popular opinion, which values the quotable put-down and likes to think of critics as scandalous fellows, in the style of Waldo Lydecker and Addison De Witt, the best criticism, criticism that transcends its normal function as an adjunct of publicity, should take the form of appreciation, for no one can sustain the act of analysis for any length of time when one totally despises the work or the sensibility one has taken in hand. This applies especially to Sarris, who strikes me as the one regular commentator on film who has actually grown in the openness of his responses while the rest of us fight the shrinking effects of the dutiful years.

Still, the obvious danger in the appreciative mode is ... appreciativeness. Its white light can blind a critic to some fairly obvious defects in an artist's work, and though, as it happens, I find Anderson's reading of Ford's last years more persuasive than Sarris's, I think he, too, finally misses the essential point about him. It is this: Ford very largely failed to realize on film what he was trying to say, and not only because of age and a falling off of mental and physical capacities. He failed because the matter in hand—his sense of loss, his sense that the world was heading in a direction he could not apprehend even for purposes of criticism—was a matter too subtle for his art. And it would have been, I believe, even in his prime.

It seems to me that the weaknesses that become so painfully apparent to Anderson in Ford's late years—weaknesses which Anderson, like Sarris, sometimes reads as strengths—were always there, a part of his sensibility as powerful as his gifts. Another way of putting it is that films like, say, *The Wings of Eagles* or *The Last Hurrah* are not isolated phenomena; there is a little bit of them in almost everything Ford ever made. Indeed, in their carelessness and superficiality they seem like reversions to Ford's young manhood in the movies, that is, to such perfunctory early talkies as *Air Mail, The Lost Patrol, The Whole Town's Talking,* genre pieces quite inferior to similar pieces made in the same era by less revered hands. Finally, these defects of craft and conscientiousness, visible throughout his career, cannot be blamed on the studio system or his collaborators (Dudley Nichols, the screenwriter, who pushed Ford to his more self-conscious poeticizing, gets bad marks from both Sarris and Anderson) or the zeitgeist. No, the truly damaging elements in his work are projections of something essential in the man.

Among them we might list, for example, his utter failure to create memorable female characters. They run to Madonnas and whores, unless they are entirely desexualized by age or by grotesqueness of appearance. To be sure, it's not always easy to work a woman into the genres where Ford worked most comfortably. But I would point out that women are inevitably a part of almost any community and that they ought to have had more prominence and particularity than he granted them as his males ventured forth on their protective duties. Nor does it seem entirely churlish to observe that Howard Hawks, whose great subject was a much more self-consciously male community, found ways of granting women not just admission to, but delightful centrality in, his films.

Then there is the matter of the raucousness of the other ranks. How tiresome it was constantly to find Victor McLaglen and his pals boozing and brawling their way through the subplots. It was not very funny at the time, and it is even less so in retrospect. Again, a comparison with Raoul Walsh seems in order. He was an Irishman, too, and he had a certain natural affection for Celtic hijinks. But he tended to stop short of glorifying their excesses and to get something tender and even wistful into his portrayals of his fellows' wayward ways. One thinks of the delicacy of *Strawberry Blonde* in this respect, even the affectionately done roistering and railing of *On the Bowery*. And then there are other, perhaps more minor matters, Ford's execrable taste in music, which ran toward military airs and sentimental Irish and western ballads, for example. More than one of his splendid images has been vitiated by the thunderings or whimperings of his score. Finally, there was the way he seemed to lose interest in his work, to let the slack or the careless scene stand rather than to work it up.

Quibbles? Not if a man is to be defined as a "poet." The subject of film may or may not be film, but the subject of poetry is assuredly poetry. That is to say, in the end what we value in a poet is his manner, his style. I agree with Anderson (and with Sarris) that Ford's heart was generally in the right place. His conservative, but not reactionary, stress on duty, on self-sacrifice, on the need to build and defend shared values, to create communities, even if they were only temporary communities of interest—and even when he overstressed a gaseous sort of patriotism as both a cause and an effect of this enterprise—was valuable and sometimes movingly stated in his artfully simplified narratives. I do miss them, particularly in this age of radical selfhood. I could even make a case that the body politic misses them. But still . . .

It is, I think, too much to claim that he generally succeeded in poeticizing these themes. Apart from the crudenesses I have already mentioned, the sheer inarticulateness of his films, their failure to state precisely what was on his mind in any but the most platitudinous verbal terms, vitiates their claim on the poetic. He was in no sense a sophisticated or subtle vernacularist. In thinking of him, neither Robert Frost nor William Carlos Williams springs to mind. Carl Sandburg, maybe. Or possibly that earliest poet-movie fan, Vachel Lindsay.

Looking back, I suspect that everyone's lingering affection for Ford—including my own—largely depends on that crusty, rebellious legend he created and on the superb first impression he made when he placed his unquestionable gift for imagery in the service of stories a youngster could appreciate. Almost alone of the great American popular directors he brought this imagistic gift over from the silent films, and almost alone of them he continued to develop it when the main thrust of movies was elsewhere. (King Vidor did the same thing, but his stories grew increasingly exotic, not to say weird, and groping desperately for words, he gathered them to him in lush armloads.) When he was just starting out to make movies, Elia Kazan tells us in his autobiography, he sought out Ford to ask his advice on directing. He was told that once he got on the stage or location, he should throw the script away and look for ways of realizing its intentions through action and imagery. It is good advice—particularly to a director coming from the stage, where of course, dialogue is paramount. But it was, at that time (the late forties), bad advice for Ford himself. He needed to learn to trust words as badly as a man like Kazan needed to learn to trust the expressive power of the image. For words were requisite to his task as "a rememberer of things past." Judiciously used, carefully shaped, they were what he needed to redeem and transform lost time and to address subtly the other topics that activity inevitably proposed: the recession of youth; the diminution of certain gallant traditions; the fading of certain crucial values in American life. Pictorialism, mime, slapstick, broadly archetypal characters and situations—these were always insufficient to the high intent imputed to him. And the lack of more subtle resources grew deadly in the last decades of his career.

We are left, finally, with one or two masterpieces of radically simplified, but authentic, emotion, perhaps a dozen movies, the consistently striking pictorialism of which is vitiated by countless banalities of narrative, characterization, and dialogue, and an astonishing number of pictures—close to fifty of them, among the sound films alone—that are at best respectable genre pieces, at worst historical curiosities to be rather grimly borne. Memory, of course, makes deconstructionists of us all: Details of story, of specific scenes—especially bad ones— tend to escape it as the years pass, while powerful images abide. And

55

this has served Ford very well. Those great classical compositions of his, at once so spacious and so stark, so resonant with large, inarticulated thoughts and feelings—indelible impressions of our impressionable years—do not fade even when their contexts do. Those images of Monument Valley, with a brave little stagecoach bucketing through it or a troop of cavalry outlined against one of its ridges, seem to be lodged permanently in certain masculine hearts. To reject them totally would be to reject not just an aspect of the American past and the movie past, but something essential in our personal histories as well. Yet when we honestly confront them anew, we must regretfully admit, I think, that they now partake of an unintended poignancy—for roads not fully explored by their creator, for roads that are now forever closed to all American males, however profoundly he may yearn for the lost romantic spirit of young manhood.

PRESTON STURGES
ELEGY FOR THE WIENIE KING

*I*t is time to set aside all those pop Freudian explanations of the life and art of Preston Sturges. Enough about the giddy aesthete mother dragging him around the galleries and theaters of Europe, thereby instilling in him a lifelong distrust of high, formal culture. Enough about the down-to-earth stepfather in Chicago, the athlete-inventor-businessman whose values—principally his definition of success in purely economic terms—Sturges so desperately tried to emulate. Enough about how little Preston's psyche was split down the middle by their conflicting demands and how that split affected his movies, mostly adversely.

How did we get off on that sidetrack anyway? Brian Henderson, in his introduction to a collection of some of the master's best screenplays, says it's all James Agee's fault. By the time Sturges became Hollywood's hottest director—the first and at that time the only one who wrote all his own pictures single-handedly—and the interviewers from the popular magazines were coming around to do their standard eccentric movie genius numbers, Sturges realized that there was good copy for them in his admittedly curious background. It would be diverting for their readers and diversionary for him. As Henderson says, it did not do in those days for an American movie director to wear his artist's heart on his sleeve. It was much more comforting to the bosses and to the typical moviegoer to play it a little dumb. And so Sturges alleged that he shared none of his mother's high aspirations, that all he wanted to do was make funny, knockabout comedies that turned a tidy profit—the goal to which Daddy had taught him all real American men must aspire. Never a man to prune back his best inventions, Sturges permitted this tale to grow lush and purple in the retelling, though it appears that one aspect of it—the fact that it was his mother who presented Isadora Duncan with the scarf that killed her when it became entangled in the spokes of a car wheel—was a true believe-it-or-not.

In any case, all this glorious Technicolor served Agee especially well. He was emotionally committed to a different kind of comedy—silent comedy, the values of which (obviously) were kinetic, not verbal, the air of which was more austere (to put it mildly) than anything Sturges was doing. The tale was used by the critic to explain why Sturges's films, which he seems to have admired more than he could bring himself to admit openly, so often failed to meet the formal standards he felt obliged to apply to comedy. Sturges's work appeared to Agee less well made than that of Agee's childhood idols, the silent comedians. Moreover, this prefabrication permitted the critic to fit the director into the preexistent, overarching, and apparently permanent Hollywood myth in which the man of talent goes west and is corrupted by the vulgar values present there. Sturges, it seemed, was a prime candidate for yet another reenactment of this cautionary yarn, even gave evidence that he welcomed the casting.

Since Agee is for some reason Agee, a "great" critic who never got around to creating a great or even a sustained body of critical work (he had a silky, confidential style, approachably middlebrow tastes and the good sense to die young, with several promises unfulfilled), everyone who has since written about Sturges has had to contend with his fly-by-the-slicks psychologizing. Even if one were disputing it, as, variously, Manny Farber, Andrew Sarris, and Richard Corliss somewhat have, some of Agee's theory has stuck to their revisionisms. Not that Henderson, having done his best to strike down Agee on Sturges, offers anything useful by way of a replacement. Indeed, Henderson's performance both in his introduction and in his essays on each script in his collection *(The Great McGinty, Christmas in July, The Lady Eve, Sullivan's Travels, Hail the Conquering Hero)* is exceeding strange. He seems to have mislaid whatever critical sensibility he has among the reams of Sturges's papers to which he had access. It is interesting, to be sure, to learn that the seemingly profligate Sturges never really abandoned even his half-developed ideas. He was always hauling them out of his trunk, refurbishing them, and using them as the basis for new projects. On the other hand, it is not at all interesting, or profitable, to follow his progress on a script from one stage of revision to the next. The main thing we learn from Henderson's dogged pursuit of variously expanding and contracting ideas from draft to draft (with the final polish occurring when Sturges was on his feet, directing) is that he was a very craftsmanlike writer, an intelligent and reasonably ruthless self-editor, as, given the overall quality of his work, one suspected. In any event, this information, presented in mind-bending detail, argues neither for nor against Agee's reading of Sturges's character. But then Henderson appears to be a scholar in pursuit of an "edition," not a critic in pursuit of an insight.

He therefore misses a timely opportunity to start fresh on Sturges, unburdened by preconceptions. More than four decades have now passed since Sturges's great run of Paramount successes, beginning with *McGinty,* abruptly halted with *Hero.* It now ought to be possible not only to correct Agee's misapprehensions but also to abandon some of the estimable, but entirely inappropriate, critical principles with which people have been yes-butting Sturges for years. There is, for example, the question of whether or not Sturges was truly a satirist, and if not, why not? (He wasn't, but who cares?) And the matter of whether his failure to accede to the formal demands of the genre in which he seemed to be working was willful or careless. (It was neither; he just didn't give a damn.) And the endless critical cluckings about his sudden descents into broad farce, which looked to some writers like failures of the imagination or, worse, like pandering to the lowest tastes of his audience. (They were neither; they were integral to his vision, and they worked brilliantly as often as they failed miserably.) It is the same with his happy endings, which Corliss in particular finds to be "cop-outs," though I think a case can be made that they express his true, and utterly singular, authorial nature in roughly the same degree that the disconcerting black passages (notably in *Sullivan's Travels*) also express that nature's mercurial qualities.

All of this is easy enough for me to say—easier, anyway, than it was for most of the critics who have preceded me. When Sturges was at the height of his Hollywood celebrity, I was in the depths of preadolescence. His was a name I heard around, and I think I watched one or two of his movies sail over my head; but he was not a moviemaker I could appreciate at all. Then there was a long period in the fifties and sixties when he became a kind of legend of the lost, his work hard to find even in the more esoteric revival houses. It was not until the seventies, when his repute slowly began to revive, that I came delightedly to his films. Not only was I finally old enough to appreciate them, but so were a lot of people who, like me, were now sufficiently detached from the issues that not only had agitated and distracted his contemporary reviewers but had conditioned so much of the discussion that had followed in cinéaste circles.

I can sum up my view of Sturges very simply. Sturges was not, and never intended to be, the social critic, the satirist that Agee and the rest wanted him to be. James Curtis's biography *Between Flops,* a straightforward, well-researched, and admiring volume, makes it clear that Sturges was an utterly apolitical character without an ideological bone in his body; which explains why his politician characters (in *McGinty* and *Hero*) are so enduringly funny. He saw the typical American pol for what he timelessly is—a venal windbag—and was utterly undistracted by the thought that a true liberal (or conservative) commitment might cure that condition. In other words, Sturges was not, and never meant to be, a politicized social critic. He was, rather, an uncommitted observer, bemused and compassionate, but without any cures in mind for the conditions he observed. These were, he seemed to say, specifically American adjustments to, and evasions of, dull reality. The best we could hope for was the temporary palliative of a good laugh; that is, of course, the entire point of *Sullivan's Travels,* a movie I take to be emotionally autobiographical, in its gentle contempt for the social-critical aspirations of his Hollywood contemporaries, but not a statement about any frustrated ambitions of his own.

That his viewpoint, his genius, if you will, was decisively formed by his early personal history goes without saying, but not in the narrow sense that Agee proposed. If it had been, surely we would have seen at least one female in his movies who was a determined culture vulture like his mother—not exactly an unknown comic type in American movies of the time. But there is none. On the contrary, the women in Sturges movies always represent, charmingly, the reality principle stated in sweetly patient, deflationary terms. Some aspects of his beloved stepfather do possibly influence his characterizations of men—they tend to be rather quizzically loving when they get around to thinking about their relationships, which is not very often—but they tend to be far goofier than Solomon Sturges seems to have been, and much less practical.

No, I think the influence of his earlier years on his work is much simpler to understand. He was away from the United States so much, and his education was so oddly catch-as-catch-can, that when he returned, he was mildly but permanently an alien—no matter what his passport said. That is to say, most of the assumptions his fellow citizens had learned to take for granted from childhood on, all the premises they saw no reason to examine, struck him as strange and wondrous, very much worth pausing and mulling over.

It took him awhile—the better part of two up-and-down decades as a Broadway playwright and a Hollywood scenarist (he was past forty before he directed his first film)—to catalog his anthropological finds and to discover a manner of presenting them that was worthy of, and fully expressive of, their value. He has been justly praised for the structure of what is, perhaps, the most famous of the early screenplays he did not direct, *The Power and the Glory,* a recollection, from more than one point of view, of an American tycoon's career in the immediate aftermath of his death, which must have influenced the Welles-Herman Mankiewicz approach to *Citizen Kane*. The prints that survive—the original negative was lost in a fire—have a severely truncated air, as if what we are seeing may be a version cut down to fit on double-feature programs after the failure of the original road show presentation of the 1933 film. Allegedly inspired by the rise of cereal magnate C. W. Post (Sturges had been married to his granddaughter), it traces the rise from illiteracy to presidency of a railroad of one Tom Garner (Spencer Tracy in one of his best early roles), ambivalently celebrating the nerve, energy, and native shrewdness of an archetypal American yeoman. Like many of Sturges's later characters, he generally proves his worth at the expense of more conventional-minded middle-class and wealthy figures, though interestingly (considering the historical moment at which he appeared), he shares the establishment's antilabor views (an antiunion speech to striking employees is the dramatic high point of the film). There is irony in his undoing: He abandons the faithful wife, who, by teaching him to read and write and by believing in him, was greatly responsible for his rise, and is then himself abandoned by the younger woman who replaced her and who, it is strongly implied, has an incestuous relationship with his son by his first marriage. But clearly this is not yet comic irony, nor is the typical Sturgesian music for American voices yet heard in the dialogue, which is flatly realistic, and not much helped by William K. Howard's pedestrian direction.

His next attempt at an American theme, *Diamond Jim* (Brady), edges Sturges a little closer to what would become his home territory. Brady is like Sturges himself in that he is a man who knows how to make money (a great Hollywood controversy arose around Sturges's deal for *Power,* which appears to have been the first in which a screenwriter was awarded a percentage of the gross), without having much interest in using it to make more. The picture contains one pure Sturgesian madness, the invasion of a bar by a horse, and a climax in which Brady commits suicide in a unique fashion—by eating himself to death.

But it was really not until 1937 and his script for *Easy Living* that Sturges began to find his truest tone as a screenwriter. Directed by the talented Mitchell Leisen (who was Paramount's George Cukor, though apparently not so likable, especially to Sturges, who was now ambitious to direct), it tells what happens after a fur coat descends from the sky onto the head of a secretary (Jean Arthur) as she rides on the open top of a Fifth Avenue bus. This, obviously, is a screwball premise, and the film contains many stock screwball situations and characters, notably the choleric yet down-to-earth tycoon (Edward Arnold) who heaves the coat out his penthouse window in a fit of anger at his spendthrift wife and his good-natured, useless heir (Ray Milland), who

61

must learn a thing or two about life by briefly falling downward through society. This occurs as the secretary (with whom, naturally, he falls in love) rises in the world, precisely because the coat gives her credentials among the easily impressionable. But in addition to these predictable (but well-orchestrated) generic elements, one hears Sturges's voice piping above the chaos. The play of the film's language is unmistakly his—richer, more lunatic than one usually finds in films of this kind.

But even though it was a success, and Sturges's contribution to that success was widely acknowledged, he still had to wait three years for his first directorial opportunity, finally giving his *McGinty* script (worth perhaps thirty thousand dollars at his normal rates) to Paramount for ten dollars on condition he be allowed to direct. For the next few years, making the seven movies on which his immortality rests, he was like a man possessed. Everyone speaks—correctly—of their density, both verbal and visual: the way he packed his often inelegant, but (given his needs) highly practical, frames with American eccentrics, the kinds of faces that the fully acculturated native passes without noticing but that apparently stopped Sturges in his tracks; the way his sound tracks resounded with their relentlessly articulate expression of their wayward but passionately held ideas, right down to the one-line day player, whose one line was almost sure to be a lulu.

It is, indeed, his concern for language—the American language, that is—that best proves my point about the way his partial alienation shaped his sensibility. He reminds me of certain émigré artists—Nabokov comes to mind only in this one respect—for whom our clichés, our slang, which the rest of us are too familiar with to hear, ring sharply, comically. In the case of Sturges, his fascination with common speech extends to promotional sloganeering—mere existential wallpaper to most of us growing up in a heavily commercial culture. For him it provides more than just a source for an odd gag or two. It is one of the major motifs of his work. The entire plot of *Christmas in July,* it should be recalled, revolves around the hopes for rising out of the slums and his dead-end job that Jimmy, its central character, has staked on winning a coffee company's contest for a new catchphrase. (His awful, wonderful entry, designed to go with pictures of insomniac citizens, is: "It isn't the coffee, it's the bunk.") But this obsession is everywhere in Sturges movies. Don't forget that Sullivan sets out on his travels to prove his worthiness to direct the movie version of a proletarian novel hilariously entitled *Oh Brother, Where Art Thou?* (I don't know of a literary critic who has observed how often leftist political fiction of the thirties sought to broaden its popular appeal by fake biblical evocations.) Don't forget that the source of the fortune that causes the cardsharps of *The Lady Eve* to fix their cheating hearts on hapless Hopsie Pike, heir to a great brewery, is a slogan—"The Ale

That Won for Yale." And don't forget the delirious homemade sloganeering of the small-town political campaign in *Hail the Conquering
Hero,* for example, this placard: UP OUR HERO GOES, DOWN THIS ZERO GOES.

It is not too much to say, finally, that it is wartime rhetoric—
sloganeering on the grandest and most pervasive scale—that leads
poor, innocent Trudy Kockenlocker into all that trouble in *The Miracle
of Morgan's Creek.* Explaining why she ignored her father's orders not
to attend a dance for soldiers—the one at which the man known in
her dim memory only as Private Ratsky-Watsky impregnated her (unless,
of course, her sextuplets were, in fact, a new example of virgin
birth)—she says: "Soldiers aren't like they used to be when he [her
father] was a soldier. They're fine, clean young boys from good homes
and we can't send them off maybe to be killed—the rockets' red glare,
the bombs bursting in air [an inspired touch, that quotation]—without
anybody to say goodbye to them." She pauses for a moment's giddy
thought and concedes they do perhaps have families to bid them adieu,
but "How about the orphans? Who says goodbye to them?" (Another
inspiration, that linkage of peacetime's common-consent neediest case
with wartime's, the departing soldier.)

This diatribe, played in a fever combined equally of sexual excitement and patriotic fervor by Betty Hutton may be the greatest of all
Sturges's satirical epiphanies, a brilliant commentary on the mad media
rhetoric of wartime (remember "The Kid in Upper 4" lying awake in
his berth, a tear trembling on his eyelid, as he thinks about "a dog
named Shucks or Spot or Barnacle Bill" in the famous railroad ad?).
It is also an act of considerable artistic bravery since no other movie
of the war years dared send up either the official version of why we
fought or the carefully sanitized image of those who were doing the
fighting. In the movies there was no such thing as a man who enjoyed
killing, just as there were no hardened criminals or other antisocial
types among democracy's defenders. As far as the movies and the rest
of the media were concerned, America's soldiery was drawn exclusively
from the working middle class, and mainly the small towns at that,
except for the comic relief from Brooklyn and Texas. Even the mildly
out-of-step soldier—the griper or the slacker—existed merely to reform in the final reel, and no one—absolutely no one—got knocked
up after a USO dance.

But weird distortions of language of every kind, not only those of
the advertising culture, endlessly fascinated Sturges. The most endearing moment in that first directorial effort of his, *The Great McGinty,*
arises out of wordplay, which, besides being in itself a comic invention
of rare felicity, also reveals, with offhanded grace, how tough Dan
McGinty's character has been softened by marriage. He is reading a
story to his stepchildren: "I'll give you three guesses and then three

more and three other ones, but you could guess all night without guessing who it really was, because it was none other than—" His wife interrupts this splendid parody of icky children's literature to point out that the kids have nodded off. But the semiliterate McGinty, caught up in what may be the first fiction he has ever read, presses on: "... none other than our friend Muggledy-Wump the tortoys." That mispronunciation is breathtaking. And so is its capper, McGinty's delighted "That's who I thought it was." This scene is the emotional turning point of the movie, telling us that if McGinty is capable of this comprehension, then he is capable of comprehending political corruption and of opposition to it. As well, this moment, so soft amidst the general ruckus of the movie, may be a tribute to Solomon Sturges's gentle stepfatherhood.

McGinty is—shall we say?—incapable of sustained linguistic analysis. But other Sturges creations are. And they have the spunk to wrangle determinedly over these delicate matters. In *Christmas in July,* for example, Jimmy is in love with the play on words that is the basis for his slogan. But his girl friend, faithfully supportive in all other respects, is not. She simply does not understand how he expects to win a contest with a phrase that is manifestly a lie. Everyone knows that coffee keeps you awake—no matter what is claimed by the fancy Viennese doctor, whose theory about its being a soporific Jimmy has read in the Sunday paper. It is their only contentious moment. There is a little throwaway scene of a similar nature in *Sullivan's Travels.* The studio, protecting its investment in its wayward director, has sent a trailer, staffed with cook, secretary, and press agent, to follow Sullivan on his wanderings. As he trudges ahead of it, the publicist begins dictating a press release to the secretary: "Thus begins this remarkable expedition into the valley of the shadow of adversity." "The shadow of the what?" she inquires. Whereupon the van's driver speaks up in a voice as rough as his countenance: "The valley of shadow of adversity. It's a paraphrase." Sturges's America was full of autodidacts, proud of their hard-won knowledge and determined to insist on making fine distinctions based on it.

One of the best scenes in *Hail the Conquering Hero* involves a similar dispute, this time between the town mayor, who is dictating a speech to his son and commits a grammatical error. The lad corrects him. The mayor has a typically choleric fit. And ends up firing the secretary, who agrees with his son. The issue here, as it is in Jimmy's squabble with his girl, lies between the literalists and the poets, between those who see language as purely functional and those for whom it is the clothing of dreams. The mayor points out that good grammar has never been a plank in his platforms, that part of his success is based on deliberate misusage. "It gives that homey quality," he says, before drifting off into beloved clichés—"horny hands and honest hearts."

Beneath the ancient commonplaces of democracy one senses, as well, and despite his corruption, the pull of an ancient belief, now honored only in the comic breach. Bear in mind that this character's name is Everett *Noble*.

He is, finally, only another of Sturges's near-grotesque caricatures. But like all his villains, Mr. Noble is impossible to hate. For they all seem once to have dreamed some great American dream. Their problem is that they lost it—or never found its redeeming implications and now are trapped in their quotidian crassnesses. They should be seen by Sturges's heroes as cautionary figures, but the bright young men rarely make that recognition. For them the dream is so fresh, so utterly compelling. They cannot imagine its having a dark downside because they are still suffused in the glow of original innocence.

Yes, the opposite of original sin. By this I mean Sturges operated as a sort of Henry James in reverse. He came back from Europe to discover in blooming health that quality that the novelist found ever-imperiled. And the point he is making is a variant on James's. Isolated behind our oceans walls, untainted by the major corruptions of the Old World—high culture, exquisite manners, a rigid class system—we are (or were) permitted to dream on undisturbed. And even when we fall from this state of grace (which none of his heroes ever does permanently), we fall only into tolerably petty crookedness, comic eccentricity, or, at worst, those farcical kafuffles that so distressed Sturges's early critics.

How determined he was to permit his American Dreamers to preserve their dreams unvexed! Of the five central figures preserved for close study in the published screenplays—which read enchantingly, by the way—only one, Dan McGinty, comes late to the dream. It requires the love of a good woman to convert him to reluctant idealism. But once he is caught in its grips, he is willing to sacrifice everything he has just won for it—his governorship, his family, the comforts that might have crowned and rewarded a discomfited lifetime. He comes not to consciousness but to a willed unconsciousness of venal practicalities, the reason why Sturges permits him to escape to a banana republic which lacks an extradition treaty with the United States. The others, of course, are far purer. Jimmy, the coffee sloganeer, is convinced that he will win this prize because he has lost so many others. As he sees it, when he lost the how-many-peanuts-in-the-window contest, it doubled his chances in the you-fill-in-the-missing-word contest. "But you lost that one, too," says the girl. "Fine. So I was eight to one when I went into the limerick contest." "But you didn't win it, Jimmy." "That's what makes me such a cinch in this one."

And so it goes. Why can't Hopsie Pike see that Jean, the cardsharp he falls for, is not what she seems to be? Similarly, when she is working her revenge plot on him, why can't he penetrate her transparent disguise as the Lady Eve? The answer is simple: Hopsie, as he tells us, has actually dreamed a dream girl, and Jean-Eve is her living incarnation. He cannot and will not abandon that ideal image made flesh, no matter what the provocations.

It's the same way with Woodrow Lafayette Pershing Truesmith, of *Hail the Conquering Hero*. A medical discharge (for unromantic hay fever) has spoiled his chances of being the marine hero his father was and he has dreamed of becoming since boyhood. But he has been unable to abandon that fancy totally, indeed, engages in elaborate deceptions of his mother and girl friend back home rather than admit his failure. It is when they sense that in his way Woodrow lives the corps motto (*Semper Fidelis*—Always Faithful) better than they do that the six marines he meets in a bar force him into impersonating a military hero and claiming the acclaim of his hometown. Given that Truesmith has been the true smithy of his soul, loyal to his own best self all along, given that all his deceptions have been harmless—none of his business what the social consequences of other people's self-deceptions are—can one really argue that his fable requires a punishing ending?

In *The Miracle of Morgan's Creek* Sturges goes even farther. Dear, ditsy Trudy, unable to find the unholy ghost that impregnated her, carries his issue to term—and delivers herself of sextuplets. And delivers herself of *the* American dream—a first *and* a most. She is famous, and fame forgives anything, everything. Morgan's Creek, the great world, are now willing to accept her story, to make of her a home front heroine who gave her all for the cause and to provide her with her just rewards. No need to belabor the parallels between this myth and the central myth of Western civilization—the virgin Trudy, the Virgin Mary. Sturges certainly does not, though even hinting at it at any time in a Hollywood movie, let alone in the midst of World War II, is an act of staggering daring. But parallelism is not the point. The dream is the point. And in this film it is not just the beleaguered individual who sets aside reality in order to embrace the improbably inspirational. It is the whole world that finally does so.

It was, of course, the obviously genial spirit in which *Miracle* was made—no village atheism here—that permitted Sturges to get away with what in any other hands would have seemed sacrilege. That was a crucial element in all of Sturges's successes: his ability to escape the consequences of his satire. He was always ducking away into the melees he created.

Was this shrewdness—cynicism—on his part? Or was it an aspect of his vision? America as hubbub, an infinitely distractable society, incapable of concentrating very long on abstractions. No matter, probably. Historically it looks like a vision. Certainly we know Sturges despised ideologues, reformers, people whose ideas impose burdens on their fellow citizens instead of lifting them with a useful invention, or a moment of delight. It was a point he addressed directly only once, but brilliantly—in *Sullivan's Travels.* John L. "Sully" Sullivan, wildly successful auteur of *Hey, Hey in the Hayloft* and *Ants in Your Plants of 1939* dreams a dream, too, but it is for Sturges an unworthy one: that of using commercial movies to propagate what he believes to be the higher philosophical truths—as it happens, Marxist (i.e., European) theories about the class struggle and all that. This was not, in 1941, an unknown moviemaker's dream, and if there was sometimes something innocently admirable about the earnestness with which it was pursued, there was something inappropriate about it, too, not just because Hollywood was what it was but because America was what it was—politically in a state of invincible ideological ignorance.

And a good thing, too, in Sturges's view. Sully is presented not as a grim Stalinist but rather as someone possibly capable of fellow-traveling with them. In other words, he is another of Sturges's rich, good-natured, dangerously educable nitwits—an articulate Hopsie Pike. There is something sweet in his lack of cynicism and his bravery in search of direct experience of poverty. Surely abundant America can provide that, too, if you ask it nicely. Everyone, from the kindly studio bosses (their humanity irritates observers, who do not enjoy having their mythic Hollywood disturbed) to the down-to-earth girl he meets on his travels, tries to dissuade him. But he must endure the film's bleak middle passage, and we must endure that brutal break with comic conventions—one of the most daring structural strokes in American movie history, I think—in order for Sully to learn what Sturges most deeply believed—at least in those glory days. Simply stated, it is not that it is impossible to tell the "truth" in Hollywood films but that the "truth" everybody was always hectoring them to tell was a lie.

If we are a nation of eccentric and volatile individualists, each absorbed in his own private variant on the American dream, if much of the time we cannot even agree on a language with which to express this infinite multiplicity, then of what use to us are generalizations, dragooning us into the conformities of class consciousness? Or, for that matter, those of the tragic sense of life? All we can agree on is that everyone else we meet is likely to be—thank God—some kind of a weirdo. That is to say, we can reach agreement only on one point: the absolute necessity of laughing at each other—ruefully and not unkindly. That is, of course, how we laugh at Sullivan and how we imagine his audience will laugh at his characters in the comedies he vows to make after his travels have revealed to him what the girl knew all along: that "there's nothing like a deep dish movie to send you out in the open."

If there is a problem with this movie, it is not that its conclusion is "happy." It is that it is too easy, not complex enough to resolve fully the rich set of questions that preceded it. Probably this is what critics of Sturges "happy" endings are complaining about. Too many of his wildly unconventional tales end with the hasty application of conventional good cheer.

Alas, poor Sturges. The neat conclusion he always found for his movies eluded him in life. He reached the point his characters always reached at the end of his movies. He pursued his dream and enjoyed its triumphant fulfillment. The eccentric inventor hit the jackpot. He was famous. He was rich. He was honored by a grateful nation. But life is not a movie. It doesn't always end where it's supposed to. Sturges had to go on living in postwar America when the country he had discovered with his innocent émigré's eye, realized on film with a freshness unmatched by anyone, was smothered by the great wet blanket of prosperity, the price for which was near-universal corporatization, stunting and stifling the juking, jiving waywardness which Sturges, better than anyone, had crammed onto the movie screen, the very act of cramming increasing the energy of the work. Bitter decline followed. He wandered the world, his money gone, scratching away at scripts and plays that sometimes came close to production but almost never made it. He lived the unhappy ending he would not permit Sully or anyone else in his pictures to endure. True to his code, he died optimistic, believing he was merely "between fortunes" as an actor is often between roles, believing his autobiography, his impending television deal, or something was about to rescue him. Who knows? He may have been right, for we know with certainty that he was, at that moment, only between reputations.

If, now, much of the criticism he endured seems niggling and namby-pamby, irrelevant to his enterprise, one must yet admit that one's growing love for his work is in part based on nostalgia for a world that, truly though he reflected it, is now gone beyond recall. But one suspects Sturges sensed even in his glory years how quickly it was passing. Maybe it was one of the things that accounted for his energy in those years—the need to get as much of it as he could down before the colors faded. In those last sad years did he perhaps remember the poem of the *The Palm Beach Story*'s Wienie King?

> *Cold are the hands of time—*
> *that creep along relentlessly*
> *Destroying slowly*
> *but without pity*
> *That which yesterday was young.*
> *Alone our memories*
> *resist this disintegration—*
> *And grow more lovely with the passing years.*

It always gets one of the best laughs in the picture. It even appears to break up Claudette Colbert, to whom the poem (which Sturges originally composed for Rouben Mamoulian's guest book) is spoken. Its success, of course, partly depends on the fact that it is recited by a funny little man who represented the wacky way wealth can descend on you in America (he invented a variation on the hot dog which he advises Colbert not to try). But its claim on memory—on immortality, in my judgment—depends on the perfection with which it captures the essence of the hot dogs Sturges used to peddle—a farcical filling, spiced with wonder and wistfulness, wrapped in a tough-tender casing, and hawked in the most astonishing version of the American language ever to issue from a movie sound track.

ALFRED HITCHCOCK
AFTERNOONS OF AN
AUTEUR

*A*t a moderate hour each week-day morning—not too early, not too late—a moderate black automobile—not too long, not too short (and driven by an unliveried chauffeur)—slid unobtrusively through the main gate of Universal City Studios, eased up the main street—sound stages to the left, postproduction facilities on the right—and pulled up at the side door of an unprepossessing stucco bungalow. There it discharged a rotund black-clad figure who quickly negotiated the two or three steps leading to the side door of his suite of offices. Inside, it was always cool and dark and hushed, a safe sanctuary not only from the Southern California sun but from the endless hurly-burly of show business trundling back and forth all day just outside its heavily draped windows. Unless he had to report to a set to direct a picture—a business he did his best to organize so it required an absolute minimum of time and (above all) tribulation—Alfred Hitchcock did not leave this building until it was time to go home.

Not for lunch. Not even for Lew Wasserman. At the time we are talking about, the head of the studio, and then, as now, the most powerful man in the motion picture industry, came to Hitchcock. Wasserman's democratic habit has always been to take his lunch in the studio commissary and to forbid room service to his employees. But for Hitchcock he made an exception to both rules. Hitch's meal—never anything but steak or sole, with french fries for visitors—was always brought over and served in his conference/dining room. And when they both were in town, Wasserman joined him there on Fridays.

What was good enough for Lew Wasserman—who was a friend, and agent, before he became Hitch's indulgent employer—was good enough for the rest of the world. Whether we were movie mogul or movie star, screenwriter or journalist, our needs for him, his needs for us were mutual. But we recognized there was no middle ground where he could meet us comfortably, so profound were his anxieties about the unknown and its potential for the unplanned, unprepared-for incident. So we came to him.

He talked about this anxiety quite openly in interviews. But the idea was so preposterous that a fair number of readers assumed it was a put-on, something like the persona he created for the television shows he used to host—the slightly macabre, perversely jolly fat man—so obviously designed to preserve from prying eyes his private nature. It was, after all, difficult to believe that a man as wealthy, celebrated, and powerful as Hitchcock was so frightened he might get a traffic ticket that he never learned to drive. Or that when he traveled, he always booked the same rooms in the same hotels in order to avoid the unusual. Or that he would not venture out of these hostelries for days on end for fear of encountering the untoward. But the habit of caution extended to the smallest details of his life—the unvarying diet, the unvarying black suit, for example. And I came to think the very naiveté, the almost comical childishness, of his methods of eluding (or was it placating?) ill chance (by which, of course, he really meant malevolent fate) was the best evidence that he was in earnest about his anxiety.

One of his habits was more curious than the rest. He kept on his desk a copy of the master European railway timetable, a thick, densely printed tome. On idle afternoons, when he was between pictures, and between planning pictures (which took him much more time), he would thumb through this volume, planning long, complicated, entirely imaginary journeys marked by many very close connections. His approach to this pastime was like his approach to moviemaking: first imagining a trip fraught with as many perils as possible and then imagining interesting, exciting ways of avoiding them by the narrowest possible margins. The ability to outwit fate within the imaginary narratives he created, and safely, sanely to conduct the process of creating them, granted him a sense of mastery that no amount of money or honors or respect could give him in life.

No wonder he could speak of, think of little else but his work. To him everything else was an infinitely menacing mystery. But movies, especially Hitchcockian movies, are a highly compressed narrative form, one which requires, unlike the novel, great selectivity in order to eliminate the kind of ambiguities and digressions that disturbed Hitch in real life. Moreover, though a movie set always reverberates with potential chaos, the closed doors of the sound stage and the director's status on that stage contain the chaos, give it finite, control-lable dimensions. (Hitch naturally hated location work, probably the main reason his movies are so full of matte and process shots, which bring the outdoors in in a fully manageable form).

I loved listening to Hitch talk about the movies. We met when he agreed to appear in the pilot episode of a television series about movie directors that I was doing, and of course, he insisted on as much planning as possible. (Later we repeated these encounters when he asked me to host a closed-circuit TV press conference in aid of his next, and last, picture, *Family Plot.*) As he was not busy just then—*Frenzy* had just opened and he had not found his next project—he was inclined to be free with his time. Moreover, he sensed in me someone who wanted to learn as much as possible about the technical aspects of his work—how he had accomplished this shot or that—and that encouraged his loquacity, too. There was a final element in his generosity. He had reached an age—seventy-three—when he was tak-ing an interest in his posthumous reputation. If he judged an inquirer to be sympathetic and responsible, he was inclined to think of him as a keeper of the flame, someone who would help protect his reputation when mortality, the greatest mischance of all, left him vulnerable to his enemies.

He even tried to be autobiographically open with me, I think, though there a lifetime's habit of circumspection continued to tie his tongue. He would make an effort at personal recall, but it would render him uncharacteristically inarticulate. Like everyone else, I had to be content with the little anecdotes he had long ago worked up to explain how anxiety had entered his life. In one of them he is a very small boy sent with a sealed note by his father to a neighborhood police station. The Bobby on duty at the desk reads it, beckons him to follow, and without a word of explanation locks him in a cell. Five minutes later he reappears to let little Alfred out, saying he has been instructed to perform this small but infinitely sadistic act by the boy's father, so he would know the inevitable fate of naughty little boys. In another an-ecdote he is sent off to a Jesuit school the principal of which disciplines its students by beating their outstretched hands with a gutta-percha strap. "The awful part of this thing—to, say, a little boy of ten—was that having been sentenced, it was up to him whenever he should take it. He could take it at the first morning break, lunchtime, midafternoon, or the end of the day. And always it was deferred to the end of the day. And then you would go into this room and the priest would enter your name in a book and then grab the hand that was to be punished and lay this thing in. Never more than three on a hand because the hand became numb.... So then they started on the other hand. And if, by chance, the crime was so great that you were sent for twelve ...

you could only have six one day and then the other six the following day. Well, this was . . . it was like going to the gallows."

Biographers have thrown some doubt on the literal truth of these stories, and there was something a little too practiced in Hitch's telling of them. But it really doesn't make any difference if they are untrue or half true. The first story is clearly a representation of Hitchcock's controlling fear, of false arrest and punishment; the second, of his abiding interest in anxious narrative. And both are little examples of how he discharged those concerns: by creating controlled stories about them. "Psychiatrists tell you that if you trace your psychological problems back to childhood, all will be well," Hitch said. "Of course, I don't believe that at all." No, patting them into a shapely tale was his way.

Psychiatry, of course, was an institution in his rather innocent eyes. It requires confession and in return offers the consolations of belief in a creed or ideology. It was thus uncomfortably like the Catholic Church of Hitchcock's childhood, something he was drawn to and could not entirely trust. Too many bad things either are done in its name or escape its eye. Almost all of Hitchcock's films begin with the failure of the institutions that we depend on to maintain a sense of order, security, and continuity in everyday life—especially the law. They show people either unjustly accused of crimes or accidentally privy to compromising information about them. The former, of course, cannot expect help from the police in clearing their names, and it often works out that for some reason or other, the latter can't get official help either.

These situations, in turn, propel them into what amounts to waking dreams, where, for example, they find themselves running across great, open spaces but putting no distance between themselves and their pursuers. Or conversely, they find themselves trapped in some claustrophobic space or in an indifferent crowd where a cry for help would be either impolitic or unheeded. Or maybe they end up simply hanging from some very high place in imminent danger of falling . . . falling . . . falling. Simple stuff. Archetypal dreamwork to a shrink. But the director's casual implication was that it can happen here, in real life, in daylight, in the most familiar surroundings. In other words, he concretized and objectified his own obsessive fears in fictions wonderfully designed to take advantage of the cinema's natural, indeed irresistible propensity to transform reality into dreamscapes without announcing (or sometimes being aware of) what it is doing. Since most of us share those fears in mild, denied forms, he tapped into something universally compelling.

People were slow to see what he was doing, partly because he was himself slow to articulate his intentions firmly and self-consciously, and because his marvelously elliptical style, in which a twelve-frame cut could proclaim a world of menace, had not yet been fully developed.

73

The little English pictures of the 1930's *(The Lady Vanishes, The 39 Steps)* adumbrated these themes, but in a witty, agreeable, rather backed-off manner. His first American films *(Rebecca, Suspicion)* were distractingly romantic in tone and pace. He himself did not think he began to get at the heart of his matter until *Shadow of a Doubt* in 1943. It is, of course, the story of a girl discovering that a beloved Uncle Charlie is, in fact, a psychopath, what we would now call a serial killer and was then called a bluebeard—abnormality intruding on a very normal, small-town family's well-ordered life.

The critics were not very helpful in spotting what Hitch was up to. They kept stressing his technical virtuosity and his skill as an entertainer. The "master of suspense" and all that. At the same time many chided him for wasting his skills on what they persistently misread as simple thrillers. And yet as early as his 1926 silent, *The Lodger,* he had taken up his "wrong man" theme. And in his first sound film, *Blackmail* (1929), he had found a way of demonstrating visually just how thinly the membrane of civilization is stretched over the skin of irrationality, how vulnerable our institutions are to disorder. The film's concluding chase is set in the British Museum with the police pursuing a criminal past its priceless artifacts, the former endangering them with their zeal to restore order, the latter with his zeal to maintain his career in disruption. And he kept coming back to this idea. The chase at the Statue of Liberty in *Saboteur,* the one at Mount Rushmore in *North by Northwest* suggest that the most massive monuments to tradition, historical pride are vulnerable to anarchy. The attempted murder in the concert hall in both versions of *The Man Who Knew Too Much,* even the little chase in the china factory in *Topaz* make the same point about cultural institutions. And he used to like to muse about other such sequences: a chase through the House of Representatives, perhaps, or the queen reading her speech at the opening of Parliament and someone in the back of the hall shouting, "Liar."

"You take an average courtroom which is dealing with evil, examining it, processing it every day," he said to me. "The interesting, the contrapuntal thing is the remark of the usher who says, 'Order in the court.' As though that was a special thing." It was, of course, to Hitch. To him it was not empty ritual. It was a cry from the heart, a plea for a miracle in a chaotic world.

On these matters, for some reason, Hitch was more open with me, I thought, than he was with some others. Around the time I was seeing him, another prominent critic emerged from a conversation with him to complain in print that the Master seemed to have only two topics of conversation. One was true crime—a subject he kept up with through the newspapers, television, and an obsessive perusal of books on the subject—an addiction more common in England than America, he used to say. The other was film theory and technique, especially the solutions he had found for difficult problems of staging and structure. He could remember in detail glass shots he had made during his apprentice days, and he would delightedly discuss them, and all their successors, as long as anyone cared to listen.

Well, he did have this boyish fascination with mechanisms and processes, how things work. And there was more than a little show-off in him. For example, he loved painting himself into corners—all those closed-space films like *Lifeboat, Rope, Dial M for Murder, Rear Window*—and then getting out with no loss of cinematic values. More important, he really had thought much about technique, had developed a manner that was uniquely his, and had been consciously refining it over the decades. It was based on an instinct for subjectivity. "It seemed natural for me to put the audience in the mind of a particular character," to use his camera to force them gently to confront the world as he or she does, compelling a surrender of passivity and comforting objectivity. It is possibly the great glory of the movies that they can accomplish this imagistically, without resort to the awkwardnesses of interior monologue, for example.

No less important to Hitch was the fact that "the stress on the pictorial enables you to reach the widest possible audience, to appeal to a world audience in any language"—it was a legacy of his beginnings in silent films. But if his initial impulse toward the subjective was driven by instinct, he was insistently proud of the fact that he had come to a conscious understanding of that instinct and had worked out intellectually the techniques to implement it in all kinds of situations, thus achieving the best of all possible worlds for an artist; he was working at the highest, most uncompromising levels of his art (as he defined it) while at the same time holding the mass audience in thrall.

He loved to demonstrate the self-consciousness of his working methods, rather innocently believing that if he could make people see that there was nothing lucky about his inspirations, that they were the product of hard work, they would take him more seriously as an artist. He would talk about throwing away the books he adopted, working with his screenwriter for months to reimagine the story in purely cinematic terms by creating a shot-by-shot scenario perhaps a hundred pages long but containing no dialogue. By the time he finished this process, he would say he knew every shot, every angle by heart, so that when he went on the stage, he was in the position of "a conductor conducting an orchestra without a score." He would never look through the camera's viewfinder, or shoot alternative angles to protect himself, so well had he planned his montage in advance. There were, he said, seventy-eight shots in the forty-five-second shower murder sequence in *Psycho,* and every one of them was scripted in advance. Here, of course, the dictates of art happily conformed to his own demand for order and a lack of surprise, even a happy one. "I wish I didn't have to go on the stage and shoot the film, because from a creative point of view one has already gone through that process," he often said. Or words to that effect. For the only things that can happen in shooting are bad—an actor on an ego trip, a technician screwing up, a piece of equipment going awry.

All this purity, he seemed to feel, linked him to the traditions of modernism in the other arts. "We don't have pages to fill, we have a rectangular screen in a movie house," he said, and it "has got to be filled by a succession of images." It was from this succession, not out of plot or character or moral view, that ideas arose, and to think otherwise, he said, "would be the same as a painter worrying about whether the apples he's painting are sweet or sour. Who cares? It's his style, his manner of painting them—that's where the emotion comes." One understood his motives. He knew he was something more than the master of suspense, that he was doing something more interesting than making thrillers, and he was intent on making those who had so casually dismissed him as a technically facile entertainer see the true worth of his work in his terms. He was also increasingly aware of his influence on a rising generation of young directors, critics, and film historians, so he played to both audiences by turning away from old-fashioned, self-conscious moralism in his public statements.

There was considerable truth in this position, but it really was not the whole truth, or the latest truth, about Alfred Hitchcock. At some point in the postwar world, it began to be borne in on large numbers of people that considering the amount of motiveless—that is to say, irrational, psychopathic—malignity loose in the world, its effect on all of us amplified by the blare of the media, the question of what constituted pure and impure art was a fairly paltry and irrelevant one. Disorder of this kind was not quite the same thing as being falsely arrested for a traffic violation. Uncle Charlie was now everywhere. And Andrew Sarris could write, acutely: "Hitchcock's repeated invasions of everyday life with the most outrageous melodramatic devices have shaken the foundations of the facile humanism that insists that people are good, and only systems evil, as if the systems themselves were not functions of human experience." Whatever humor and felicity of style he offered to ease our way—Hitch called it "nursing" the audience— he insisted, as Sarris put it, "almost intolerantly, upon a moral reckoning for his character and his audience."

Or should one say, "Once a Catholic, always a Catholic"? For something like original sin was in his view always operating in the world, and his films universally reflected that fact, though I am not sure he ever openly acknowledged this, to me, self-evident fact. One day, over lunch, he said he had read somewhere that Ingmar Bergman had confessed admiration for his work, and it puzzled him. He could not see anything they held in common. "Well," I ventured, "you are both post-Christian artists." He looked at me quite blankly, and quickly returned the conversation to its original track, which was, as I recall, some true crimes he had been studying.

I believe there was nothing feigned about his puzzlement. He really did not see the connection between the theology that had been hammered into him as a child and the way things tended to work out for the protagonists in his movies. There was, for all his fussy, carefully thought-through attention to detail in his work, a curious innocence in his refusal to make quite simple conscious connections between behavior—whether it was his own or that of his characters—and autobiography. Those connections appear to have been purely instinctive with him. And the salient virtue of his "subjective" style lay in the way it forced us to think—or should one say, see?—as he did. That is, instinctively, in childish terror, stripped of our recourse to comforting ratiocination or ideological structure, sacred or secular.

Consider just one example, the perverse way his shooting makes us identify with the brutal sex criminal of *Frenzy*, as he tries to make his escape, with the body of his latest victim hidden (humorously, if you can allow yourself laughter) under a truckload of potatoes. Hitchcock's frequent return to a favorite topic—the falsely accused individual forced to flee from the law—is similarly motivated. The man may not be guilty as charged, but he is guilty of something. Take Cary Grant in *North by Northwest*. He didn't murder anyone, of course, but he is guilty of the sins of pride and avarice and general carelessness in his human relations. He must be stripped of his complacent veneer by increasingly deadly circumstances, must expiate his venial sins before he can be released from suspicion of mortal ones. The line between good and evil was, for Hitch, at the end, almost invisibly thin. James Stewart in *Rear Window* may solve a murder, but only because he is himself an obsessive voyeur. Marnie may be a compulsive thief, but the man who uncovers the root of this compulsion does so because he is a fetishist who must sleep with a criminal. And our identification with these figures, the ease with which Hitch created it, makes us, in effect, accomplices to their crimes.

Hitch was aware that "evil has spread . . . every little town has its share of evil," a situation he contrasted, perhaps too naively, with earlier times, "when the world was very placid in many ways." But he was much less smoothly articulate on this subject than he was on some others, much more visibly appalled—shaken—by the brutality of sin in, as it were, modernist dress. One time when we talked, he had seen something on television which caused the normally steady flow of his sentences to break into ellipses: "An interview with two . . . condemned men . . . they'd murdered six people. . . . But there the element of evil . . . was so exemplified by their attitudes. . . . The complete lack of remorse or . . . didn't even apologize. They were . . . almost . . . giggling over it. And that struck me as being . . . the epitome of evil . . . the attitudes of those men."

It is no wonder that in his later films the Hitchcock who once averted his camera's eye from the act of murder, or skimmed quickly over it, now lingered over horrifying detail: Janet Leigh's dreadful death in *Psycho;* the brutal killing in the farmhouse in *Torn Curtain* (the victim won't stay dead); the rape-murder in *Frenzy.* The psychopaths of these sequences, Hitchcock came to acknowledge, were humanity's bottom line, the ultimate disturbers of our illusory peace, creators of horrors that defy reason. Worse, they pass among us unnoticed all the time, their lunacy unrecognized until it is too late—until they have us, locked in a tiny room or fleeing across some endless open space, anyplace where our cries for help must go unheeded.

Hitch's withdrawals and silences, his narrow routines and compulsive habits were placatory. His art symbolically imitated life as he saw it. But his life was not going to imitate any aspect of his art in even a minor way. In the end, he said to me one day, the only thing he truly trusted was his talent, "the one thing they can't take away from me." I thought of that remark a few years after he died.

The last time I had gone to seen him was to request permission to use, for another television program I was working on, a clip from *Vertigo,* that subtlest of all his explorations of the obsessive personality and of the interpenetration of good, bad, and, above all, hidden motives. By quirk of contract he had full control over just five of the fifty-four features he had made, and he had been holding this one (along with *Rope, Rear Window, The Trouble with Harry,* and the 1958 *The Man Who Knew Too Much*) out of all markets for some years. We had a nice lunch, I made my pitch, saying a teasing, tempting glimpse of this masterpiece could only enhance its value, and he seemed interested. But no, he finally said, he intended these films, well rested, eagerly awaited by a younger generation to whom they had become only rumors, as a legacy for his wife and daughter.

At the time it seemed reasonable to me. Then, after a while, it didn't. In his late years he had grown enormously wealthy; he needed to harbor no fears, reasonable or unreasonable, about his family's future welfare. And even so, an accountant could have argued that the continuing distribution of these films over the two decades he withheld them might well have netted him as much as, if not more than, might be realized from a posthumous release. It occurred to me that this cache of film represented insurance not for his heirs but for his own reputation.

The idea was perfectly consistent with his habits of mind. He had always protected himself against mischance, and now in his seventies he was confronting the greatest mischance of all—death. He would no longer be around to protect and burnish his image, a task to which he had assiduously addressed himself throughout his career. The libel laws would no longer be applicable. His friends would have preoccupations more pressing than the defense of his image. And of course, he had his guilts. Of course he did. It was in his view, as we have seen, a—perhaps *the*—ruling existential condition. He could not reasonably exempt himself from it. Or from the sure and certain knowledge that there were in the world people who would come sniffing around in search of his secret sins. People are ever willing to believe the worst of their fellows and to pay good money for evidence that supports these dark imaginings.

There is not much a public man can do to protect himself against these eventualities. Hitch had always refused to erect the conventional autobiographical defense. Too much danger of self-exposure there. But these films? They included his arguable masterpiece *(Vertigo)*, two bold technical experiments *(Rope* and *Rear Window), The Man Who Knew Too Much,* which, whatever its other defects, contains what is perhaps his most brilliant suspense sequence, the murder attempt in the concert hall, and *The Trouble with Harry,* a macabre comedy that is modestly funny, modestly engaging. Moreover, these all were color films, featuring popular and even beloved stars (James Stewart is in four of them). Going to see them would be instructive for some, but pleasurable to all—not like going off to see some silent classic, which, alas, excites only specialists. Relaunching them as a group would be a minor media event, an occasion for learned reassessments of his achievements, something that would counteract whatever they might be saying now that his back was permanently turned.

Preposterous? Not if you knew Hitch. But what in the world was he guilty of? Not much, in my judgment. Both his public poses—that of the ghoulishly punning jokester on TV, that of the earnest artist charming the cinéaste in his office—were partial fictions, hiding an emotionally stunted nature. In most matters having to do with human relations, particularly relations between men and women, Hitch seemed to me permanently arrested at about the age of fourteen. Under that dark suit and bland manner there always beat the heart of a chubby, unpopular, God-haunted, sexually inhibited schoolboy, convinced that at any moment he was going to be given three (or six) of the best for impure thoughts. The only time he ever embarrassed me was when I asked him about his predilection for cool, blond heroines and he started gibbering about what one of them might be like if you got her alone in the backseat of a taxicab. It was of a piece with the other innocences I've discussed. And I've run into worse childishness in my time, and unaccompanied by genius at that. I judged it to be the product not of an excessively evil nature but of an excessively innocent and repressed one. Thing to do was change the subject.

Not Donald Spoto, though. This sometime Catholic priest loved this topic almost as much as Hitch did, though from a different perspective, needless to say. Three years after Hitch's death he published his biography, *The Dark Side of Genius,* in which he rounded up evidence of every slight, cruelty, coldness, foolishness anyone could remember Hitch committing, climaxing with the unsupported allegation that he had fallen obsessively in love with his "discovery," Tippi Hedren, star of *The Birds* and *Marnie.* When she rebuffed him, it was said, he visited unconscionable cruelty on her in the course of shooting several rigorous scenes in which she was obliged to appear. There was, perhaps, some truth in all this—but not the whole truth. Spoto neglected to balance his gossip with a critical evaluation of Hitchcock's work. But even without that effort, it should have been possible to acknowledge that like all men of large gifts, he was also, inevitably, a driven man. In his perfectionism he undoubtedly spoke sharply to colleagues and employees. Other directors, less gifted, have done far worse. And he may well have misinterpreted something Hedren did or said and, in his unworldliness, come on to her in an unpleasant fashion. Or, after years of repression, abandoned his reserve. Who can say? What one can assuredly say is that Spoto's study, widely read and in its more gossipy implications much more widely discussed, was a very unbalanced book, working off the entirely erroneous, but quite common, popular assumption that good art must somehow stem from high moral—or anyway behavioral—rigor.

Be that as it may, the damage was done. And uncannily, just as Hitchcock had fearfully imagined it might be—with accusations, true, false, and in between that he could not answer from beyond the grave. He was, or might have been, in worse condition than one of his protagonists, whom he always let off for good behavior in the last reel. But all that was in the spring of 1983. By the fall the first and best of the reissues, *Vertigo* and *Rear Window,* were in the theaters, and sure enough, there was not a movie critic in the country who did not write an awed piece about his mastery. And the lines, composed mostly of young people, started forming, just as Hitch had planned, or so I believe. These movies, which had been no more than rumors to them, were suddenly realities—and attractive, interesting ones, at that. The bright side of genius now banished the dark side to the edge of consciousness, where it belongs. The films abide. Doubtless someday there will be a movie called *Alfred,* which, like *Amadeus,* will demonstrate anew that God often presents his gifts to us in strange and unlikely forms. In the meantime, we have reason to be pleased that canny, slightly paranoid Alfred Hitchcock's clever estate planning helps us bear that point in mind. Once I asked Hitch what his idea of happiness was, and he replied, "Nothing. An empty sky." We may imagine him now, I suppose, happy at last.

STANLEY KUBRICK
THE UNBEARABLE BREVITY OF BEING

"*L*ife is too short."

Is it possible? Can it be? Could one reasonably, soberly, in full command of one's critical faculties, in full knowledge of one's critical responsibilities when confronting a major portion of a major artist's work, advance the possibility that from such a commonplace, there arose this uncommon sublimity—*Dr. Strangelove, 2001: A Space Odyssey, A Clockwork Orange*—Stanley Kubrick's marvelously varied, wonderfully ingenious, curiously gnomic contemplations of where we have arrived in the history of the race and where we might yet be going?

"Life is too short." Surely all this virtuosity, technical and otherwise, has not been lavished on the illustration of so ordinary a cliché? And surely all the speculative frenzy, and all the outrage, too, that were vented on these films when they were initially released cannot be made to dance on this pinhead phrase.

Probably not. Probably the facts of the case are more complicated than that. For Kubrick is one of the few true intellectuals (as opposed to people who merely like to play that role) ever to make movies, which is to say that the range of his interests (not to mention his reading), as well as the modernist taste for ambiguity that he shares with his kind, makes one resist any attempt to understand his work too easily. Moreover, he has honed to a very high degree the intelligent artist's capacity to cover his creative tracks with superbly misleading ex posto facto rationalizations. That, too, compels a certain caution when confronting his work critically.

But still that wretched incautious phrase keeps recurring: "Life is too short." It bustles back time and time again into the mind that has repeatedly banished it for the sin of oversimplification, elbowing aside all the more delicate formulations. And so in the end, however reluctantly, one grants it headway. Somehow the phrase seems to link Kubrick's three futuristic films better than any other: It directs one's attention away from the political, scientific, and social metaphors that have (in the order of their appearance) controlled the discussion of these films; it has textual support in statements Kubrick himself has made about his work; and, most useful of all, it has double meaning in the context of both his art and his personal preoccupations that is, I'm convinced, crucial to our understanding of the issues with which both are most centrally concerned.

Kubrick's virtuosity as a filmmaker, and the range of his subjects, have served to disguise his near-obsessive concern with these two matters—the brutal brevity of the individual's span on earth and the indifference of the spheres to that span, whatever its length, whatever achievements are recorded over its course. His works, whatever their ostensible themes, must always be seen as acts of defiance against this tragic fate.

On both points he has been quite specific. Here, for example, is Kubrick on the subject of individual mortality: "Man is the only creature aware of his own mortality and is at the same time generally incapable of coming to grips with this awareness and all its implications. Millions of people thus, to a greater or lesser degree, experience emotional anxieties, tensions and unresolved conflicts that frequently express themselves in the form of neuroses and a general joylessness that permeates their lives with frustration and bitterness and increases as they grow older and see the grave yawning before them." (This was, of course, the theme of the great, and greatly misunderstood, *Barry Lyndon,* in which Kubrick time-traveled deeper into the past than he ever has into the future. At the end of a movie full of pointless (and chance-dictated) adventures, endless, equally meaningless duplicity, all in aid of trivial social advantage, he brings his eponymous antihero to precisely the point described in the preceding quotation. The film's last words belong to an anonymous, narrator (godlike, as a novelist is), who comments simply that the people of this long-ago tale, however they stood in relationship to one another in life, "are all equal now." That is to say, they are all in their graves.

It can, of course, be argued that existence was ever thus, and for any reasonably intelligent person thoughts along these lines are, at this late date in history, only a short crawl up—or perhaps sideways—from the banal. But in fairness, one must also argue that it is in the fear of mortality that all creative work begins. Every truly interesting sensibility must entertain it, and the most interesting ones, though not very often moviemakers, tend to entertain it consciously. This is perhaps because, as Kubrick has observed, most films—even those that are made with high intent and great technical facility (Kubrick: "I mean the world is not as it's presented in Frank Capra films. People love those films—which are beautifully made—but I wouldn't describe them as a true picture of life")—consciously or not, are trying to ingratiate themselves with the audience. One feels compelled to add only this: that the ingratiatory impulse remains more visible at the highest levels of film-making than it does at the highest levels of the other great narrative forms, the novel and the theater. It is demanded critically, too, which is one reason that Kubrick films so often get reviews that range from the dim to the hostile on initial release.

But the fact remains that in the modernist (or postmodernist) world the gloom surrounding the contemplation of mortality is deeper and more pervasive than it was in any earlier time. The obvious reason for this, of course, is the loss of religious faith and the consoling promise of immortality it once offered the believer. About that also little more need be said at this late date. But as the depth and breadth of the cosmos have been made ever more evident to us by twentieth-century science, our other hope for immortality—our last hope, as it were—also diminishes. In this vastness all our accomplishments dwindle to microscopic size; our best works, our proudest achievements, get lost in the stars. And man, most especially artistic man, despairs still more. Or as Kubrick once put it, "Why, he must ask himself, should he bother to write a great symphony, or strive to make a living, or even to love another, when he is no more than a momentary microbe on a dust mote whirling through the unimaginable immensity of space?" Why, indeed? Especially when it becomes more and more clear that our universe was created by chance, is ruled by chance, and may well be snuffed out by chance.

It was the last of these matters that Kubrick spoke of first in his work, and it is the one (I venture to say on the basis of some firsthand knowledge of his way of life) that has the most effect on his day-to-day existence. About mortality and about the universal indifference one can do little except confront them with an acceptant mind. But about chance one can actually do something; one can take a few precautions that will, at least, diminish its more malevolent workings. Kubrick thus refuses to fly. Nor will he work outside the studio if he can possibly avoid it, closed environments being infinitely more controllable than open ones, especially for directors of his undisputed stature, kings in kingdoms of their own devising. He lives, too, behind gates, in well-guarded isolation, selecting those visitors he chooses to see, ordering in the books and films he omnivorously devours, reaching out by telephone and telex when he needs to get in touch with the outside world. When he sends forth his films, he does what he can to protect them from mischance. He personally inspects, for instance, every print that goes to the first-run theaters, and he keeps a file of those houses, complete with detailed descriptions, even pictures, so he can be sure his movies are not booked into environments he regards as unhealthy for them.

In this connection one thinks of his first important picture, *The Killing* (1956), in which a perfect crime, the meticulously planned robbery of a day's takings at a racetrack, is undone at the last moment by chance operating at its most absurd levels. This silly woman with her stupid dog—we don't expect to encounter such creatures in heist movies; we expect to encounter them in life, where we think of them as annoyances, not as deadly dangers to our best-laid plans. For Kubrick, of course, their sudden intrusion in his story, setting in motion the near-farcical and distinctly ironic sequence of events that results in the loot blowing away in the prop wash of what was to have been the getaway airplane, is more than a well-calculated coda; it is the whole point of the film, an expression of Kubrick's deepest sense of how the world works—refuses to work, actually. As he sees it, the lady and her dog, or something like them, must logically put in a blundering appearance at some point in all our venturings if, indeed, it is chance that rules our universe. What he is saying is that there is nothing chancy about chance's arrival in our affairs; the only unpredictable things about it are the form it will take and the precise moment of its appearance.

If this be so, then obviously the prudent man, the prudent society will take what precautions they can against the workings of this omnipresent force, try to minimize the damage it must inevitably wreck. This point is, in fact, so clear that even the dim-witted governments of the superpowers have, in one instance, made such prudence into elaborate official policy, surrounding those weapon systems which have doomsday capability and are most vulnerable to the mischief of chance—the atomic weapons—with not one but many fail-safe precautions. These are, naturally, as foolproof as the similarly elaborate fail-safe systems which surrounded *The Killing*'s robbery scheme. As a result (to borrow a subtitle), we have all "learned to stop worrying and love the bomb." Yes. Absolutely.

Dr. Strangelove is not to be read solely as a cautionary tale comically put, though it is surely a great comedy, one that we can see, two decades after its release, is going to hold up for a very long time. That is because it is a true black comedy, a comedy that proceeds from a bleak, but deeply felt, view of human nature and is not dependent for its best thrusts on its situation—the desperate attempt by the American high command to recall an atomic strike against the Soviet Union launched by a madman—or upon its satire of the already outmoded technology of the strike and the recall effort it details. What Kubrick is contemplating here are both the ironies of accident and the failure of rationalism to estimate the effects of chance on human endeavors and to build into its contingency planning compensations for these effects.

He has clearly gone far beyond the simple statement he made about the accidental nature of existence at the end of *The Killing*. Consider just the most obvious workings of chance in *Dr. Strangelove*. There would be no film if, by chance, an unstable figure, General Jack D. Ripper, had not wormed his way into the system and if, by chance, he had not been made CO of the Burpleson Air Force Base, with access to the code that can send a SAC wing on its way to Russia and if, by chance, he had not come unglued at just the moment he did, neither sooner nor later. Certainly it is chance that sends an antiaircraft burst into the radio of one bomber (instead of destroying it or hitting it in a less crucial spot), so it cannot hear and heed the recall code when it is finally found and broadcast. It is chance, too, that dictates that command of that ship rest in the hands of Major Kong, who is one of those otherwise good-natured souls whose only flaw is that he unquestioningly obeys orders, even ones that he is dubious about.

But the point of the exercise is not merely, or most significantly, to demonstrate how disastrously the law of unintended consequences can work out. It is rather to demonstrate the impotence of the rational in dealing with it. Reason is represented in *Dr. Strangelove* as either comically ineffectual or, when it is effective, comically perverse. In both modes, of course, it is portrayed by Peter Sellers, in his justly celebrated triple performance. It is interesting that at both the field level where, as Group Captain Mandrake, who discovers what General Ripper has done and must try to undo it, and at the highest echelon, as President Muffley, who must use the hot line to try to talk his Soviet counterpart into being sensible and patient about the whole mess, Sellers adopts the wheedling tones of a parent dealing with a child caught in the grips of the terrible twos. Whether he speaks in the false-hearty terms of commonsensical Mandrake or the false-hearty terms of a President who seems to be half Eisenhower, half Stevenson—a man of common decency swimming far beyond the limits of decency's power to stay afloat—these speeches are parodies of reasonableness, hugely comic statements of its enfeeblement when it confronts this harsh reality: that however grown-up they pretend to be, most people, including the most powerful, remain at heart children. The alternative is the one chillingly offered by Dr. Strangelove himself. Crippled in body, bent of mind, he is presented as a living critique of pure reason, calculating how to turn disaster into advantage for whoever pays his salary right up to the trump of doom. Reason—for that matter, all the other human sentiments—carries no moral weight for him anyway; it has long since been drained of its human components, reduced to a set of figures in his computer's memory bank.

But whether it presents itself as hand-wringing humanism or as a set of figures on a printout, reason, as we presently conceive it, is, in Kubrick's view, a poor tool with which to confront the postmodern, postatomic age. What he is saying in this film is that though man is sufficiently advanced to imagine a rational world and to build intricately rational systems for governing it, he has not yet progressed far enough in his evolution to rid himself of his irrational impulses or to rid society of those institutions and arrangements that are projections of that irrationalism. In short, man is incapable of building fail-safe systems at a level of sophistication where they include mechanisms capable of nullifying the effects of chance or of the irrationally thrown monkey wrench (they amount to the same thing actually). He is also saying, I think, that at our present level of development we will never be able to create such systems; we're just not brainy enough. He may also be saying—though this point is both much more speculative and much more ironic—that it might not be an altogether brilliant idea to do so, since we would undoubtedly sacrifice something of our essential humanity if we managed to achieve that next evolutionary level.

Not to worry too much about that, though. As we said at the beginning, life is too short. It is clearly too short for any individual to achieve this higher consciousness; it is also too short, obviously, for the race to achieve it, since the possibility of blowing ourselves to smithereens is now upon us. Such hope as there is, in these circumstances, lies in the possibility of rebirth in a new form. It is the final irony of *Dr. Strangelove* that it suggests that possibility and places the suggestion in the mouth of its resident mad scientist, who proposes that he and his elite colleagues retreat to deep mine shafts, there to live and procreate until the clouds (of radiation) roll by and, in a few generations, their heirs stroll forth to reclaim the earth. Perhaps, given the elitist principles that will govern selection of the survivor population, they will be stronger and wiser than we are now. Certainly Dr. Strangelove seems to imply as much when he puts forward this possibility. Maybe they will be weaker—inbreeding, you know. Kubrick himself is not saying. There is just this song on the sound track: "We'll meet again someday. Don't know where, don't know when. . . ." It is certain, however, that they will be different, these inheritors; in some sense reborn. And rebirth, as Kubrick sees it, is our only hope.

Vide (to borrow a word not from the Latin but from *A Clockwork Orange*'s droog tongue) *2001: A Space Odyssey,* which, as Andrew Sarris said, "is concerned ultimately with the inner fears of Kubrick's mind as it contemplates infinity and eternity." What he is mulling here is the reverse of what he considered in *Strangelove*. It is not the triumph of unreason but the triumph of reason which is presented here as cause for alarm. The opening passages of the film make that painfully clear, for the everyday reality of 2001, despite the ease with which man has mastered space travel, is one in which the banalities of our own everyday life are writ parodistically large. People ride from star to star, eating the same plastic food, enduring the same plastic smiles from the cabin attendants, as we now do making the LA–NY connection. They look out the windows at space slipping by with the same bored expressions with which we watch the Middle West slip by beneath our jets. They meet with the same false cordiality, exchange information in the same bureaucratically flattened language. Even when space travelers venture deeper into the darker reaches of the galaxy on their quasi-military missions, their rounds are dismally like those of today's astronauts. They tend to their physical fitness, occupy themselves with routine tasks, do everything possible to drain their adventure of a sense of adventure. Indeed, the mission of the space ship *Discovery*, which is to try to trace the origins of a mysterious signal-sending obelisk that has been discovered on the moon, a sign that superior life-forms visited us sometime in the distant past, though ostensibly commanded by Dave Bowman, is actually controlled by the superrational computer HAL. He is, in fact, by far the most interesting "character" (in the conventional sense of the term) present in the film. He has wit, and it would seem he is touched by something like original sin, which the human space travelers show no awareness of, so programmed into their technological routines are they.

It may be that HAL represents a "mistake" on the part of his human creators. Perhaps they didn't understand that when they wired him up for extrahuman brainpower they were, willy-nilly, creating a creature capable of the higher speculation in realms other than the mathematical—like the metaphysical—thus capable, perhaps, of wishing to prevent these poor human specimens from coming into contact with the superior intelligences they are seeking. It may even be that he deems himself to be more worthy of that honor. He is, after all, more like them than poor man is, since he, too, represents a form of pure intelligence and thus, naturally, is contemptuous of humankind's progress in this regard. One thing he surely is not is a "mistake" on Kubrick's part, though he was so regarded by many of the film's first critics, who made heavy sport of the fact that poor, foolish Stanley had made a movie in which a machine was a more entertaining character than any of the humans present. The possibility of conscious calculation on the part of the era's most consciously calculating director never occurred to them. Poor dears! They were to Kubrick pretty much what Bowman was to HAL: capable of dismantling him, but not of following his logic.

Be that as it may, the future, as Kubrick projects it from the evidence of our shared present, is dismally without resonance—romantically, intellectually, culturally. It is an engineer's future, not an artist's. And *2001* is, finally, the story of a microcosmic rebellion by the one human being who survives HAL's murderous depredations among the rest of the crew. He begins by lobotomizing the computer, then proceeds, in effect, to shuck off the shell in which civilization as he knows it has encased him. He leaves his spaceship in a smaller auxiliary vehicle, proceeding toward Jupiter and then, when moons, planets, suns, and Bowman's ship are in alignment with a monolith orbiting in space, Bowman enters a "stargate" and is eventually transported into a room where the decor is half that of the eighteenth century (the Age of Reason), half *moderne.* There he confronts his aged self, dies, and is reborn as the "starchild," a fetuslike creature, with enormous brain and eyes, who is last seen whirling through space toward some new, unimaginable destiny.

For a film that was so puzzling to its first critics (mostly because it insisted on telling its tale in the one language movie reviewers, with their unacknowledged literary bias, do not understand, the language of images rather than words—another reason Kubrick fares badly with this crowd) the meaning of *2001* seems in retrospect very clear. It is, in fact, less ambiguous than that of any other works of Kubrick's maturity. It says, quite frankly, that our present "lines of play" (to borrow a chess expression Kubrick himself likes to employ when discussing his work) are used up, without creative force or possibility. Again, our opening phrase recurs to mind: "Life is too short"—that is to say (in this context), the individual does not have time, in the space of a brief lifetime, to await patiently the arrival of circumstances that might be helpful in his efforts to evolve upwardly. Nor can he expect much help in that regard from society, which is bent on routinizing him. Nor, finally, can he put much faith in that old liberal hope, the idea of progress, the notion that somehow, automatically, technology and our developing social institutions are edging us upward toward a higher plane of being. No, Kubrick seems to be saying here, nothing short of the most daring rebellion, a rebellion that takes us to the threshold of the unknown, and then propels us over that threshold, will do. Somehow, like Bowman, we must will ourselves toward the higher consciousness, open ourselves to it. It is no accident that the film's principal musical theme is from *Thus Spoke Zarathustra,* music inspired by Nietzsche.

But one cannot leave this remarkable movie without speaking of its history since its release in 1968. Opening to puzzlement, outrage, dismissal, and the worst kind of criticism—contemptuous dismissal on the one hand, mystified awe on the other—it has become, in the few

years since, one of the major milestones on the postmodernist path—
so far the only movie that has achieved that status. Its imagery is now
burned into almost everyone's consciousness, is almost universal in its
familiarity, so much so that people refer to it in the other visual media
without seeming to be aware that they are quoting it. And that leads
one to yet another interpretation of the film's central symbol, those
monoliths scattered about the universe by the superior race on their
long-ago star voyagings. The Arthur C. Clarke short story from which
2001 evolved was called "The Sentinel," and it posited the possibility
that these enigmatic creations were just that, warning devices to tell
the superior beings when a new race evolved to a point where its
consciousness might be of interest to them. They perhaps function
similarly in the film, but I think Kubrick means us to see them in
another way as well, as art objects which signal us aesthetically as well
as electronically across the millennia, suggesting the possibility that
there are present among us superior beings, beings capable of creating
works that, even if they are buried and lost in the short term, may
speak to the beings of the future, whether or not they are shaped like
men, may indeed speak more clearly to a reborn race than they speak
to us. It would be characteristic of a man oppressed as Kubrick is by
time's fleeting quality and the fragility of man's works to suggest this
faint hope, and to express it enigmatically, as a nonverbal sign amidst
his more voluble pessimism.

His next film, *A Clockwork Orange,* also takes up the matter of
creativity just as it takes up some of the other themes of its two immediate predecessors: the limits of rationalism, for instance, and the
possibilities of rebirth. Lacking the antic spirit of *Dr. Strangelove* or
the soaring optimism of *2001,* it is a grimly comic piece, more bitterly
ironic in tone than any of Kubrick's other films. It is also, in terms of
sheer technique, Kubrick's most arresting work as well as his most
morally ambivalent one.

Alex, its central figure (superbly played by Malcolm McDowell), is
a projection into a future not much more distant than 2001, of the
contemporary spirit of juvenile delinquency, amoral and anarchistic,
yet with a certain cheekiness as well. His style is also a projection of
the contemporary punk manner, which Kubrick presciently caught
practically at the moment of its birth in London. Alex and his three
droogs (friends) devote themselves almost entirely to mugging and
rape, and—no other way to describe it—they have a flair for these
activities. In the dismal world of the future—all telescreens, cellblock
housing developments, and a dispassionate, institutionalized, welfare
state liberalism—Alex in particular represents the life-force. He has
energy, a twisted creative intelligence, a strangely compelling charm.

And one saving grace of a traditional kind: his obsessive passion for the music of "Ludwig Van" (Beethoven).

The scenes in which he leads his gang on their depredations—most notably the invasion of a country house, where a writer is savagely beaten and his wife savagely raped (to the tune of "Singin' in the Rain")—are among the most shockingly perverse in all cinema, for they are shot and edited and played to stress not the victim's horror but the victimizer's pleasure (more Nietzsche). They are, in short, extremely erotic—and imaginative, even darkly humorous in their vicious way. Another way of putting it is that they are emotionally expressive—however unpleasant the emotions expressed—in a way that nothing else is in the society Kubrick presents.

But of course, that won't do. Civility, if not civilization, must be served. Apprehended for his crimes and jailed, bold Alex volunteers for a radical new reeducation program being advanced by a "progressive" minister for home affairs. He, too, believes life is too short. Society cannot afford to wait years for prison to accomplish the moral regeneration of its inmates, which mostly it doesn't do anyway. In the new program drugs are used to open up the subject emotionally, so he can respond with proper loathing to documentary film footage recounting man's inhumanity to man. And the program works; it turns Alex into a perfect wimp, docile, passive, a good citizen. But remember, crime is his form of creativity, and when the impulse to crime is programmed out of him, so is his capacity to respond to any of the other higher impulses. Now he will retch at the thought of committing a rape in his born-again state. But he will also lose his capacity to love Ludwig Van, too. The irony is superb.

And prepares the way for a new and final irony. For the reeducated Alex now becomes, in the eyes of the liberal-humanist party, a victim of the state's technocratic and bureaucratic impulse to meddle with psyche and spirit. Such an outcry is raised that the state must now agree to reeducate the reeducated, and the film ends with a close-up of Alex's wickedly glinting eyes as he contemplates a return to a life of crime.

A Clockwork Orange is obviously cautionary in the same way that Kubrick's other probes of the future are, in that it offers a radical critique of contemporary society—its politics, culture, and moral values. It also forms a coda to 2001 by making manifest the point that rebirth cannot be achieved on the cheap, through simple technological or chemical means—a point that the earlier film's prime audience, sixties youth, responding to the film through a haze of pot and self-indulgence, mostly missed.

Taken together, these films form a sort of intellectual trilogy. The first of them mourns the failure of rationalism as we have, until now, understood it. The second of them proposes a redemptive myth, something to live for in place of conventional rationalism and, for that matter, conventional religion. The superior beings of *2001* are superior not only intellectually, not only spiritually, but in both respects. And Kubrick is surely saying that the development of our powers in one of these areas at the expense of the other would grant us only a false and illusory power. Finally, in the last film, he is again reminding us—his main theme—of the awful brevity of man's span, that salvation, rebirth of the kind he has proposed, is not a matter of hasty reform, not something to be easily achieved, as our present society with its addiction to self-help books, pop psychologizing, and the quick political fix likes to think it is. Rebirth is, to put the matter simply, a millennial matter. In the meantime, though, he is saying that short of the millennium, the good society will in some measure be a violent society, if only because questing and adventuring—even if they are merely intellectual—are violent enterprises. He is also saying that only a tumultuous society is capable of leaving its mark on the centuries or, to put the matter properly, is capable of nurturing individuals who, needing to defy their mortality, must try to leave their marks on society—some obelisks to guide and goad, whoever, whatever come later, reminding them that some superior beings, an unhappy few, preceded them.

III
A BLOODY CROSSROADS: TWO ESSAYS ON POLITICS AND MOVIES

THE HOLLYWOOD TEN
PRINTING THE LEGEND

*I*n 1970, when he was presented with the Writers Guild of America Laurel Award, annually bestowed upon a veteran of the screenwriting craft for the body of his work, Dalton Trumbo, by that time surely the most famous of the Hollywood Ten, used the occasion to make what has almost as surely become one of the few memorable formal addresses in Hollywood history. Known now as the "Only Victims" speech, he entered a moving and eloquent plea for reconciliation between groups that had become, over a period of about two decades, relentless adversaries—those former (and not-so-former) leftists who had refused to testify before the House Un-American Activities Committee about their onetime Communist party affiliations and those who had, mostly in reluctance and terrible guilt, "named names" in order to protect their careers and their families.

Trumbo took the position that the time of the blacklist was a moment of such evil that the "situation" of those required to testify "had passed beyond the control of mere individuals," so that each person "reacted as his nature, his needs, his convictions, and his particular circumstances compelled him to." There was, said Trumbo, "bad faith and good, honesty and dishonesty, courage and cowardice, selflessness and opportunism, wisdom and stupidity, good and bad on both sides. . . ." In the end, he said, it was useless to search for villains and heroes in the history of that time because "Some suffered less than others, some grew and some diminished, but in the final tally we were *all* victims because almost without exception each of us felt compelled to say things he did not want to say, to do things he did not want to do, to deliver and receive wounds he truly did not want to exchange." None, he concluded, "emerged from that long nightmare without sin."

It was—there is no other word for it—a noble utterance, quite characteristic of a man whose wit and style, whose feisty breadth of spirit were not entirely characteristic either of his fellows on the Hollywood left in particular or of screenwriters (by and large a gloomy crowd of injustice collectors) in general. It was also characteristic of him in other ways, for there was no one better than Trumbo, with his gloriously twirled and pointed mustache, his jaunty cigarette holder, and his dramatically gravelly voice, at flamboyantly seizing an occasion and making the dramatic most of it. It was that spirit, supported by an indefatigable energy, that had allowed him to sail triumphantly through the blacklist period, winning his only Oscar (for *The Brave One,* under the pseudonym Robert Rich) and writing his best script (for *Gun Crazy,* using a front). There would have been high poetic justice if this man, the most gallant and humane of the Hollywood Ten and, among its writers, the most successful (therefore, the one who lost the most professionally through blacklisting), had succeeded in recasting the moral-historical view of the era he had himself named, in a 1949 pamphlet, *The Time of the Toad* (Trumbo was never one to waste time looking for words).

In this, however, he failed dismally. The terms for discussion of the blacklist were set by the Ten themselves and by their supporters, while the drama's last act was still being played out in the early 1950's, and they thereafter permitted no deviation from the stark dialectic they insisted upon, not even by one of their own number. (Of the surviving members of the group, only the likably humane Ring Lardner, Jr., supported Trumbo's 1970 position.) Later on their interpretation of the events in which they had been caught up was taken over, unquestioningly and in its entirety, by the New Left historians of the 1970's. They completed the task of turning what anyone with the slightest degree of objectivity ought to see as an incomplete and highly sectarian view of those occurrences into inarguable gospel.

One good measure of their success came in the fall of 1987. It was then that PBS marked the fortieth anniversary of the HUAC hearings at which the Ten earned the contempt citations that eventually led to their jailing by running a documentary entitled *Legacy of the Hollywood Blacklist.* This film, partially funded and heavily promoted by the Writers Guild, contained no mention of Trumbo's apostasy, and its creators took no testimony from anyone but the blacklistees and their families. No one who took the opposite course, who agreed to testify before HUAC or any other investigatory body, was permitted to defend himself. Nor, for that matter, was any liberal anti-Communist participant in the events under examination interviewed, and no politically uncommitted student of them was heard from either. The film did allow that the Ten were Communists (though it was less forthcoming about the affiliations of others who were blacklisted), but it refused to admit that there were ever any substantial ideological distinctions between Communist party members and other leftists and liberals. As far as it was concerned, the history of the American left 1930–1950 was that of one big, happy Popular Front in which no serious sectarian warfare took place, no mortal enemies were made, until the astonishing chain of events that began with the 1947 hearings devastated paradise.

As *Legacy* would have it, sympathy for the downtrodden and the disenfranchised—stock footage of breadlines and violent strikes—and the rise of fascism abroad—shots of goose-stepping soldiers—moved large numbers of good American folk leftward, into something euphemistically known as the "progressive movement," during the Depression decade, where they remained a united band of brothers and sisters until, after World War II, the American ruling class invented the cold war out of whole cloth, mostly as a way of scaring "progressives" into conformity. Thus the darkness that came to be known as McCarthyism crept across the land, with government agencies attempting to silence political dissent by noisy, threatening inquiries into the political beliefs of quite innocent—indeed, it would seem, almost randomly chosen —American citizens. A small, heroic band resisted this madness, enduring jail sentences and the loss of their customary employment rather than bend to it. Another group cooperated with the inquisitors, ignominiously betraying friends and colleagues in the process, for no better cause than the desire to protect their own comfort. The former are to be regarded as flawlessly heroic figures. The latter are to be seen as cowards and stool pigeons and as objects of unrelenting contempt— and not only by us. For we are to understand that what took place in this country some four decades ago was a great and timeless moral drama, susceptible to only one clear and simple interpretation, which must guide our footsteps in the future, when, inevitably, the toads return looking for new toadies.

Legacy is a childish film, beneath even the routine contempt most television documentaries that attempt to take up serious and subtle issues deservedly earn, and beneath extended criticism, too. But it is apparently the work of youngish people, and so it demonstrates how thoroughly the old Communist left, a group that never fully declared its interest in an ancient quarrel, has imposed its position on posterity. Aside from the suspect hysterics of the New Right and a few members of that aging, dwindling crowd of complication mongers, the old anti-Stalinist left, there is virtually no one to whom a citizen under forty can resort for an alternative interpretation of the blacklist era.

The library is also unhelpful in this regard. The two standard, fairly recent volumes on the subject are *The Inquisition in Hollywood,* by Larry Ceplair and Steven Englund, and *Naming Names,* by Victor S.

97

Navasky. Both are well researched, with the former particularly strong on Hollywood political and labor history in the thirties and early forties, the latter especially generous in its quotations from those looking back in varying degrees of anger and anguish on their decisions regarding testimony. Ceplair and Englund are not graceful writers, and they are uninterested in moral nuance. For them, there is only one correct position in this matter, and that was silence before the inquisitors' questions. Little space and no mercy are granted to those disagreeing with them. Trumbo's speech is not mentioned in their book, and the issues he raised are of no interest to its authors.

Navasky, by contrast, uses the speech as one of the stars by which he sets his course, though he ends up at the opposite end of the world from Trumbo. His book grew out of a piece he wrote for *The New York Times Magazine* three years after Trumbo spoke, and there is no doubt that the continuing vehemence of the quarrel between the screenwriter and the critics of Trumbo's ameliorative position—most notably with another member of the Hollywood Ten, Albert Maltz—that he then uncovered led Navasky to believe that a more detailed treatment was needed, one that would not merely be an interesting narrative of a curious moment in time but also have didactic value, as a guide for right behavior, in times to come. In any event, his book reaches its climax, and throughout draws its intellectual tension from, an examination of the issues that were first publicly joined when Maltz used Navasky's original article as a platform from which to attack the position Trumbo advanced in his Writers Guild speech. Thereafter the two men expanded their arguments in a correspondence to which Navasky had access, though Maltz refused to permit direct quotation from his portion of it.

Navasky's volume was more enthusiastically received than Englund and Ceplair's had been. There was not, in fact, a negative notice of it in the general press at the time of publication, and it is easy to see why. Aside from its stylistic superiority to *Inquisition,* Navasky's willingness to grant unlimited space to those who informed under governmental duress and the sympathetic air he affects in dealing with them give his work a certain novelty. No one else, before or since, has gone quite so far out of his way to track down these people and grant them a lengthy say. Finally, aside from a couple of cases, he has not been thumpingly judgmental about their behavior. Mostly, he is all sweet reason. Or so it superficially seems.

Nevertheless, his carefully humane pose is no more than that—a pose. It is dictated more by the demands of strategy than the dictates of the heart. For in the end, no more than Maltz, who died a few years after the book appeared, was he prepared to forgive, or even genuinely to understand, the position of those who "named names." Nor was he prepared to admit that there were not only errors but (to borrow a word from Trumbo's speech) "sins" on the part of the Stalinist left, which must be taken into account in any history that pretends to definitiveness and at least a degree of judiciousness. But sins there were among Maltz and his cohorts, and by his failure to acknowledge them, Navasky leaves himself open to charges of being a less-than-forthright follower of the revisionist line in cold war historiography. It remains, for me, a minor scandal that he was so little challenged, not so much about what he has said as about what he has left unsaid.

In taking up that challenge, I want to borrow another phrase and "make one thing perfectly clear"—namely, that nothing in what follows is to be construed as an endorsement of HUAC or of the practices of witch-hunting and blacklisting by anyone, anytime, anywhere. I am not a neoconservative. I remain a liberal of a rather old-fashioned kind and a lifelong anti-Stalinist. Therefore, my natural antipathy to the know-nothing bullying of bodies like HUAC is matched by an equally strong antipathy to those whose actions are dictated by party discipline. They, too, are "victims," not heroes in my view. Indeed, I think that's what Trumbo was trying to say, without openly breaking with his old comrades.

Be that as it may, the issue, as Maltz stated it—with Navasky finally endorsing it ("Viscerally one responds to his sense of outrage")—is that it is morally bewildering to insist that everyone, committee resisters and informers alike, was equally victimized in the time of the toad. "To say 'None of us emerged from that long nightmare without sin' is to me ridiculous," Navasky quotes Maltz as saying. "To say we're equally without sin—what does that mean? What did we fight for? What did people suffer for?" Maltz even evoked a melodramatic analogy between those who named names and members of the French resistance whose betrayals sent friends to the torture chambers in World War II.

Such zeal! Such passion! And to have maintained this primal fury over the lengthening years, which saw the Ten's triumphant entrance into history not as film craftsmen of the second rank (which is what, in all objectivity, their work entitled them to) but as cultural heroes of the first rank! One understands the human impulse to avoid contact with former friends who have become enemies through what you judge to have been acts of betrayal. Trumbo himself admitted to his inability to have anything like normal social intercourse with such figures from his past. But Maltz and his fellow travelers always went farther than that. They were the ones who publicly and endlessly insisted on the irredeemability of the informers. More important, they also insisted that there were no nuances in the history they had shared, that the full story could be contained in a simple dialectic: good versus evil.

It puzzled Trumbo. He raised the sensible point that if we generally parole murderers and rapists after a suitable period of punishment, believing it is possible for them to return to society as useful citizens, it ought to be possible to extend the same treatment to perpetrators of less heinous crimes. He also felt that by focusing history's attention on the informers, Maltz and friends were diverting it from the true villains of the piece—HUAC and its moronic (and often venal) supporters. It puzzled me. When I wrote the first version of this essay, I speculated that perhaps to maintain their own heroic posture, Maltz and his comrades required, for purposes of comparison, constant reference to others whose stance was visibly more bent.

I still think there is something, perhaps a great deal, in what I said initially. But as I read and thought more about this ever-vexing subject, it began to seem that it required both more "back story" (to borrow a term of art from the screenwriters) and an attempt to draw finer moral distinctions than I—or anyone else that I have read—have so far managed. To put a complex matter simply, the unforgiving position adopted by Maltz and his fellow "progressives" was not merely a way of defending their future in history but also, intellectually and tactically, the logical extension of those ugly habits of thought that define the Communist mentality: the need to recast every situation, no matter how complex, as a simple dialectic between correct and incorrect ideological positions; the need to impose the doctrine of democratic centralism (that is, to permit no deviation from the party line once it has been set) on all and sundry; the inhuman disregard of individual circumstances in favor of the party's demands; and, of course, the need to rewrite history so that it also always favors the party.

In effect, as I hope to show, they were making, from the time of the hearings onward, a tragic and ludicrous attempt retroactively to impose their mind-set, and the strategies it proposed, on people who had broken with them, often in great bitterness, and had every reason to distrust and deplore them. If we are ever to have a balanced, judicious history of this period, some acknowledgment of this effort must be written into it. And to do that, we must also enter into the record some notion of how the show business Communists lived and operated in the years prior to the HUAC hearings. Otherwise that history is going to continue playing as it now does, like one of the World War II movies the Communists so frequently wrote, full of characters both falsely heroic and falsely villainous, overacting improbably manipulated scenes on the way to a conclusion stressing everyone's obligation to self-sacrifice—with inspirational music up and out (to borrow another term from the screenwriter's lexicon) and covering dubious dramaturgy with fake emotion.

Both professionally and politically the life of the Communists in

Hollywood was frustrating. That is the most basic fact about them. When all was said and done, they could claim only perhaps one or two major directors for their cause, no great stars, and, in the area of their deepest penetration of the industry, only a handful of significant writers. In the first, and in many ways still the best, study of movie communism, "The Day of the Locust" chapter in *Part of Our Time,* Murray Kempton noted that of the 17 individuals listed by Leo Rosten in his sociological study of the film industry as its highest-paid writers in 1938, only one was later identified as a CP member. In a place where influence has always been directly correlated with earning power, that is a telling statistic. Even more revealing is this one: When it finally tallied up the results of its investigations in 1952, HUAC announced that precisely 222 movie employees (or their spouses) had been named as party members—by Kempton's estimate, less than one half of one percent of the industry's total population. And mind, the 222 were never massed together for even a single moment. That's the total of those who drifted in and out of the party's orbit over a span of some two decades—not much to show for a great deal of sound and fury.

Nor does it seem that this tiny band had the kind of disproportionate influence that the revolutionary cadres that haunt the nightmares of the right are supposed to have. The apolitical F. Scott Fitzgerald observed their busy comings and goings and advised that they be handled "as you might treat a set of extremely fanatical Roman Catholics among whom you find yourself"—that is, as people capable of twisting an interloper's arguments "into shapes which put you in some lower order of mankind . . . and disparage you both intellectually and personally in the process." They even treated their own badly. In a recent article on Sterling Hayden's brief, but ultimately devastating, party membership, the actor's stepson, Scott McConnell, recounts a day when Hayden attempted to introduce his new comrades to his passion, which was sailing. He took them out for a day on his boat, which they passed reading, drinking, and discussing politics, rudely ignoring their host, and sparing not a moment for the pleasures of the experience. McConnell reports that in the first draft of his autobiography, *Wanderer,* Hayden began his chapter about his party days with this anecdote and that it was cut out by Angus Cameron, the Stalinist who was the book's editor.

Such behavior by the Hollywood Communists was not uncommon. These true believers were disagreeable to encounter and easy for most people to discount. As a result, their influence was peripheral. Philip Dunne, the screenwriter and director, who was among the town's doughtiest liberal political activists, wrote in his autobiography that— another disappointment for conservative fantasy—Hollywood's Communists generally found it necessary to fellow-travel with the liberals

101

when pressure groups and fund raisers in aid of good political causes were being organized, instead of the other way around. In other words, despite the secrecy with which they surrounded themselves, and despite Hollywood's reputation for political naiveté, it seems that the Communists were readily recognizable by their dourness, if nothing else, and consequently of small influence outside their own small circle.

That social failure is not insignificant—not in a community that has always mingled business and pleasure indiscriminately. But there are three more important realms in which to test the Communists' influence on Hollywood: We need to know how successful they were in providing money for their own organization and such fronts as they did control; we need to have an accurate estimate of their role in the founding and functioning of its unions; we need to determine how influential they were in shaping the content of movies on which they worked. In all three realms the record must be read as a disappointment to themselves and to the only other group that greatly cared about their activities, the hysterics of the right.

On the first of these questions HUAC provided what we may be sure was as accurate a record as can be humanly aspired to, and it was not alarming. Hollywood was "a fat cow to be milked," in the inelegant phrase of one party bagman (whose truthfulness earned him quick reassignment to fields less Elysian), and such lapses aside, its faithful were treated rather more gingerly than other, less well-off adherents because of their relative prosperity. Still, the committee's gumshoes reported that less than a million dollars was squeezed out of the movie industry in the prewar years—not bad, but not great either. People responsible for collecting party dues later reported that theirs was a not entirely grateful task. The class enemy appears to have been the business manager, keeping his clients on allowances which restricted their discretionary political expenditures. On the whole, it appears the Hollywood Communists were never quite able to buy the full respect of their coreligionists, let alone a wider following.

Similarly, their influence in Hollywood's unions was never large, despite rumors and charges to the contrary. Indeed, in the bloodiest labor confrontation in Hollywood history, a jurisdictional dispute between IATSE and a group of craft workers calling itself the Conference of Studio Unions in 1945–46, the Communists conspicuously failed to support the latter, more liberal group until it was too late. It was claimed by the right that around the same time the Communists made an attempt to gain control of the Directors Guild, but there was more fantasy than reality in the charge. Ronald Reagan seems to believe that he led a defense of the Screen Actors Guild against Red infiltration, but again the threat does not seem to have been very serious. Communists were, of course, active in the struggle to establish the Screen Writers Guild, an effort that consumed much of the 1930's, and in this, more than in any other guild, their names figure prominently as officers and board members until the period after the HUAC hearings, when party members were barred from guild membership. They obviously had an influence on the guild's philosophy and actions, and there has been some retrospective grumbling about the harsh manipulativeness of their tactics within its counsels. But was their influence a dominant one? Probably not. They always shared power with anti-Communist liberals and with people whose primary interests were nonideological, bread-and-butter issues. Dunne's memoir, for example, records many an ideological squabble with Communists in public organizations, but no significant disputes with them inside the guild—and no attempt by them to take it over either overtly or covertly. In other words, the militant factionalism the Communists displayed elsewhere in the labor movement in the thirties and forties was not vividly demonstrated in the struggle to organize the motion picture industry.

Perhaps, then, they were diverted by goals they judged more important? Like inserting doctrinaire messages in the pictures they worked on. Kempton was neither the first nor the last to make mordant sport of that notion. He repeats the legend of the screenwriter managing to work some lines from La Pasionaria into a football coach's pep talk in one of his scripts. And then there's the one about the actor who, asked to improvise some business to cover a pause in a scene, whistled a few bars of the "Internationale." He also devotes an amusing page to a listing of representative scripts that bore the credits of CP members during the thirties. They ranged from the good *(Angels with Dirty Faces)* to the bad *(The General Died at Dawn)* to the irrelevant *(Winter Carnival)*, and many, as Kempton ironically documents, earned high marks for the correctness of their "Americanism" from a source no less troglodytic than the DAR's movie rating service.

Kempton has been the only writer to introduce aesthetic considerations into the discussion of the Hollywood Ten, but after making a good start on that useful project, he shies away from specific engagement with their work in favor of contemptuous, and dubious, generalities. Still, it is necessary to say, as he does, that it is a latter-day myth "that communism in the thirties had a special attraction for the best talents." In fact, as he observes, the flirtations of the truly gifted, like John Dos Passos, Edmund Wilson, and Richard Wright, tended to be brief, not least because of the vulgar and inhuman qualities of party rhetoric. He quotes Richard Rovere, another journalist who, like Kempton himself, did not tarry long with the Reds: "The American intellectuals who fell hardest for Communism were men, not of aristocratic tastes in art, but of tastes at once conventional and execrable. Many of them, of course, had no literary taste at all. . . ." Irving Howe put the

103

point even more bluntly: "Those who supported Stalinism and its political enterprises, either here or abroad, helped befoul the cultural atmosphere."

What Kempton failed to notice was that this point could be applied to the movies as successfully as it could to the other art forms. But he shared his generation of intellectuals' contempt for American movies and so, he busied himself instead with a superficially attractive analogy between the tastes of the movies' tyrannical moguls and that infinitely more monstrous tyrant Joseph Stalin. But that analogy does not contain the full truth, for Stalin's Russia was monomaniacally concerned that art should uphold official virtue, while Hollywood interest in this issue was much more occasional. Now and then some studio chieftain would pull himself up short and spare a thought for the moral obligations and educational power of the medium, especially when some self-righteous pressure group inquired about such matters. Mostly, though, the moguls thought about making money, and what made money most consistently in the thirties and early forties were scripts of high wit and romantic elegance, and it is precisely here that Kempton might have most profitably applied Rovere's or Howe's thoughts to his subject.

For the fact is that this delicious (and, as it has turned out, immortal) manner was created by the "aristocrats" of the screenwriting trade. These men were as disparate in their backgrounds and styles as Samson Raphaelson, Ben Hecht, Jules Furthman, and the Billy Wilder-Charles Brackett team, to name just a few of the best. Kempton didn't notice it later any more than the Communist writers did at the time, but if this was only arguably the golden age of the movies, it was inarguably the golden age of the screenplay, when a premium was placed on sharply honed, wonderfully polished dialogue. A few party liners were capable of joining the fun—Donald Ogden Stewart *(The Philadelphia Story)*, Ring Lardner, Jr. *(Woman of the Year)*, and the most consistent of them all, Sidney Buchman *(Theodora Goes Wild, Holiday, Mr. Smith Goes to Washington)*—but most were not light enough on their feet for it. They worked mainly as movers of heavy furniture. They did not notice that the social commentary they kept whining that they were not being allowed to make, and Kempton scorns them for not making, was actually being done—but mainly, and most effectively, in comedy. Think not only of the works of all the aforementioned, but of Robert Riskin's many scripts for Capra, Preston Sturges's scripts for Preston Sturges, and, possibly the high point of it all, Herman Mankiewicz's brilliant satirical and structural contributions to *Citizen Kane*. Remember, too, that Dudley Nichols, a liberal who wrote some of the more highly praised dramas of the time, had sole credit for that most marvelous of screwball farces *Bringing Up Baby*. But of course, none of these movies was revolutionary in intent or manner, so they didn't count. In other words, blinkered by their ideology and hobbled by the lameness of their talents, the Communists' professional successes were no greater than their social ones.

Except for one brief shining hour, during the war, when the planets of the political zodiac lined up in a conjunction astonishingly favorable to the Hollywood Communists. It is perfectly true that Stalinists wrote most of the handful of pro-Soviet films that so bemused HUAC a few years later (*Song of Russia, The North Star, Mission to Moscow, Counterattack,* to name most of them), but the fact remains that they did not initiate these projects. Washington wanted pictures that would quickly counter the prewar stereotyping of Russia in the mass media, and the laws of typecasting suggested to their bosses that these were suitable assignments for their in-house Reds. No, their professional sins were more subtle than that—aesthetic, rather than political, though certainly it was the blunting of their sensibilities by their politics that made them so valuable during the war years. And here Kempton's observations about the ease with which a Stalinist could turn out prose to suit any monolithic master are particularly well taken.

The government's commitment to total war required, so Washington believed, a similar commitment on the part of the movie industry. And since film, the actual celluloid on which movies were made, was regarded as a strategic material, the bureaucrats had the power to enforce patriotic enthusiasm on the studios through their allocations policy, though in fact, there was no need to do so. The war was a great Hollywood subject, full of action, suspense, and romantic possibilities, and as always, the moguls, immigrants and the sons of immigrants, were eager both to cooperate with the powers that were and to prove their patriotic fealty. Most of these films were "recruiting films" (Kempton's phrase) only in the broadest sense of the word. The theme of cheerful sacrifice, by soldiers and civilians, was much prized both in the nation's capital and the film capital. So were stories in which the recalcitrant individual, in or out of uniform, sets aside his private preoccupations in order to join the group marching forward to victory. Often in the course of these tales someone would pause to make a speech against racial or religious prejudice or about the universal brotherhood of man or about the brave new postwar world everyone was fighting for. The point was that everyone, no matter how humble or how far from the fighting front, had a valuable contribution to make to the war effort. In a sense, everyone was being asked to sign up for a great crusade by these movies and was then continuously encouraged to believe he had done the right thing.

The ideas were pure Popular Front, and so was the ghastly rhetoric by which they were expressed, platitudinous and inhuman. But the Communist ear was perfectly tuned to it. They could grind this stuff out by the yard, and for four years they prospered as never before. Their commissar—he uncannily suited George Orwell's description of the breed, "half gramophone, half gangster"—was John Howard Lawson. The movies credited to this once bright hope of the left-wing theater had often been quite apolitical before the outbreak of hostilities (*Algiers,* the lugubrious American remake of *Pepe le Moko,* and *They Shall Have Music,* a musical featuring Jascha Heifetz, playing a concert for the benefit of a music school located in a slum) and, when political, indecipherable ideologically *(Blockade* and *Four Sons).* The war brought him and the movies to a point where they could happily harmonize—two Bogart pictures *(Sahara* and *Action in the North Atlantic),* as well as the pro-Russian *Counter-attack,* all of which provided him with plenty of opportunities for noble, if entirely unrealistic, speech writing.

It was the same with the others. Albert Maltz and Lester Cole rose from B pictures to A's, like *Destination Tokyo* and *Cloak and Dagger* by the former, *Blood on the Sun* and *Objective, Burma!* by the latter. Dalton Trumbo had the best war of all. He, too, had been writing minor entertainments until the war came along. But he demonstrated a gift for low sentiment in *Tender Comrade,* which concludes with Ginger Rogers reciting a monologue about her husband who has been killed in action, which she directs at their infant son: "No million dollars or country clubs or long shining cars for you, little guy. He only left you the best world a boy could ever grow up in. He bought it for you with his life." This is the way a Hollywood "progressive" thought the plain people talked—eerie, isn't it?—but the sentimentality, if not the underlying sentiments, appealed to Louis B. Mayer, and MGM hired Trumbo at what he believed was the highest salary ever paid a screenwriter to that time. There he prospered with fables about the heroism of ordinary folks *(Thirty Seconds over Tokyo, A Guy Named Joe, Our Vines Have Tender Grapes).* Appropriately his own largest victory in those days was a modest one—a scene in the first-named picture in which a character specifically refuses to indulge in hatred for the enemy. His colleagues on the left were generally less fastidious. The Japanese were customarily treated as less than human in Hollywood war films—"monkeys" was a favorite epithet—but Maltz in *Destination Tokyo* and Cole (leading a triumvirate of leftists) in *Objective, Burma!* went out of their way to prove that their belief in human brotherhood did not extend to the Oriental enemy. The anti-Japanese screeds they wrote for these pictures were shamelessly racist—and hysterical.

Be that as it may, the Hollywood Communists did well for themselves in this period. They momentarily moved from the fringe of the industry to a place closer to the center, and many of their careers flourished as never before. Indeed, this time of prosperity and general good feeling caused many of them to start drifting out of the party's orbit in those years. Most of them were not rancorous when they broke. Many seem to have retained friendships with those who remained in. The latter, in their turn, had reason to believe that whatever their politics, they were valuable to the studios and could count not only on their employers' support but on that of their old comrades and the Hollywood community at large when trouble arose. In this, of course, they disastrously miscalculated.

Central to that miscalculation was their habit of secrecy. However obvious their allegiance seemed to people who knew and worked with them in various political activities, the fact remained that most American Communists not openly identifiable as party functionaries or as employees of its publications, were not forthright about their highest allegiance. This does not mean they were spies or secret agents, but in the thirties and forties their refusal to openly state the premises from which they were operating earned them the disgust and distrust of liberals, with whom from time to time they shared some political positions, and the hatred of the non-Stalinist radical left, who, particularly in the thirties, observed that party secrecy was often the cloak for murderous depredations, particularly against anarchists, syndicalists and, of course, Trotskyites. Ultimately, of course, party secrecy played into the hands of the no-nothing right, which correctly judged that it would be anathema to ordinary American citizens; the politics of the cellar has none of the romance here that it does—or had—in Europe.

Writing about the Hiss-Chambers case in 1951, Leslie Fiedler called the unacknowledged Communist a "new-model Bolshevik . . . the more valuable as he seemed less radical. Far from being urged to sell the party press, he was even discouraged from reading it. These new secret workers had never been open members of the party; they did not merely hide, but pretended to be what they were not. For the first time a corps of Communists existed for whom 'treason,' in the sense of real deceit, was possible. These were not revolutionaries but Machiavellians, men with double allegiances, making the best of two worlds and often, like Hiss, profiting immensely within the society they worked so hard to destroy."

In 1955 Kempton put the matter this way: "The Communists are the only political party in our history with a great body of members consistently embarrassed to admit their allegiance. They tried at once to possess their dream and live outside it. When men follow that course for twenty years and are finally brought to crisis under it, they tend to behave badly . . ." In the end, and despite disputes among themselves over this matter, the Communists' contribution to the tragedy that followed the HUAC Hollywood inquisition stems from the conflict that developed between the need for openness if they were to prevail in the court of public opinion and their inability to abandon their clandestine ways.

After preliminary investigations in Los Angeles, HUAC issued subpoenas to nineteen "unfriendly" Hollywood figures in September 1947, requiring their presence at hearings scheduled for the following month in Washington. Almost all of those served were, or until very recently had been, party members. But whatever their status, they agreed to act as one in this matter, and various tactics, ranging from full denial of the committee's authority to inquire into their beliefs to full disclosure of those beliefs, were discussed by them before their Washington appearance. The latter course, it would seem, had substantial backing within the group at first—and not just from those whose loyalty to the party was now wavering or over. Of course, admission of party membership by an individual would have opened him to questioning about others he knew in the party; but if all had agreed to speak, no moral opprobrium could have been attached to anyone, and as we can see now, both the blacklist and all the ugliness it spawned might have been avoided or mitigated.

On the other hand, as Trumbo later argued, the unfriendly witnesses were "virgins." They could not predict how things would go for them, and they had no special gift for foretelling the farther future either. They made a judgment call that turned out to be wrong. But there was an obvious and understandable appeal in taking a principled stand, denying under the First Amendment's guarantees of free assembly, association, and speech the right of the committee to inquire into their political and union affiliations. They imagined—correctly—that it would play well in the press, among liberals, for that matter to the ordinary American's sense of privacy and fair play, though they underestimated another simple American instinct, which is a distrust of stealthy conclave.

They were, however, too optimistic about their chances in the courts after they were served with the contempt citations they knew their recalcitrance would provoke. In later years the Communists would claim that the First Amendment strategy was undone by a change in the composition of the Supreme Court, with a liberal majority, which might have found for them, giving way to the conservative one, which refused even to hear their case over the years it was in the lower courts. But in fact, the legal precedents in cases of this kind were ambiguous. For every decision holding that legislative bodies did not have a right to inquire into the beliefs of witnesses, there was another holding that they did. Indeed, the president of the Writers Guild, Emmett Lavery, who was also the author of *The Magnificent Yankee,* a play (and subsequently a movie) based on the life of the great liberal Supreme Court justice, Oliver Wendell Holmes, when he testified at the hearings, opened with a challenge to the committee's right of inquiry about an individual's membership in any organization, but having established that point for the record, went on to testify as to his affiliations. This was, or so it seems to me, the only justifiable position a liberal could take in these circumstances, though the Hollywood radicals consistently pilloried Lavery thereafter as a "conservative," which manifestly he was not. By doing as he did, he recognized what the Communists did not, that it was possible that even a liberal court might find against their position on purely, and quite justifiable, legal grounds. In any event, their implicit claim, at the time, and in history, that they were merely victims of a temporary aberration, a cold war hysteria that infected even the judicial system, is at best clouded.

But, then, nothing worked out as they imagined. Not in the short run. Not in the long run. In the event only eleven of the nineteen were called to testify, and Bertolt Brecht, granted a special dispensation by his colleagues, denied party affiliation and quickly decamped to East Germany, beyond the reach of the committee. The performances of his remaining associates when they testified were dismaying. The leader of their little flock, John Howard Lawson, was the first to testify, and he was strident, argumentative, unsympathetic. The newsreel footage reveals not a reasonable, put-upon liberal but a bragging, braying ideologue, so far removed from the realities of American life that he had not the faintest idea of how to win sympathy from anyone not previously committed to the cause that dared not speak its name. The rest, excepting Ring Lardner, Jr. ("I could answer that question, but I'd hate myself in the morning"), were equally unappealing.

Were they determined to provoke the most violent possible confrontation, hoping thereby to prove that their tormentors were "Fascists"? But they were not. They were figures much more common in American political life, especially American congressional life; they were ignorant yahoos, much better approached in the satirical spirit of Mark Twain, H. L. Mencken, or, for that matter, Philip Dunne's father, Finley Peter Dunne, which draws upon our traditional populist suspicion of legislators. Were the unfriendly witnesses so convinced of the rightousness of their cause that they believed people would rally to them no matter how they comported themselves? There they were on somewhat steadier ground. Even after they testified, polls showed that the majority of Americans either did not believe Communists should be punished for their beliefs or were at least still unsure on the point. But whatever revisionist historians now write, the fact remains that Soviet actions in this period were threatening and people were justifiably anxious about them, thus eager for reassurances and openness from domestic Communists on the question of where their first loyalties lay. To put it mildly, this was not an unreasonable desire.

Finally, one must ask if they overplayed their hand as a result of their recent wartime successes, believing they were now so valuable to the industry that its rulers would rally behind them? Or was the opposite true? Were the most committed of the unfriendlies, Lawson, Maltz, and Cole, together with the equally devoted Herbert Biberman (a truly awful director) and Alvah Bessie (a writer with few credits, but with deeds—he fought in Spain—to authenticate his revolutionary credentials), already seeing the possibility of fame, even immortality, by turning themselves into martyrs? The history of the radical left is, after all, studded with people ranging from Sacco and Vanzetti to the Scottsboro Boys to Tom Mooney, around whose causes—some of them dubious—the faithful had rallied, and whose names, as a result, had gloriously gone down in the only history that counts with Communists, the history they write themselves. After all those years in the political shadows, and with little to show for them artistically either, was it possible that such a moment was being seized here?

All these questions are speculative. But whatever their motivations, the unfriendly witnesses undoubtedly did themselves harm in their appearance before HUAC, though it did not seem to be at first irreparable. For one thing, HUAC's chairman, J. Parnell Thomas, abruptly canceled the hearings before the last nine of them were called to the stand. Apparently he felt public opinion was running against the committee, and in any event he was having great (and understandable) difficulty documenting any harm they had done. Some—Kempton among them—believe he would not even have called for a blacklist if support among the groups the unfriendly witnesses required had not immediately begun to erode.

Philip Dunne recalls that the mood among the Committee for the First Amendment, the unfriendly witnesses' chief liberal support group as they returned to Hollywood, was elated. To be sure, the Hollywood right, led by fanatics like the director Sam Wood and Adolphe Menjou, had recruited one or two relative innocents like Gary Cooper to appear with them as friendly witnesses at the committee's revels, and the right was to grow more and more voluble in the years immediately ahead; but many more famous faces had appeared in support of the unfriendly group, and if some of them had been dismayed by their champions' demeanors, for the moment many believed they still had a chance of winning the fight.

Almost immediately, however, something distinctly unpleasant occurred. Back in Hollywood, Dunne and director William Wyler had what they thought was a bright idea. Their committee would purchase network radio time, put all the unfriendlies on, have them take an oath, and then testify freely on their political beliefs. Dunne put the idea to some of their lawyers, pointing out that if more than a few of the group were Communists, the ploy would backfire. This caveat outraged Bartley Crum, one of the attorneys. All his clients had sworn to him that they were not party members, and Dunne's mild hint of concern riled his innocent Republican heart. That very evening, however, Adrian Scott, who was, as we shall see, the most tragic of the ten, quietly advised Dunne to abandon his idea, on the ground that it would backfire. (Later, of course, Crum and the other lawyers learned that at least some of their clients had indeed lied to them.) When the nineteen officially, and contemptuously, rejected the committee's offer, support in the liberal community began to erode. Many committee members continued to offer financial and moral support to the unfriendly witnesses as individuals (Dunne was ready to quit his job at Twentieth Century-Fox in protest when the studio fired Ring Lardner, Jr.; and was dissuaded by Lardner himself), but their organization was effectively disarmed by the continuing refusal of the nineteen to speak forthrightly about their political convictions.

But now events were passing out of community hands. The Hollywood Ten, as they were beginning to be known, had been widely defended in the civilized press, but down at the American Legion level of American life, some boycotts against films on which the unfriendly witnesses, and even some of their liberal supporters, had worked were organized. Hollywood had always overreacted to such tactics; the threat of them, by any minority, however minuscule or mad, is what has always made the industry timorous and self-censorious. True to this spirit, the group that was most crucial to the leftists' defense, their employers, deserted them. A month after the suspension of the hearings, industry leaders met at the Waldorf-Astoria in New York and, after two days of deliberation, issued the notorious statement in which they promised not to employ "the ten Hollywood men who have been cited for contempt" until they had been acquitted of the charge or had otherwise purged themselves of it. Moreover, they promised not knowingly to employ a Communist or anyone else advocating the overthrow of the government by force or by illegal or unconstitutional means in the future. There was one notable dissenter, Samuel Goldwyn, most independent of the independent producers, and the most legendary of the mogul-ogres, Harry Cohn, railed against anyone trying to tell him how to run his business. But as with the unfriendlies themselves, democratic centralism prevailed; once the group decision was reached, all were expected to abide by it, whatever their private reservations.

In his evaluation of this history, one of Dalton Trumbo's arguments for forgiving the defectors on the left was that the exclusive concentration on their sins by Maltz and his ilk was that "to concentrate on them was to forget the enemy. The enemy was the goddamned committee." He should have included the goddamned pusillanimous moguls, tyrants in their own backyards, cowards whenever they ventured into the great world. For remember, at the moment they issued their statement they were truly monarchs of all they surveyed. Television was not yet a force threatening their existence; they had yet to divest themselves of their theater chains, as they were forced to do the next year to settle a long-standing antitrust action against them. They were, in short, men of enormous power and enormous resources to assert their will—if they had wanted to.

Their motivations are beyond the purview of this essay, but in *An Empire of Their Own*, the best study of the Jewish immigrants and sons of immigrants who founded the motion picture industry and who, at that time, still remained in control of their creation, Neal Gabler attributes their action to fear of anti-Semitism. As the most visibly prosperous Jews in America, they had always been particularly attuned to this disease, and they saw HUAC as chiefly motivated by it. They may have been overreacting, but anti-Semitism was certainly the great unspoken element in the committee's activities. At any rate, as Gabler writes, "the choice between abetting HUAC and unleashing anti-Semitic forces which they believed might soon be aimed at them, or opposing HUAC and risking charges of anti-Americanism, posed a terrible dilemma, far more excruciating than the left-wing writers thought—for it placed the means of their life's work against the end. Their control of Hollywood, which would be endangered if they did not support HUAC, had been the avenue for gaining American respectability, which would be doomed if they didn't." That is putting it kindly, but it is also the only kindness one can imagine extending to them in this circumstance.

In effect, the professional fates of the Hollywood Ten were sealed by their employers within a month of their Washington appearances, but it was two years before they exhausted all their legal appeals and reported to serve their sentences—a year for eight of them, six months for two who drew a lenient judge—in various minimum-security prisons. None of them would work openly in the movies until 1960—a harsh price to pay for one's political convictions, though not so harsh, obviously, as the one demanded of dissidents in the Soviet Union.

HUAC paused in its persecutions while the Ten's cases were adjudicated. But soon after they went to jail (along with the man who chaired their hearings, J. Parnell Thomas, who was convicted, as one might expect of a petty politician of his ilk, of minor corruption), the committee returned to its investigations of film industry communism. The First Amendment defense having been held invalid by the courts, a witness now had no principled retort he could make to queries about his past associations. He could, as the saying went, "take the Fifth"— that is, invoke the right not to incriminate himself for "crimes" he did not really believe were crimes—or he could answer the investigators' questions. The first course allowed him to avoid jail but, because of the policy first enunciated in the Waldorf statement, barred him from open employment in films and, latterly, in television. A full response to committee questions had to include the names of former associates, and it was obviously repugnant. But it did permit one to go on working, and fifty-eight Hollywood people chose this course. Most did their best to confine the damage by naming persons who had previously been identified as Communists, but the committee's staff had done its work well. They were eager to jog reluctant memories with specific queries.

That, as it happens, is a crucial point. The questions were pure ritual. The committee already knew everything any witness might conceivably have to say. Even Ceplair and Englund admit this point, though in their customarily loaded language:

> Contrary to the victims' angry feelings, the informers did not *cause* [their italics] the destruction which overtook their uncompromising colleagues. By April 1951 it was eminently clear even to the most blithe Hollywood radical that HUAC did not need the exposés provided by the informers; that the Committee had sufficient nails, wood and bloodthirsty onlookers for all the crucifixions. Even if no one had "confessed" it is clear that [John S.] Wood [the new committee chairman] and his cohorts would have coldly, briskly and efficiently marched the entire list of "Hollywood Communists" through the witness box, one at a time, listened to their recitals of the Fifth and waited for the studios to blacklist them.

That being the case, and with the constitutional issue involving the First Amendment defense now unhappily resolved, what point was there in further resistance?

The answer is none, unless personal honor demanded it. In ordinary democratic politics it is customary, when a cause is lost, to release delegates, to allow them to take whatever course is necessary to minimize personal damage from a debacle. In this case, in fact, the Communists and their allies might have done a signal social service by at last lifting the shroud of secrecy they had wrapped about themselves. They might well have ended the blacklist before it got started. And they might well have changed the entire atmosphere of the fifties by so doing. But of course, they had no interest in such a course because Marxists have no interest in peaceful, ameliorative solutions to any social issue. In this instance, as they had to see it, their continued presence as victims of an unjust and reactionary society was further proof that their revolutionary critique of that society was valid. Never mind that there were available better villains, ones that suited Marxist theory better: an arm of the state and the leaders of a substantial element of corporate America. For purposes of agitprop theater, something for politically naive Americans, gathering information on the fly from the media, a different, less complicated drama played better. And it continues to play better in history: brave, principled, innocent victims brought low by weak and venal former comrades. We've all seen that story a hundred times at the movies. We know how to respond to it without thinking.

But history—serious history—is not a movie. And it should not be surrendered, as it has been, to not-very-good screenwriters who were beholden to a not-very-good cause. Let us return to Maltz and the dramatic (or, as Hollywood would now say, "high-concept") analogy he drew between the situation of the Hollywood Ten after the hearings and that of resistance fighters in occupied Europe during the war. Here is how he developed his point: "To put the point sharply: If an informer in the French underground who sent a friend to the torture chambers of the Gestapo was equally a victim, then there can be no right or wrong in the life that I understand." Well, yes. Of course. But wait. This analogy between torture by the Gestapo and an appearance before HUAC strikes one as just a trifle overstated. But let that pass. Let us take up instead the question raised by the word "friend." Throughout the blacklist period people like Maltz kept insisting on the word, implying that their closest party collaborators were ratting on bosom buddies when they supplied names to the committee. But many, if not most, of these friendships were not friendships at all; they were nodding acquaintances from years back. And most of them had dissolved into the vaguest of recollections as lives moved along their separate paths, as the ties which might have been formed in the course of brief encounters past were dissolved by sectarian political differences, by the ups and downs of social life in a careerist town. A question that should at least be raised in this context is not what we owe to intimates, or to colleagues we have knowingly joined in a dangerous enterprise like the resistance, but what we owe to casual acquaintances from activities in which we no longer believe and which were never presented as dangerous.

Then, too, there is the matter of timing. One understands that the resistance operated under sensible rules in this matter. A captured underground fighter was not expected to hold out forever under torture. The French were too humane and too aware of human weakness to insist on prodigies of masochism. You were supposed to hold out for a couple of days, to give your immediate colleagues a chance to make their escape. After that you were free to end the agony—no questions asked.

Certainly it would seem that as the blacklist era dragged on, as the process of obtaining clearance by naming names became more and more a stylized ritual, with (after a certain time) no one adding anyone new to the HUAC list, such opprobrium as attached to undergoing this "degradation ritual," as Navasky insists on calling it, should have diminished. In the circumstances an informal statute of limitations might well have come into play. And certainly there should have been some understanding of why a man or woman might, after a decent interval, decide to go before the committee and speak. In one of his exchanges with Maltz, the key exchange in my view, Trumbo puts this matter very well. Why, he asks, did the informers do what they did? Here is his answer:

> ... a man, to support a business venture, had hypothecated everything he possessed in anticipation of future income, without which he would be bankrupted; a man caught in a homosexual act and given the choice of informing or facing exposure and prosecution in a time when it was more disgraceful to be a homosexual than a Communist; a woman who has worked her way from secretary to writer, now three months pregnant, the sole support of herself and ... husband, whose brother has a long record of crime and imprisonment; a man who had left the CP to avoid constant attempts to meddle with the ideological content of his writing; a foreign-born citizen threatened with revocation of his naturalization papers; a man who left the Party because he could not stomach its insistence that the early phase of World War II offered no choice between Hitler and the West; a person whose spouse suffered from recurrent spells of melancholia which, in such a crisis as political exposure, could have resulted in suicide; a person whose disagreement with the CP had turned to forthright hostility and who, when the crunch came, saw no reason to sacrifice his career in defense of the rights of people he now hated....

The list continues, and ends, justifiably, with "the weak, the cunning, the ambitious and the greedy."

It might have included, I think, one other category: people who defined themselves as artists and who, unlike the screenwriters (who could at least labor anonymously, at cut rates, on the black market), could not face years cut off from the work from which they derived not only the prime satisfaction of their lives but their very sense of themselves. High on the list of those excoriated for their "betrayal" of old loyalties in the blacklist period are Lee J. Cobb, Elia Kazan, Clifford Odets, Budd Schulberg, Robert Rossen, and, of course, the one apostate among the Ten themselves, Edward Dmytryk. They may not qualify for the American Pantheon, but still, their list of accomplishments is on the whole stronger than that of the group they left behind, and it is impossible to believe that they were motivated solely by the hope of monetary gain. It is reasonable to suppose that having held out for a decent interval, having made, as most of them did, substantial financial sacrifices in support of their old allegiances, they could not imagine lives cut off from their vocations. Or to quote the unforgettable line from *Dodsworth,* William Wyler's best picture, "Love has to stop short of suicide."

That judgments of this kind are difficult to understand for a man who defines himself through political engagement goes without saying. But must one assume that the latter is a higher, more morally valuable calling than the artistic? Perhaps, if one wishes to use this matter as yet another excuse for Hollywood bashing. That is to say, if you assume, as many on the left did in the thirties and forties, that movies had nothing to do with art and that one worked in them solely for gain. But even Kempton, who generally shared in this attitude, did not raise it when discussing the so-called informers. Writing close to the events, in 1955, he is notably unjudgmental about their behavior. For example, he notes that though Dmytryk had withdrawn from the party before the hearings, he went along quietly with the Ten and their tactics, even serving his jail term, before openly breaking with the party. Similarly, he observes that Rossen passed on at least one major deal that was contingent on his clearing himself with the committee before going back to testify about his past associations. He thought this would clear him of suspicion of having acted for gain. (It is also worth noting that he was out of work for four years before reluctantly naming names.) As far as Kempton was concerned, these actions constituted payment in full of past dues to a group that no longer claimed their allegiance.

Implicit in Kempton's work is a subtext entirely lost on later writers: The quarrel between the Stalinists and those who broke with them clearly read to Kempton exactly like all the sectarian quarrels that had divided the American left for decades. They were always more bitter than their quarrels with their real enemies, and they always seemed to bring out the worst in everybody. In the concluding chapter of his marvelous and poignant work he writes: "I do not think it entirely my jaundice which has left these studies so barren of remembered acts of mercy or kindness or fraternity; I think that void exists because there was less kindness, justice and brotherhood in the radicals of the thirties than of any other group of radicals in our history." I would add only that that is because Stalinism was, finally, the issue around which everyone on the left had to define himself, and there has been no more heartless or inhuman doctrine at that end of the political spectrum.

116

Even Navasky has to admit that—at least in passing. Unlike Ceplair and Englund, he concedes that in Hollywood and out, there were several historical moments at which decent people, by the thousands, deserted communism. The list of these moments is a familiar one: the Moscow purge trials; the invasion of Finland; the Hitler-Stalin pact. Anyone who had to wait for the invasion of Hungary in 1956, or Khrushchev's revelations of Stalin's domestic horrors, to perceive the true face of Soviet communism was a very dull fellow indeed. But let that pass. Let us imagine that many Hollywood Reds suffered the cultural lag that is apparently endemic to the movie world in every era. There were local issues that offered revealing glimpses of what citizens of less ingrown societies were seeing.

The first of these occurred in the late thirties, when Budd Schulberg (scion of one of Hollywood's founding fathers, B. P. Schulberg), then a party member, announced his intention of turning a story he had published in *Liberty* into the novel he eventually published as *What Makes Sammy Run?* Before he had written a word, he was set upon by the party hacks Lawson and V. J. Jerome, who was at the time commissar of all party cultural activity. They fretted that the original material did not pay sufficient heed to the workings of the "progressive movement" in Hollywood and was too individualistic in viewpoint. They did not explain what relevance these criticisms might have to a portrait of a sweaty little hustler cutting and thrusting his way upward in the business, but they sufficiently alarmed Schulberg so that he decamped for Vermont to write the book free of ideological hassles. He was back in Hollywood in 1940, when the novel was published and a reviewer for the *Daily Worker* praised it, without noting the aforementioned defects or others that appeared to Lawson and his ilk when they read the finished work. These now included insufficient attention to the party's crusade for world peace and, it would seem, a generally demeaning portrayal of Hollywood manners and morals, which the party always avoided making—it didn't do to sour the milk of their cash cow. The *Worker*'s reviewer was summoned for public criticism, and he wrote a second notice recanting his first. Schulberg, who had already quit the party, refused an invitation to defend his work at another party meeting and took up a virulent antiparty, but never illiberal, stance, particularly calling attention to the silencing of dissident writers inside the Soviet bloc. When he was named as a sometime Communist (by one of the men who had led the fight against *Sammy*), he had no compunctions against naming his old enemies within the party. You want to play hardball? Fine, let's play hardball.

Dmytryk and his producer colleague Adrian Scott faced similar circumstances in 1945. Working on the film *Cornered,* they engaged John Wexley, a party member, to work on the screenplay. They were themselves party members, but they found Wexley's work on this story, about a man seeking vengeance against a Nazi who had murdered his fiancée, too blatantly ideological in tone. They reasoned that the story itself contained such an obvious anti-Fascist message that there was no reason to further underline it, so they hired another, apolitical writer to do the final draft, which they shot. Thereupon Wexley accused them of something akin to counterrevolutionary thought and turned them in to Lawson, who summoned eight of the faithful to what amounted to a trial of the offenders. They refused to recant and pointed out that since their film was in the can, they could not go back to the studio (RKO) and ask to shoot Wexley's scenes and insert them. Not only would the frugal studio bosses refuse on practical grounds, but they would suspect Scott and Dmytryk must be acting under party orders. At the end of this meeting Lawson in effect suspended them and so far as one can tell did not officially reinstate them even after they became one fifth of the Ten.

According to Dmytryk, this incident led directly to the most famous incident of thought control in Hollywood party history. Albert Maltz had enlisted on his and Scott's side in the *Cornered* debate. Brooding on the matter, he wrote a famous article for the *New Masses,* "What Shall We Ask of Writers?" In it he argues what would seem to non-Communist (or non-Fascist) writers an unexceptionable point: You cannot judge creative works *primarily* by their formal ideology. "Having a tactical ax to grind usually requires the artificial manipulation of character," he adds in the course of arguing his case for permitting a hundred flowers to bloom. He was briefly a hero among the Hollywood leftists, but then came the deluge: page after page of denunciations from party stalwarts in the magazine; meetings in Hollywood where he was bitterly excoriated to his face and made to feel he was a pariah. A few months later he published his recantation. He later said the issue was too minor for him to break with the party over, but it was not for several who witnessed this degradation ceremony. It was the grounds several of them later cited for taking their leave.

A little later it was Robert Rossen's turn, and his experience was perhaps the weirdest of all. He announced his intention to write, produce, and direct an adaptation of Robert Penn Warren's *All the King's Men,* which is, of course, an account of the rise and fall of an American demagogue, tracing his path from populism to something akin to native fascism. On the face of it, it would seem to have been a project to warm the party's heart. Not so. One night John Howard Lawson came knocking on Rossen's door to argue against making the film on the ground that it could be perceived as a thinly disguised tract against Stalin. Well, after all, both Willie Stark and the Soviet leader were power-mad, weren't they? Hard to imagine Lawson's being that perceptive about his Supreme Leader. Doubtless he argued that the infinitely clever class enemies would see it that way, whatever the writer's true intention. Rossen was not to be dissuaded by this sophistry. But Lawson was not easily turned aside either. When the film, which ultimately won the Academy Award as best picture of 1948, was released, Rossen was summoned to another of Lawson's degradation ceremonies, did his best to defend himself, then angrily walked out.

The myth of revolutionary comradeship dies in the toils of these anecdotes. In them one surely reads some of the "sins" Trumbo refers to in discreetly general terms in his Laurel Award speech. And of course, he specifically addresses the issues raised by them in the list of possible reasons for turning against the party that he later provided the unhappy Maltz. It was, as I said earlier, pure fantasy to imagine that the Communists could retroactively continue to maintain discipline over people they had treated as they had these men. It is equally a fantasy to imagine they could reassert control over others whose connection with the party had been brief and long ago. Elia Kazan, for example, was not beaten with ideological truncheons. But his flirtation with the party had lasted only a year and a half and had ended in 1935, when he was twenty-six years old. How could they imagine he would spare himself very long on their behalf? The same is true of Odets, who was a party member for six months in the same period.

As for the actors, the demand for silence was inhuman. They have no alternative but to work in public, and if one honors the simple resister's courage displayed by the likes of Albert Dekker, Howard Da Silva, and Zero Mostel—nothing but off-Broadway and the farther reaches of the road were open to them—one also understands it as exceptional, not a norm to which many can easily aspire. One would surely rather have been one of them than Larry Parks, pitifully groveling before the committee. But would one rather have been Sterling Hayden, who, after naming names, spent the rest of an alcoholic life noisily fellow-traveling in order to reingratiate himself with the Stalinoid left? It worked for him; he found some kind of community. But he was always in emotional conflict over his course and his association with people who did not appeal to his essentially anarchical spirit. As for the rest—the less famous, the less accomplished, the less economically secure—seeing in the fifties what the Ten could not have foreseen when they took the stand—the blacklist—how could they forever be expected to hold their tongues, especially if they no longer held with the party line?

In the end, and with just one exception that I can discern, the only people who finally did not inform were those who remained under party discipline. The others—the "stool pigeons"—were those who could no longer tolerate that embrace. It makes perfect sense, and this

is a point that no one, so far as I know, has raised: The only emotional
and financial support available to those who would not inform was the
party and its ever-dwindling band of fellow travelers. But if, on principle, you had left them, how could you now return to them? That,
too, would have been a form of dishonor for most people. It would
seem that of them all, only Adrian Scott, apparently as ideologically
disenchanted as anyone caught up in this nightmare, and at quite an
early moment, adopted this solution. He was manifestly a decent man,
much respected by all who encountered him, whatever their political
biases, and equally clearly a man who defined honor in some subtle
recess of his soul unavailable to others. On the evidence, he appears
to be the one true martyr in a crowd jostling all too eagerly for that
distinction. Again, Trumbo seems to have had the last word about him.
Responding to the comparison of his career with Dmytryk's, which
Maltz insisted upon, he wrote: "I reject your remarks about Adrian
altogether. Had you loved him more, you could not have found it
possible to score a mere debater's point by invoking his illness and
death."

Debater's points. Yes. Finally, that is what it came down to. But the
stake in the debate was not a small one. In the end what was under
discussion—and perhaps still is, if anyone really cares—was history
and its interpretation of events in a rapidly receding and increasingly
mythified past. It has, for now, entirely succumbed to the Communist
historical line about the Hollywood Ten and the era of the blacklist in
the entertainment industry. Its stalwarts are firmly installed in the role
of heroes, their opponents in the role of heavies. It is the one and only
victory communism has scored on American soil, and it has been won
by the same methods it has scored its victories in third world countries,
by seizing not the high ground but the simple ground, that terrain
which can be defined by easily read and understood slogans, which
the young, who have never run head-on into a Stalinist, can bounce
blithely across in their sneakers. Another famous movie line is apposite:
"When the truth becomes legend, print the legend."

Let me say it again. I do not endorse HUAC or the motion picture
industry's collapse before it and its deplorable allies. I believe that the
Hollywood Communists were wronged and that they were entitled to
whatever redress, whatever consolations, the passing years granted
them. But I do not believe they and their heirs and assigns are entitled
to command the historical record unchallenged. It is, as I have tried
to suggest, more subtly shaded than it now seems to most people—a
darkling plain, perhaps, where increasingly ignorant armies clash by
night.

RONALD REAGAN
THE REST OF HIM

*I*t will probably help if, finally, we radically reformulate the terms of our bemusement. The problem is not that the former President of the United States, the Leader of the Free World, the Occupant of the World's Loneliest Office, etc., used to be a movie actor, a creator of make-believe. The problem is that he used to be—probably still is—a movie *fan,* a consumer of make-believe, just possibly an addict of it.

This is a disturbing conclusion. So much so that even bold Garry Wills, whose *Reagan's America: Innocents at Home* leads one inescapably toward it, stops short of baldly setting it forth. And for good reason: It implies the most depressing things not only about Ronald Reagan but about ourselves and our infinite capacity for delusion, political and otherwise.

During his term of office we all learned to stop worrying and live with, if not love, the idea of an actor-President. This is no small matter. It is, in fact, an aspect of one of the more interesting unremarked social phenomena of postwar American life, the general acceptance of the idea that acting is a profession, demanding of its practitioners a training, discipline, and sobriety comparable with those required of lawyers, doctors, and the other grown-up occupations.

To earlier generations this notion would have been unimaginable, dumbfounding. But there it is. Three decades of journalistic and talk-show debates about the Actors Studio and the Method, a similar span of general concern about Marlon Brando's integrity, the rise of graduate education in the theatrical arts and crafts, the decline of the term contract in Hollywood, which freed performers to pursue highly personal projects at the same time they were freed to express themselves with impunity on public issues and, for that matter, private morals—all these encouraged even movie actors to take their work, and their duties as citizens, more seriously. And encouraged the general public to join them in this activity. It is ironic that Ronald Reagan, that least serious and least actorish of actors, a man no one ever really conjured with as a major talent or screen presence, should be the chief beneficiary of this change in our attitudes. It is a point that, quite correctly, worries Wills.

"On the one hand, some try to explain Reagan's extraordinary success in politics by saying he gets by because he is 'just an actor.' On the other hand, we are told he was not even a good actor—which seems to make his political success more mysterious. Which is it to be? Is he just reading lines, following his script, using theatrical skills, as President? Or did a man lacking the depth for great roles in the theater somehow acquire a knack for filling the most responsible role in the world?" How pleasant it would be if one felt these questions to be apposite. For then we could fit the rise of Ronald Reagan into our standard explanation of success in America: natural talent, solid training, honorable conduct in an honorable line of work, and then, finally, the respect of peers and public, translated in his case into the greatest gift it is in our power to bestow.

Wills's rhetorical questions are quite unanswerable as posed. Reagan was clearly not a distinguished actor, and though he was sometimes a respectable one, he was equally often an incompetent one. Similarly, it is hard to find any evidence that he possessed a genius for the political gesture that awaited unlocking by changing times and circumstances. No, you cannot get hold of this character with questions as convenient as those posed by Wills in this passage. Reagan's astonishing success in not one but two careers that have defeated men with far higher gifts and far more ferocious ambitions begins to make sense only if you view it in utterly unconventional, if you will, in utterly un-American terms. This way:

He succeeded as an actor, in the theatrical sense of the word, precisely because he refused to act in the nontheatrical sense of the word—refused, that is, to try to impose himself on events, to shape them to his uses. Rather, the opposite is true: He succeeded because he—correctly—saw his movie career as a lucky opportunity proffered him by rich and powerful men, men much cleverer than he was, to live within one of the most delicious of American fantasies. All he had to do, as he saw it, was go along with them agreeably—show up on time, learn his lines, submit to the publicity process, and, above all, not question the wisdom of their decisions about his career. The result was little short of miraculous. In his rise, as Wills nicely puts it, he was "a winner, not a stunner; in his fall he was a fader, not a loser." And when as a movie star he had reached near-ectoplasmic condition, his mentors, having accumulated no grievances against him, had no reason to indulge the usually irresistible Hollywood habit, which is to punish the weakened star for his past arrogances. Instead, they pointed Ron in a new direction, toward the political illusion, within which one may also succeed simply by showing up on time, learning one's lines, etc., etc. . . .

I do not wish to imply that Ronald Reagan was without gift. In fact, he was hugely gifted—as a fantasist. Which is an occupation that, until he showed us the way, no one had ever regarded as likely to lead anybody to anything except a bad case of pimples. But which now, perhaps, we might find a certain profit in reexamining.

We can begin, prosaically enough, with the observation that Reagan was of the generation that came of age as the movies came of age. The year in which he was born was the year the first studio opened in Hollywood; the year he graduated from high school was also the year talkies came in; the first year he was in college was, as well, the first year of the Academy Awards. And so on. In other words, his crowd was the one on which the mythmaking power of the movies shone with the piercing power of the new. He was also of a place—small-town middle America—and of a class—the lumpen bourgeoisie—that had a particular need for the transfiguring power of this mythology. In other words, the kind of glory dreaming in which he has his whole life long indulged himself was by no means unique to him.

What was singular about him was that he probably would have dreamed his dreams even if the movies had not been there to provide model scenarios for them. The evidence is that he possesses, is possessed by, a unique—no, awesome—capacity to project himself into fantastic narratives, to turn personal history into wish-fulfilling and morally exemplary fiction of the kind that the movies, as he was growing up, were learning to conventionalize so that such stories could be read easily by the mass audience. And, of course, easily and endlessly replicated by the moviemakers themselves. Indeed, so powerful was this capacity of his to create starring roles for himself in the genre movies he wrote, produced, and directed for projection exclusively on his own brainpan that it survived—perhaps even battened on—his rise within the moviemaking community, a process that usually generates the kind of cynical heat that eventually dries out most of the imaginations that devote themselves for very long to this line of work. Reagan's capacity to stay fresh, delighted by the workings of his own easy-striding imagination is one of his strengths, perhaps the source of his remarkable youthfulness of manner.

Reagan somehow contrived to remain what he was long before he came to the movies, profoundly suggestible. We all know, of course, that he entered show biz as a radio sports reporter for small stations in Iowa, where his specialty was, to use the polite contemporary word, "visualization" of baseball games. In other words, the bare facts of a game proceeding in far-off Chicago were telegraphed to him, and he was required to create, on the spot, a full word picture of the contest, right down to little red-haired boys making spectacular catches of balls fouled into the stands. In later years one of Reagan's favorite anecdotes has the line going dead as a ball left the pitcher's hand, leaving silver-tongued Dutch Reagan to improvise many, many foul balls—utterly untraceable in the next day's box score—until service was restored. Harmless fun, of course, and arguably a service to the higher truth. That is to say, Reagan's fictive embroidery did not distort the account of the game as it progressed—the hits, runs, and errors were all present and accounted for—and the rest was just entertainment. Also, possibly, good training in those on-your-feet skills requisite to the successful conduct of a presidential press conference.

In any case, as Wills observes, Dutch Reagan became in those years an uncritical admirer of that school of sports reporting—exemplified in print by the likes of Grantland Rice, on the air by a line of performers beginning with Graham McNamee and culminating with Bill Stern—who could not resist improving on the historical record, particularly if their inventions lent an uplifting moral point to an anecdote. It was at this stage that Reagan began his fascinating lifelong association with George Gipp by retelling Rice's basic "win one for the Gipper" legend on one of his radio shows. The story stayed with him so powerfully that he proposed it as a screenplay soon after signing his Warner Brothers contract and well before he was himself cast as the Gipper in *Knute Rockne—All-American*. He was still telling it, essentially unchanged, when he received an honorary degree from Notre Dame in 1981.

A little research of the kind that White House staffs can easily command and that indeed, Reagan himself might have conducted at any point in his half century's obsession with the Gipper would have revealed a number of interesting points about his story. The first is that Gipp himself was a thoroughly undesirable character, a pool hustler who smoked, drank, played pro football on the side, and regularly bet on Notre Dame games in which he played. In life, incidentally, he was never referred to as the Gipper, and his death, before graduation, appears to have been hastened by his dissipations, which he never recanted. Still more interesting is the fact that no one ever heard of his deathbed request that Rockne invoke his name sometime when a Notre Dame team was in need of inspiration until the coach brought his weakest team into New York for the Army game of 1928. He spent the evening before it with Rice, trying out this preposterous inspirational yarn on the sportswriter before feeding it to his team the next day. This may have been Rockne's biggest whopper, but it was by no means his only inspirational invention, for it turns out that this most sacred icon of the American sports pantheon, this legendary builder of youthful character was—naturally, how can it be otherwise?—a congenital liar, or, if you prefer the politer term, suitable to Presidents as well as folk heroes, a mythomaniac. But, as the Leader of the Free World himself inquired at Notre Dame, "Is there anything wrong with young people having an experience, feeling something so deeply, thinking of someone else to the point where they can give ... completely of themselves?"

Well ... er ... um ... gosh. One wonders: Are these higher truths, arrived at by climbing a ladder of smaller untruths, really worth the cynicism they will ultimately, inevitably engender? One also wonders: How high, really, are these higher truths? They are not exactly Grecian in their mythic richness, are they? Not exactly the sort of legends around which you would want to organize your life or your society. At best, they are fables for a high school sports banquet.

But Reagan has a million of them, and he goes on telling them to this day. One favorite has a World War II B-17 pilot ordering his crew to bail out after their plane has been crippled by antiaircraft fire, then finding one of his gunners wounded and immovably trapped as the plane starts to spiral earthward. The boy is frightened, but the pilot cradles him in his arms and says, "Never mind, son, we'll ride it down together." Terrific. And the Leader of the Free World likes to use the story as evidence of how our political system creates a morality superior to that of the Communist system. He neglects to observe one point. If the only two witnesses to this exchange indeed rode their crippled plane down together, who survived to recount their dialogue?

For a long time people wondered: Is it from some old war movie the rest of us have forgotten or a radio drama or a pulp story? Film history to the rescue. The scene occurs in the 1944 movie, *Wing and a Prayer,* written by one Jerome Cady and directed by the redoubtable Henry Hathaway for Twentieth Century-Fox. Though Reagan in his retellings locates the action over the English Channel, the movie setting was the South Pacific, and it is about a torpedo plane squadron based on an aircraft carrier. The White House, pressed by reporters to find a somewhat grander provenance for this yarn, set the Air Force Historical Office to work tracing it down in the annals of war, instead of movie annals. That was four years ago, and the Pentagon has yet to be heard from. While we are waiting, it is amusing to speculate on why this, among the many heroic improbabilities of World War II cinema, stuck in the Leader of the Free World's mind. Could it be because one of the principal characters in the film (played by William Eythe) is supposed to be a movie star, who, if memory serves, carried his Oscar around with him? And whose actor's ego had to be tamed so that he fit into the group? Agreeable Ronnie Reagan never had that problem, one imagines, during his less daring war service, but surely he must have been, or become, very interested in a story featuring an actor performing bravely on a stage larger and scarier than a sound stage.

Be that as it may, one does feel confident in observing that Reagan's taste for these slices of life according to *Reader's Digest* has obviously had an influence on his autobiographical impulse. His life, as he likes to retell it, is at every stage illuminated by similarly shapely and instructive dramatic sequences. For example, he is playing football for Dixon High School and at a crucial juncture in a game commits an infraction undetected by the officials but protested by the opposing players; one of the zebras puts it to young Dutch: Did he or didn't he perpetrate a foul? Alas, "truth telling had been whaled into me," so Reagan fesses up, apparently costing his team a chance for the one touchdown by which it ultimately lost the game. We owe to the relentlessly researching Wills the information that no game with an outcome of the kind Reagan describes took place while he was playing for Dixon.

As he grows older, the line between provable and improvable truth grows ever more blurry—and, possibly, ever more important in evaluating his character and his "performances." Another example: He has honorably served his country in war, abandoning his screen career just as he was making the transition from B pictures to A's, and "By the time I got out of the Army Air Corps, all I wanted to do—in common with several million other veterans—was to rest up for a while, make love to my wife and come up refreshed to a better job in a better world." Right. Unexceptionable sentiments. Except that they imply lengthy service far from the comforts of home. But Reagan passed the war entirely in Hollywood, assigned to "Fort Roach" (normally Hal Roach's Culver City studio), where he worked on Air Corps training films. He went home to wife, Jane Wyman, every night, except for a period when she was away on a bond-selling tour. Indeed, it's possible that her wartime duties took her away from their bedroom for a longer period than his did.

And now memory grows even loopier. It is 1983, and President Reagan is entertaining the prime minister of Israel and implies, or seems to imply, or something, that he was part of a Signal Corps unit filming the Nazi death camps as they are liberated. Moreover, he moreovers, there was this one particularly moving piece of footage that he felt he ought to sequester because he thought someday people would question the authenticity of the Holocaust and—sure, sure, that's the ticket—one day someone did exactly that in his presence and he had this footage and ... Mr. Shamir was duly moved and impressed and so were Simon Wiesenthal and Rabbi Marvin Hier when they came to the White House a little later and were treated to the same story. It was only after it was repeated in the Israeli press and people here and elsewhere started checking on it that Reagan's staff had to launch what some observers called the most strenuous "containment" effort of his presidency up to that time. Ahem. Cough-cough. You see what he meant to say was : ... Or perhaps the visiting dignitaries misunderstood Reagan; after all, English is not their native language ... If you see what we mean. Obviously, if Reagan passed the war entirely in Hollywood, it would have been a little difficult for him to be with a Signal Corps unit as the camps were freed. "Bill Stern, the Colgate shave cream man, is on his way. ..."

Outrageous, on the face of it. Yet we have trouble working ourselves up to outrage. For we recognize in Reagan something we indulge in ourselves and in our friends—namely, our not entirely conscious, not entirely unconscious desire to reshape the maddening ambiguities of reality as we commonly experience it into the narratively neat, psychologically gratifying form of an old-fashioned movie, with a beginning, a middle, an end, and, above all, a central figure we have no trouble rooting for—who is, of course, ourselves. This brings us to an amusing pair of questions. Does this represent a basic human need in search of a form that the dreamy movies kindly provided? Or did the suddenly pervasive movies propose for us kinds of transformations we had never before known we wanted or needed to make? Who can say? What we can say is that this is one of the forms modernism takes at the popular, unselfconscious level and that Ronald Reagan is obviously, if astonishingly, one of the masters of modernism, in his way the equal of those we more commonly recognize as such—Picasso, Joyce, Stein, et al. Life is, for him, a collage, a juxtaposition of materials not normally brought into close congress. Or else, like some Leopold Bloom, he is simply borne along through his days on the stream of his consciousness.

Maybe the name we should actually be evoking here, for purposes of comparison, is that of a postmodernist, whose background class and geographic background are not dissimilar from Reagan's and who, like the President, just sort of seemed to dream himself to fame and fortune. I am speaking, of course, of Andy Warhol. For as with the Factory's late foreman, Reagan created a wonderfully seamless and seemingly unconscious join between life and imagery, self and works. I mean, it is interesting how learned exegetes of both Reagan's works and Warhol's works endlessly debate the question of whether or not it is art—that is to say, how consciously they shaped the products that bear the stamp of their personalities. It is similarly curious to observe the similarity of the stances both men took toward their work: modestly amused by

the fuss it has caused, unassertive, unegocentric in their claims for it
—and innocently delighted in how much fame they achieved with so
little apparent effort on their own behalf. Indeed, Reagan seems to see
his movie career very much as Warhol saw his career as an artist: as a
swell movie in which he was lucky enough to obtain the leading role.

Ronald Reagan did not break a sweat breaking in. He was out
covering the Chicago Cubs' spring training season on Catalina Island,
off Los Angeles, when he took a few hours off for screen tests and
obtained for himself the modest Warner Brothers contract that was to
be his first step on the road to the White House. He seems to have
found life around the studio fun, and both his own accounts and those
of others show him in these days to be a young man of no temperament
and no image of himself as an actor at all. This would be his salvation,
of course. For recall that Warner Brothers in the days of his apprenticeship there was aroil with rebellion. His latter-day pal James Cagney,
Bette Davis, Olivia De Havilland, Bogart, Flynn, even—yes—Joan Leslie
were in constant noisy conflict with Jack Warner, seeking better parts,
more money, a role in the choice of their roles. Not young Ron. He
unassumingly did leads in program features, small parts in a few A's.
He established himself most usefully as Brass Bancroft, in the four
pictures constituting the Secret Service of the Air series that Brynie
Foy's B picture unit ground out. These pictures, it has been hinted
here and there, (1) prepared Reagan emotionally for his later role as
a real-life FBI informer against suspected Communists (Brass did a bit
of undercover work in his time) and (2) may account for his devotion
to the "Star Wars" concept since in the last of these pictures Brass must
defend from enemy agents the "Inertia Projector," a device capable of
knocking enemy planes out of the air from a distance of four miles.
Life may occasionally imitate art for everyone, but it did so repeatedly
in Ronald Reagan's career.

In any event, he had no cause for complaint. His career was moving
ahead at a nice, but not unnerving, pace. It did not cost him sleep or
recreation time—loss of which are known to make him cranky, even
now. He got his good showy bit in *Knute Rockne* and immediately
thereafter an excellent second lead as George Armstrong Custer vying
anachronistically with Flynn's Jeb Stuart for De Havilland's hand in
Santa Fe Trail. The thing was not at all the western it sounds, but rather
a preparedness preachment, in which the two are in pursuit of Raymond
Massey's John Brown, who is made to stand in for Hitler, with good
men being urged to stand up to his raving bigotry before it is too late.
It was also, improbably, about half the time, a romantic comedy, with
Flynn playing the smooth seducer and Reagan playing Custer as the
one thing he surely was not, an amiable goof, the butt of Flynn's jokes

and schemes, and ultimately the loser to him in their contest for the girl. Reagan hated the way Flynn kept upstaging him, but the picture established once and for all Reagan's viability in big-budget pictures, and two years later he got his common-consent best role, the one that stays everyone's critical hand when they attempt to evaluate his acting career, that of Drake McHugh in *King's Row*. His next good part, and his last before entering the service himself, was again with Flynn and Massey in Raoul Walsh's *Desperate Journey,* in which he was a Yank in an RAF crew, downed in occupied Europe and trying to fight their way back to England. Much of it was played as knockabout comedy, and rather refreshingly so, it must be said. Aside from *This Is the Army,* for which Warner's was able to borrow him back from the Air Corps to play the romantic lead in a revue the profits of which went to Army and Navy Relief, that was it for Reagan until 1947 and *Stallion Road.*

Reagan's prewar movies repay study, for they are the ones that define the limits of the untutored talent that once he had asserted it, he did nothing to develop or refine (again the analogy with Warhol suggests itself). Obviously *King's Row* is central to this consideration, for though it must tiptoe around the incest theme that was crucial to the success of the best seller on which it was based, and though poor, bland Robert Cummings was, as always, a hopeless leading man, it was an energetic and more than usually memorable picture, with good character people like Claude Rains and Charles Coburn, an interesting cast, a wonderful look to it (the joint creation of cinematographer James Wong Howe and production designer William Cameron Menzies), a grand Erich Korngold score, and the always adorable Ann Sheridan deliciously present and down-to-earth. Above all, of course, it gave Reagan what everyone pretending to movie stardom must somehow obtain, a riveting scene, with (he or she may hope) a line as unforgettable as his "Where's the rest of me?" delivered when he wakes up to discover that a sadistic doctor has needlessly amputated both his legs after an accident in a railyard.

In his reading of this movie, Wills, I think, errs seriously. He wants to take even this one small thespic triumph away from Reagan, and so he insists that his big scene is really Sheridan's (and Korngold's). But I ran it over and over one night recently, and it is just not so. To be sure, the preparation for it is all Sheridan's. The camera is long on her as she anxiously awaits Drake McHugh's awakening from shock and anesthesia and his discovery that he has been mutilated. But once she responds to his first cry, mounts the stairs, and enters his room, they share the scene equally. She has three close-ups, he has two, and there are three two-shots, two of which distinctly favor him. Moreover, he does his famous line unimprovably—anguish and panic in his voice, in his facial expression, in his thrashing movements under the covers. Hard to ask for anything more from any actor—and one gets no sense that the director, Sam Wood, had to cheat to cover for Reagan.

No, Reagan's problems in *King's Row* occur earlier, when he is called upon to represent himself as a careless womanizer and ne'er-do-well heir to a small fortune. He is supposed to provide a contrast with Cummings, playing an earnest and idealistic medical student. At this stage of the movie Drake McHugh is not a nice guy, and Reagan is visibly uncomfortable, straining, in these passages. He does not exhibit the born actor's relish at playing a heel. Instead, he exhibits the born public figure's discomfort at being mistaken for one. He has no technique to help him get under this character's skin or to distract us from his own discomfort. Before he loses his legs, Drake loses his inheritance, and that returns Reagan's character to the social level which was familiar to the actor in life and to the emotional range where he was—and is—comfortable in reality. It is the only realm where he ever learned to live comfortably, persuasively on the screen.

His other work in the period reinforces this point. Take his Custer, for example. The relationship with Jeb Stuart is not the only anachronism in *Santa Fe Trail*. Reagan plays his role as a modern youth improbably dressed up in a nineteenth-century soldier suit, and though he is kind of funny, sometimes, he is also kind of jarring, too. Things work out for him a little better in *Desperate Journey*. He is supposed to be a breezy American kid, who, under interrogation by Massey (playing a Gestapo officer), resorts to jive talk in order to evade awkward questions, and he is genuinely funny in the scene. Timing was the experienced radio performer's strong suit, his only reliable technical skill, and he used it to good effect here. As for *This Is the Army,* he was straight man to a vast troupe putting on a soldier show, their stage manager, and the movie's only male romantic interest, trying to evade Joan Leslie's advances on the ground that it was irresponsible to marry while there was a war on and he might be killed—yes, *that* one. But again, it was comfortably within his modest range.

As we look back on his work, it is clear to us—was it ever clear to him?—that he lacked the art to transform himself through art. He was trapped within himself on the screen as well as off. Real actors are in essence escape artists or maybe quick-change artists. It is the opportunity to strut that gift that provides such fascination—and payoffs—as that line of work offers, the thing that makes a difficult and frustrating business occasionally worthwhile. It is also, of course, the thing that goads them, makes them difficult, hard for studio managers to manage. They are, in effect, junkies ever in search of their fix, their passage out of entrapping reality. For Reagan, lacking the gift of transcendence, acting could provide only an extension of reality, not an escape from it. Like the rest of us "non-pros" (to borrow *Variety's* old contemptuous term), he had to rely on private fantasies to make his way out of the quotidian. And like those of the rest of us, these were fed, polluted perhaps, by mechanized dreamworks, by movies of the very kind he unimaginatively worked in. And by the movielike fantasies provided by the rest of the media—sportscasters, political commentators, storytellers of every "nonfictional" kind who had mastered the basic American movie trick, which is to tell whoppers in a realistic-seeming manner, tell whoppers of the kind Reagan is still genially telling and believing. Oh, yes, absolutely believing, as Colonel North and Admiral Poindexter discovered to their delight. They looked like old-fashioned heroes to him, and so they could tell him just about anything and make him believe it—especially spy stories that must have sounded a lot like movie treatments as they outlined them to him, keeping them brief and punchy, the way Jack Warner used to like them.

This limit under which he worked was not so important back before the war. He was a cute guy, and young, and, as noted, a pleasant relief from all those artist types yearning to breathe free. After the war, though, it was different. He wasn't so young anymore, and the movies were changing. Genre films, the conventions of which had done a lot of the actors' work for them, were losing their hold on the public. Now you had to bring something of your subtler awarenesses of self and world to the party up there on the screen. Hard for everybody, especially hard for Reagan.

His wife of the time caught this drift early. "Button-nose," better known as Jane Wyman, came from a background similar to, and not more tony than, Reagan's. When they were courting, she was making B's at Warner's, too, and she fitted in chipperly with the gang of middle western transplants, nonpros the lot of them, with whom Reagan ran socially—mostly to the beach and (odd for movie folk) to the movies, where they paid their money and took their place with the other nonpros in the audience. But instinctively the starlet sniffed the profession's possibilities for healthy escape from self and ordinariness. By 1945 she had *The Lost Weekend,* by 1947 her first Oscar nomination (for *The Yearling*), a year later the big prize itself, for *Johnny Belinda.* Hubby was left behind to make a bitter quip: that he should name Belinda as corespondent in his divorce action. In other words, she had found and entered the country of the imagination—one feels like writing the *healthy* imagination—he could never locate.

The people who ran the town tried to help him. Unlike most of the other actors, he had always treated them politely, gratefully, according them the respect he had never been able to grant his alcoholic father, the shiftless shoe salesman who had more than once shamed him. He had been loyal to Jack Warner; more important, he had remained faithful to the only agency he had ever had, Lew Wasserman's increasingly powerful MCA. They all saw him as an actor who had to stay within himself (these people really are not stupid about their business; it's all they ever think about). Basically that meant light comedy and romance, contemporary stuff. It also meant perpetual youth, which is actually easier to maintain and project in real life (and on television, where Presidents star) than it is on the cruelly magnifying big screen, which makes all the wrinkles and wattles loom large.

Still, he could get away with it. For a while. He had the nice-guy, other-guy roles in *The Hasty Heart* and in *Storm Warning,* where the showy parts (as, respectively, a bitter man on his deathbed and a brutally bigoted Ku Klux Klan leader, who actually starts to flog Ginger Rogers) went respectively to Richard Todd and to Steve Cochran. He could get true leads only in light and minor comedies like *Bedtime for Bonzo.* In later years it served him as *The Horn Blows at Midnight* served Jack Benny: It was a funny-sounding title around which gag writers could cluster deflationary jokes about his career, the film that put ironic quotation marks around his "stardom." Also, of course, liberals and other cruel people could use it as a symbol of his fundamental lack of seriousness. Actually, though, it is an agreeable farce, and he is expert in it as a professor trying to maintain his dignity while conducting an experiment in behavioral psychology, raising a baby chimp as a human baby.

The next year they found another professor for him to play, in *She's Working Her Way Through College,* which is a dismal remake of the James Thurber-Elliott Nugent play and film, *The Male Animal,* with songs added. In it he appears as the liberal-minded teacher who risks his tenure to defend a sometime stripteaser's right to attend the stuffy college of her choice. The students all are on his side, of course, but not the president or the chairman of the board of trustees. Though it is amusing now to see him as a man playing the anti-McCarthy role and though he is quite all right in the part, he had turned forty the year before. It was obvious to him, if not to everyone else, that he could not perpetually perpetuate youth in these silly little pictures. It may even have been obvious to him that the television sitcom was about to render them obsolete as movie fare. And then where would he be?

He needed to do grown-up roles, roles without jokes. He loved the outdoors, was proud of his skills as a horseman (that was director Allan Dwan's chief memory of him), and from youth and like every other male of his age, he had wanted to encompass the western myth, internalize and then project it. Maybe he could rescue his career as another aging juvenile had done, by embodying that myth on screen. But though he now had the crags to match the landscape's crags, Ronnie

Reagan was no Jimmy Stewart. Watch him in *Cattle Queen of Montana.* He lacks the *gravitas* one expects of the classic westerner. He seems to float above this countryside, unrooted in it or in its history. Above all, he is innocent of that radical self-sufficiency that is the essence of the heroic westerner. Or of the true loner's toughness that Stewart found in himself in the westerns he made with Anthony Mann in this period.

It is the same way with most of Reagan's other attempts to break away from the selfhood that he was at last beginning to sense as a professional imprisonment. Maybe he should have played more soldiers and sailors. *Hellcats of the Navy,* the picture now famous because Nancy was his costar in it, is interesting not merely because it reveals what prevented her from becoming a star (coarse jawline), but as, perhaps, a signpost on a road not taken by him. Somehow, in a uniform, going by the military book, he is granted an authority, a maturity unexpressed in his other postwar roles. This costume does a job for him that westerner's garb cannot. For to borrow from David Riesman, whose terms were much on everyone's lips in those days, a military man is classically other-directed (like Reagan himself) while a westerner is classically inner-directed (utterly unlike him).

In any event, a trip to the corner video parlor will demonstrate to anyone that off-casting was not the answer for him. His last picture, *The Killers,* was his most ludicrous. He's supposed to be this mysteriously crooked businessman, keeping Angie Dickinson, hinting at off-screen sadism in his relationship with her, while he plots the mail heist that will bring him the wealth with which he intends to buy respectability. But he cannot project menace now any better than he could project sexual banditry two decades earlier as Drake McHugh. The picture offers him only one scene within his range. For purposes of plot he has to impersonate a cop and direct traffic away from the scene of his crime. He has to be chatty, amiable, as he misleads motorists, and he is as relaxed and agreeable as can be. A nice and totally believable liar. In short, he is postively presidential in the scene. Presidential, that is, as he has redefined the term in recent years.

By the time he made *The Killers* in nineteen sixty-four solutions to the Ronald Reagan problem were in sight. He had made his own significant contributions to this effort. In show biz the unions are generally presided over by either has-beens or never-weres, people who take themselves seriously and thus seriously feel it when they are denied proper stages on which to assert their gifts. Reagan was not a dynamic SAG prexy. In Doug McClelland's useful compilation of eyewitness accounts of his rise and decline in the business, *Hollywood on Ronald Reagan,* Olivia De Havilland is quoted thus on his leadership: "What comes to mind is his affability and his gift for conducting

133

Screen Actors Guild meetings with adroitness and good humor. I think he was always an instinctive politician, and a genial one."

Yes. Sounds right. He was finding a way to play a president that was within his range. He was not taking charge of that presidency any more than he could be said to have taken charge of his subsequent governorship or his larger presidency, substituting agreeableness for authority, letting the mantle of office—the generic conventions of the role, as it were—substitute for true characterization. It is the *Hellcats of the Navy* illusion writ large.

There is, piled up in the Reagan biographies, a huge body of evidence that his grasp of the complex issues confronting his union presidency was no more subtle than it was in his later presidency. Indeed, an astonishing moment is recorded in which, talking with a paid union staffer, he wonders why they need to go on insisting on a union shop in their negotiations with employers. He thought the union was so popular, and doing such a good job, that it could prosper as a purely voluntary organization. We know, of course, that Reagan vastly simplified—that is, recast in starkly melodramatic terms, B movie terms, if you will, the whole issue of Communist penetration of the unions. We know, too, because investigative journalists keep returning to the subject, that he was instrumental in granting the SAG waiver that permitted his own agency, MCA, to enter film and TV production, thus facilitating its rise to its present eminence as the most powerful—and stable—institution in the moving-image industry. We know that ultimately it was MCA functionaries who arranged the real estate transactions that provided him with the wealth to run for the presidency.

But the real payoff was both more subtle and immediate. His agents looked upon his performance as SAG's leader and saw that it was good. That is, that if it played for an audience of professionals like Olivia De Havilland, it would play for a broader, less demanding audience. Reagan did not object or disbelieve. These men had been so good to him for so long, had been so, well, fatherly, in a way that his own father never had been, so gently undisruptive of his dreamy ways, why not follow the drift they pointed out for him now? Why not give up the exhausting effort to be something other than himself, which is what his late screen career kept demanding of him? Why not relax back into the old simple, perpetually youthful self he had been so contented playing in his earlier movie days? Obviously, they had the right of it: That too-temperate naturalism, that lack of imaginative fire may have limited his screen career, but these very deficiencies had, they could sense, quite limitless possibilities in different venues. TV hosting, for starters . . . And after that . . .

No, even Lew Wasserman is not that smart. He was clearly a great agent in his day—whom else can we imagine getting a million-dollar contract for Reagan out of Jack Warner?—but we cannot imagine even him imagining that politics was about to become a branch of television in a wink of history's eye. Or imagine him imagining this agreeable second-string client of his as the man who would seal that deal. Show biz is a novel by someone named Irving. It is not Mann's *Doctor Faustus*.

This much, however, Wasserman knows, Reagan knows, everyone in show biz knows: "One day they tell you you will not go far/The next day on your dressing room they've hung a star." In other words, the art of show biz survival consists largely in riding the ups and the downs patiently—gracefully if you can manage it. Look at Joan Collins. Look at Dennis Hopper. Look at Jane Wyman, for heaven's sake. While her former mate was getting elected to all kinds of things, she couldn't —or maybe wouldn't—get elected to *Love Boat*. But it is said she now gets a $150,000 an episode for *Falcon Crest*. That's the harum-scarum way of it.

Now, of course, he got and-how lucky. Until a couple of historical minutes before his second term expired. When it was rather forcefully borne in on him that Presidents really must behave presidentially every once in a while. What a rude and puzzling awakening. For most of his adult life he operated under the unspoken, but very firm, agreement that rules the relationship between "talent" and its agents and managers. It holds that the former is to be spared all the unpleasant details of career management. The idea is to free creative people from those distractions that might dilute or divert their creative energies. Or from just having fun or dreaming along, enjoying one's fame and fortune if, as it was with Reagan, creativity was not a high priority—or, truth to tell, much of a possibility. The business types like this. They are pleased to think of their clients as willful children in need of practical guidance. And they are inclined to believe that when these clients mix too assertively into business affairs, they blunt the creativity of the dealmaking process. Modern movie stars tend to get a bit scratchy with this arrangement, but a lot of the old-timers like Reagan got quite used to it. And quite liked it. One imagines him feeling he could leave things to Don Regan the same way he used to leave things to Lew Wasserman and enjoy the best part he ever had—all entrances and exits and a musical theme all his own ("Hail to the Chief"), which is more than Erich Korngold ever gave him. He has observed that as president he gets a schedule of his next day's activities and that it is comforting in the same way that the call sheet, which outlines the next day's work, is for a movie's cast and crew. One imagines him even less prepared for characters like Poindexter and North, with their hidden ideological agendas, not to mention the starring roles they were intent on playing in the phantasmagoric spy movies running in *their* heads. Show biz agents—the good ones—do not have hidden agendas—not where their clients' interests are concerned.

One is saddened. To be awakened so close to the end of this long-running dreamwork of his, and to have the instrument of his awakening be the yawping and baying of the press, which Lew and his crowd had always been so good at tranquilizing. No movie fan—and who among us is not, finally, something of a fan?—can be anything but touched by his plight as he stood outside the theater, blinking at the light, trying to recapture the sweet cheats he had so long and happily enjoyed inside. My God, one suddenly thought—he even looks, and acts, his age. Still, as he begins his retirement, he has this consolation: His picture ran longer and prospered better than any our minds' eyes ever contemplated. And none of us, it need hardly be said, had plot devices to match the boldness of his: a mental movie in which the star becomes a real movie star? And then President? He is to this form of dreaming what Alexander Portnoy was to another less dangerous and less interesting kind.

IV
STAR TURNS

DOUGLAS FAIRBANKS, SR.
"BY THE CLOCK"

*T*o see him at work—even now, sixty, seventy years since his finest films, almost a half century since his premature death—is to sense, as if for the first time, the full possibilities of a certain kind of movement in the movies. The stunts have been imitated and parodied, and so has the screen personality, which was an improbable combination of the laughing cavalier and the dashing democrat. But no one has quite recaptured the freshness, the sense of perpetually innocent, perpetually adolescent narcissism that Douglas Fairbanks, Sr., brought to the screen. There was, of course, an element of the show-off in what he did. But it was (and it still remains) deliciously palatable because he managed to communicate a feeling that he was as amazed and delighted as his audience by what that miraculous machine, his body, could accomplish when he launched it into trajectory to rescue the maiden fair, humiliate the villain, or escape the blundering soldiery that fruitlessly pursued him, in different uniforms but with consistent clumsiness, through a dozen pictures.

Watching him—and contemplating his ever-diminishing repute— one feels that somehow we have lost the knack, not to mention the spirit, for what he did and that the loss is permanent. Undoubtedly there are many people around to equal, even to surpass Fairbanks's athletic gift. But there are none, one sadly imagines, who could or would orchestrate that gift as he did, creating out of a series of runs, jumps, leaps, vaults, climbs, swings, handsprings, and somersaults those miraculously long, marvelously melodic lines of movement through which he flung himself with such heedless grace. The problem is that even among acting's most youthful spirits there is no disposition to see their aim as simply taking joy from the job and giving it back—enhanced—to the audience. For since the end of World War II, actors have grown distressingly sober about their mission in life. If they are not engaged in agonizing debate about the theory of their art, they are devoting their celebrity prestige to good causes of every kind. It is the same with the popular genre films in which they appear. Comedy is now generally a much more inward, self-consciously psychological matter than it formerly was—"post-funny," Richard Corliss has memorably called it. Romance is tormented in analogous ways, and action is devoid of the elegant wit and grace with which Fairbanks imbued it. It is all rending metal, explosive charges, and glum hunks like Sly Stallone, who might be better off in silent pictures, where the subtitles, at least, could supply the literacy they cannot handle.

Fairbanks, of course, was the product and exemplar of an age that, if not quite so innocent as we like to suppose, was nevertheless not quite so grand in its artistic aspirations—especially in the movies, which only a few zealots then imagined as an art form—as we have become. There is absolutely no evidence that Douglas Fairbanks conceived of himself as anything more than a fabulist and fantasist. The idea that he might have held a mirror up to life would probably have appalled him. What he did was hold a mirror up to himself—to endlessly boyish Doug—and invite his audience to join him in pleased contemplation of the image he found there, an image that very accurately reflected a shallow, callow, charming man who lived by the simplest of American codes and eventually died by it.

It is fair to say that of the great silent-screen stars, Fairbanks probably expressed more of his true self on-screen than anyone. Mary Pickford, with whom he was to contract Hollywood's first royal marriage, had created, of course, the classic American girl—spunky, virginal, with a beauty bathed in perpetual golden sunlight. But she was, in fact, a tough, shrewd woman, and it would appear that her character began as a fantasy shared by her mother (the archetypal stage mom) and her first film director, D. W. Griffith. Certainly her Golden Girl image was sustained more by the demands of commerce than by the demands of artistic conscience. Chaplin's Little Fellow was a more complicated construct and represented a part of his complex nature—but only a part of it. William S. Hart, the first great western good-bad man, came in time to identify very strongly with his screen character; but his real-life western experience was limited, and before the movies found him, he had been an actor in stage melodramas (notably *Ben Hur*) that had precious little to do with frontier days in the United States. As for vamps and other exotic sex symbols, from Theda Bara to Rudolph Valentino, they were mostly the offspring of the fevered imaginings of producers

140

and publicists and, more often than not, desperate and, ultimately, despairing in their efforts to disguise the gap between fantasy's finery and reality's frumpery.

But Fairbanks was always—triumphantly, irritatingly, ingratiatingly—Fairbanks, both on the screen and away from it. In fact, there is about his career a certain inevitability; one can't quite imagine what he would have done with himself if the movies had not come into existence and provided him with precisely the kind of showcase his spirit and his talents required. Many of his peers might have been just as successful (if not quite so wildly prosperous) as stage personalities. But there was no stage that could contain Fairbanks's energy or permit him to fully exploit his natural gifts. Indeed, even the screen could not entirely absorb him.

Therein lies his modest tragedy. For it is as the founder of the most imitatable of the life-styles of the rich and famous—the high Hollywood manner, the great house, the breathlessly reported travels, the friends from all walks of celebrity life—that he is recalled (if at all) by later generations. His films, which captured the best of the man, his sweet cheekiness and his easy grace, are scarcely seen at all now. And his quite successful efforts to expand the expressive range of the screen —he virtually invented the most delicious form of spectacle, the humorously romantic form, which in his time stood (or rather floated) in such delightful contrast with the humorless galumphings of De Mille and Griffith—go unremarked, except possibly by George Lucas. So great was his fame in the last decades of his life and so affectionate was the regard in which the millions held him that this latter-day neglect would surely have sobered, if not completely shocked, this perpetual optimist. Or then again it might not have. For he did outlive his gift, which was entirely bound up with the illusion of perpetual youth, perpetual energy, and he did die before his time in a state of puzzlement over where the magic had gone. One would, if one could, rescue his innocent and quite lovely art for this dwindling century's latecomers. But since no one cares much anymore about the silent screen, that is impractical. What one can perhaps do is rescue certain aspects of his life from increasingly vague legend and show how, to this day, his personal history influenced—unacknowledged—other personal histories, hence the creation of other legends, and, indeed, the celebrity system that now rules so many of our perceptions of public life.

The record of his earliest years imparts to one a sense that as with so many performers, none of the more usual livelihoods could possibly have satisfied him, that he had no choice but to put himself forward in ways that would provide him with immediate attention, even if that attention was often negative. He was, as a child, different from other youngsters in ways that no one at the time could quite specify. At the very beginning, in fact, there was some fear that he might be "exceptional" in the most dismal sense of the term—that is, retarded, though it may be that, later in life, Fairbanks exaggerated these family fears in order to create an exemplary contrast: dark past versus triumphantly sunny present. Still, he was by all accounts a curiously gloomy infant, incapable of sending out the signals of contentment—smiles, cooings, gurglings—that parents wait so anxiously to observe. His principal pleasure, observable apparently even in the crawling stage, was risk taking. By the time he was three he had, according to his niece Letitia, who (with a journalist's assistance) wrote an excessively discreet biography, "climbed everything in the yard and had swung from every limb and rail." Indeed, on his third birthday his mother, overseeing the preparation of the celebratory cake, was interrupted by Robert Fairbanks, Douglas's senior by a year, crying, "Mama, he's on the roof again." And sure enough, there he was, on top of the barn, having climbed a trellis to achieve his precarious perch. What bothered Mrs. Fairbanks more than the physical danger was his owlish expression.

There were reasons for the withdrawn nature Fairbanks exhibited in early childhood. For one thing, he had a remarkably dark complexion. "I was so dark ... my mother was ashamed of me. When all the neighbors came around to look at the new baby, Mother would say, 'Oh, I don't want to disturb him now—he's asleep and I'd rather not.'" In later life that darkness, burnished by the Southern California sun, would be largely responsible for the tanning craze that proved to be among the most enduring of twenties fads. There is reason to believe he also exaggerated the effect of skin tone on shaping his personality in his later years. But there is no question it contributed to the prevailing mood of his formative years, a sense that he was unloved and somewhat isolate.

One always distrusts easy psychological explanations for the basic patterns of a man's behavior; but Fairbanks was a simple man, and in his case a simple explanation will probably suffice. As a child he needed more affection than he received; his best weapon in the fight for approval was his natural athletic talent, and since a depressed athlete seems (or seemed in those more innocent days) a contradiction in terms, he developed a personal style that would suit his strongest skill. Everything began and ended for Fairbanks with his zealously guarded physical skills and well-being. Almost all the other prominent features of his character were based on his athletic ability: the bounding, boundless optimism; the perpetually youthful manner; the lack of concern about the future; even his taste for practical jokes of a very physical kind.

The wounds he tried to heal with this balm were of the psychologically classic kind—an unhappy and domineering mother; a failed and finally absent father. Ella, his mother, was New England-born, brought up in socially secure, carefully sheltered comfort, which did not prepare her for the vicissitudes she was shortly to experience. By the time she bore Douglas, her fourth child, she had been once widowed and once divorced. The first marriage had been a happy one, though when John Fairbanks, who ultimately contributed his name but nothing else to the children she later bore, died, it was discovered that he had been swindled out of much of his wealth by business partners. She retreated to New York, where she married again, this time a drunkard named Wilcox. The union was brief and ended in the divorce obtained for her in New York by attorney H. Charles Ulman, whom she soon married. Shortly thereafter they decamped for Denver in search of a silver fortune that stubbornly eluded him. The boy they christened Douglas Elton Ulman was born on May 23, 1883, two years after their arrival in Colorado and a year after the birth of his brother, Robert, with whom he remained close all his life.

There is no doubt that in time Ella came to love both these sons in an excessive, even smothering sort of way. But for the moment, trying to maintain a prosperous front without adequate help, she resented them because they added to her feeling that she had been ill used by life and that under its pressures she had betrayed her best self. For one thing, she had been raised a Catholic and had, of course, been forced to abandon her faith when she divorced her second husband. Then her third husband was partially Jewish, which reinforced her feeling that she had strayed far too far from her background. Her pain might have been eased had Ulman's mining ventures worked out, but they all proved worthless. And so did he. In 1888 Ulman took a position as a paid speaker for Benjamin Harrison, the Republican presidential candidate. His family was forced to move into a smaller home, and Ella took in boarders to eke out a livelihood. Ulman eventually settled in New York and returned only once to Denver on some mysterious business. Douglas, then twelve years old, encountered him on the street during that stay and persuaded him to come home and visit Ella, but the reunion was painfully strained. Douglas did not see or hear from his father again until he achieved his first Broadway successes, when the old man would occasionally drop around the theater to cadge small loans.

In later years Douglas attributed his interest in the stage to his father, who had been an amateur Shakespeare scholar wont to recite from the Bard at the smallest excuse. A modern observer is more likely to attribute his theatrical bent not to anything in his father's presence, but to his absence. It is an uncanny thing, but a disproportionate number of actors, both male and female—particularly of this period—are the children of fathers who absented themselves from their childhoods.

143

Very often, when one even lightly probes the lives of those whose fathers did not stray, one discovers that they were emotionally absent. The stage, in those days, required very little formal training, so it was a logical place for young people to look for work to help out with the family finances. But one cannot help thinking that the approval so readily obtained from an audience was a highly seductive substitute for the fatherly approval that is so important in developing a healthy ego.

Be that as it may, there were other, more concrete factors directing young Fairbanks to the stage. He was a poor student and an inveterate and much-punished prankster who obviously needed to be the center of attention. The reward for his transgressions was often the enforced memorization of some Shakespearean passage, and that work—along with the one part of the school week that he looked forward to, the Friday recitations—surely helped shape his future. In any case his neighbor Burns Mantle (later to become a well-known drama critic and editor of the annual *Best Plays* volume) said that by the time Fairbanks was in his teens, "he would recite you as fine and florid an Antony's speech to the Romans as you ever heard. With gestures, too." He performed for his mother's boarders, organized a backyard theater one summer, and achieved a certain skill in dialects by imitating the street peddlers—Irish, Italian, Jewish—who hawked their wares from carts passing his home. He even got a bit with a touring company, using one of the accents he had acquired to play an Italian newsboy.

Douglas's mother was not altogether happy about her son's interest in drama, but that was less worrisome to her than his perpetual high spirits, for the gloomy infant had turned into a lighthearted delinquent, and visits to the school principal's office were almost weekly occurrences. The exact nature of most of his offenses is lost to history, but it is said that he and Robert once loosed a carton of water snakes on a crowded trolley car and that on another occasion, when Douglas was serving as an altar boy, he spiked the sacramental wine with vinegar All the while, of course, he was busy turning the world into a gym, making ordinary structures—steps, fences, porch roofs—into props for crowd-pleasing displays of a boy in graceful motion.

Meanwhile, Ella tried to turn the clock back. She divorced Ulman (for desertion) and resumed her first husband's name of Fairbanks, which she induced her third husband's boys to adopt as well. She also saw to it that they were raised in the Catholic faith, from which she had lapsed, and, for good measure, insisted that Douglas take the temperance pledge. This he kept for the rest of his life, although his church affiliation was lost through divorce, as his mother's had been.

Whether "Mrs. Fairbanks" achieved through these expedients a measure of contentment we do not know. It is clear, however, that she was never able to take and hold a firm line with rambunctious Douglas. She tried sternness—two years of military school she could ill afford —but that had no discernible effect on him. Thereafter she enrolled him in an extracurricular drama school, no doubt thinking he might thus, finally, get acting out of his system.

It was too late. His teacher, Margaret Fealy, was a retired actress of some repute, and she apparently sensed a genuine gift in the energetic young man, though she was never quite able to name what it was. At any rate, he confirmed his sense of vocation under her tutelage. In one of the productions in which Miss Fealy exhibited her school's talent, Frederick Warde, a well-regarded, rather scholarly actor-manager who had made his career on the road, saw Fairbanks act. Though he scarcely gave Doug a rave—"That dark-haired youngster has more vigor than virtuosity"—the optimistic young actor somehow managed to parlay this faint praise into a promise of employment in Warde's company should he be able to leave high school.

Quitting school was easy. On St. Patrick's Day he placed green hats and bows on all the busts of the famous men that lined the school corridors and was expelled. Talking his mother into letting him go into the theater was more difficult. Here a friendly parish priest helped out, slyly suggesting that Douglas might find a suitably adventurous life by becoming a missionary in Africa. Ella, as the priest expected, decided that if acting lacked something in respectability, it at least did not put her son in imminent peril of the cannibals' pot, and so, partially financed by Robert Fairbanks, by then a traveling salesman, she and Douglas set out to seek his fortune in New York. The year was 1900, and Fairbanks was seventeen.

Warde kept his word: Douglas got a job doing bits and understudying in his touring company. He went on for the first time as "a lackey" in something called *The Duke's Jester,* and Warde, in the title role, began to get nervous whenever the script called for him to ring for his servant since Fairbanks tended to vary his entrances—one time through a window, another time from the ceiling, only rarely from the wings, from which he was supposed to enter. His big chance came in Duluth, where he went on as Laertes in *Hamlet* on short notice. "Mr. Warde's supporting company was bad, but worst of all was Douglas Fairbanks ..." the local critic wrote. Warde himself was to call the young actor's first season "a catch-as-catch-can encounter with the immortal bard." Warde discharged him at the end of the tour with the advice that he gain more experience of the world.

There followed two years of miscellaneous adventures—a short try at a "special course" for high school dropouts at Harvard, a cattle boat to Europe, an office job on Wall Street, hardware wholesaling—before he was back on the stage in a touring company of *A Rose o' Plymouth*

Town, the leading lady of which later said that he seemed to have "a bad case of St. Vitus's dance."

Apparently two years of worldly experience had not notably contributed to his thespian skills, but he had established a pattern he was to repeat during his fourteen-year, on-again, off-again career on the legitimate stage. He was ever willing to take a flier on some other occupation or simply to take off and see some new part of the world. Clearly his dedication was not to his art but to himself, and he had other desires that required satisfaction. All his life the periodic need simply to be footloose came upon him. As an international star he was later to indulge this taste in luxury though, alas, never in anonymity. He later claimed that in this period he occasionally abandoned the stage—for a walking tour of Cuba, for example, or a long voyage to the Orient—though his son doubted these tales, thinking they were but imaginary projections of his wanderlust and glamorous cover for periods when he was simply unemployed as an actor. About this, however, there can be no doubt: His mother's yearnings for respectability had been transmitted to him, and so he became a fellow traveler of New York's young socialites, a group he observed rather more closely and satirically than he was perhaps conscious of doing at the time. At any rate his first film success was in part based on his ability to make fun of their pretensions and preoccupations. (Nothing vicious about this; it was just good, clean amusement for the honest yeomanry that was his basic audience and whose contempt for the smart set was matched only by its envious curiosity about it.)

Meanwhile, stories of his athleticism began to get around. A director paused during the rehearsal of one play to wonder how Fairbanks might quickly ascend to a balcony without slowing the pace of the production, to which Fairbanks replied by leaping, pulling, and then flipping himself up onto the second story. On another occasion producer William Brady was astonished to find him filling time during a break by walking up and down stairs on his hands.

Nobody thought much of him as an actor, but everyone had to admit that he had a way with him, that there was . . . well . . . something about him. . . . So the roles, the billing, and the salary got bigger. For three seasons, indeed, he was under contract and working steadily for the prolific Brady, whose wife, the actress Gladys George, had noticed Fairbanks toiling in a Shubert chorus and brought him to her husband's attention.

Then, however, his devotion to his craft wavered. The cause of his distraction was blond, plump, pretty Beth Sully, eldest daughter of Daniel Sully, popularly known as the Cotton King. In his way Fairbanks loved her, though his decision to marry was undoubtedly influenced by her wealth and social position. In any event, after their marriage in 1907 he abandoned the stage, possibly because he could find no employment there, possibly because his father-in-law disapproved of his profession—accounts differ on this point. Anyway, he found himself employed as a salesman for the Buchan Soap Corporation, one of Sully's many interests, where he was wont to demonstrate his product's purity by taking a bite of it and swallowing it, to the bemusement of potential customers.

Fairbanks was rescued by the short, sharp recession of 1907–08, which washed out not only Sully's soap business but the cotton market as well. Back he went to the stage. And from here on his career as an engaging young leading man specializing in light comedy was steadily ascendant—and his marriage was steadily descendant. He was never much good in the role of husband and father—too egocentric for either part. In the beginning his son, Douglas junior irritated him with his boyish clumsiness. Later, when "Junior" went into the movies (mostly to help support his family, which had run through the money his father settled upon them when he finally divorced Beth), Douglas senior resented the boy's seeming capitalization on his name and even conceived the faintly absurd notion that he was deliberately competing with the old man, although young Doug avoided, during his father's lifetime, roles that were anything like the sort associated with the older man. It was not until his own career had begun to fade that hurt and bewildered, he reached out for such consolations as a fraternal rather than a paternal relationship with his son could offer. Even then he made up names for them to call each other, so much had he come to resent the fact that they shared the same one. He got Doug junior to call him Pete, and he called his son Jayar—for the letters in the abbreviation *Jr.*

All that, however, was far in the future when he picked up his stage career again in August 1908. He was almost never out of work for the next six years. The plays all have been forgotten, but his penultimate Broadway vehicle, *He Comes Up Smiling,* seems to have been quite typical of them and, indeed, of the movie roles he was shortly to be playing. It is about a bank clerk bored with his job who undertakes a life of adventurous vagabondage and, after many cheery thrills, finds fortune and romance. *The New York Times* called it "a gay story of great adventure" and noted that Fairbanks's performance "justified" his star billing.

He was equally successful in his final Broadway engagement, *The Show Shop,* which was a genial satire of theatrical folkways. By this time his name was firmly established, and so was his public personality; he was now a known quantity that audiences could count on to deliver a certain kind of entertainment. In fact, unknowingly he had been creating out of the raw materials of his essential self precisely the kind of image that the movies at the moment required.

Fairbanks was lured to Hollywood by a now almost forgotten "pioneer of the industry," as filmland's ceremonial phrase goes. Harry Aitkin had broken in as an owner of middle western theaters and film exchanges and had then shifted into production with dizzying success, most notably as the man who pulled together the financing for the movies' first great—if tainted—masterpiece, and their first blockbuster financial success, *The Birth of a Nation*. Indeed, it was that film's huge box-office takings that enabled Aitkin to attract investors to his new company, the Triangle Film Corporation. Its director, D. W. Griffith, was part of the company supervising one third of its production on the Fine Arts lot in Hollywood (where *Birth* had been made), while the other two thirds of the company, Mack Sennett and Thomas Ince, concentrated, respectively, on comedy and action films. Aitkin, with a corner on name directors, knew that they were not enough to ensure prosperity. He also needed actors to compete with such luminaries as Chaplin and Mary Pickford, and he signed some sixty stars of the legitimate stage, among them Sir Herbert Beerbohm Tree, De Wolf Hopper, Billie Burke, Texas Guinan, Weber and Fields, and, in the second rank, almost as an afterthought, Douglas Fairbanks.

His salary was two thousand dollars a week, which compensated for what he regarded as a loss of status in shifting from the stage to the movies. The trouble was that Griffith, in whose unit he was placed, couldn't figure out what to do with him. His bounding energy irritated the humorless master, as did his breezy personal style. It was, in any case, one of the tragedies of Griffith's career that though he had an uncanny eye for feminine screen talent (Pickford, the Gish sisters, Mae Marsh, and Blanche Sweet all began their careers with him), he was, it would seem, quite uncomprehending about what constituted star quality in men (he was later to have Rudolph Valentino in his employ and entirely miss his appeal). Besides, he was just then greatly preoccupied with expanding a short film he had in production into an epic that might match *Birth*'s stature and profitability (it eventually became *Intolerance*). Finally, he was in a chronic state of disaffection with Aitkin, who was vastly overextended financially and unable to rationalize the day-to-day operations of his fractious producers.

In short, Fairbanks seemed to Griffith yet another of his backer's harebrained ideas, and he tried to evade the issue he presented by suggesting that perhaps the actor would be happier working in Sennett's unit. The idea did not appeal. Fairbanks was a physical actor, no question about that, but his gift was grace, not knockabout farce. So he hung on, drawing his salary, perhaps consoling himself that most

of the other stage actors caught up in Aitkin's net were similarly un-
derutilized, since everyone was beginning to realize that stage stardom
was not necessarily transferable to the screen. Youth and naturalism
of style were the desiderata for actors in the new medium, and those
were commodities the movie people, most of whom, like Griffith himself, had come to film precisely because they had failed in theater,
were ever pleased to find lacking in the strangers from legit.

Still, after a summer of idleness Fairbanks finally got something to
do—a script (author unknown) called *The Lamb,* which Christy Cabanne, a longtime Griffith assistant, directed with D. W. "supervising"
from as great a distance as he could. In this film a great deal of Fairbanks's essential screen personality was set forth. It was the tale of an
effete eastern snob invited to join a house party in the Wild West and
forced, through a chain of unlikely circumstances, to rescue and defend
from marauding Indians Seena Owen, playing a girl who had earlier
scorned his love. This was a transformation that fascinated Fairbanks.
In one after the other of his short, early films he was a sissy or a
seriously inhibited youth who found within himself the surprising resources to rise to difficult challenges. Even when he began rummaging
through history for stories, the character he played often used the role
of the unconcerned, uninvolved playboy as a way of disguising his true,
heroic nature (see *The Mark of Zorro,* for instance). There can be no
doubt that Fairbanks thought that he had himself effected an analogous
transformation when he escaped from the respectability his mother
had sought to impose upon him.

At this point, however, no one saw what he was driving at. On the
set of *The Lamb* he irritated the crew with his irrepressible between-
takes gymnastics, and they retaliated by making him up to look like a
victim of anemia. The film was shipped to New York with no confidence
at all, and Fairbanks followed, pretty well convinced he had no future
in the movies.

Nevertheless, quite apart from its leading man, *The Lamb* turned
out to be important in film history: Aitkin wanted to see if he could
get away with charging prices comparable with those of a stage attraction for ordinary, program movies. For this experiment (the top price
was three dollars) Aitkin needed something by each of the Triangle
producers, and this was the best work available from the Griffith unit
at that moment. Sitting down with *The Lamb* on the night of September
23, 1915, were such lions of New York's artistic circles as Paderewski,
painter Howard Chandler Christy, writers Rupert Hughes and Irvin
Cobb—and, as it happened, they were amused. So was the press, which
proclaimed Fairbanks a very satisfactory hero.

Fairbanks had been present on this great occasion, and he returned
to Hollywood more irrepressible than ever. On the train trip back he

was accompanied by the owner of the Algonquin Hotel, Frank Case, and Fairbanks amused himself by dressing in full Indian regalia to waken Case from his slumbers one night. After he got over his fright, Case retaliated by telling the porter that Fairbanks was a mental case on a strict diet and that his frequent requests for fruit, candy, ice cream, and other amenities were to be sternly ignored. Fairbanks doted on this sort of adolescent japery, and he and his companions spent untold hours creating elaborate practical jokes. Indeed, in later years Fairbanks had a chair in his office wired so that he could administer electric shocks to unsuspecting visitors and much effort was devoted to maneuvering the unwary into the hot seat. (Later the widely unlamented mogul Harry Cohn had a similarly rigged chair in the executive dining room at Columbia, where it was seen in quite an opposite light, as evidence of its owner's sadism, not of his boyish high spirits.)

As of the fall of 1915, Griffith was not willing to concede star status to Fairbanks, no matter how successful *The Lamb* had been. He did, however, approve another Cabanne project, *Double Trouble* (with Fairbanks playing twins), and still found his sense of decorum offended by the star. At that point John Emerson, an actor turned director, appeared on Griffith's lot. Emerson had been a friend of Fairbanks's in New York, and he asked for a change to do something with his old pal. Rummaging around in the files, Emerson discovered a bundle of comedy scenarios by the very young Anita Loos and was enthused about their possibilities as Fairbanks vehicles. Griffith, who had little regard for Emerson anyway, was unexcited. "Don't let that material fool you," he said, "because the laughs are all in the lines; there's no way to get them onto the screen." Why couldn't the gags be printed as subtitles? Emerson asked. Because, said Griffith, people don't come to the movies to read; they go to look at pictures. Why, then, Emerson inquired, had Griffith purchased these scripts? "I like to read them myself," he replied. "They make me laugh."

Perhaps Griffith noted a certain illogic in his position as he stated it to Emerson. Or perhaps, preoccupied as he was with *Intolerance,* he was merely seeking a quick solution to the nagging Fairbanks problem. Anyway, he finally told Emerson to have a meeting with Loos (eventually they were to extend their collaboration into marriage), who was persuaded to add more gags, both verbal and visual, to one of the scenarios, and according to her, they had a high old time shooting the thing, which was called *His Picture in the Papers.* When it was finished, Emerson and Fairbanks screened it for Griffith, who told them that if they cut their five reels to two, he would see if, possibly, he could find a way to release it.

So the picture was shelved. Or so everyone thought. But now, uncannily, a second accident, even more fortunate than the one that had attended *The Lamb*'s premiere, occurred. An uncut print was some-how shipped to New York despite Griffith's dubiety, and it was sent over to Roxy Rothafel at the Strand Theater as a substitute for a picture that he had booked but had got lost in transit. By the end of the first reel of *His Picture* the theater, according to Miss Loos, "was fairly rocking with laughter." By the next day *The New York Times* had pro-claimed it a hit, and Roxy kept it on.

The Loos-Emerson formula was quite a simple one. She put much more wit into the subtitles than had been present in the two earlier Fairbanks films, and Emerson, as Alistair Cooke was to put in his study of Fairbanks, had the good sense "to let Fairbanks' own restlessness set the pace of the shooting and his gymnastics be the true improvi-sations on a simple scenario." In these films all the "acting" took place in the early going, when Fairbanks might be discovered, in monocle and spats, idling about some mansion or watering place, good-natured but a figure of fun to everyone but himself. As a variation he might be seen as a repressed or an inhibited dreamer, trapped in some routine job and longing for adventure. The point was simply to set up a situation where the true Fairbanks—resourceful, daring, gallant—could emerge from an improbable cocoon and gaily, dartingly demonstrate his re-markable heroic gifts. In that very first Loos-Emerson film, for example, he boxed six rounds with a professional fighter, dived from the deck of an ocean liner into the sea, and took a mighty leap from a speeding train. In subsequent films he was to be observed fighting forest fires, climbing the sheer walls of canyons, being a "human submarine."

Of course, there was more to the popularity of these cheerful little dramas than good humor and great stunting. These transformations of his from spectacular ineptitude to even more spectacular eptitude gen-erally signaled an implicit conversion of another sort—to "American-ism," for want of a better word. That is to say, he set aside vaguely foreign or effeminate ways (they were really the same thing as far as most males of the time were concerned) and faced his troubles forth-rightly but with quick, improvisatory cleverness. The time was ripe for such a figure, and Fairbanks's rise to fame coincided with a great popular interest in the application of those virtues to world problems. In 1916, the year he made ten films—a quarter of his lifetime's production—America was standing ambivalently aloof from the Great War in Europe, and there was a major debate over whether the nation as a whole should undertake a transformation not unlike the one Fair-banks repeatedly undertook. Ultimately, of course, it did—with results far more ambiguous than those he so happily achieved.

But even if the war had not been going on, Fairbanks would have had a fundamental appeal to his audiences. A room, as Cooke so nicely put it, was for him "a machine for escape," and to see Doug at bay and fighting off his enemies, the while casing the place for possibilities (this staircase here, that balcony there, and how about the chandelier?—let's see how can I put them together to befuddle these fools), was always the moment of highest deliciousness in his work. The potentialities were always apparent to the audience but not the sequence of their employment, not the variations he could ring on simple action. (Who else, for example, would have thought of, let alone dared, a handspring powered and supported by only one arm?) Lightning pragmatism, that was the heart of his style, and to combine pragmatism—America's only major contribution to world philosophy —with instant action—our national obsession—was no trivial invention.

Its appeal abides, perhaps better than the relentless optimism of Fairbanks's nature. He was a man who in adulthood naturally looked on the bright side of things, but the books he wrote (or had ghosted) were a bit too much. *Laugh and Live, Making Life Worthwhile, Whistle and Hoe—Sing as We Go* (to name less than half his literary output) set the teeth on edge. Yet one must admit that at this time he had better reason than almost anyone else to believe that anything was possible for a plucky, lucky young man, for by 1920 he had achieved not merely wealth but (because he was the first to recognize consciously the celebrity power the film medium could confer on its chosen few) also social position and influence on the world of affairs—beyond the dreams of any previous actor.

His economic rise is easy to trace. In 1917 he left Aitkin to form his own company, taking Loos, Emerson, and another favorite director, Allan Dwan, with him; three years after that he joined with Pickford, Chaplin, and Griffith to form United Artists, in whose councils his and Pickford's became by far the most powerful voices. Silent films were relatively inexpensive to make, and in those days of absurdly low income taxes it was easy for stars who controlled their own negatives to make, and keep, astonishing sums of money. By 1920 Fairbanks was unquestionably a millionaire many times over and equally unquestionably the most popular leading man of the screen.

His rise in social stature took more time and subtlety to achieve. Looking back, one can discern that much of it was based on his relationship with Mary Pickford. They met at a house party in 1915, when both were more or less unhappily married, and the circumstances of their meeting could not have been more romantic. She, of course, was already the most important screen star of the day, and in the pecking order of the guests at the country home of musical comedy and vaudeville star Elsie Janis—the historic Philipse Manor near Tarrytown, New York—she far outranked him, the moderately popular stage actor just beginning his assault on the movies. Still, he was highly complimentary, and she was very disappointed in her marriage to hard-drinking Owen Moore, a Griffith leading man she had married over her mother's strenuous objections. At that time, she says in her autobiography, "I was resolved to take my marital punishment with a grin. I had carved out my future in my career. It was my solace, my high fortress, where no one and nothing could molest or harm me." So she paid little heed to Fairbanks until, later in the day, she attempted to cross an icy stream on a narrow and slippery log. Halfway across, she found herself trapped, immobilized by fear. Others in the party shouted advice and comfort, but it was Fairbanks who resolved her contretemps in typical fashion —leaping agilely onto the log, sweeping her up in his arms, and nimbly depositing her on dry ground in a single graceful action.

It was, in short, a perfect meeting—both behaving in perfect public character. Indeed, they continued in character throughout the five years of courtship that followed, he avidly pursuing, she nobly resisting his advances. According to her autobiography and his official biography, they were never, or at least rarely, unchaperoned. Still, when his mother died suddenly in 1916, it was to Little Mary that he turned for comfort. She had written him a note of sympathy, he asked if he could see her, they went for a drive in Central Park, and there Fairbanks broke down and wept for the first time in his bereavement. She consoled him as best she could, and when the storm passed, they looked up to discover (so the legend goes) that the clock on their car's dashboard had stopped at the exact moment of his mother's death. Thereafter in moments of stress they swore love and fealty to each other by invoking the phrase "by the clock."

From then on their affair grew steadily in intensity. Miss Loos recalled that Fairbanks, in order to meet his inamorata, took to sleeping on a porch well away from his wife's bedroom in their Hollywood mansion, so that after she was asleep, he could slide down an Ionic pillar, roll his car silently downhill before starting the motor, and then speed over to Mary's house. The difficulty was getting home—pushing the car back up the hill (so says Miss Loos) and shimmying back up the pillar. It is probable that no other screen actor, before or since, was fit enough to carry on such a strenuous courtship. Still, there were problems. Both would have to renounce their Catholicism, which was more of a wrench for her than it was for him. ("Why shouldn't I divorce?" he cried. "Caesar did it. Napoleon did it.") Although his intended was America's Sweetheart, Fairbanks knew she had been born plain Gladys Smith in Toronto and therefore lacked the excellence of birth and breeding that all his life he envied. But as he approached the top of the movie pinnacle, where she had reigned virtually alone (only Chaplin's popularity equaled hers), he must have seen that he and Mary together could found a new aristocracy every bit as potent as that of the "old money" back East.

In order to accomplish this, they and other stars of the first rank had first to create a system by which they could cope, economically and personally, with a sudden access of wealth and fame combined in unprecedented measure. One gains an understanding of how difficult it was by listing their contemporaries who failed at the task. The number of them who died broke is legion. The number of them who eventually succumbed to drink, mental illness, or the urge to self-destruction is equally impressive. Nowadays there is a well-articulated structure designed to serve those who must endure the accident of stardom. Agents, accountants, lawyers, and public relations advisers staff this structure, and the possibility of emerging more or less intact from the ordeal of stardom is reasonable, if never entirely certain. But Fairbanks, Pickford, and their peers had to begin creating that system under the pressure of fast-moving, unpredictable careers. Whatever one thinks of the way they handled the task, it must be seen as a problem for which they had no convenient models.

In any case, after United Artists came into being in 1920, and in fear and trembling over what divorces and a quick remarriage might do to their images (especially hers), Doug and Mary were joined in wedlock. The public forgave all, and their European honeymoon turned into a triumphal procession (for they were true international stars), although the noisy, jostling crowds they attracted whenever they ventured forth in public often frightened them with their size and unruliness. Once, for example, as they were moving slowly in an open car through a London mob, those nearest Mary laid hands upon her, and if her husband had not grabbed her ankles, she would have been pulled from the car. There is a still picture of this moment, and the terror on Pickford's face is profound—and haunting.

Indeed, it would seem that these experiences permanently traumatized her. As the years passed, she went less and less into public, spent more and more time in seclusion, which was, in any event, her natural preference. They were a genuinely loving couple, and there is no question that if it had been up to her, they would have kept very much to themselves. For example, when Doug and Mary accepted invitations, they sent engraved cards to their hosts to be, requesting that they be seated next to each other at the table. Each morning she appeared in his dressing room to help him select which of his forty suits and innumerable shirts and ties he would wear to the studio that day, though both knew that as soon as he arrived at work, he would shuck this finery in favor of flannels and a sweater or polo shirt. When they were not entertaining, they let it be known that they favored simplicity—screening a new movie, perhaps, and chewing peanut brittle as the action proceeded.

The trouble was that Doug was incurably restless. He loved travel and relished the adoration of the public, and this created what was perhaps the largest of the several strains that began tearing at their marriage before the decade was out. It did not show at first, for the world was pleased to beat a path to their door and Mary's husband was pleased to join her in welcoming it. The house that was christened Pickfair (by the press, not by its owners) and was to become the most legendary of all the seats of the movie mighty was already under construction when Fairbanks and Pickford married, and it soon proved to be a splendid place from which to conduct their splendid reign over what people used to call "the movie colony."

It was not overwhelming in outward appearance, agreeably hugging a hilltop in Beverly Hills; inside, it was furnished somewhat in the manner of a stately English country home. Again, "comfortable" seems the right word; but it was spacious, and there was no amenity, from swimming pool to tennis court, that it lacked. Walter Wanger, the producer, commented on the suddenness with which it replaced Mack Sennett's house as *the* Hollywood place to be invited. And perhaps not a moment too soon, since at Sennett's, "If you didn't take the young lady on your right upstairs between the soup and the entrée, you were considered homosexual." Doubtless he exaggerated, but in a new journalistic era the press was eagerly covering Hollywood's offscreen doings, regularly shocking and titillating readers with those scandals that have long since become a staple of popular social history. In that atmosphere the movie industry would have had to invent something like the morally reassuring Lord and Lady of Pickfair if it had not already done so. For as a pleasantly wicked contemporary journalist, Allene Talmey, put it, they provided "the necessary air of dignity, sobriety, and aristocracy. Gravely they attend movie openings, cornerstone layings, gravely they sit at the head of the table at the long dinners in honor of the cinema great, Douglas making graceful speeches, Mary conducting herself with the self-abnegation of Queen Mary of Britain ... they understand thoroughly their obligation to be present, in the best interest of the motion picture industry."

Wanger later recalled a possibly apocryphal story about their receiving a message that Princess Vera Romanoff was in town. Since they hated to miss any titled visitor to Hollywood, "they sent a car over to the Biltmore and brought her up there and gave her a wonderful weekend, with parties for her all the time. She was actually a little secretary from San Francisco who went back on Monday morning, having thanked them very much." But she was a rare fake. As one Hollywood wit summarized the matter, "Doug goes to Europe each year to book his royal visitors for the coming year." In the famous gymnasium at his studio the star fenced with the Duke of Alba, asked Prince George of England to join him in a wrestling match, and invited the king of Siam to try his mechanical horse. Prince William of Sweden, not unnaturally, did Swedish exercises there. And if Fairbanks ran short of titled guests, there was always the world of achievement to draw upon. The guest list was marvelously democratic and eclectic. Fairbanks played leapfrog with Babe Ruth, sparred with Gene Tunney and Jack Dempsey, encouraged Conan Doyle to try his punching bag. Pavlova danced for his home movie camera (one of but two motion picture records of her art); Bill Tilden joined him on the tennis court; Winston Churchill rested from his lecture tours at Pickfair.

The high point of a visit to Pickfair was likely to be a predawn ride through the nearby hills and canyons (subdivision had not yet reached the hills above Los Angeles). The visiting notables were routed out of bed at an ungodly hour, placed groaning atop horses, and taken for a strenuous jog through the darkness to a campsite, where breakfast—sent out by truck in advance—was served. Steak, Florida grapefruit, and croissants might be on the menu; the star himself might tell the tale of a legendary bandit, Tiburcio Vasquez, whose hideout Doug claimed had been in the very canyon where they were breakfasting.

It was all larger than any life outside a royal palace had ever been. For Fairbanks was the first to perceive that fame of any and every kind creates, among those who possess it, a unique community of interest. Whatever the original source of one's celebrity—politics, the arts, birth, or business (show or plain)—one finally becomes known for one's well-knownness, as the more recent formulation has it. As a result, one shares with other, similarly blessed individuals, no matter what they do, overriding common concerns, the most important of which is the need to confirm one's status by breaking bread and rubbing shoulders with (to borrow another recent phrase) one's fellow "lords of the universe." And as transportation and communications sped up, that was increasingly easy and pleasant to accomplish. Also, of course, all this was good for Fairbanks's medium, conferring on the movies, just emerging from disreputable beginnings, respectability by association. And that, finally, was good for him, though to his credit, he was always rather playful and without pomposity as he went about his status seeking—as visibly and innocently delighted by these leaps as he was by his on-screen acrobatics.

While Fairbanks was recasting everyone's idea of what constituted the good life, he was also recasting his on-screen persona, a possibly more dangerous operation. "Douglas Fairbanks is a tonic. He laughs and you feel relieved," a critic had written of his early films, and there were those who believed that his medicinal effect would be diluted if he ceased to show himself in contemporary settings in simple little films that he could effortlessly dominate. Indeed, the consensus among film critics and historians is that he did, in fact, bury much of his best self in the costume dramas he concentrated upon exclusively after 1920. For example, Alexander Walker, a modern critic, writes that in these later films "the armies of period historians, costume designers, special-effects men and art directors . . . do not support their leader so much as swamp him. . . . Where once he danced on air Doug now stands on ceremony."

There is truth, too, in the idea that he was much more appealing performing marvelous acrobatics on commonplace objects instead of on a castle wall, in the rigging of a sailing ship, or in an Arabian Nights palace. Walker compares these feats in the later pictures with such winning stunts as his avoidance of a black cat that threatens to cross his path in an early movie—up a drainpipe and over a balcony in a single flip without ruffling his city suit or losing his dignified black homburg—and one must agree that the simple charm and sheer inventiveness of the modern-dress trick are the more engaging. There were other defects in these later films. Sometimes it seemed that things, inanimate objects, now controlled Fairbanks and that he had lost his ability to dominate them, as he had done in the beginning. Sometimes, too, his confidence seemed to deteriorate into braggadocio and narcissism, and the cruel element, always present in physical comedy, whether practiced by Chaplin or Mickey Mouse, sometimes became too obvious as increasingly, Fairbanks used people rather thoughtlessly—playing casually off their weaknesses to make himself look good. Finally, all too often he cast himself as that creature he most envied, the nobleman. To be sure, his sword was always placed in the service of the people, of democratic ideals, but it is also true that there was a heavy touch of noblesse oblige, hence of condescension, in these movies.

In short, these later films have their discomfiting aspects. But they also have high virtues, more apparent, perhaps, to viewers coming on them uncommitted to the earlier work, which was the sweet stuff of their adolescence to older critics. The language of film was expanding exponentially in the postwar era. It was not just a matter of length, though the knowledge that the public's attention span was longer than moviemakers had believed in the previous decade was liberating. It was also a matter of technique—of vastly increased subtlety in editing, of an escape from naturalism in both camera work and settings. (The Russians, led by Eisenstein, were offering lessons in the former subject; the German Expressionists, in the latter.) There was enough of the native American booster in Fairbanks to want Hollywood to compete with these foreign innovations. As for himself, the emerging leader of his industry, he could not rest on his laurels, be content with short and unprepossessing films which did not match his status. If everyone else of importance in Hollywood was making superproductions, then he had no choice but to embrace the new lavishness, too. Not that his calculations were entirely, or even primarily, cynical. If Fairbanks did not conceive of himself as an artist—he always said his friend Chaplin and his wife Mary had genius, while he only had talent—he certainly perceived in these developments ways of expanding himself expressively; they offered him the chance to convert himself from athlete into conjurer, and that must have seemed to him an irresistible step upward.

The change did not occur all of a sudden. His first costume dramas, *The Mark of Zorro* (1920) and *The Three Musketeers* (1921), are almost as unpretentious as the earlier comedies—strong, sharply edited narratives that modestly expand his range since they allow him to demonstrate his remarkable gifts as a swordsman. The blade was somehow a natural extension of his quick, thrusting personality, and its employment often provided him with an easy and natural rationale for bounding about his sets. In some respects his broad gestures seemed even better suited to costume dramas than to the earlier naturalistic films.

The turning point was *Robin Hood,* in 1922. Fairbanks plunged grandly ahead with the idea, then, as the great castle set—the largest movie set since Griffith's Babylonian walls for *Intolerance*—began to rise, seemed to lose confidence in the enterprise. He was apparently afraid this mighty edifice would be the true star of the picture. The director, Allan Dwan, and Robert Fairbanks, now Doug's very able production manager, both were trained engineers, and they had built into the structure many opportunities to show off his athleticism. (The trick, Dwan later explained, was to rig things so that Fairbanks's stunts never seemed to strain him; if that meant cutting down a table's legs to make a vault look more graceful or hiding a trampoline behind a castle wall for the same purpose, so be it.) But Fairbanks—that "very actorish, petulant, shrewd, creative man," in Dwan's memorable description—took off on one of his journeys rather than confront the stage they had erected for him. Finally, though, Dwan was able to conduct him through a detailed inspection, showing him that the set was really a giant set of monkey bars, just waiting for him to swing through. Fairbanks especially loved a huge set of draperies that concealed a slide. When evil's troops had him trapped, he flipped into these folds and slid merrily to safety, several stories below.

Once he saw the castle's potential, Fairbanks's attitude toward it changed completely. He took to showing friends around it, demonstrating the tricks he intended to perform on it. (Chaplin, always a minimalist in such matters, got tired of the brag and one day had Dwan lure Doug out to the set on some pretext. The huge drawbridge cranked down, Chaplin, clad in a nightshirt, tottered across it, set out a cat and an empty milk bottle, then stretched, yawned, and returned whence he had come, the great gate creaking up behind him. It was a perfect parody of modern suburban ritual and a sight gag of surpassing wit.)

As it turned out, the public loved Doug in this new context as much as he did himself, and in general, contemporary critics saw nothing distracting in the spectacle now surrounding Doug. Indeed, these films, whatever their defects, gave him unprecedented opportunities not merely to transcend reality but to defy gravity itself. They are the repository, therefore, of some of the most memorable imagery in the history of the silent film, and in the end it is imagery, not plausibility of plot or character, that grants a few films perpetual life in our memories.

Robert Sherwood, a movie critic before he became a playwright and adviser to presidents, was positively ecstatic about Fairbanks's next effort, *The Thief of Bagdad*. "I now know what it means to be able to say, 'Well, I've been to the top,' " he wrote. More important, he singled out the quality that gives this picture, grievously abused by later critics, its special appeal. "Fairbanks has gone far beyond the mere bound of possibility; he has performed the superhuman feat of making his magic seem probable."

It is important to bear these comments in mind, for *The Thief* represented the culmination of the star's trip into the heavily fantastic. His artisans, led by the great designer William Cameron Menzies, fashioned a strikingly stylized vision of the Arabian Nights city; his special-effects men created flying carpets, mythical beasts for him to slay, a magical rope that, flung skyward, stiffened so he could climb it. In short, it was full of wonders that, if often imitated since (and in most cases technically improved upon), have never been surpassed in their ability to delight. There is something childlike and innocent about these visions; they are immortally disarming. And as Sherwood said, the story of a happy-go-lucky thief who learns that "happiness must be earned . . . is sound and workable, and proceeds rhythmically and gracefully at a steadily increasing rate of speed."

The real defect of the film is Fairbanks's performance. Here, as elsewhere in the later works, he seems to be uncomfortable competing with the spectacles he caused to be created—and to be forcing himself beyond his natural limits as an actor. His grin is often too broad; his gestures are too sweeping. Still, this could be seen as a kind of trade-off. If some of the old easy Doug was lost, he managed to transfer some of his essential spirit to the productions themselves. Precisely because they are so genial, the films, taken on the whole, stand the test of time better than many more pretentiously conceived movies of their day. Which is to say that on balance the posthumous reputation of at least some of his late films—they include *The Black Pirate* (with its memorable slide down a sail, Fairbanks clinging to a dagger as it knifes down the canvas); *Don Q, Son of Zorro; The Gaucho; The Iron Mask* —should probably be revised upward. Who can seriously complain of movie forms generous enough to support the gorgeous flummery, the sheer showmanship of these pictures, which remain among the most watchable of silent movies today?

There is another point to be made about these films, a point that earlier critics were either unaware of or unable to face. That is that they were the works of a man who was, in fact, older than he seemed, and certainly older than he wanted to be. Fairbanks, for all his youthful spirit, had come rather late to the movies, and in 1923 he turned forty. For a man who had staked not just his career but his style and his sensibility on eternal youth, the date had a terrible significance. His constant training (he kept two boxers on his payroll) had actually served him ill. He was becoming stiff and muscle-bound, in part—ironically —because he worked out so much using training methods far less sophisticated than they now are. (His regimen, it would seem, also contributed to the circulatory problems that led to his death in his mid-fifties.)

There were other reminders of time's passage. As early as 1924 his son, seeking to aid the dwindling fortunes of his mother and her family (Douglas senior had not been generous in his settlement with her), signed a Paramount contract and appeared in his first feature. His father was sulfurous about this matter. He claimed that his good name—and a boy's youth—were being exploited by unscrupulous promoters (there was a certain truth in his argument). But what really rankled, and frightened, was the fact that the notoriety accruing to his almost grown son was bound to remind the public that the old man was getting on in years. Then, one day in 1927, dropping in on the set of his wife's picture, *My Best Girl,* he thought he detected unusual ardor in her response to the lovemaking of Buddy Rogers, her young costar (whom she, of course, married some years later). This flirtation—if one can even call it that—was innocent, but it scared him, too. And then came the scariest thing of all: sound.

Realistically it should have bothered him less than many screen stars; after all, he was well spoken and stage-trained. And the thing that he said worried him most about the new technology—that the obligation to dialogue would interrupt the arc of his action—might have been perceived as an advantage for him. If he could not manage stunts as he formerly did, talk could distract attention from his physical falling off; a new sedentariness had been widely noted in his 1927 release, *The Gaucho,* where his best tricks were with the bola, the Argentine lariat, which required dexterity, but little movement, as well as a religiosity that some felt imitated the less grateful aspects of Cecil B. De Mille's spectacles. But Fairbanks was not thinking practically. Socially acute, as always, he saw what many in Hollywood did not: that sound was a force potent enough to overturn the old hierarchies, to install new people, a new generation, in the seats of power.

He decided to make one last film in the old manner—*The Iron Mask*. But he chose to make it as a silent, though sound was available to him and though he had earlier enjoyed pioneering another new technology when he shot his 1926 release, *The Black Pirate*, in two-stripe Technicolor. Even more significant, impersonating D'Artagnan for a second time, he contrived to kill off his swashbuckling screen character, never to return. It was done with sentiment aforethought. At the end of the film Athos, Porthos, and Aramis all have died, and their friend, too, is felled. They appear to him as ghosts and cry out to him to follow them into the next world—"Come on, there's greater adventure to come," the subtitle reads—and off he goes, laughing, eager. It is one of the most strangely touching moments in movies, a carefully planned and beautifully executed (by Dwan) statement of the way the star wished to be remembered, gallant and cheerful even in the face of the final adversity.

Would that life were as easily arranged as a movie. But there was no "greater adventure to come" for him. In reality his exit was slow and stumbling, agonizing for him to endure and for everyone else to witness. He and Pickford decided to confront the challenge of sound together, as costars of a version of *The Taming of the Shrew*. But he was far from himself as they worked on it. She reported in her autobiography that though they both were due on the set at 9:00 A.M., he stretched his morning exercise and rubdown period until noon, while cast and crew waited, running up charges that deeply offended his wife's frugal soul. When he did appear, he often did not have his lines learned and had to have them chalked on a blackboard out of camera range. And he refused to do retakes. It was a very petulant act, though he was, all in all, quite good—more comfortable seemingly than his leading lady—in the finished film.

It was not, however, a great success. And Fairbanks's mood was not improved by the great crash, which did him no good financially and, worse, seemed to challenge the verities that had formed such intellectual underpinnings as his work had. The individualist ethic, the notion that one man with grace, charm, and courage could right all wrongs, was shattered for everyone; but few people this side of Herbert Hoover had as much staked on that oversimplification as Fairbanks had.

Time did not heal the trauma of this spiritual shock. He seemed to shrink, visibly so in the photographic record of his final years. He turned rather unpleasant in his personal dealings, and while his wife worked on a second talkie, which she junked at a cost of three hundred thousand dollars and no little damage to her pride, he went off to Europe. It is said that alcoholism—a disease the entire Pickford family was prey to—accounted for some of Mary's reclusiveness. It is said that womanizing motivated some of his wanderlust. The combination of afflictions surely accounted for their growing estrangement.

This time, though, reports of an imminent separation reached the press, and the beginning of the end of what many regarded as the age's perfect romance may be dated from this period, although appearances were kept up for almost five more years. In 1931 he attempted a musical, *Reaching for the Moon,* which, despite a score by Irving Berlin and the presence of a young crooner named Bing Crosby, failed. Thereafter he did a truly disastrous travelogue (*Around the World in 80 Minutes*), the chief function of which was to provide him with an excuse to get out of Hollywood and keep moving. Globe-trotting is essentially all he did for the last decade of his life, trying to escape the growing sense that he was never going to find an adequate substitute for the kind of work he had once done.

There were two more sad attempts at features, but mostly he was preoccupied with affairs of the heart during his final years. He met a former chorus girl in London, Sylvia Hawkes, who was married to Lord Ashley, heir to the ninth duke of Shaftesbury, and carelessly got himself named corespondent in that noble gentleman's divorce proceedings. This outraged him; gentlemen were supposed to manage these matters more discreetly. Moreover, there is this irony to contemplate: He and Mary, whatever their troubles, still loved each other—and went on doing so until the end of their days. Much back-and-forthing now ensued. She ostentatiously accompanied him to New York to see him off on one of his trips publicly. On another occasion she met him in Europe for a similarly well-reported display of affection. Hearing that she had joined Rogers when the band he led was appearing in Chicago, he—dosed with his own medicine—flew to Albuquerque to join her homeward-bound train and effect another reconciliation. Still later, when everyone was convinced the end of the marriage was finally at hand, he hastily flew to Los Angeles and staved off the final breach with public and private displays of devotion.

Finally, though, a divorce was agreed to, and he took ship for London and Sylvia. But even then a last faint hope hovered between them, and only a farcical mishap—a hotel clerk mislaid a reconciliatory telegram from Mary—prevented yet another stay of execution. His son belatedly recovered the wire and called his father on the ship-to-shore telephone to read it to him. But by now the elder Fairbanks's mood was fatalistic; he had had enough of this dither and decided to proceed along the course that it seemed the very gods of chance had endorsed.

In 1935 Pickford obtained her divorce, and a year later he married Sylvia in Paris. The pictures of him as he returned from Europe and during his final years in Los Angeles show a shrunken, haunted man, bearing more resemblance to the tragic John Gilbert than to his former self.

He was consumed with self-pity and, perhaps, not a little self-loathing. "When a man finds himself sliding down hill he should do everything to reach the bottom in a hurry and pass out of the picture in a hurry," he had said to Mary toward the end of their marriage. If his life now had any meaning for him—and it is impossible to say how consciously he embraced it—it was as a kind of cautionary gloss on the success ethic and the cult of youth. He had intently followed the commonly accepted rules and practices of American life in the twentieth century. He had, in fact, helped invent and propagate them. And he had enjoyed the promised rewards. Indeed, another man might yet have found a way to go on taking pleasure in them, for he was still rich and still generally admired.

I observed earlier that his was one of those rare personalities that flourished best under the light of public attention, that needed to be up and doing, out and about. Privacy, the putterings of retirement, a reconciliation with his son who was carrying on his tradition quite successfully at that point—none of these had a truly saving charm for him. Of all the people who have been called to that most curious of professions, international movie stardom, none more profoundly required its hubbubs—its importunings and distractions, its comings and goings—than the man who had invented it.

Stardom at this level encompasses all the roles a man or a woman may play on the screen—and transcends them. And it was Fairbanks who demonstrated—it was by far his most fabulous stunt—that anyone of talent, or merely will, could play this larger role. He had found the machinery of the media there, waiting for him, like one of his sets, and he had bounded daringly, childishly, wonderfully, about in it, a delight to the eye, an example to many. He forgot only to check some of the handholds, make sure there was an escape route at the end of the routine.

There was not. And so he had to endure what must have been for him the greatest humiliation of all—public clumsiness. No wonder at the end he seemed to welcome death. One Sunday in December 1939 he was stricken with a seemingly mild heart attack. Bed rest and nursing care were ordered, but the situation was not especially alarming. Still, he told his brother that he feared incapacity more than death. And through him he passed one last message to Mary: It was, of course, "By the clock." By now one discerns a certain irony in this phrase of his. Was it not the clock—well, anyway, the calendar—that had betrayed him? No matter. A second attack carried him off in his sleep the next night, at the age of fifty-six.

Clear-eyed Allene Talmey, prefiguring F. Scott Fitzgerald's more famous apothegm for American life, had spoken his epitaph twelve years earlier: "There are no third acts for him." One cannot help thinking that if Fitzgerald, fascinated by the unfinished qualities of American lives, had lived long enough to finish *The Last Tycoon,* he might have worked something about Fairbanks into it. He belonged, certainly, in someone's Hollywood novel, though of course, there is a little bit of him in all of them—and, whether younger generations know it or not, in the collective novel about celebrity that all of us are reading, writing, revising in our minds all of the time now.

HAROLD LLOYD
FROM THE CLOCK

*B*y the time he died, on March 8, 1971, at the age of seventy-seven, Harold Lloyd had become an obligatory name on the short, nostalgic—sometimes falsely nostalgic—list of the great comedians of the silent screen, which also included Chaplin, Keaton, Harry Langdon, and sometimes Laurel and Hardy. No one dared omit his name. He had been so greatly popular in his time and he was obviously such a nice man, living in prosperous retirement in his legendary home in Beverly Hills, that it would have seemed an affront both to the man and to history not to mention him at least in passing. Besides, no illustrated history of the movies—indeed, of the social history of twentieth-century America—seemed complete without that famous still from *Safety Last:* Lloyd hanging from the hands of a clock, its face itself dangling from the huge timepiece's mainspring, some twelve stories above a busy downtown street. Somehow, better than any other, that picture seemed to summarize the inordinate lengths to which Lloyd and his peers in the great, lost art of silent comedy would go for a laugh. If few knew exactly how and why Lloyd came to this unlikely and obviously temporary predicament, fewer still cared to investigate the matter. It was difficult to see his films since they had long since gone out of general release and two compilations of their better sequences, put together by Lloyd himself in the early sixties, had aroused only mild, and certainly not critically acute, interest. There were no calls for a revival of his work, as there were for that of Chaplin and Keaton. It would have been fair to say that when he died, Harold Lloyd was recalled fondly, and even warmly, by those who had grown up on his films in the 1920's. But he was not remembered, not in the fullest sense of the word.

There were two reasons for this. In 1971, when Richard Griffith, former curator of the Museum of Modern Art film library, came to write an introduction to the reprint of Lloyd's reticent, primitive venture into the as-told-to autobiography, *An American Comedy,* he noted the lack of interest in Lloyd, a lack of interest so profound that not a single substantial book had been written about him. This reflected, Griffith commented, "the disesteem in which he had traditionally been held by the movie highbrows. They do not like his optimism. His calculated comedy methods have been labeled 'mechanical' and let go at that. His wealth and success have been held against him. . . ." So far as these remarks go—and Griffith did not live to finish the introductory essay—they are entirely accurate. To them, we might add another point. Lloyd, who was a generous man, and enjoyed the process of group creation, was always careful to share credit for his work. Though there could be no question that he was the auteur of his films, directorial and scenario credits were always given to his collaborators, and that, too, has made him seem less a "genius" in posterity's eyes.

These biases were kindly expressed by James Agee, whose 1949 piece "Comedy's Greatest Era" did more than any single work to revive interest in the silent comedians. Agee thought it necessary to balance his generally affectionate remarks about Lloyd by remarking, "If great comedy must involve something beyond laughter, Lloyd was not a great comedian." In *The Comic Mind,* a study devoted entirely to screen comedy, and largely to silent comedy at that, Gerald Mast spares but sixteen pages for Lloyd, and though he gives grudging acknowledgments to Lloyd's skill as a creator of incredibly long and intricate gag sequences, he calls him "deliberate, cold-blooded, and detached . . . superficial." Ultimately, Mast tells us, "Lloyd comedies say nothing about life." The problem, as he sees it, is that Lloyd (and Langdon) lacked "that perfect unity between soul and surface, internal feeling and external gag, comic business and serious implication, subjective reaction to human life and objective depiction of it in the film medium."

Such writing strikes me as gibberish. Its hidden message is that comedy must be damped down with tears and must not attempt to fly in dry desert airs. To be sure, Lloyd's comic persona, pretty much what we would now call a nerd, was not as rich as Chaplin's, or as attractively enigmatic as Keaton's, or as downright weird as Langdon's. On the other hand, it had a sort of everyday humanity about it, something audiences could easily identify with and take to heart. He really was a modern everyman—with the emphasis on "modern." In this sense, Lloyd's work seems to me to have plenty to say "about life": about the malevolence of the modern mechanical world; about how the twenties (and, for that matter, the eighties) dream of rising socially and economically can betray us; about the taxes the new—at the time—gods of speed and efficiency impose upon ordinarily thoughtless people. Walter Kerr, in *The Silent Clowns,* gets much closer to the heart of the matter—the heart of Lloyd's achievement—when he writes: "Unable to create for himself an outsized figure sufficiently bizarre and ambivalent to function as myth, he fell, almost without thinking, and because of who and what he was, into a myth that already existed: the myth of the good American." This was surely a different accomplishment from that of his competitors, perhaps a lesser one, but by no means the inconsiderable one writers like Mast would have us think.

Lloyd's troubles with posterity were compounded by his mild and seemingly undramatic private life. If his critics found a lack of what we would now call "soul" in Lloyd's films, they found a similar lack of emotional resonance in his life offscreen. It seems to have contained only one serious crisis—a comedy bomb blew up in his hand, taking a couple of fingers with it—but (typically) Lloyd went to great lengths to disguise his handicap (which, of course, made his thrill sequences even more perilous to execute than they seemed) and soldiered on uncomplainingly. So far as anyone outside his immediate circle knew, no tragedies afflicted his private life, though again there was more unhappiness in it than this discreet man permitted the world to know. But essentially his road to success—an enormous success in his time, quite comparable with Chaplin's, economically—had been a smooth one. His childhood was apparently emotionally stable, if less geographically rooted than most—though interestingly, all the great silent comics had rather footloose beginnings. Lloyd's struggle to establish himself professionally was both brief and without major frustration. He made the transition to the sound era more easily and more profitably than most of his peers, though without the legendary results that Chaplin, after much creative anguish, achieved in *City Lights* and *Modern Times*—if, indeed, it is fair to call these sound films in the full sense of the term. In any event, Lloyd was not economically ruined as Keaton and Langdon were, not forced into the sometimes humiliating low-budget pictures that Laurel and Hardy had to make in order to keep going. Then, when the public taste gently, without rancor or shocking haste, veered away from him, he was able quietly to withdraw, never officially announcing a retirement, and indeed, keeping himself before the public in a variety of dignified ways during the last three decades of his life—as a producer, as the host of a radio show for a brief time, and, most important to him, as Imperial Potentate (the national president) of the Shrine. He was even the star of a Preston Sturges movie, though it turned into a famous mess, at least in part because the producer was Howard Hughes. Later, of course, there were his compilation films to attend to and the inevitable old star's round of retrospectives, film festivals, seminars, and lectures, as well as extensive real estate holdings to oversee and a succession of obsessive hobbies to fill the hours between his public and business engagements.

Of such things legendary status as a cultural hero is not made. What is required is some sort of tragedy. An artist who dies before his time is, in a sense, fortunate; if he had any ability at all, we mourn not only for the indifference visited upon him by a world that underestimated his mortality but also for the work that might have been. But death is not necessary to achieve tragic status. For example, Buster Keaton was effectively silenced as an artist by drink and by the incredible insensitivity to his gifts of his last employer, Metro-Goldwyn-Mayer (and its strangely revered production chief Irving Thalberg), who tried to turn him into a verbal comedian, even teaming him with Jimmy Durante, of all people, then brutally abandoned him when these first sound films proved unprofitable. Charles Chaplin, in a sense, produced and directed his own fall from grace. His marital difficulties and his earnest, if innocent, left-wing political views (and his insistence on lecturing about them on- and offscreen) did not jibe with the benign image of the Little Fellow. Unable or unwilling to sue for a renewal of the affection he had once found in his adopted country, he withdrew in bitter exile and did not return until he could return to the prodigal's welcome that was arranged for him on the occasion of his receipt of a special Academy Award in 1972—an event that, not accidentally, coincided with the carefully managed reissue of his old films by shrewd promoters. Even poor Harry Langdon, the least self-aware of silent comedians and the one with the briefest period of stardom, came to be seen as a tragic figure. As Frank Capra, who was part of the team at Mack Sennett's studio that concocted a screen character for him—something close to the Good Soldier Schweik—and who directed his first independent feature, tells it, Langdon was afflicted with a sudden swelling of the head. He dismissed most of the group, Capra included, who had helped create his success, floundered for a bit, and, after the coming of sound, quickly sank low—into short subjects, then bit parts, finally silence. Agee's article did not so much rescue Langdon's reputation as make it, for he had never really established himself in his time, as Chaplin, Keaton, and Lloyd had; without the critic's intervention, Langdon would have been almost completely forgotten. Now, if anything, his ranking exceeds Lloyd's in the estimate of many scholars.

Thus the congeries of factors that have condemned Harold Lloyd to the fringe of historical consciousness. And thus the need to reexamine his achievements. I am not going to argue that received opinion about him is completely wrong. Nor am I going to attempt to prove that there was some hidden psychological wound or some previously unsuspected depth of vision or feeling that only now, at some distance in time, we can perceive and thereby find new values in his films. Yet it seems to me self-evident that any performer who achieved and sustained over a period of years the enormous popularity that Lloyd enjoyed must have had virtues that his more recent critics have ignored. It also seems to me, having had the opportunity to study the complete body of his work, that it has, for the most part, an overriding virtue that is so obvious it is easy to overlook—namely, it is simply and more consistently hilarious than the work of any contemporary other than Keaton. Or, as Agee immediately added after acknowledging that Lloyd, for lack of heart, might not be a "great" comedian, "If plain laughter is any criterion—and it is a healthy counterbalance to the others—few people have equalled him, and nobody has ever beaten him."

It is a point to be borne firmly in mind. And there are others that suggest themselves as his work unfolds before one, a half century and more after it was completed. For one thing, Lloyd's was the "realest" of all the comic worlds of the silent screen, the freest of exaggeration and stylization, both physically and in terms of the other characters encountered by Lloyd's character, often identified in the credits only as "The Boy." There are few freaks or grotesques here, and the streets, shops, and homes he moved through were more often than not locations rented for a few days' shooting and, so far as one can tell, scarcely changed or decorated by the moviemakers. And because Lloyd himself is usually such a normal, everyday sort of chap, fitting so easily into these ordinary surroundings, one gains from the films a quite extraordinary sense of the physical reality of a period fast receding from living memory.

One point seems particularly worth emphasizing, if only because Lloyd and his co-workers (probably unconsciously) emphasized it. That is that the decade or so between the end of World War I and the stock market crash in 1929 was a period of contrast between the older, essentially rural America—nineteenth-century America that had, in fact, continued to flourish, at least as a repository of traditional values, for the first two decades of this century—and the new urban America that was fast developing. This new nation inside the old seemed nothing less than a miracle to a goodly portion of the citizenry, especially to those who, like Lloyd himself, had been born in small-town America, but had been irresistibly drawn to the glamour and opportunities of the growing cities.

This all seems odd to us today, oppressed as so many of us are by the ugliness and decay of city life. Though Lloyd was quite capable of mourning the passing of the old, slow, gentle way of life (one of his best, and most overlooked works, *Speedy,* is about an attempt to save a horse-drawn streetcar line from being taken over by traction magnates bent on electifying it), the fact remains that to him and his contemporaries the city mostly seemed fresh and enthralling. The automobile, for instance, represented a wondrous convenience, an object of almost indescribable longing, not a source of pollution and, indeed, mass death. No wonder one of his greatest comic sequences—Harold taking his wife and his in-laws for the first spin in a new car in *Hot Water*—is so beautifully orchestrated and so curiously touching. One understands what the car means to its new owner as a first symbolization of rising status and as a demonstration to his thoroughly awful relatives that he is a more substantial figure than they reckoned him to be. Thus its gradual demolition as he attempts to master both the vehicle's mechanical intricacies and the confusions of the city's traffic regulations is more than merely suspenseful and funny; it has emotional richness, too. One gains the sense from this sequence that Lloyd's befuddlement and his increasingly desperate attempts to maintain his savoir faire, to project mastery in a situation for which he had no training, emotional or otherwise, were instantly and entirely recognizable to his audience—and that they evoked instant empathy. Indeed, one does not have to work very hard to rekindle, more than sixty years later, a similar emotional response, for there are still complicated objects we long for but which can undo our dignity, our amour propre, when we attempt to bring them under our control. Simply replace the *Hot Water* car with something like a camper and place in it an urban American attempting to embrace the outdoor life, from which we are now as alienated by birth and training as Lloyd and his generation were from the city and its tools for living, and the comic point becomes self-evident.

Similarly, Lloyd's obsession with skyscrapers makes perfect sense for his time—and has a resonance for us as well. *Safety Last* may contain the most famous of these sequences, but he had begun experimenting with similar work in his two- and three-reelers of 1920 and 1921, *High and Dizzy* and *Never Weaken,* and he may have topped all these "thrill" sequences with the one contained in an otherwise indifferent sound film, 1930's *Feet First.* At any rate, they all were products of a period in which the whole nation was mightily impressed by our relatively newfound ability to build upward, ever upward. The skyscraper was perhaps the greatest symbol of the age's technological achievements —a thrilling, yet in some sense a scary, thing. (It still is; only now anxiety outruns pride—witness the number of films and television programs that revolve around innocent citizens' becoming trapped, for one reason or another, on the high floors of an office building.) In any event, there is no need to emphasize that skyscrapers almost immediately became a feature of our dreamworld, as any psychoanalyst can testify. Nor is there much need to stress the dreamy quality of Lloyd's high-rise thrill sequences, the (again unconscious) surrealistic air about them. They afford us, now, the opportunity to reflect on how recently our attitudes toward our environment were diametrically opposed to what they have become, how quickly we have reversed ourselves, and—perhaps more to the point—how Lloyd's always disastrous entanglements with the contraptions of modernism seem to predict the exasperation with them that more and more of us were to feel in the years to come. Again, it is impossible to believe that this rather narrow-minded pursuit of the strongest possible gag line had anything like social criticism in mind. He was not writing on film an early version of *Future Shock*. But it is there to see if one has the eyes to see it.

It is also quite interesting to observe how accurately his pictures reflect the exquisite confusions of a time of vast environmental transition. For example, in that same sequence in *Hot Water,* one of the things Lloyd, his family, and his car get entangled with is a fire engine answering an alarm. The engine is horse-drawn. Yet this encounter with a remnant of nineteenth-century technology follows almost immediately their eluding a traffic cop who is mounted on what appears to be the latest-model motorcycle. Similarly, there is a great sequence in the immediately preceding film, *Girl Shy,* in which Lloyd must stop a wedding before the girl he loves marries a sly bigamist. He must get from city to country, and in the process he uses—or attempts to use—every mode of land transportation then available (including, most spectacularly, a runaway trolley car). The point is not merely that this is as beautifully orchestrated a sequence as anything in Keaton but that horses and horse-drawn vehicles come as readily to his desperate hand as motor-driven conveyances. The confusion of the old-fashioned and the modern, doubtless accepted without thought by audiences of the day since it is accepted unblinkingly by Lloyd, adds a note of peculiar interest to the movies today—a strange displacing note—that often occurs in other Lloyd movies as well and gives them a special value on rediscovery. Indeed, there is something of this quality—the familiar made casually unfamiliar by quirks of costume, decor, or what have you—lurking in the corner of nearly every frame of every silent film. It is one of the sources of their continuing fascination today—an unintentional benison of an art increasingly lost on younger audiences.

In reviewing Lloyd's work today, one is also struck by how purely it seems to be the product of the movies and of nothing else. This is often held against him by critics like Mast, who point out that Chaplin and Keaton were "international" stars of vaudeville and music hall before coming to film, that even Langdon served a long, if not particularly distinguished, apprenticeship in the same environs. It is perfectly true that aside from the most modest kind of work in amateur theatricals and a few professional stock companies, Lloyd had only a small amount of stage training and no vaudeville background whatsoever. It is also undoubtedly accurate to say that he knew next to nothing of the comedic traditions, established in the dim reaches of theatrical history, that informed Chaplin's work in particular. Lloyd's schools were the movie comedy factories, mainly Hal Roach's but also, for a brief interval, Mack Sennett's. And as Agee said, "The early silent comedians never strove for or consciously thought of anything which could be called artistic 'form,'" although, as he also says, "they achieved it."

The basic Sennett and Roach films, especially in the early days when Lloyd was apprenticing, consisted of setting up an excuse for a chase or "rally" (as the device was known around Sennett's) and then getting it going—at undercranked speeds, of course, so movement would be (Agee's phrase again) "just a shade faster and fizzier than life." Sennett, in particular, was uninterested in the comedy of character (though perhaps he achieved a comedy of humors from time to time), and while William K. Everson finds more character development in the Roach films, it remains difficult to advance very elaborate claims for them either in this respect. At any rate, Chaplin left Sennett precisely because the opportunities for his delicate pantomimic characterizations were few and he feared being lost in the general uproar. Keaton also had only brief Sennett experience, taking a cut from his $250-a-week vaudeville salary to learn the craft of film comedy for a starting fee of $40 a week, at first working mainly in the Fatty Arbuckle series. In fact, of the legendary top bananas of the silent screen, only Lloyd worked for any length of time at either of the premier comedy studios. And that may very well account for the fact that it was he who developed to its highest point the comedy of thrills and movements—the rally raised to its highest levels—though there is nothing in Lloyd's work that suggests the balletic parallels a number of critics, especially the French, have found in Sennett's rallies.

But that's all right, too. Sennett himself used to reserve his bluntest derision for critics of that school, noting happily that he had never seen a ballet in his life. What's more important is that Sennett in the beginning, then Keaton and Lloyd with greater sophistication were able to use the first machine capable of capturing and reproducing motion in order to satirize an age of machines that had set the whole society into accelerated motion. It scarcely detracts from Chaplin to say that except for *Modern Times* his feature films seem unaware of the mechanization of life. The Little Fellow had other fish to fry. Similarly, it seems unfair to criticize Lloyd for his failure to develop a tragic sense of life. He, too, had his eye on other matters. Besides, there do not seem to have been any incidents in his early life that might have set him to brooding about injustice, about the pathetic and the absurd qualities of existence.

In his films he did suffer, as Andrew Sarris has acutely pointed out, "terrible humiliation . . . on the social ladder," and these moments can

172

generate more potent shocks of recognition than most critics care to admit (*The Freshman,* for example, is full of them). Still, it is fair to say that Harold Lloyd had every reason to suppose that the most banal of American philosophies—the pluck-and-luck dream by which a poor but eager youth is elevated above the crowd because he is willing to work hard to develop his God-given talents—actually worked. It had for him, and he had the good fortune to place before the public his best and most carefully developed work at precisely the historical moment when that public as a whole had every reason to share his belief in this most common form of the American dream. He was comedian to the Age of Prosperity, and no more than his audience did he have reason to suppose that the age would not last, that a moment ought to be spared for the thought that trouble and tragedy are timeless and, for the individual, quite resistant to the movements of the business cycle. But if, in fact, Chaplin and to a degree Keaton had the depth and sensitivity to comprehend this and to encompass it in their art, one may note that Lloyd's sublime unawareness of it can be refreshing in its innocence. Or should one say in its Americanism?

Indeed, it might be more nearly correct to suggest that Lloyd is rather unfairly lumped with Chaplin, Keaton, and Langdon. They are considered together largely, it would seem, because they were the leading producer-stars of feature-length comedies in the 1920's. But even a superficial glance at their appearances tells us Lloyd should be somewhat set apart from the others. For they all clung to the conventions of the comic stage, which insisted that "low" comedians announce their identities with antic makeup and costumes. Chaplin's look was, of course, a construct so singular that he was able to leave rights to his character to his estate, preventing anyone from adopting it without paying royalties to his heirs. Langdon affected too-small clothing and whiteface. The austere Keaton, in this respect as in most others superior to his competitors, required little assistance from paintpot or costumier; he often (but not always) wore an extraordinarily flat porkpie hat, but otherwise his "makeup" consisted entirely of freezing his face into his characteristic expressionless mask. Lloyd's eager youth, slender and well groomed, used only his famous lensless glasses—themselves a completely natural, everyday sort of appurtenance—to establish his "character."

Psychologically this figure owed more to the early Douglas Fairbanks screen character than it did to stage convention. Fairbanks, like Lloyd, though on a grander scale, had come from legit, where he had been mostly a juvenile, and the character he played in his early movies, before he turned to historical spectacles, was a variation on the kind of youths he had been playing onstage. This figure was introduced either as an inept and wealthy idler who discovers within himself untapped depths of courage and physical inventiveness when he stumbles into some sort of danger or as a rather dreamy lower-class youth entertaining fantasies of heroism behind his clerkly counter and then given the opportunity to act out those dreams in reality—usually because the girl he loves requires rescuing from some peril or other. These are the two characterological variations Lloyd employed in his features, and these, precisely, are the situations Lloyd found himself coping with in them. It is also important to observe that Fairbanks made the last picture of this kind (*The Nut*) in 1921, a year after he had made the first of his swashbucklers, *The Mark of Zorro,* the success of which determined his new direction. For in that same year Lloyd, who had begun in 1918 to experiment with his "glasses character," as he liked to call his only enduring screen persona, made his first feature, *A Sailor-Made Man,* which is astonishingly close to the early Fairbanks formula. In other words, consciously or not, Lloyd saw a niche in the process of being vacated and nimbly hopped into it.

It did not take him long to make it his own. Fairbanks had never been averse to getting a laugh, but he also fancied himself, quite correctly, as a considerable romantic figure, and his stunts, though often edged with comedy, were primarily designed to show off his graceful and dashing athleticism. Lloyd, however, depended on looking as comically awkward as possible when he was confronted by difficult circumstances, and, of course, he was required to draw out his chases to the point where an audience's fears for him were converted first into nervous laughter, then into the pure boffo thing. This, obviously, left but small space in which to build up the romantic side of his character, which also had its ridiculous side—this shy, pale four-eyes, the kind of kid who plays clarinet in the high school band, has trouble getting a date for the prom, and hopefully takes the business course (though it is hard to imagine his mastering the courage to sell anything except from behind a modest notions counter).

Still, it is the comparison with Fairbanks, not with the other comedians of his era, that is most helpful in illuminating Lloyd's achievements and restoring them to their proper place in film history. Chaplin self-consciously reached for the "timeless," the "universal"—and sometimes achieved it. Keaton appears never to have entertained this ambition but, in his stoicism, to have achieved it anyway. Lloyd didn't think much about the long run, either, and never achieved anything like the surreal brilliance of Keaton at his best (in *Sherlock, Jr.,* for instance). But it is possible that more effectively than anyone else of his period, Lloyd both summarized and satirized the go-getter values of his American moment. And at his best (*The Freshman*) he exposed—willingly or not, it is hard to say—their shallowness.

That film is, without question, his masterpiece, and on it alone his reputation may be quite safely staked. It is best remembered, of course, for its hilarious concluding football sequence, where Harold, the water boy, comes off the bench and wins Tate College's big game. It also contains another, perhaps more subtly orchestrated gag sequence, in which Lloyd, wearing a tuxedo, hastily basted but not fully sewn together by a drunken tailor, goes to a college dance where his finery disintegrates under the pressure of his social exertions. That scene is typical of *The Freshman*. The notion that higher education was both a right and a rite that middle-class youths must not be denied, that the path to success had to begin with a trip through university gates, first gained general credence in this period. The popular culture was bedazzled by tales of college humor and college heroics, and this picture is a devastating satire on that fascination. For Lloyd's character, the poor and naive youth who unwisely believes this myth, is, in his eagerness to live within it, constantly led on by his collegiate social betters, then cruelly let down by them. Finally, the film becomes a study in scapegoating, mob psychology. And anyone who blindly believes Harold Lloyd was incapable of social satire—or of touching the heart—is advised to study this work more closely. If his other movies are not as fully developed or as brilliantly sustained in these ways, most of them do manage to say something interesting and ambiguous about the prevailing optimistic mood of the time to which they are so closely tied, and by extension to all such periods (like our own) when we tend to forget that even the prosperous foot must ever remain prey to the banana peel. That Lloyd's films constantly testify to this point, and do so with a kind of innocent acuity and an awareness of his medium's expressive power (he was technically a far livelier and more ambitious moviemaker than Chaplin), is also a reward not to be lightly dismissed.

Let us reconsider for a moment Agee's backhand shot: "If great comedy must involve something beyond laughter, Lloyd was not a great comedian." Strictly applied, it rules the Marx Brothers out of the pantheon, and Monty Python's Flying Circus, and maybe W. C. Fields, too—all kinds of people who cannot be said to have addressed our higher sympathies, but merely—merely?—reduced us to helpless laughter. What's worse, this standard opens the door to the likes of Danny Kaye, Danny Thomas, and Jerry Lewis, doubtless good citizens all, but also men who are not at the core of their beings essentially merry. In the end they belong to the annals of charity, not comedy.

Lloyd, for all his modesty, certainly lacked the divine madness. He was a very practical comedian, as his sometime rival Stan Laurel once said, "the best of the smart comedians." Thus he asserts his claims on posterity shyly, modestly, rather like the way his screen character asserted his repressed claims to romantic fulfillment. But that is a manner critics, scholars, such members of the audience who care about the

175

past must train themselves to recognize. Our tendency as we look back on movie history, which suddenly looks longer (and thus more complex) than it seemed only a few years ago, when the men and women who founded the medium were alive and available for seemingly authoritative interviews, is to view it through the lens of simplifying legend. The tragic myths of rebelliousness thwarted, of talents unfulfilled or disastrously distorted claim our largest attention: Griffith, Von Stroheim, Welles, Louise Brooks, Marilyn Monroe. We search through the wreckage of such lives, seeking clues to fit them into the great movie monomyth, which holds that most of the truly great artists of the medium, particularly in America, are destroyed by commercial crassness, celebrity exploitation. Large and hugely significant bodies of work, ironically, are lost to view because we so eagerly seek out the cautionary rather than the exemplary tale. Harold Lloyd is among the victims of this willed incapacity to see. But of course, we are self-victimized by it, bereft of the simple pleasures his films, requiring but little allowance for changing times, are still able to evoke—and in a measure richer than the uninitiated can possibly imagine.

GARY COOPER
AN AMERICAN
ABROAD

... but the traces of national origin are a matter of expression even more than of feature, and it was in this respect that our friend's countenance was supremely eloquent.... It had that typical vagueness which is not vacuity, that blankness which is not simplicity, that look of being committed to nothing in particular, of standing in an attitude of general hospitality to the chances of life, of being very much at one's own disposal, so characteristic of many American faces. It was our friend's eye that chiefly told his story; an eye in which innocence and experience were singularly blended. It was full of contradictory suggestions ... you could find in it almost anything you looked for. Frigid and yet friendly, frank yet cautious, shrewd yet credulous, positive yet skeptical, confident yet shy, extremely intelligent and extremely good-humoured, there was something vaguely defiant in its concessions, and something profoundly reassuring in its reserve.

The description is of Christopher Newman, protagonist of one of Henry James's most approachable and entrancing novels, *The American,* his most conscious attempt to give particular form to the general characteristics he found most admirable in his countrymen. It occurs within the first few pages of the book, and from that point onward Newman moves through its pages—in one reader's imagination, anyway—in the lineaments of Gary Cooper despite the fact that James carelessly endowed his hero with a mustache, an adornment with which the actor only rarely trifled.

It was in 1960, a year before Cooper's death, that I read *The American,* and so powerful was the connection I made between the two fictions—the formal one and the informal one that any star's career eventually becomes—that I have never been able to separate them since. That linkage would have seemed eccentric at the time if I had let it stray from my thoughts to print, and indeed, it may seem even more so now, almost a quarter of a century later. To moviegoers either older or younger than I am, Cooper seems to be a much more limited, regional sort of icon. He is to them, to borrow the title of one of his best-known films, *The Westerner,* nothing more resonant than that. It's understandable. Everyone knows he was born in Montana, a fact that colored his accent and manner, no matter whom he was playing, and that he broke into the movies as a rider in the herd thundering after Tom Mix and his ilk in inexpensive cowboy pictures. The older generation first noticed him in a small part in a western, *The Winning of Barbara Worth,* in 1926 and took him to heart seriously after his talking-picture debut in a version of that most classic of western tales *The Virginian* in 1929. Conservative of temperament and closely attuned to his own limits, Cooper was careful not to stray too far or too long from the good first impression he had made. Especially in his later years he tried to make every third or fourth picture a western. It reminded him and his lifelong fans of his roots and, as he once said, "gives me a chance to shoot off guns."

As for the younger crowd, who came to his career late, their sense of him was even more limited. For the most famous of his postwar pictures was 1952's *High Noon,* that carefully self-conscious restatement of what were thought to be—that word again—"classic" western themes. In memory it is forever linked with *Shane* in this regard, as westerns for people who don't really like westerns—that is, as films for middlebrows who generally held themselves aloof from the genre unless they could find "serious" or "important statements" in them. That was particularly true of *High Noon,* with its I-can-read allegorical overtones—anti-McCarthyite in intent—which gave it a special "relevance" for the politically conscious liberal, quite disaffected in Eisenhower's American and grateful to grasp at any straw. In any event, the success of this highly stylized picture, for which Cooper supplied a badly needed human authenticity and won his second Academy Award, returned his slightly flagging career to full speed. It was to define the last decade of his career and fix a particular image of him in the popular imagination forever. Of course, he might have done more westerns than anything else in this period even without *High Noon.* Many a star who found himself in his fifties in the fifties discovered that his weather-beaten visage suited the weather-beaten vistas of the West better than it did any other setting. Be that as it may, for whatever reason, or combination of them, this linkage of particular man to particular landscape and, by implication, particular traditions and values, seems to me to have cost Cooper's posthumous reputation greatly. In most people's memories he seems to have sunk back to his movie beginnings. He is just a cowboy, and not even the greatest cowboy (John Wayne is that).

Oh, one occasionally runs into a woman of a certain age who, contemplating the manner and appearance of what passes for a movie star nowadays, will sigh a nostalgic sigh for the perfect masculine grace of Gary Cooper, who was the only truly beautiful actor who did not spoil the effect of his handsomeness by seeming vain or self-absorbed. Even more rarely one encounters a cinéaste, critic, or historian, who, remembering Cooper's appearances in *A Farewell to Arms* and *For Whom the Bell Tolls,* knowing of their long friendship and being aware of how much his protagonists' famous "code" derives from the equally famous "code" of the westerner, will concede Cooper might even more often have succeeded in personifying Ernest Hemingway's major literary conceit. But the ladies' memories grow less lively with the passing years, and Hemingway has been at a discount in the better literary circles for many years now and seems no more likely than Cooper to enjoy a resonant revival in the near future. Indeed, so far have we drifted from our former ideals of masculine virtue, so often is the American male now urged to "share his feelings" or "express his pain," that the very laconicism of a Cooper or a Hemingway hero is bound to be held against him, made to seem quaint and retrograde.

But Cooper was always better than that, at once capable of a wider range of effective work—more enigmatic, therefore more interesting—than this literary model or his own westerner's image suggested. Had to have been, else he would not have been what he demonstrably was: the greatest star of his era and one of the two or three greatest stars in the history of the sound film. Exaggeration? Hyperbole? The desperate assertions of a writer desperate to justify his interest in a subject that appears too increasingly arcane? Not at all. One hard, simple fact proves the validity of this claim on Cooper's behalf: From 1936, when he first appeared there, until 1957, when he dropped off it for the last time, his name appeared no fewer than eighteen times on the annual poll of motion picture exhibitors, in which they are asked to name the stars who bring the most customers into their theaters. It is a highly unsentimental exercise, conducted in a constituency of no discernible standard other than the purely material. And the fact remains that no star of this era—not Gable or Grant, not Tracy or Cagney or Bogart—appeared on these lists with anything like Cooper's consistency. In fact, in the history of this balloting only John Wayne was chosen more times (twenty-five), and of the current performers only

Clint Eastwood seems likely to surpass Cooper and, conceivably, challenge Wayne's supremacy as the movie star with the longest-running popularity.

It is important to understand that when he made the list for the first time, Cooper had not appeared in any western at all for six years and that in the next fourteen years he appeared in not more than a half dozen such films, a figure that includes a rather lame comedy-romance, in which he played a contemporary rodeo cowboy, and two quasi-westerns, one of which was set in Canada, the other in colonial America, when the frontier was located in the Greater Pittsburgh Area. No, when he was at the height of his popularity (and, incidentally, appearing regularly on another sociologically significant list, that of the highest-salaried Americans), he was not thought of by anybody as a man exclusively or even predominantly on horseback. He was, in fact, more often to be found either in military uniform or in a lounge suit appropriate to "salon flirtations," as David Thomson has put it.

The great horseman was, in fact, a great clotheshorse. To look through a collection of still photographs of Cooper is to become enviously aware that the ease with which he wore everything from tweeds to top hats was a very real part of his appeal. Everything seemed to fit him comfortably and helped him to fit comfortably everywhere. In interviews he sometimes spoke of the way that playing with a hat, tilting it this way and that, helped him find his characters, and his best scene in *Morocco* is one in which, contemplating desertion from the Foreign Legion, he confronts a mirror and studies himself, first in his kepi, then in a civilian's homburg. There is great honesty in his playing, no vanity, and he speaks volumes about his conflict with self-mocking humor and without actually saying a word.

This was not the last time in this first decade of authentic stardom that he donned the kepi. And his other uniforms were equally exotic: those of the British and Italian armies, the British submarine service, Canada's Northwest Mounted Police, and, of course, the Bengal Lancers. As for the pictures in which his handsomely draped suits hinted heavily of Savile Row, these, too, were often set in faraway places, and (Thomson's phrase again) "it was remarkable how the haltingly eloquent Cooper overawed sophisticated women," among whom we can number characters played by the likes of Marlene Dietrich, Carole Lombard, Tallulah Bankhead, Miriam Hopkins, and Madeleine Carroll. Moreover, during this period he worked with many of Hollywood's most sophisticated directors, including Howard Hawks, Frank Capra, Josef Von Sternberg, Frank Borzage, and, most significantly, that most elegant of drawing-room (and boudoir) wits Ernst Lubitsch. The master directed the adaptation of Noel Coward's *Design for Living* in 1933 and *Blue-*

beard's Eighth Wife in 1938 and gave *Desire* to Borzage in 1936, though keeping an obvious hand in as producer.

In all the Lubitsch films and in many of the other thirties films in which he was permitted to wear his elegant civvies, Cooper played an American abroad, as if both producers and audience understood that his kind of understated Americanism was best illuminated by placing it in a setting that was remote from the landscapes that formed his character and vividly in contrast with them. Sometimes the audience was even asked to accept him as a foreigner, but in those instances that background information was usually whispered softly and hastily in its collective ear, so that its basic sense of who and what he was— the American Democrat, Nature's Nobleman as he was defined in our nineteenth-century literature, both high and low—remained essentially undisturbed. It was really quite uncanny. He might be cast as the title Venetian in *The Adventures of Marco Polo* (1938) or as the title aristocrat in *Beau Geste* (1939), but no matter what the script claimed for him by way of birth and breeding, we subjectively, unconsciously rewrote it so that in the movie running in our minds he was what he most familiarly was, a displaced Yankee showing them foreigners a thing or two: about being polite and mannerly despite the provocations of fancy talk and fancy ways; about the virtues of instinctive fair play, polite curiosity, common decency, and modestly asserted courage.

> The world, to his sense, was a great bazaar, where one might stroll about and purchase handsome things, but he was no more conscious, individually, of social pressure than he admitted the existence of such a thing as an obligatory purchase. He had not only a dislike, but a sort of moral mistrust, of uncomfortable thoughts, and it was both uncomfortable and slightly contemptible to feel obliged to square oneself with a standard. One's standard was one's own good-humoured prosperity, the prosperity which enabled one to give as well as take. To expand, without bothering about it—without shiftless timidity on one side, or loquacious eagerness on the other—to the full compass of what he would have called a "pleasant" experience, was [his] most definite programme in life.

So runs our last borrowing from Henry James's description of Cooper's analogue, Christopher Newman. And if the world had stopped and stood still at some point in the middle of the 1930's, we might well have let it stand as the last word on our subject. For Frank J. Cooper, to call our subject by his rightful name, was in many respects a nineteenth-century sort of character, and the United States was still very much a nineteenth-century sort of a country at that time—no matter what the popular social historians, ever in search of the easy generalization, like to pretend. It might have been disillusioned by its venture onto the international political stage during World War I. It had at best imperfectly absorbed the revolution in manners, morals, and aesthetic values which had so preoccupied its younger tastemakers in the first postwar decade. It was certainly in the midst of a profound economic dislocation which called into question all the assumptions on which its conventional political and social wisdom was based. Yet away from its one truly cosmopolitan center, New York, and away from Washington, where the young New Dealers fed off one another's excitement over the institutional changes they were effecting, most Americans, through a combination of willed inattention and censoriousness, were shutting their ears to the cacophony of rude noises being sent up by modernism in all its multitude of forms. People might now set their watches by the radio rather than the whistle of the 4:12 as it passed through, but the horse-drawn ice and dairy trucks still clopped lazily down the drowsy streets, the lemonade went around on the twilit porches, and the whirring clatter of the hand-propelled lawn mower was heard in the land.

The man who would be christened *Gary* Cooper, by an agent borrowing the name of her own hometown in order to help the young actor avoid a conflict with another performer called Frank Cooper, was formed at least as much by the comfortable yet aspiring bourgeoisie as he was by the western plains. To be sure, he was born in Helena, Montana (in 1901); but both his parents were immigrants from England, and his father, Charles, was an ambitious man who prospered modestly as a salesman, then attended a combination business and law college, after which he clerked in a law office while studying to pass his bar examinations. He became a respected trial lawyer, served briefly as secretary to one of Montana's territorial governors, and eventually won election to the state's Supreme Court. At the time Frank, his second son, was growing up, the family lived in a solid two-story brick house in Helena in a style befitting a rising professional man. By the time the boy was an adolescent his father had purchased a ranch along the Missouri River, where horses and a herd of some five hundred cattle were raised. It was there, of course, that Frank learned to ride and shoot and acquired his lifelong taste for the outdoors. Before that, however, he had tasted another kind of life, that of a student in an English preparatory school, where he and his brother spent three years not quite so unhappily as Cooper sometimes liked to make out in later interviews. By that time Cooper had developed his interest in art, which he hoped to pursue professionally. An auto accident which left him

182

with a problem hip that plagued him all his life interrupted his education for two years, but he attended one of the Middle West's more sophisticated liberal arts colleges, Grinnell, in Iowa, for two years, then decided to withdraw in favor of an art school (he had never cared much for formal education at any level). Before enrolling, however, he paid a visit to his parents in Los Angeles, where his father had removed, partly it is said for his health, partly to help a relative manage his investments. There Cooper encountered some boyhood pals who were earning ten dollars a day as movie stunt riders, and they encouraged Cooper to try their trade. He rode anonymously in about thirty pictures in 1925 and 1926, then graduated to small parts, notably in *The Winning of Barbara Worth* (1926), *It,* and *Wings* (both in 1927). Thanks in part to his romantic relationship with Clara Bow, he had the second lead in her *Children of Divorce* (also in 1927), and he played some leads in modest westerns that same year. By 1928 he was starring in such major releases as *Beau Sabreur, Legion of the Condemned,* and *Lilac Time.*

This list of early titles indicates that even then Hollywood was more interested in rescuing him from westerns than it was in burying him in them. *Beau Sabreur,* for example, was a sequel to Ronald Colman's great silent-film success *Beau Geste* (which Cooper would, of course, remake as a sound film). In it he played a French officer, while the other significant 1928 releases were aviation pictures, in which Cooper played World War I fliers. The point is that wherever he was born, however he had come into pictures, the studio executives sensed in him something more elegant, more glamorous than a mere cowboy, and one must wonder if Cooper himself did not see himself that way, too. His parents, more than usually literate for their time and place, as well as more cosmopolitan and perhaps more socially ambitious than most, may have well imparted, almost unconsciously, a sense of the world's wideness and the idea that there were pleasures available elsewhere in it that could not be sampled in Helena. And his preternatural good looks as well as the quick success he achieved in the movies gave him easy access to almost any circle he cared to explore. To put it simply, he was in life what he so often seemed to be on the screen in his early days: the kind of young man the American provinces had been sending out into the great world long before James typified him in his wonderful fiction. Perhaps these young men were not quite "the last best hope of earth," to borrow the jingoistic phrase so prevalent in the nineteenth century, but they did have a way about them. They were exemplary without being overbearing, courtly without being mannered, attentive without being overbearing, intelligent without being assertive about it, and sexy without being threatening, either to the objects of their desire or to other men.

The underlying assumption was that only a young democratic nation, still closely in touch with the natural world it was still in the process of "taming" (as another old-fashioned term put it) could produce men so naturally at ease in any situation. His sometime costar Ingrid Bergman, a woman who worked in the same vein, said it directly: "He is the most natural actor I ever worked with." Others expressed the same thought in a somewhat more complicated fashion. For example, Anthony Mann, the director: "Something in those eyes tell you fantastic things. . . . They are at once electric, honest, devastating. And he knows how to look through them. . . . No one can so graphically reveal his thoughts by the look on his face." Like others who directed him, he doubtless had the experience of watching Cooper underplay on the set, thinking retakes would be necessary, and then finding everything the scene required on film when he viewed the dailies.

To be sure, Cooper had his minimalist mannerisms—a gulp he affected when his leading lady seemed to be encouraging him to express himself emotionallly, a shy, downward, sideways glance he employed as an alternative—but mostly his art consisted of a show of artlessness. Simon Callow, in his recent biography of Charles Laughton, has recorded that most artful actor's admiration of Cooper. Laughton, his biographer writes, divided actors into two types, the presentational and the representational, that is to say, actors who simply presented themselves as simply and forcefully as they could, and actors who had to seek their characters through observation of others, the close analysis and breakdown of their roles. Laughton, who costarred with Cooper (*and* Tallulah Bankhead *and* Cary Grant) in a risible drama about submariners and their passions, *The Devil and the Deep,* early in all their careers, and been smitten by his—to some eyes—adrogynous beauty. But he found in Cooper, and others of his breed, great artistic purity. Nobody else could do what they did, he said, because what they did was so closely allied to their essential natures, so little reliant on potentially distorting, corrupting intellectual processes. Cooper, in short, had as a gift what highly trained and self-conscious actors have to struggle for, often despairingly: utter naturalism.

More recently, another Englishman, Rex Harrison, spoke to the writer Gerald Clarke about why Cooper's seeming lack of technique worked so well in the movies. "Film is a visual art," he said, "and screen audiences don't hear the words as they do in the theater. Cooper had learned early on not to bother with dialogue. He used to go through his scripts cutting long speeches. He was good at looking, thinking and listening." He was always extremely, and genuinely, modest about his abilities, the least egocentric of actors. He was famous for taking naps on the set, apparently without a care in the world. He was also, however, famous for freezing on camera, especially during the early days of his career. These moments, people noticed, always occurred when he was required to exchange high emotions, particularly with women. His whole system, it seems, balked at this demand. He was, it should be noted, quite good at making a speech, as long as anyone wanted, when he was isolated in the shot, addressing a group of any size. His career is, in fact, marked out by these scenes: the courtroom defense of his altruistic plans in *Mr. Deeds Goes to Town;* the assault on the Fascist-minded businessmen in *Meet John Doe;* Lou Gehrig's farewell (a much longer affair than most people, recalling only its magnificent dying fall, remember) in *Pride of the Yankees;* the courtroom harangue that concludes *The Fountainhead;* the lengthy stay in the witness chair in *The Court-Martial of Billy Mitchell.*

But this only makes his character an even more typically American character—shy when it comes to expressing intimate feelings, good at spouting abstract idealism. In his prime time, which was very likely the nation's (at least in this century), neither quality was regarded as a defect. Far from it. His silences and refusals, in what we would now call "interpersonal relations," implied that for Americans questions of behavior at this level were—or should be—embarrassing, even taste-less, to talk about. Good instinct would adequately tutor passion. On the more public level, of course, sermons were sometimes required. And if people wouldn't listen to reason, well, it was sometimes necessary, though only as a final, reluctant resort, to enforce it with a gun.

Now, in all justice, how could we reserve such a paragon to ourselves? Did we not have a positive duty to share such an exemplar with the rest of the world? And did not the rest of the world find him romantic and delightful—such a divine contrast with the chattering magpies of its wearisome salons, its damnable doubts and ambiguities? Best of all, did we not get a kick out of watching our hero pleasantly teach those outlanders a thing or two? Of course we did.

And it may be that Cooper himself, in his life offscreen enjoyed this role, too. When he was a young actor, his affairs with such tempestuous temptresses as Clara Bow and Lupe Velez greatly titillated the gossips. But that was nothing compared with his first foray to Europe, a journey that reads like the scenario for one of his pictures of the period. For there he met the countess Dorothy di Frasso, actually an American heiress born plain Dorothy Taylor, who was one of the leaders of what the newspapers loved to refer to in those days either as "cafe society" or the "international set." She caught Cooper at a vulnerable moment, for he was lonely and somewhat depressed at the lack of recognition he was accorded in Europe, where, in 1931, he was not yet the star he had become in the United States. She took him in hand, "like the lost lad I was," Cooper was heard to say, all innocence (after all, the countess was married). He claimed that "rubbing elbows with assorted noblemen, heiresses and celebrated characters" at her villa "made me forget my fears." Actually the pair disported themselves quite openly as lovers in various glamorous venues, and the Di Frassos eventually turned up in New York, where Cooper was allowed to make a picture at Paramount's East Coast studios so he could stay close to his new friends. A year later he and the countess went on safari together in Africa—very Hemingwayish—and after that the Di Frassos took a home near his in Beverly Hills. He brought back a chimpanzee from Africa as a pet.

The point here is not to retail ancient gossip. It is rather to suggest that from this time until his death Cooper always traveled with the social elite and some part of its artistic elite as well. His marriage, in 1933, to Veronica Balfe, known as Rocky, cemented this connection. She was invariably described in the press as a "debutante" or a "socialite," and indeed, her father was a respected Wall Street figure who became eventually one of the governors of the New York Stock Exchange. In the years before the war the Coopers nearly always summered in Southampton, moving in what was called a conservative circle, though they were not infrequently observed at the Stork Club and El Morocco (as was appropriate since Mrs. Cooper claimed to have developed a schoolgirl crush on the man who was to become her husband when she saw him opposite Dietrich in *Morocco*). They frequented Sun Valley in the winter for the skiing when that was anything but a commoner's sport, and Mrs. Cooper achieved championship caliber in skeet shooting, better than her husband with a *loaded* gun in a sport that was then also chiefly an avocation of the wealthy. In this period the famous connection with Ernest Hemingway was established. They frequently joined him and other show folk with social and literary pretensions on hunting and fishing expeditions. For example, in a famous *Life* act, the Coopers and the Hemingways (he was married to Martha Gellhorn, the writer, at the time) were seen roughing it in Utah with the likes of Howard Hawks, the director who was to guide Cooper to his first Oscar in *Sergeant York,* and Leland Hayward and his wife, Margaret Sullavan, whose background was not unlike Rocky Cooper's. In time Hemingway let it be known that he used Cooper as at least a partial model for Robert Jordan, the protagonist of *For Whom the Bell Tolls,* whom Cooper, of course, played in the movie adaptation. In later years Cooper's friendship with Pablo Picasso also became a subject for photojournalism, and we learned that the actor who attributed the longevity of his career to playing Mr. Average Joe American had adorned the walls of his home with paintings by the likes of Renoir and Bonnard.

If he was not a Jamesian figure, he was assuredly a Lubitsch character: "The world, to his sense, was a great bazaar...." Yet he remained—always—very unassuming about the way he lived, fitting in wherever he went with casual, unstudied elegance, doing his best not to embarrass his hosts with his fame or to disillusion his public, which did indeed see him as (his words) "Gary Cooper, an Average Charlie who became a movie star." He once proclaimed to a reporter that glamour was "all right . . . to ease the pain of disiliusionment during the beginning of a career, but it drugs the brain during success." He added: "I don't like to see exaggerated airs and exploding egos in people who are already established. . . . No player ever rises to prominence solely on his or her extraordinary talent. Players are moulded by forces other than themselves. They should remember this . . . and at least twice a week drop down on their knees and thank Providence for elevating them from cow ranches, dimestore ribbon counters and bookkeeping desks."

Christopher Newman, that wryly proportionate man, that softly smiling observer of the world's passionate follies, could not have said it better. And one can imagine Cooper speaking the lines—halting yet forceful, a shy smile on his face, as if he were self-astonished by this burst of unaccustomed eloquence. Perhaps in the course of the speech his eyes glance away from his listener, as if fearful he might be embarrassed by the other's attention. Yet even as he spoke, in 1939, the ground was shifting under him. This did not affect the private man, insofar as the distant observer of his life can tell. He would remain what he had always been, a nineteenth-century figure operating out of certain assumptions of coherency about the world and his enviable place in it, self-deprecating about his talent, albeit soberly pleased with the good life it provided him. But what was true of Cooper personally could not, would not remain true of the character he played. Sometime in the 1930's the previous century's notions of what constituted ideal manliness finally began to slip away from us, and the joke of loosing Cooper on the salons of Europe started to lose its force. The Democratic Prince was losing his roots in felt reality and becoming a fairy-tale figure.

This was not a sudden thing. Cooper's character did not suffer a wrenching overnight transformation. But the perplexed look that etched his face in later years began to be visible in flashes here. And it is impossible to dispute David Thomson's identification of the source of that concern, which was over the question of how "the American hero could remain a good man in this world." It may well be that Frank Capra was the first to propose this anxiety to Cooper, as early as 1936 and *Mr. Deeds Goes to Town.* The picture operated out of this basic instinct: that Cooper's character did not have to leave his native shores in order to discover pseudosophistication in need of unmasking, that there were plenty of homegrown shysters who required lessons in recognizing simple virtue when they were confronted with it. Now,

187

Longfellow Deeds, who writes greeting card verse for a living and plays the tuba in his New England town band as a hobby, is perhaps more sweetly shy on first impression than even Cooper naturally was. But that quality is not to be mistaken for stupidity, as the shysters discover when Mr. Deeds actually gets to town. He is there, of course, to claim his surprise inheritance from his long-lost uncle. They are there, of course, to try to do him out of it, a task that begins to look easy for them when he concocts a plan to give most of his money away in the form of grants to the deserving poor, so that they may start little farms and become self-sufficient landholders in the oldest and perhaps best American tradition, the Jeffersonian one. The opposition to this altruistic enterprise on the part of the city swells is per se evidence of how far they have drifted from the basic values of their native land. Truly, they are made to seem as alien as any noble fop Cooper might have encountered abroad. And when they try to have Mr. Deeds declared legally insane for his act of faith in the American yeomanry, they are calling into question not just the sanity of an heroic icon but the sanity of our most treasured traditions.

Capra gets Cooper, and himself, out of this mess unscathed—with a punch on the nose and a laugh. But there is a dark prefiguring of Cooper's screen future here. In fact, it is possible to say that, excepting his final job for Lubitsch, in *Bluebeard's Eighth Wife* (1938), he was never quite his old self again. Take *The Plainsman* in 1937, when he was a fatalistic Wild Bill Hickok, shot in the back and killed at the end by a historically accurate, but absurdistly aimed, bullet. What about *Beau Geste* (1939), which requires of him a martyr's death? It was heroic enough, and he was supposed to be a noble Englishman, in which breed the tradition of the self-sacrificing end is more firmly established than it is among its American counterparts. But still, it defied the American belief that *everything* must come right in the end. And what of *The Westerner,* in which it was noticed for the first time that his shyness could be a perfect mask for slyness? Yes, of course, he employs his con man's skills mostly for good ends—to prevent Walter Brennan's strangely touching Judge Roy Bean from hanging him and, later, to thwart his war on the civilizing homesteaders intent on pacifying the judge's violent territory. But still, the absence of forthrightness, especially when he was back on home ground, in a western, was notable, enjoyable—and vaguely discomfiting.

One can perhaps see these films as preparation for the astonishment of *Meet John Doe* in 1941, in which Capra abandoned the optimistic populism on which his fame and fortune rested in the 1930's and required of Cooper that the innocence that had formerly armored him be shown for what it was, a malleable weakness when it was attacked by truly malevolent experts. Cooper is introduced as a baseball pitcher whose career has been ended by a sore arm. On the bum he is discovered by a Fascist-minded press baron who is seeking the archetypal Common Man to front what appears to be a high-minded populist movement but is, in fact, an American version of the Blackshirts. Once again Capra was insisting that Cooper's character did not have to go across the seas in order to discover wickedly un-American ideas; they were germinating right here at home. Why, the very manners of Edward Arnold, playing the evil publisher—and no performer of this period more perfectly personified capitalism (in both its wicked and its benign manifestations) than this good actor repeatedly did—betrayed the alien nature of the ideas they were trying to propagate. At least in memory it seems that every time Cooper's title character confronts Arnold and his coconspirators they were in their dinner jackets, puffing cigars and sipping brandy, circumstantial, but irrefutable evidence that they were prey to bad—that is to say, undemocratic—values. But this time there is no easy victory for Cooper; in fact, there is no victory at all. Duped and then betrayed by his sponsor, suicide comes to seem the only honorable course for him. Suicide! Gary Cooper? It is unimaginable. And indeed, Capra pulls back from it, though it is actually one of the three endings he shot for the picture, finally going with one that is at least ambiguously uplifting. (The common people who had briefly permitted themselves to be misled and had earlier mocked and scorned Cooper in a magnificently staged Calvary sequence come to their senses—and to his rescue.)

Almost simultaneously with *Meet John Doe,* it is only fair to note, Cooper made *Sergeant York,* winning his first Academy Award for playing perhaps the most innocent of all his heroes, the Tennessee hillbilly who, abandoning his pacifist principles, became the most decorated American soldier of World War I for killing and capturing hundreds of Germans. It was a tract for the time, a non-too-subtle symbolic plea that the United States abandon its pacifism and prepare to take arms against a new German threat. As such, it is well taken—and well made by Howard Hawks, working somewhat off his usual line. But it does require its hero to abandon a devoutly held personal principle in order to support what is presented as the greater social good. And that, too, represents a new dilemma for Cooper's figure. Before this the linkage between the values of a good man and good society was ironclad, unquestioned. Even John Doe was never required to change his mind about his basic beliefs; he had only to defend them against sophisticated opponents representing clearly opposite views. But Alvin York had to abandon his code of belief, and the movie even enlists God—in the form of a windstorm that riffles the pages of a Bible so that it falls open at an appropriately inspiring passage ("Render unto Caesar . . .") while he is thinking over this matter of killing for your country—in order to compel his revision of principle.

Hawks almost immediately cast him in what may be Cooper's best comic portrayal, that of an absentminded professor, resident in a think tank, the cerebrations of which are interrupted by Barbara Stanwyck as a stripper on the lam. But even in *Ball of Fire* the cream of the jest was that the once-omnicompetent hero was hopelessly befuddled by the belated appearance of a sexual object in his life. Still, the shrewd Hawks made sublime use of Cooper's inarticulate shyness.

By and large, however, Cooper's war years were clouded by all sorts of ambiguities. In *Pride of the Yankees* (1942) he played Lou Gehrig, the baseball star who was struck down in his prime by incurable illness—a motiveless malignity that is morally equivalent to the shot that killed Bill Hickok. Until tragedy creeps up on it, the film is played mostly as a romantic comedy, with Cooper doing his shy klutz routine as he pursues a wealthy young woman (Teresa Wright) and incidentally plays a little baseball. But the conclusion, Gehrig's famous farewell to the fans in Yankee Stadium, is affectingly underplayed by him. Wartime audiences responded to the film's implicit message, which proposed that a simple, ordinary man could respond with high but unfalutin bravery to the threat of death before one's time. When Cooper toured the South Pacific, entertaining troops, he was frequently asked to do that speech for young soldiers confronting the possibility of such an end.

In *For Whom the Bell Tolls* (1943) his idealistic college teacher, having enlisted on the Loyalist side in the Spanish Civil War, finds himself buffeted by the personal and political crosscurrents running through the guerrilla band that is supposed to aid him in dynamiting a bridge behind enemy lines, destruction of which is crucial to preventing effective response by the Fascists to an offensive the Republicans are launching. Worse than that, Jordan's message urging delay in the attack—because the enemy has already moved reinforcements across the span—is shunted aside in the confusion of war. Except insofar as his desperate rearguard action at the bridge permits his guerrilla friends and his new love, Maria (Ingrid Bergman) to escape, his sacrifice is rendered meaningless in terms of his cause, if not in terms of his—and Hemingway's—personal code. If we see the Spanish conflict not merely as a rehearsal for World War II but as a rehearsal for all the ideological confusions of the postwar years as well, then Robert Jordan—especially in this movie reduction of the novel, which deliberately blurred the issues of that conflict—can be seen as one of the first American victims of inhumane, ideologically justified megapolitics, the other victims of which, all over the world, number by now in the tens of millions.

190

This may perhaps be the place to note Cooper's own victimization by ideology. Conservative but scarcely reactionary in his political views, he was recruited by the House Un-American Activities Committee to testify as a "friendly" witness at its infamous 1947 hearings on Communist "infiltration" of the motion picture industry. This was theater of the absurd on a grander scale than Cooper had ever known or would ever know in his professional life, and the spectacle of him trying to demonstrate concern for what he thought (or was trying to make himself think) were the committee's laudable general aims while trying at the same time to avoid the specific mention of people he vaguely suspected might be of the undemocratic left was really rather touching. He was a fair-minded and tolerant man, and never did he resort more broadly to his shitkicker's image than he did in this appearance. Innocence, naiveté, little-boyishness, indeed—this was the loophole through which he successfully squirmed in what was definitely not his finest hour.

The newsreels show that if he did not cover himself with glory, he at least did not cover himself with shame. But still, he obviously felt guilty over this performance. In the years of the blacklist he is known to have offered financial support to its victims. In fact, *High Noon* was written by one of them, Carl Foreman, who, shortly after the film was released, was forced to leave the country and find anonymous work in England and to abandon plans for an independent production company in which Cooper had agreed to invest. He withdrew his money —but only after his fellow investors had pulled out, rendering Foreman's plans inoperable. And he issued a statement saying, "I had indicated a willingness to purchase stock because I was convinced of Foreman's loyalty and Americanism and of his ability as a picture maker. My opinion of Foreman has not changed."

Politics aside, however, it is clear that from World War II onward —and with accelerating speed in the postwar years—Cooper's career was drifting more or less unconsciously in new directions, just as American values were. The old-fashioned hero, repository of simple, individualistic, nineteenth-century American virtues, which were as an honestly honed and wielded blade, cutting through the fancy words and inscrutable motives of his tormentors, was now, and increasingly would be, a rather distant and psychologically inert figure to audiences, viable to them more as victim than as exemplar. Of course, Cooper would not proceed in a straight line down this path. There would be plenty of conventionally heroic roles, whether in *The Story of Dr. Wassell* for De Mille during the war or in the same director's supremely silly *Unconquered* right after it, not to mention a long string of action-adventure titles that were utterly unmemorable. He was all right in all of them—always the unassuming professional, submitting himself agreeably to the camera, never in danger of wearing out his welcome as more visibly forceful or highly mannered actors are. But perhaps precisely because he could blend so easily with conventional movie backgrounds, it began to be clear that at the very least he required something more in the way of settings if his writers and directors could not provide him with some curious character or situation against which to play. It became clearer than ever that it had been very smart to insert him into all those early thirties drawing rooms—or even into a baseball uniform. They tested his power of accommodation, forced his screen character toward a higher degree of resolution. Speaking purely dramatically, and setting aside all questions about how the fate of his hero grew more depressing with the changing times, Cooper needed to appear in an edgy context of some kind.

Example: *Cloak and Dagger* (1946), in which he plays an atomic physicist—a very unlikely, therefore very good, choice of professions for him—who is recruited by the OSS for work in occupied Europe. He is utterly innocent about espionage work, the sort of naif that director Fritz Lang loved to put into dangerously ambiguous situations, where it is difficult to tell who is a friend and who is an enemy, and then watch him squirm out. This was a version of the old Cooper character adrift in Europe, but operating now in its bombed-out cellars instead of its glittering salons.

Example: *The Fountainhead* (1949), in which Hollywood's least egocentric actor was cast as fiction's most egomaniacal architect, Ayn Rand's Howard Roark, a man so insistent upon the sanctity of his own singular vision that he blows up a housing development rather than permit its builders to tamper with his designs. The product of what Andrew Sarris has called King Vidor's "delirious" period, the film also offers Cooper the least characteristic love scene he ever played, in which he literally beats proud Dominique Francon (Patricia Neal) into submission.

It should not have worked, and maybe overall it doesn't work, considering the inescapably loopy Rand text (she wrote the screenplay). But Cooper does cut the required passions and keeps his character grounded in recognizable reality—no small feat, and an interesting one. Indeed, at the end of the picture he accomplishes a piece of acting that is near the virtuoso level. It is a courtroom scene, in which he must defend his sabotage of the housing project, in the process, of course, invoking (endlessly) Rand's perverse "philosophy" (which holds that pure selfishness is the "fountainhead" of all that is good in the world, altruism the source of all our troubles). For an inarticulate man, he has an awful lot of words to handle—and essentially incomprehensible ones at that. But he manages them gracefully. And because he was who he was, his presence grants them a certain dignity, even persuasiveness, for he links Rand's ravings to a decent and civilized heroic tradition.

Still, this was a bad time for Cooper, maybe the first he had ever endured in an extraordinarily favored life, in which fame, fortune, a stable personal life, and the good regard of his professional community all had come easy and early and had never once been seriously threatened. It was while he was making *The Fountainhead*'s immediate predecessor and direct philosophical opposite, *Good Sam* (an uncomfortable Leo McCarey fable about a man continuously sacrificing his own and his family's wealth and well-being to help strangers), that he had been called to make his distressing appearance before the House Un-American Activities Committee. Now he and his *Fountainhead* costar, Patricia Neal, fell in love. Despite a happy marriage, he had not been immune to other women, but unlike his previous strayings, this was no casual affair. He moved out of the family home, and the press reported that fact, while dropping broad hints about who the other woman was. ("He was the most gorgeously attractive man—bright, too—though some people didn't think so," Neal later said. "I lived this secret life for years and I was so ashamed, yet there was the fact of it.") For several years Cooper washed this way and that, on tides of ambivalence. He traveled a good deal, passed much time with Neal, but also appeared frequently at his own front door, looking woebegone.

In the meantime, his career suffered. He made cameo appearances in three films and worked longer stints in such forgettable epics as *Task Force, Bright Leaf, Dallas, You're in the Navy Now,* and *Distant Drums*—easily the poorest run of pictures he had ever endured. It was *High Noon,* which he campaigned to star in and cut his price to do, that rescued him. It fits our basic generalization about Cooper's late career. At heart it was a conventional western—the one about the good man who has trouble rounding up a posse to help him out against the bad men, the difference being that this time he never does get any assistance—but the pounding score and the powerful, recurring visual nucleus director Fred Zinnemann concocted (cut to clock ticking off the minutes till high noon; cut to shot of empty train tracks, down which the train bearing Frank Miller, sworn to kill Sheriff Will Kane—Cooper—must come at the appointed hour; cut to an increasingly frantic Kane, his pleas for assistance being rejected on every hand and his fiancée, Grace Kelly, begging him to run) effectively stylize the film, forcing it up from routine western realism toward the level of morality play. And of course, Cooper's character does register genuine doubt about the rightness of his course, perhaps even flashes of genuine fear about going up against Miller and his gang. And that is a substantial variant of the western hero's traditional emotional impermeability. In other words, the picture modestly but intelligently varied both the conventions of the western genre and Cooper's highly well established screen character. It was, in short, original, but not too much so, attracting the interest of critics and the sophisticated audience, while remaining undismaying to genre traditionalists—the kind of picture stars must periodically get in order to revive their careers.

Certainly all the significant films he made in the decade left to him would represent, as *High Noon* did, similar variants on the formal conventions of genre and character that had previously ruled his work. In order, these films included *The Court-martial of Billy Mitchell* (1955), in which the visionary proponent of military air power is cashiered from the service for advancing his views too forcefully. He is like a more tight-lipped Howard Roark, but an individualist who does not live to see history vindicate his opposition to the conventional wisdom. Cooper has a particularly fine passage in the film, in which Rod Steiger, a Method actor of—in those days—great force, plays the prosecuting attorney, tearing into Mitchell's intellectual defenses, trying to show that no high principles underlay his insubordinations. The scene was also, in effect, the new Hollywood versus the old, the new acting style against the old. And the cannily counterpunching Cooper more than holds his own against the younger man. In *Friendly Persuasion* (1956) he again plays a pacifist, a Quaker this time, who, like Alvin York, is forced to set aside nonviolent beliefs in order to defend his community. *Love in the Afternoon* (1957) found him back in fashionable Europe, this time as a worldly and wealthy man—and a famous womanizer— who is seduced against his better judgment by a girl (Audrey Hepburn) scarcely out of adolescence. Billy Wilder's film is a very odd blend of charm and discomfort—more of the latter than the former, as one looks at it now, but very popular in its day. *Ten North Frederick* (1958) found him in a similar, distinctly un-Cooperish situation as a man forced to counterbalance position (and, more important, ambitions) against the call on his heart made by another youngster. This time she was played by Suzy Parker. And this time the discomfort was paramount, the charm nearly invisible.

But still there was one good role left to him, in tough Anthony Mann's *Man of the West* (1958). Cooper was showing his age now and perhaps the first signs of the cancer that carried him off three years later. But the harrowed quality of his presence suited his role as Link Jones (that name, combining the diminutive of Lincoln and the most commonplace of surnames, is an inspiration), sometime member of Dock Tobin's bandit gang, trying to go straight but forced into deadly conflict with them in order to protect the virtue of Billie Ellis, a woman no better than she should be but wonderfully played by the singer Julie London. Cooper had only once appeared as a man with a criminal record (as a gentle, naive mobster in Rouben Mamoulian's elegantly shot and edited *City Streets* in 1931), and he had never had to go against a scruffier gang of cutthroats. That last word is to be taken literally. For in the picture's most memorable scene, one of the Tobin boys actually has a knife at Link's throat, cutting deeper, deeper, until Billie agrees to strip before the lewd assemblage of criminals. He is impotent to help her, and only some shrewd manipulation of the situation, not a display of conventional valor, saves her from total nakedness and who knows what degradations beyond that.

It is an astonishing scene, one it would have been impossible to imagine Cooper's ever playing even a decade previously, especially in a western. If, in the end, Cooper was to defeat Dock Tobin and his gang, one also saw that there was truly no place for his old, innocent self in revisionist westerns of this sort. Permanent shadows had fallen across both the genre and his screen persona, and they would never lift. The form had now lost touch with the frontier Eden that had inspired it, lost touch with the men who matched its mountains. All of America had. Well into the forties, authentic frontiersmen, people who, like Cooper, knew at least the vivid afterglow of pioneering days made westerns—as directors; as stars; as humble, invaluable riders in the Hollywood posse. Even men like John Ford, although raised in Maine, were drawn to westerns in part because in their turn-of-the-century youths the nation was powerfully aware that the frontier was closing, a shaping influence on the national sensibility diminishing. In the fifties this generation was dying out, and the western movie, which had for so long been the repository of their celebratory impulses, began to reflect the more dubious attitudes of younger people whose connection with the West was *only* through the movies. Now the West was viable, in movie terms, only to the degree that it could be made to prefigure the modern world. Comedians told jokes about psychological westerns; Tom Lehrer, the cabaret performer, had a funny song about a gunslinger with an Oedipal problem.

There is a certain irony in the fact that at the moment when westerns were more significant in his career than they had been at any point since its very beginnings, Cooper was required to play in them troubled figures so at odds with the simple, confident men he had formerly played. Not that these haunted characters existed only in films like *Man of the West* or its immediate successor, *The Hanging Tree,* in which he played a mining camp doctor with a mysterious past. In *The Wreck of the Mary Deare* he was a ship's officer on trial for suspected dereliction of duty. In Robert Rossen's underrated *They Came to Cordura* (1959) he was an out-and-out coward.

The story was set in Mexico in 1916, when an American expeditionary force was pursuing the bandit army of Pancho Villa. Historically this was the last American military campaign in which the horse cavalry played a significant role—fighting beside motor-driven vehicles and with airplanes sputtering in the sky overhead. Thus the movie was perhaps the first of the end-of-the-West westerns which signaled the end of the genre in the 1960's. Cooper was cast as a major who has hidden in a ditch during a surprise attack by the insurgents and is enduring punishment through irony: He has been appointed the expedition's awards officer. It is his task to identify heroic conduct and to write up citations for decorations. He is also required to conduct a party of these "heroes" back to a base camp in the title town, taking with them a woman, played by Rita Hayworth, who is suspected of collaborating with the enemy. Along the way he gets a chance to inquire into the nature of the soldiers' gallantry by interviewing them about their deeds. They, in turn, reveal themselves to be anything but exemplary figures; all are moral delinquents in one colorfully unpleasant way or another. By the end they are attempting to murder Cooper and, incidentally, have their way with the Hayworth character. Cooper ultimately demonstrates to them, to us, most important, to himself that almost anyone can be brave for a self-abandoned moment under fire, but that true heroism is never a sometime thing; it consists of modestly doing one's duty day in, day out.

If, in setting, the film looks forward to movies to come, (i.e., *The Wild Bunch*) this theme is very much of its fifties moment, while Cooper's role is very consistent with most of the others he was playing at this time (by choice, one must add, since his own production company was involved in most of these late pictures). To see him play a character who was even momentarily a coward—and the movie never excuses his moment of weakness—measures the distance he, and the world, had traveled since his screen beginnings. That his very last movie, *The Naked Edge,* released in 1961, after his death, would generate such minor suspense as it did over the question of whether or not Cooper was a murderer (he was not) provides proof we do not require of the bleakness of the road he traveled in his final years.

For one who cannot claim to have grown up with Cooper, but who became aware of his powerful screen presence in the 1940's, when he was at the height of his career, unquestionably the greatest star of the day, there is, however, one final irony to contemplate. That is the way he has seemed to recede from historical consciousness. It is understandable, of course, that contemporaries who outlived him, men like James Stewart, James Cagney, and Cary Grant (who received his first movie contract because Paramount wanted a threat to keep Cooper's contractual demands at a minimum, thereby proving our point about the studio's perception of Cooper in his early days) remained more firmly fixed in people's minds. But it is odd that performers actually no more intriguing in their ways than he was in his and possessing not much more range, come right down to it, exercise a larger claim on our imaginations. One can only think that they seem more relevant to us, more easily taken into the contemporary frame of reference than Cooper can be.

In this regard one cannot help but think of John Wayne, also an actor most commonly thought of as a western hero though in fact, like Cooper, he was much more often seen in other contexts. Iconographically he certainly replaced Cooper as the symbolic repository of the traditional American heroic virtues. Yet how significantly different he was. The essence of his screen character was actually the opposite of Cooper's. Where the latter seemed nearly always to be trying to find a way of gracefully, peaceably fitting into an alien landscape or situation, bestirring himself reluctantly to action only when his patience and suppleness went unrewarded or scorned, the core of Wayne's character was his grumbling, often angry refusal from the outset to accept his circumstances. Even when he was playing a native-born westerner, a man supposedly skilled since childhood in the ways of the frontier, awkwardness was his salient quality. As a tamer of the wilderness, of women, of his country's enemies, it was Wayne's habit simply to overpower them, beat them down with main strength. Even in a historically situated drama he was always very much the twentieth-century man, fuming his frustration with the intractable world he never made and would never much like—especially since it often presented to him evidence that it was falling away from stern rectitude into liberal and relativistic ways. In short, he represented us as we now frequently are; Cooper represented us always as we nostalgically liked to dream that we had been, wistfully to dream that we might become again. You could see this even in the way they departed from this world. Cooper worked uncomplainingly until he died, then just quietly slipped away, without fuss or drama—even after his old friend James Stewart let the secret of Cooper's illness slip by breaking down as he accepted an honorary Oscar on his behalf in the spring of 1961. Wayne, to put it mildly, did not go gentle into that good night. We sensed him raging against it, and the world stood vigil at his deathbed. Nothing wrong with that, of course. We are talking of styles here, not of moral imperatives, and there was truth, and personal integrity, in the manners of both men. What we implicitly understand when we confront Gary Cooper's image on television screen or memory's screen is that with each passing year the time and the place that formed him recede more deeply into the past, making it ever more certain that we will not see his like again. The "reserve" from which once we derived such profound "reassurance" now vaguely saddens us. He is—now—pure fantasy, an ideal belonging entirely to another time, another place, another world.

JAMES CAGNEY
SUCCESS AS FAILURE

One day in 1929 James Cagney, then thirty years old, up out of vaudeville and beginning to make a modest mark for himself in musical and straight plays, both on and off Broadway, found himself with twenty or thirty other players of roughly his age and station in life in the outer office of a Broadway producer awaiting a chance to audition for a role in a new play. It was called *Maggie, the Magnificent,* and it was by George Kelly, who was also going to direct. Glancing through the open door, Kelly's shrewd eye fell upon Cagney. "Send that boy in," he said to an assistant. "And I went in and I got the job," James Cagney recalled. "It was easy."

Recounting the tale over a half century later, James Cagney laughed and added, "He said I looked like a fresh mutt. I said, 'Is that the reason?' He said, 'Yes, everything that you are is in your face.' I didn't know what he was talking about, but it didn't matter to me. It was a job."

"It was a job." The phrase was almost liturgical with him. It occurred and recurred in every interview with him, the principal bulwark in his defense of creative privacy. Or perhaps he fancied it as the best explanation he could offer of that which is to anyone inexplicable, his or her own gift. Or perhaps, in his seventies and eighties, he was just tired of the whole subject, this essentially modest man, and wished to turn it aside as politely as he could.

Still, in the anecdote there appeared to be an opening. And the canny interviewer attempted to squirm through it. "Do you know what he was talking about?"

Pause. Reflection. "Yeah, I guess I do. Yeah ... fresh mutt." He laughed. "Sure."

Sure. In the beginning, before he developed his screen character, before he permitted people to know him—it—a little better, that explanation would have done. But later . . . ? When a certain vulnerability, even an air of victimization were allowed to show? And still later, when he took his character into realms of psychopathy where no major screen star dared to linger as long as he did? No, it wouldn't do. Of course, in his later years everyone stopped thinking about him critically at all, permitting him to make the transition from mere celebrity status (where, as the celebrated phrase goes, one is known for one's well-knownness) to the status of legend (where, naturally, one is known for one's legendariness). This was an impermeable state, impenetrable by conventional journalistic means, because neither the journalists nor their audience were interested in returning him to the land of the living. It was so much easier, so much more comfortable to love, honor, obey, and, above all, cherish the image, the impossible (or anyway improbable) image.

But yet . . . Here he is. And here I am. And if decent impulse, common politeness, wishes to leave the man to his silences, the mystery of what he created, the force with which it struck us and continues to work on our collective consciousness abides. And tantalizes. May as well go ahead and ask the questions, create some kind of objective text to supplement the subjective one, that compound of imperfectly remembered movies and publicity that has accreted to him these many years.

It was November 1980. James Cagney and I were seated at a table in the center of the largest stage at the Shepperton Studios outside London. Workmen were putting the finishing touches on the set for what was to be the most lavish interior sequence of *Ragtime,* the film adaptation of E. L. Doctorow's novel. The set was a reconstruction of the rooftop restaurant of the first Madison Square Garden in New York. In it, in a few days, director Milos Forman was to stage a reenactment of the first (but by no means last) "crime of the century," the shooting there, in 1906, of Stanford White, famous architect and notorious sexual decadent, by Harry K. Thaw, the millionaire madman who conceived that White had "ruined" his wife, the show girl Evelyn Nesbit.

For the moment my documentary crew and I were borrowing light and atmosphere as well as the star of the picture to conduct the interview that formed the basis of a television film about Cagney that was broadcast in the United States a year later, coincident with *Ragtime*'s theatrical release. It had been two decades since Cagney appeared in a film, and Forman's success in luring him out of retirement had been a publicity coup for his project, though the actor seemed at most distantly bemused to find himself at the center of attention again. But his doctor had advised him that it would be good for his health to busy himself again professionally. Forman was a trusted friend (the director lived near the actor's Dutchess County farm, a little more than an hour out of New York City), and the part, though showy, was not large; it was something he could comfortably handle.

Equally important, aside from one brief, silent cutaway to him in a distant window, all his work could be accomplished in England, within the security of the Shepperton lot or on a couple of easily policed locations around London. There would be no problems controlling crowds or press access. This was no small matter. Cagney looked well, but in fact, he was physically very frail, so unsteady on his feet that Forman had to use a double in the few shots where Cagney's character, Police Commissioner Rhinelander Waldo (a man who was supposed to be about twenty years younger than Cagney), had to walk a few steps.

There was something fragile about him psychologically as well. He appeared nowhere without a woman named Marge Zimmermann at his side. She and her husband, also neighbors of Cagney's, had obliged him by helping him and his wife out with various chores and errands, and as the years passed and his health weakened, Marge became a full-time aide. She was then a large, blunt, ferociously loyal woman in her late fifties, notable for a particularly short fuse on her temper, yet in her way quite likable. She and Cagney had a rather nice, humorously bantering relationship. Still, one could not help noticing that in their partnership she seemed to make all the decisions, both large and small, and that he was clearly the passive partner, constantly deferring to her. Considering the image we all have carried away from his movies, the force and energy of his public personality, this relationship, and his manner in it, excited a certain amount of speculation that later spilled over into the press in an unpleasant fashion. (A couple of years later a *Life* magazine article retailed ugly innuendos regarding her financial arrangements with the Cagneys and claimed that she had cut him off from contact with old friends and family. Cagney responded with a hot denial of the allegations.)

Be that as it may, from what I could see at the time I judged Marge's influence to be benign and essential, assuming (as I do) that the decision to return to the screen was not imposed on Cagney. The *Ragtime* cast and crew were ever solicitous, ever respectful (whenever he appeared on the set, he was greeted with applause). But of course, Forman, directing a complex and expensive production, could not guard and guide Cagney full-time, and the rest of his people had their own professional imperatives to attend. In this situation Cagney required someone like Marge, whose only interest was his interest.

This was particularly true when Cagney ventured away from studio or hotel. Crowds of unruly autograph seekers and paparazzi stalked him whenever he made an announced appearance in public. Beyond that even the more respectable press was clamoring for time with him, and those requests required constant sorting, constant diplomacy, balancing the star's need for privacy against the production's desire for publicity. Finally, there was a need to occupy Cagney's time pleasantly since his scenes were scheduled intermittently over several weeks, and the periods between them hung heavily upon him—a stranger virtually immobilized in a strange land.

It is perhaps fair to say that I and my television crew were given access to Cagney because, in some measure, we were perceived to be part of the solution to the problems of both guarding his privacy and giving him something safely entertaining to do with some of his free time. We could conduct our business in Shepperton's safe confines, it could be put about that he had granted exclusive right to a television interview to us, and that could be used to limit access to him by others.

He was not, and never had been, an easy man to interview. Colleagues who had encountered him the last time he had made himself generally available to the press, when he was presented with the American Film Institute's Life Achievement Award in 1974, had told me that though Cagney was polite, pleasant, and obviously trying to be as helpful as he could, his memory was strangely selective. And so it proved to be. He was capable of great warmth of feeling and much anecdotal detail about his early life, which he recounted in a wry and very winning style. Of his mother, of his three brothers and his sister (two other children died in infancy), and of the loving, decent life they shared as they strove to stay above the poverty line in turn-of-the-century Manhattan, of the children's struggle for the educations they had been firmly taught would provide them with a route out of the ghetto, he drew a vivid portrait, but his father, a bartender with a taste for the product he retailed, remained a rather shadowy figure. He was also good about his friends, the boys with whom he grew up on the streets of New York, and about his first forays into show business—about everything, in short, in which he could cast himself in a humorous light, as an innocent making foolish mistakes or tripping over himself in his eagerness for experience and a modest paycheck that would help out at home. It was only when he had to come to grips with his first minor success in the theater that one began to sense a diminution of Cagney's interest in autobiography. When he arrived at the movies, the sense of alienation from his own professional past that he imparted was almost total.

Oh, he could manage something agreeable but unrevealing about his movie friends and colleagues, and he would allow that especially in the early thirties the hours were long, the work was physically demanding and even, on occasion, risky. He would permit himself the mild observation that he and his co-workers, particularly the leading players and the director, frequently had to improve their scripts as they went along, improvising dialogue and business to plug the holes they discovered in them as they attempted to give them believable life on film. He seemed particularly pleased with himself that socially he had always refused to tread the Hollywood fast track. Once he had established himself, it became his habit to leave town immediately after he finished work on a picture, in flight to one of his farms.

But of the texture of his life during the three decades he worked in the movies he had almost nothing to say. That he had a perfect right to guard his personal life closely, no one can dispute. But there were purely professional matters one would have liked to know more about, something that would give a sense of the quality of his working days. What ambitions did he harbor that were frustrated? Which ones did he exert himself heavily to attain? What projects did he care about passionately? Which ones surprised him by turning out better, or worse, than he had imagined? If he didn't want to talk about the directors he came to dislike, could he at least try to recall those he came to trust? What made him laugh, at least for a moment? What gave him a sleepless night? Or sent him into rage or sulk or rebellion? More than that, since he had had another two decades to contemplate in comfortable tranquillity those years of great and greatly beloved stardom, it did not seem unreasonable to seek from him some summarizing sense of what the experience meant to him, looking back on it. Nothing elaborate. Nothing pretentious. But something suggesting some continuing engagement with his own history even if he could not bring himself to an engagement with the history of the medium with which he was formatively involved.

But no, that was not to be. When it came to his movies, there were only a handful of them he could recall at all, and those were the ones about which he was most often queried, so that he has worked up little responses—*The Public Enemy, Yankee Doodle Dandy,* of course, *White Heat,* and perhaps one or two others. The rest seemed to have run together in his mind, and he repeated over and over his litany: "It was just a job." I haven't counted how often the phrase occurs in the transcript of our interview, but it must be there well over a dozen times. The impression he created was that he approached his work as any man might, as a means of putting food on his family's table and a roof over their heads. The implication was that there was nothing more singular about his activities than there might be about an insurance salesman's, perhaps, or even of someone still humbler in a social order, a truck driver, maybe, or a factory foreman. There was an implication throughout that acting, even when one is extraordinarily successful at it, certainly cannot and should not be compared with the professions, especially to medicine, which his two older brothers took up and to which Cagney himself at one time briefly aspired.

There were, or there might have been, many explanations for this reticence. The most obvious was that because he was an octogenarian, the victim of at least one minor stroke and heir to several other ills of the aging, his memory simply was not all it might be. His insistence that what he was doing all those years was no more memorable or generally interesting than anyone's daily anonymous doings could have been a means of covering his embarrassment at being unable to bring to mind the material that most interested his interlocutors. But the clippings reveal he was dim on this material, and indifferent to it, long before illness was visited upon him. Besides, his ability to recall events more distant and not necessarily more remarkable than his motion picture experiences must have been seems to belie this theory.

His admirable and (so far as one can tell) thoroughly ingrained habit of modesty perhaps offered a better explanation for his puzzled, puzzling silences. His reminiscences of his early family life indicated, if nothing else, that displays of selfishness, of egocentricity would not have been tolerated. His mother, one thinks, would have belted any such nonsense out of a kid. And the Cagney siblings would have hooted at it. Life was too hard, the economic problems pressing in on them were too real, too permanent to indulge any such waste of time and energy. And that view of life was surely reinforced by his early years in the lower levels of show biz, where every act, every performer were instantly replaceable by members of the hungry multitudes always in need of work. There has never been anything like the hard, precarious grind of cheap vaudeville to teach a young performer the virtues not merely of hard work but of teamwork, of not advancing oneself at the expense of one's colleagues. That ethic obviously continued to sustain him in Hollywood, where Cagney was famous for his disciplined professionalism, which by all accounts included a genuine concern for the feelings and the welfare of everyone who worked with him on his sets. (He had a temper, of course, but it was reserved for people who did not fit his definition of working stiffs—that is, for studio executives and hangers-on, people who lacked both the honest craftsmanship and the bred-in-the-bones instincts out of which shows are created and fixed up.) The fact that he came to the movies during the depths of the Depression and at the height of class consciousness in America naturally reinforced this attitude. Cagney was, in those days, of the liberal persuasion politically, and he was active in organizing the Screen Actors Guild, serving for a time as its president. No matter what his salary was, or his level of popularity with the public, no one was going to accuse him of what would nowadays be called star-tripping, throwing the weight of his ego around. That was a point of pride with him.

There was another such point, closely related to the first. It was that he wanted to make his work look easy. This was not just a matter of creating an aura of believable naturalism around his characters though of course, that was the effect his work had on audiences. No, this, too, was a question of privacy, of not wanting the people who worked with him to catch a glimpse of possibly disheartening creative insecurity, of self-doubt. A thing like that could infect an entire set with panic. It was irresponsible. Anyway, those matters were his own business and no one else's. Even many years after the fact, when an old man could indulge his past follies and enlist everyone else's indulgence of them, he refused to do so. To hear him tell it, he never had any problems with any of his roles unless, perhaps, it was getting into top physical shape for some of the more athletic ones. "No strain, no stress"—that phrase, or some close variation on it, was almost as liturgical with him as "just a job" was.

At one point in our interview, when the talk had turned to one of the several pictures in which he played a boxer, he rather shyly mentioned a compliment paid to his footwork by a professional fighter engaged to do one of the scenes in the ring with him. He dismissed his skill as the natural by-product of his training as a dancer ("It was easy," he said, of course). And then his mind strayed to a boyhood hero. "Packy McFarlane. You don't remember him? No. [No. But my father used to mention him respectfully.] He was a helluva boxer, and he was my idol. A real fighter, because he did it all and never even got a black eye. Which was great." He paused and smiled at the sweet follies of youth. "But the hero worship that was . . . there." And he held his hand up, parallel to his forehead, indicating the height of his admiration. To do your work and not get wounded or even mussed in the process, to betray nothing of what it cost you in hours and pain of preparation, that was once an ideal, surely, and not only among American males either. It was an almost universal masculine goal in the days before psychology made the agonizing plunge into subjectivity—especially by artists—a heroic act, something to trade upon in interviews, on the talk shows.

"I never understood these fellas who have to psych themselves up to get going. You know, very, very laboriously figure things out about the kind of character they are. In the first five minutes you can tell by reading the part what kind of so-and-so you are. . . ." A distant smile flickered across his face, and he added: "But mine was comparatively easy because I was generally the hoodlum, and I understood that type perfectly well. No strain."

I objected. Out of politeness. And out of respect for critical nuance. "But you did a lot of parts where you weren't a hoodlum."

"There was a hunk of it in each one. There really was." A chuckle, an acknowledgment of deviltries past, of irrepressible boyish high spirits, escaped him. "Oh, sure."

He was clearly content with that image. It was easy to hide behind because it was so simple to understand, so entirely plausible. It required no tedious and possible self-revealing explanations. And admittedly, it was the first impression he created. We all know, have always known, since our mothers first advised us on the matter, that first impressions are the ones that last, the ones it takes a lifetime to undo. So why bother to try? Especially since the public is as content with this one as its author appears to be.

Perhaps he long ago wearied of the struggle against it. Consider that almost from the beginning—that is, from the time his fifth picture, *The Public Enemy,* made him a star—he had been automatically identified in the press as "tough guy" James Cagney or, perhaps, if there was a little more space, "movie tough guy." It was always a misnomer. Nowadays we would perhaps call his character street-smart, which is a little closer to the truth of the figure as he generally appeared in the first decade of its existence. But that term was unavailable in those days, and so the more vulgar description was put forth. And continued to cling to him, despite his advanced years, despite the obvious gentleness of manner he displayed on his occasional public appearances— the tabloid deskman's hasty emblem as he bashes out caption, lead, or headline under the pressure of his always onrushing deadline.

All right then: "hoodlum," "tough guy." Implicitly agreed-upon descriptive conventions. But acceptant as Cagney appeared to be about them, acceptant as his public still appears to be with them, even posthumously, they leave at least one observer dissatisfied, edgy. The fit of these phrases is too loose. Norman Mailer was part of the *Ragtime* company, cast as Stanford White, and one day, after he had finished a scene, he delivered himself of this thought about Cagney's screen character: "Cagney was a gut fighter who was as tough as they come, and yet in nearly all the movies he made you always had the feeling, this is a very decent guy. That's one of the sweetest and most sentimental thoughts there is in all the world, that tough guys are very decent. That's what we all want. There's nothing more depressing than finding a guy as tough as nails and as mean as dirt."

This insight is utterly basic. *The Public Enemy,* vivid as it was and dirt-mean as Cagney was in two or three of its sequences—most notably, of course, the one involving him with Mae Clarke and a grapefruit—was actually an anomaly in his career. In the vast majority of his thirties movies the movement was invariably from toughness to tenderness. Cagney was usually discovered in what amounted to a state of nature—urban nature, that is—no safety valve corking his temper; his fists leading a life of their own, furiously letting fly at the slightest provocation. Also, he was frequently seen in the early reels as a bundle of mildly antisocial nerves, particularly resistant to submerging his singular self in the spirit of group enterprise even when the cause was good. What turned him around generally was the love of a good— although usually rather bland—woman. His female costars were, as a rule, drawn from the more forgettable ranks of the Warner Brothers contract players; it was as if the smarter and more spirited actresses understood that there was no standing up to his energy and chose not to try. Later Pat O'Brien, cast as priest, older brother, or senior officer, succeeded to the role of surrogate superego, and that pairing worked better dramatically; Cagney could punch at him, or threaten to, without the loss of gallantry (and sympathy) that those scenes engendered when he shared them with a woman. But no matter. Whatever the situation, the point of the exercise was to civilize Jimmy, to let his best instincts, which the audience no less than his girl friend or Pat always knew were there, get the better of him.

That was in the comedies, of course. In the melodramas of the first decade a similar progress was made, but in these his final deliverance, his discovery of his best self, did not occur until after a capital crime had been committed or until his carelessness or self-centeredness had caused him to be culpable in an innocent party's death. In either case, Cagney's character had to Pay the Price—offer his life to balance the moral books.

"Now a peculiar thing—you could kill a Cagney or a Bogart and still have a very successful picture. But you could never kill a Gable or a Cooper . . . the audience wouldn't stand for it." This observation, which Raoul Walsh, who directed four of Cagney's films, once made to me, recurred to me on that stage at Shepperton. I mentioned it to Cagney, who was mildly interested but noncommittal. One must, per- haps, stipulate the obvious: He was the most instinctive, the least in- tellectual of actors. He went where his energy carried him, where his kinetic sense of his character took him. And that was, so often, to these spectacular death scenes. Walsh said that people were always asking him why it had taken Cagney so long to die in *The Roaring Twenties,* when Cagney, wounded in a gunfight with Bogart's mob, comes stum- bling out of their lair (at top speed, of course), ricochets down a snow- covered street, bouncing off this and that impediment, then staggers up the steps of a church before finally expiring. "It takes a long time to kill an actor," Walsh would reply.

Especially this actor. There were, of course, factors other than per- sonality working on his audience's sympathies. In the comedies the

implicit understanding was that poverty, a lack of conventional opportunities, educational and otherwise, were responsible for the rough
edges that needed to be polished off this diamond. You had to blame
society, not his character's character for his lack of the social graces.
Indeed, an instant identification was made, for most of us lack what he
lacked in the way of smoothness and fine airs and could blame our
failures on the cruel trick fate played on us by denying us access to
silver spoons for teething purposes. The fun was to see Cagney triumph
over this flaw, and to do so without loss of his essential spirit. Something
of the same thing, but much darker in tone, was going on in the
melodramas.

Take the breakthrough film, *The Public Enemy,* for instance. Most
people forget now that it came equipped with a cautionary postscript,
explicitly blaming a bungled and corrupt social order for the amorality
of Tom Powers (the petty killer, played by Cagney, whose rise to criminal power the film traces). The picture asks, in effect, what a bright,
nervy boy is to do if legitimate avenues for his energy are foreclosed.
Beyond that, Cagney played Tom as if perhaps he had a genetic screw
loose—again something he could not be blamed for. In other words,
he was a criminal operating under a no-fault insurance policy. His
death may or may not have a dimension that takes us into the realms
of Greek tragedy, but it certainly has elements of the gloomier aspects
of predestination about it. Dwight Macdonald once noted that Cagney
played Tom as a "human wolf, with the heartlessness and grace and
innocence of an animal, as incapable of hypocrisy as of feeling." Ani-
mals, of course, are incapable of right reason and are denied the
kingdom of heaven on that basis. Closer to home they escape moral
opprobrium on the same basis, while gathering to them sentimental
sympathy when they are *in extremis.*

What was true of *The Public Enemy* was true of Cagney's other great
explorations of doomed gangsterism later in the decade, *Angels with
Dirty Faces* and *The Roaring Twenties.* In the former he and Pat O'Brien
play childhood chums whose paths radically diverge, the former being
twisted toward a life of crime, the latter being guided toward the
priesthood. But as O'Brien explains over a flashback, that was all a matter
of chance. Again, poverty was a factor. As boys they were down at the
railroad yards, stealing coal, when they were discovered by the police.
In the ensuing chase the boy who grows up to be a priest outruns the
cops and scrambles over a fence to freedom. The soon-to-be criminal
is caught and hustled off to reform school. Where, of course, as one
of the most persistent clichés of penology would have it, he is schooled
not in the way of righteousness but of more sophisticated crime. From
there the downward path to the electric chair is as straight as it is
preordained though, famously, Cagney is given a last-minute oppor-

tunity to find redemption in death. (Jerry, the priest, asks Rocky, Cagney's character, to pretend to face death as a sniveling coward—and no one sniveled more effectively than Cagney when it was required of him—instead of bravely, so that the slum kids who had looked up to this glamorous gangster would finally be discouraged from emulating him.) After that Jerry, who runs a settlement house for wayward slum youths, invites them to the chapel to say a prayer for "a boy who couldn't run as fast as I could." Again, the fault is not within Cagney but within the society that forms him, a society that, for example, tolerates a prison system that hardens rather than softens criminals, a society that hypocritically uses their services when it requires them, then hypocritically destroys them when they become inconvenient, embarrassing. In this picture, as in *The Public Enemy,* we understand Cagney to be a victim, but more than in the earlier picture we come to admire him for the way he stands up to his fate, accepting it without complaint. He is almost an existential hero, a figure we might find in a novel by Camus or at any rate in a *policier* influenced by him.

The last of this thirties crime trilogy, *The Roaring Twenties,* is similar. It is structured in the semidocumentary manner, complete with a voice-over narration stressing the evils of prohibition and presenting the Cagney figure as a kind of Everyman, innocently betrayed by the world he never made. A veteran, returning from heroic service in World War I, he cannot find legitimate work that fully utilizes his talents for organizing a business since as a poor lad he lacks the capital and connections he needs. He turns to bootlegging, a victimless crime. Indeed, it was a crime which, if gracefully enough handled, earned the approval of some of society's most respectable members. Couldn't blame Cagney for any of this. Or for the fact that his career begins to decline when he is distracted by his love for a nice girl who does not return his affections, ends when repeal, something he certainly would not have voted for, puts him out of action for good, shunned by the very people who could not do enough for him when a certain glamour attached to his criminality. Through it all, he is destiny's plaything, a man who accepts the system into which he was born, plays by its rules—as he understands them—and finally, gallantly, accepts its disposition of his case, even, indeed, rushes almost suicidally to meet its judgment.

It is curious how often, even in somewhat lighter films, like *Strawberry Blonde* and *Captains of the Clouds,* he touched on this theme of victimization and how uncomfortable, uprooted, his character sometimes seems when that theme was not present in the script, when, for example (and always excepting his demonic impersonation of George M. Cohan in *Yankee Doodle Dandy*), he had to try to play rather conventional heroes. It could be argued, in fact, that once intellectual fashion changed and it was no longer convenient to shift the blame for antisocial behavior to impersonal and implacable social forces, Cagney's career was in crisis, a crisis that was not resolved until 1949 and *White Heat,* when he discovered psychosis. If a man is visibly and totally daft, and apparently has been so from birth, he cannot be held responsible for his behavior either. From that point onward most of Cagney's roles—and all his memorable ones, not excluding his last, that of the possessed Coca-Cola salesman in *One Two Three*—were as more or less crazy people. We are not talking temporary insanity here or curable neurosis. We are talking irredeemable lunacy of the sort that transcends conventional moral judgment, traditional definitions of good and evil. We are also talking art of quite a high order, since somehow, playing a succession of thoroughly unappetizing figures, he retained the affection of his public.

As our interview proceeded, I began to be nagged by the feeling that there was a correlation between the man and the roles he played which, perhaps, no one had been in a position to observe before. His intimates are not critics, after all, and few people with any detailed critical knowledge of the body of his work have ever talked to him at length. What I was sensing was that all the evasions he resorted to when the subject of his movie work was raised, that strange and discomfiting sense he imparted of being totally alienated from what was—how could he deny it?—his life's work, were analogous to the sense his characters so frequently imparted of being the helpless products of social and psychological determinism, creatures whose only option was to accept their fates more or less cheerfully and, perhaps, to go down swinging. Who knows? Maybe the ferocious energy of his youth, the often manic quality he brought to his work, especially when physical action was required of him, was rooted in a sort of panic. Possibly it represented the desperate desire of his body to deny the gloomy signals it was receiving from his mind.

That may be a bridge too far for us to tread. But this much is obvious: All his talk about movie acting's being just a job, nothing very exciting or interesting about it, and something he undertook not because he especially wanted to but because it offered him the best available paycheck, represents a denial of responsibility for his actions that was, in its way, analogous to the denials of responsibility for their actions that were written into his characters. In effect, he was saying that he signed on as a sort of corporate soldier, albeit a highly visible one, then did what he was told to do. Yes, of course, as a responsible professional he tried as best he could to improve upon his assignments, but there were limits to that activity. And yes, of course, there were some lovely, lucky accidents, a handful of pictures that even he has to admit weren't bad. But overall, no, he was not proud of what he had done and was not going to take all the blame for a record that did not please him.

This position does not jibe with the public record of his movie work or with the memories of his colleagues or, for that matter, with such unguarded memories as he sometimes let slip. The portrait of Cagney on the job is of a man ferociously fussing over the work, asserting himself tirelessly to improve his films. And to improve not only his lot but that of everyone connected with making movies. His angry contract disputes with Warner Brothers are legendary and were publicly reported at the time. His political and union activities in the thirties were immediately directed at improving the lot of his fellow performers—and not just the stars either. As soon as he was able, and rather in advance of other stars of his stature, he embraced independent production, which means that some of the pictures that provided him with "jobs" were, in fact, movies he had instigated, movies that would not have been made if he had not insisted on making them.

It was all very odd, very disconcerting, this radical alienation from his past, therefore from his completely honorable and extraordinarily gifted self. It is the more so, of course, since his own judgment of his accomplishments was so widely at odds with everyone else's. His fellow actors, for instance, continue to revere him for his attack, for the purity of his instincts, for his uncanny ability to physicalize emotion. The younger ones, in particular, appear awed by his ability to do thoughtlessly, and with heedless abandon, what it requires so many years of exercise and instruction to learn to do: express (or anyway imply) a character's inner life simply and directly, without any visible cerebration. The critics and the film historians are similarly respectful from their perspective. There is a common agreement that he was one of the truly singular presences in the history of the movies, an actor utterly *sui generis,* someone who has spawned no imitative type, who has no heirs. He was also a performer whose historical significance cannot be overestimated, the first definitely and defiantly urban character in the history of a medium that had, before him, preferred heroes of either a more rustic type (if they were Americans) or a more sinuously romantic type (if they were foreign born). Finally, and perhaps most important of all, ordinary moviegoers took him to heart almost instantly, remained astonishingly loyal to "Jimmy" even though many of his later pictures were distinctly lacking in comfortable appeal. They remained loving and loyal through all the long years of his retirement and remain so after his death.

After all this he would logically have been entitled to many poses —great man, sage, egomaniac, even plutocrat. What he was not entitled to was the role he had chosen, which is that of a successful man who talks and acts like a failure. But that, finally, became the only way to sum up his private presence. If you didn't know whom you were talking to, you would think you were in the presence of a man who suffered some terrible accident early in life or endured some historical calamity, emerging from it physically intact but emotionally in a permanent state of shock, still connected with the promising and halcyon days before the disaster but unable to contemplate the central horror and its aftermath.

Talking with him, working with him, simply hanging out with him, I came to realize that movies represented a kind of betrayal for him. They had brought him wealth and fame, and the respect of others, obviously, but they had not brought him self-respect. That he might have obtained in one of the professions, as his brothers had. Or possibly on the legitimate stage. One day in his trailer Cagney and Pat O'Brien fell to speculating about which of the movies they had done together was the best. O'Brien plumped for the one almost anyone would have chosen, *Angels with Dirty Faces,* with its rich, jostling portrayal of lower-class city life and Cagney's great death house death scene, unquestionably the greatest such sequence ever filmed. Cagney disagreed. He argued for *Ceiling Zero,* in which he played a hot, irresponsible pilot for a struggling air service (O'Brien, of course, was its highly responsible manager) who redeems himself by sacrificing his life for a comrade. I was astonished. It seems to me one of his—and Howard Hawks's—weakest films: cramped; talky; stage-bound. But that was precisely the point for Cagney. He had seen, and admired, Osgood Perkins on Broadway in the role Cagney eventually took on film, and it was, in any case, the only adaptation of a sober theatrical piece Warner Brothers ever bought for him. As such it seemed more respectable to him than the cheap little movies the studio's lesser writers cobbled up for him and its less important directors rammed through on two- and three-week schedules.

From this conversation one gained this sense of his order of priorities: If he could not be a doctor, then he should have been a legit actor, and if he could not have been a theatrical star, then he should not have become, or permitted himself to become, "movie tough guy" James Cagney; they should have given him more respectable vehicles than he generally had, vehicles he (and perhaps his mother) could have been proud of; in any event, he should have been treated not merely as a "property" by Jack Warner but as a man of respect, to be carefully consulted on his films and his roles.

But all that, it seemed to him, he had been denied. That was why he was so dismissive of everyone's praise, so unable to recall so much that was to so many of us indelible. What looked to us like a shining pinnacle looked to him like a black hole. He could, perhaps, forgive his impoverished youthful self for being drawn into it, but he could not forgive his mature self for not fighting free of it sooner. In the years that have passed since I talked with him I have often wondered if, in the century of the victim, his hold on us did not derive, finally, from the implication—sometimes subtle, sometimes not so subtle— of victimization that arose from so many of his most memorable characterizations. Surely it was that aspect of his basic creation that balanced its sometimes brutal drive, its roughshod way with jokes and women. Surely it was that aspect of his screen character that permitted him to transcend in his appeal mere "decency" (which, like mere toughness, is not uncommon in the movies), permitted entry into the deeper reaches of consciousness, establishing on us an imaginative hold that only a very few actors ever achieve. Surely that tragic sense of what destiny must hold for the overreaching individual arose from something authentic in him, some congeries of genes and experience that in youth, when his preternatural energy ruled him, he could simply overwhelm but that now, in age, appeared to have overwhelmed him. As we grow older, after all, we abandon our pretenses, our self-distractions—and the illusions with which we entertain others. We no longer have the time or the energy for all that. We are reduced to our essences. And the essence of James Cagney, as I encountered him, and who moved me in ways that were both powerful and unexpected, was a sadness as deep as it was logically inexplicable.

HUMPHREY BOGART
GENTLEMAN
DECLASSED

*I*ronies abound in the life and work of Humphrey Bogart. Among the more curious of them is this: The longevity of his stardom was less than that of any of the dominant movie personalities with whom he must logically be compared. Whether one dates his emergence as a figure to be reckoned with from *High Sierra* or *The Maltese Falcon* in 1941 or from *Casablanca* two years later, the fact is that he matched his own definition of stardom—"you have to drag your weight at the box office and be recognized wherever you go"—for only about a decade and a half. That is less time than most of his contemporary peers—Astaire, Cagney, Cooper, Gable, Grant, Tracy, Wayne—enjoyed that status. It is also less time than those who followed him and are possible candidates to match his standing have prospered at the top—Brando, for instance, or Lancaster or Newman. Even people on whom the returns are still less complete—Eastwood, for example, or Redford—have been authentic stars longer than he was.

Related to that irony is another, larger one. It is that despite the relative brevity of his ascendancy, no star of his era (possibly excepting Cary Grant, who, despite his retirement from the screen, continued for decades to astound us with tantalizing glimpses of his gracefully aging and always enigmatic presence) remains such a lively presence in our imaginations.

It is true, of course, that Bogart was the first great figure of his generation of stars to go, and premature death always enhances, however briefly, a public figure's hold on his public, encouraged as they are by the cheap press to ponder sentimentally all highly visible evidence

213

of life's shocking mutability. But Gary Cooper and Clark Gable died only a little later than he did, and also before their time, and they do not share the powerful hold on posterity that Bogart does. Like other stars of that era, they are mostly treasured nostalgically by older people, for whom they remain the unsinkable dreamboats of adolescence, the first, and therefore the best, repositories of our earliest romantic fantasies. Our children may have learned a respectful thing or two about these figures from television, but they do not find them "totally awesome" (to borrow teenage America's highest current accolade). Their tendency is to nod politely when the old guys are mentioned—and start sinking down on their spines or edging out of the room.

With Bogart, though, it is different, especially if they are middleclass and collegiate. To them he is alive as no movie figure not of their moment is. Three decades after his death (in January 1957) he continues to speak for them and to them. They think they know him as they know themselves, as a man grappling with what they have just learned to called the "existential" issues.

Herein lies the largest irony Bogart presents to us. For this is the second case of mistaken identity his career offers, the first having been that he was a "tough guy." Always, it seems, the relatively simple truth about the man eludes us; always, it seems, we have gone thundering past the intersection where personal history and screen character meet and mutually inform each other. It is the purpose of this essay to linger at that crossroads and contemplate the evidence about who he was and what he was—evidence which he left plentifully scattered about in plain sight.

We may profitably begin at the beginning, with the first and simplest of his movie images, that of the entirely charmless tough guy, sort of a second-string George Raft (unimaginable as that status now seems). He was thrown into competition for roles with Raft at Warner Brothers because Bogart achieved his first movie prominence playing the gangster Duke Mantee in the mummified adaptation of Robert Sherwood's ridiculous play *The Petrified Forest*. For six years after, the studio kept him close to what it quite thoughtlessly, quite unobservantly assumed was his type. Bogart not unnaturally objected to this kind of casting, mostly because he was really rather bad, often visibly uncomfortable, in these roles. On the other hand, he also found it amusing, because it was so wildly misleading, to play a hard case offscreen. He had a fondness for a certain type of newspaperman, hardened drinkers, and sentimental cynics, and to them he was astonishingly voluble, snarling sardonically, for attribution, about his profession and the way the movie business was conducted. Since he was an alcoholic married to an alcoholic in these years (his third wife, the sometime actress Mayo Methot), their drunken battles in public and at the home to which the

police were frequently summoned to quell disturbances also lent credibility to the image of a man who, according to what seems a reliable
accounting, was hanged or electrocuted eight times, sentenced to life
imprisonment nine times, and riddled by bullets a dozen times in his
first forty-five movies.

Since even after he was rescued from the supporting roles and B
picture leads in which he suffered these indignities he continued to
play men who found themselves on the margin of legality (and sometimes on the margin of sanity), and since he did not grow notably less
outspoken or more sober in his nocturnal recreations, this aura did
not entirely dissipate in later years. Indeed, to the majority of his
contemporaries in the audience toughness, even after it was enlisted
in idealistic and romantic causes during the war, remained an essential
element—perhaps *the* essential element—in his persona. Raymond
Chandler, who knew something about this subject, spoke for the generation that met him first as a mug when he wrote: "Bogart can be
tough without a gun. Also, he has a sense of humor that contains that
grating undertone of contempt. Ladd [who emerged as a star of a similar
kind at the same time] is hard, bitter and occasionally charming, but
he is after all a small boy's idea of a tough guy. Bogart is the genuine
article."

If there had been nothing more to him than that, Bogart would
probably not have been a star—not for any length of time, anyway—
and he certainly would not have become a legend for later generations
to moon over. (For that matter, Chandler's own great creation Philip
Marlowe, whom Bogart successfully impersonated once he had found
his own character, would not have become an immortal fictional figure
if he had been merely tough.)

No, Bogart had to subtract a little something from that vulgar
image—and add a great deal to it. This he began to find the opportunity
to do in *Sierra* and *Falcon,* but unquestionably his authority as a screen
presence, both during the rest of his career and posthumously, radiates
outward from *Casablanca.* It is certainly not his best performance—
he stretched more in others, revealed more of himself in still others
—but it is good. And it is good not because he is embodying that
congeries of modern philosophical ideas that have since been imputed
to Rick/Bogie, but simply because Humphrey Bogart, the actor, is ease-
ful here, instinctively at home with his character in a way that he only
rarely had been before, and never as fully as this.

That kind of comfort with a character, that kind of blending of a
factual self with a fictive creation, in which neither the performer nor
the audience is entirely aware of where the one ends and the other
begins, is extraordinarily rare. But it is a basic requirement for screen
actors working at the star level and hoping to stay there for a while.

Many people as gifted as Bogart (or more so) never find the role in which that connection can be made. And as we have observed, and will have reason to observe again, he had to wait a long time in frustration before he could make it. In any event, one does not take up residence in a role, as Bogart did when he got under Rick Blaine's skin, through an intellectual process.

All the imputations to the contrary, all the attempts to claim Rick Blaine and Humphrey Bogart for the party of Sartre and Camus needlessly complicate what turns out to be, on not-too-arduous examination, a fairly simple identification between actor and part. These claims and imputations are rationalizations for the fad that was created around *Casablanca* and (to a slightly less impassioned extent) Bogart himself. This began, not long after the actor died, in the sixties at Harvard, spread outward from there to other American campuses, attaining cult status on its way to becoming what it now is, a rite of passage for many. (Howard Koch, who shares credit for the film's screenplay and now accompanies it as a lecturer at colleges, reports audiences chorusing the dialogue with the actors on-screen as if it were *The Rocky Horror Picture Show,* meeting students who have seen it upwards of twenty times; he particularly recalls one girl who was introduced to him as "a curiosity on exhibit" because she was seeing *Casablanca* for the first time the night of his visit.)

Astonishing, all this! And if there is an edge of resentment in my tone, it may be because long before these newer generations claimed Rick/Bogie for their own, he had been *our* own since *Casablanca*'s release, the exclusive emotional property for those of us who came to romantic and idealistic consciousness during World War II. It is very hard for us to see a character with whom each of us once had a rather personal, highly individualized relationship taken over by mass worshipers (we were not so much pack travelers as our successors, and we were not encouraged to build an unbreachable subculture of our own). But perhaps my resentment proves a point, which is, only slightly alter to the title of the unproduced play on which the film was based (and one of the latter's many famous lines): At a certain stage of life it is reasonable, perhaps inevitable that "Everybody comes to Rick." And for the best of reasons. Throughout the film he grapples with two issues every more or less sensitive individual standing on the brink of adulthood must confront for the first, but not the last, time in life. One is the attempt to weight personal desire against traditional moral imperatives and public need and strike the correct balance between them —the one you can live with the rest of your years. (Shall Rick, in short, keep Ilsa for himself now that he has regained her or shall he relinquish his claim in favor of those presented by her legal mate and by the world struggle against fascism, which she can serve by devoting herself to this allegedly inspiring leader?)

Perhaps more poignant—anyway, more subtly put—is the state of static equilibrium in which we discover Rick. The past exerts a powerful pull on him. His memories of Ilsa and their time together in Paris are bittersweet at best, but he obviously felt an intensity of emotion for her which he had not known before, which he has not known since, and which must be forever treasured. Besides, those memories are comforting in their familiarity. On the other hand, there is the future. A man could lose himself in the struggle to build it along decent lines, finding self-renewal and self-esteem in the process. As any parent has reason to observe (and remember), the late-adolescent discovery that childhood, that mixed bag of irresponsible pleasure and protective custody, is forever lost comes as an unpleasant shock. There is a tendency among young adults to indulge in instant nostalgia for it, just as Rick does his nostalgia for his quite recent affair with Ilsa. At that same time the unknown future, at once promising and scary, beckons as ambiguously to kids as it does to Rick.

These carefully encoded messages, of course, permit *Casablanca* to transcend the simple wartime metaphors, aimed at mobilizing the conscience of the audience, in which they were cloaked. They are what give it continuing relevance to young people when most pictures of its time, peddling similar inspirationalism, appear at best dated, at worst ludicrous. Naturally the artfully glamorous context in which these messages were presented helps: the exotic locale; the colorful minor characters; the seductively shadowed film noir atmosphere. So do the highly stylized dialogue, blending the tones of tough rue and cynical wit, and the serviceably suspenseful narrative, rushing everyone along past its own several improbabilities. Indeed, in his very acute essay on the movie Umberto Eco makes the point that its success depends on the fact that it is an almost perfect compendium of the conventions (or clichés) of the adventure-romance film as they had developed to date. He claims there is not a single one of them that the picture fails to evoke, with the result that its manic generosity simply overwhelms disbelief. It is, in short, one of those rare cases where less would have been ... less.

This is not to discount Bogart's contribution to the initial and continuing success of *Casablanca* but to place it in perspective. It is his presence, persuasively weary, yet persuasively wary, that grounds a movie always in danger of flightiness and unconscious risibility in a recognizable reality. Indeed, at this point one must pause to pay tribute to the concentrated power of personality he so subtly mobilized in this film. It was late in his career—this was his forty-fifth movie—and late in his life—he turned forty-four the month it was released—for him to unloose a force that would travel with undiminished velocity down the corridors of time. And he was, as the press of the time never tired of observing, an unlikely figure of romance: a small man (five feet nine inches, 155 pounds), balding, with a scar on a nerveless upper lip the most prominent defect in a face already showing the wear and tear of alcohol and life's disappointments. He was, moreover, as compact emotionally as he was in stature. He did not permit his feelings, in this film or any other, to slosh about and spill over in a way that elicits instant regard, especially nowadays, when men who "surface" their feelings are much esteemed. Clearly there was something in this role that spoke deeply to him, permitting him to transcend the obvious handicaps he brought to it.

Was it a sense that as a kind of emotional outlaw, with perhaps an anarchical admixture in his temperament, he found an objective correlative in Rick, treading reserved and uncommitted among the many shady factions of a raffish, amoral, and entirely alien environment? That's a line that some of Bogart's more impressionable fans have followed. They perhaps took their cue from Jean-Luc Godard's *Breathless,* which was released in the United States just as the collegiate Bogart cult was forming. "Ah, Bogie," sighs Jean-Paul Belmondo, the film's punk protagonist, posing against posters advertising his hero's old movies. His slightly improbable identification with Bogart's screen character, intended ironically by Godard as a comment on a petty crook's self-romanticism, was taken literally by many in the audience, who thereupon felt licensed to make similar identification.

Those licenses were all counterfeits. Bogart was never the man Belmondo's character or those who followed him thought he was. Not in life, certainly not on-screen, except when he was called upon to play a psychopath. Like Rick Blaine, most of his characters were quite aware of the general principles of conventional morality or, if you prefer, traditional masculine ethics. Therefore, he was never truly a classic existential hero, forced to define himself and his standards ad hoc, in action. It is true that he often had to improvise quite desperately in order to stay out of the law's reach or harm's way for much of the time in many of his films. It is also true that in this process he was known to exude a certain world-weariness, which lent itself to interpretation as existential despair. Finally, one sometimes sensed in Bogart's character a temptation toward the kind of overt criminality that some existential writers have been pleased to romanticize as a form of rebellion against life's tragic lack of meaning. But this posture, in particular, was of more practical than philosophical use to his character. It made him seem unpredictable, dangerous, someone to be reckoned with by the less savory figures with whom he was forced to deal. But the fact was, whatever exertions were required of him, whatever pressures were placed upon him to deviate from the path of true righteousness, the drama of the Bogart figure in his typical later movies always revolved around his eventual acknowledgment of the power of his best instincts, his better self, which was formed by values of the most old-fashioned and, indeed, cultivated kind. All atmospherics and smart dialogue aside, these were Rick Blaine's basic and, as it turned out, unshakable values.

What I'm saying is: Forget tough guy. Forget existential hero. What Bogart found in Rick Blaine was something more interesting than his first misnomer, no less complex than the second, but much more appealing—to some of us at least—than both. Above all, and most important to him in establishing emotional connection with it, was the fact that his screen character as it finally evolved was but a minor variation on the role he had been playing off-screen most of his adult life. And had taken up with particular relish when he took up permanent residence in Hollywood.

That role was ... declassed gentleman, a man of breeding and privilege who found himself, as a result of circumstances not entirely of his making, far from his native haunts, among people of rather less quality, rather fewer standards morally, socially, intellectually than he had been raised to expect among his acquaintances. To put the matter simply, Rick Blaine should not have ended up running a "gin joint" in *Casablanca,* and Humphrey Bogart should not have ended up being an actor in Hollywood.

About Rick's background, of course, we have only hints. We know that he was involved in some sort of disreputable, but not necessarily dishonorable, activities in the United States when he was a young man (left-wing politics perhaps?). We know he ran guns to the right sides (that is, the left sides) in Spain and Ethiopia prior to the outbreak of World War II in Europe. And that is about all we know for certain. But *Casablanca* makes it easy for us to imagine him as a familiar archetype of his period: the young man of good family, made restless by its pieties, cautions, and hypocrisies, rebelling against it, ultimately exercising that rebellious spirit in the dangerous and romantic ways specified by the script. In any event, his bearing and his articulateness about his values, when Ilsa's return to him dissolves his hard and bitter silence, do not suggest a humble or an underprivileged past.

About Bogart we know a great deal more, and his personal history proposes only one logical conclusion: Rick was the first screen character he ever found in whom he could discern a complete natural affinity, draw upon his own experience and attitudes to form. While he was alive, the press made much of the fact that the movies' leading "tough guy" was, in fact, the son of privilege. It was the kind of simple, readable irony the fans enjoyed. And the story was true enough—as far as it went. But it was not being born to comfort and a measure of social distinction that was crucial in shaping the actor's personality; it was the loss of them—the waste of them, really—that made him what he was.

There had been inherited wealth to begin with—one of Bogart's grandfathers had invented a commercially successful process for engraving on tin—and both his parents had prospered in their careers. His father, Belmont de Forest Bogart, was a surgeon with an upper-echelon practice. His mother, Maud Humphrey Bogart, was a prominent commercial illustrator—she used her son as a model when he was a child—and also a militant suffragette. They had two other children, both girls, and the family lived in a brownstone on Manhattan's Upper West Side, summering at another home on Lake Canandaigua in upstate New York, where Bogart developed his lifelong passion for sailing. On the surface their life appeared close to the placid ideal of their time and place. And indeed, as he grew up, Humphrey Bogart had every reason to look forward to a comfortable and not overtaxing future. He was sent first to New York's select and socially impeccable Trinity School, later to the Phillips Academy in Andover, Massachusetts, then, as now, one of the nation's leading preparatory schools. It was expected that he would go on to Yale.

Life in the Bogart family was not, however, as serene and secure as it appeared on the surface. Belmont Bogart appears to have been a weak and charming man—very likely an alcoholic—not overly devoted to his work or his family's future; he was perfectly capable of setting aside his practice for months at a time in favor of hunting and fishing expeditions. Maud, in contrast, was a regal and reserved woman, about whom Bogart was later to report: "I can't say that I ever loved my mother. I admired her."

At Andover the boy began to stray from his preordained rut. He was expelled after three semesters for "incontrollable high spirits." Actually, according to Bogart, it was because he joined a group bent on ducking an unpopular teacher in a pond one night; he was the only member of the gang the victim recognized. The United States having entered World War I by that time, and Bogart loving boats and the water, he joined the Navy. He served in a destroyer and as helmsman on a troop transport, where the repair of a wound he received from a flying wood splinter gave him his trademark scar on his upper lip. On the whole, though, he had a good war; it was peace that came as a shock to him.

When he returned home, he discovered that his father had lost most of the family's money through careless investments. Even if Bogart had been interested in returning to formal education, there was now no possibility of that. Nor was there any possibility of idleness or a long search for a comfortable job. He had to find work immediately, doing whatever presented itself to him. He tried one or two avenues —including stockbrokerage, so often the salvation of indigent young men of good breeding—then caught on with William A. Brady, a famous producer, who had been a power in all aspects of show business since before the turn of the century and was married to the actress, Gladys George. He had been a neighbor of the Bogarts, and his son, William Jr., had been one of Humphrey's best boyhood pals. The elder Brady took him on first as an office boy, then put him to work in his New York film production unit in several capacities, before appointing him company manager of one of his touring companies. Bogart took to kidding the lead in the show, Neil Hamilton, about the soft life that actors seemed to lead. On the tour's last night Hamilton dared Bogart to go on in his place. He did—and froze. But later, when he was complaining to Brady about the lack of remuneration in backstage work, the producer casually replied, "Why don't you become an actor? Actors make good money."

And so he did. There was no conviction in the decision, certainly no grand passion. Nor did he appear to have an abounding natural gift. But it seemed to Brady and others who employed him that he was ideally suited to play juveniles of the class into which he had been born. He was not at first very good. Of his second Broadway appearance, in 1922's *Swifty,* Alexander Woollcott wrote: "The young man who embodies the sprig is what is usually and mercifully described as in-adequate."

Still, he persevered, "a well-behaved, agreeable, serious young man," in the words of a colleague of those days. "I have politeness and manners. I was brought up that way," Bogart himself was to say many years later, and those qualities served him well, distracting audiences from his shortcomings in technique. And the fact that romantic comedy, of various degrees of sophistication, was a staple genre on Broadway in the 1920's helped, too. Not a year went by that he did not have at least one role in one of these feathery concoctions. Legend has it that Bogart was the first to pipe the line that seemed to sum up, in two words, the entire vanished style that sustained him and perhaps the institution of the commercial theater in those days. It was "Tennis, anyone?"

It could be argued that during this phase of his career he was more appropriately cast, wearing blue blazer and flannels, uttering breezy inanities, than he was at any time by Hollywood in the subsequent decade. In any event, he acquired a bagful of actor's tricks, a patina of professionalism, and his first two wives, both actresses he had worked with (his marriage to Helen Menken lasted fewer than two years; that to Mary Phillips, a decade). What he could not acquire, what he had to wait for the passing years to give him was that air of rue, of unspoken regret for possibly unnamable things, on which his later stardom was to rest. But as the decade drew to a close, he was beginning to outgrow juvenile roles. The theater, too, was beginning to outgrow them, or anyway the kind of plays that required them.

Hollywood, however, was learning to talk. And it swept up actors, writers, and directors who were thought to have learned in their stage work how to handle the mysteries of dialogue. Bogart was carried along by this westward-streaming exodus. In 1930, the first year of the Depression, he signed a contract with Fox at four hundred dollars a week, under which he made five films, none of them significant for him or for the history of the medium. When his option was dropped, he returned to New York for one play, got more picture work in Hollywood, then, when it dried up, returned again to New York. "I wasn't Gable, and I flopped" was his brief latter-day comment.

By then he could afford to be offhand about his youthful follies. At the time he had reason to be anxious, and he apparently was. The Depression was entering its bleakest years, and his family's economic condition had worsened with the nation's. The work he was able to get in New York was all in short-lived shows. Around this time his father died in Bogart's arms, leaving him ten thousand dollars in debts to settle and a ruby and diamond ring his son was to wear for the rest of his life. Nor was that the end of the troubles in his house. One of his sisters died, also apparently the victim of drink, and his other sister fell prey to a chronic mental illness and was, as well, left penniless by a divorce, with a young child to care for. Bogart was her support, "emotionally and financially" (as Lauren Bacall put it), for the rest of her life.

Now, however, his professional luck began to change. He was cast in a play called *Invitation to a Murder,* in which he impressed producer Arthur Hopkins, who remembered him some months later, when he was searching for someone to play the psychopathic Duke Mantee on Broadway. Playwright Robert Sherwood, who was a friend of Bogart's, wanted him for another role in the piece, but Hopkins persisted, the star, Leslie Howard (after whom Bogart was to name his daughter) liked him, and all opened to approving reviews. In the course of the play's run Howard told Bogart he would do his best to see that he got a chance to repeat the role in the screen version, and he was as good as his word. Warner Brothers tested other actors and actually announced Edward G. Robinson for the role. When Bogart heard this, he cabled Howard, vacationing in Scotland, and Howard informed the studio that he would not play in the picture if Bogart was not cast in it.

However dismal the film was—and under Archie Mayo's all-too-respectful direction it lacked the energy, conviction, and lunatic spirit of even the routine gangster movies of the time—it did impress people for its fidelity to the play and the sobriety with which it took up what the audience was led to think of as large themes in a self-consciously literate manner. Within its static, indeed, claustrophobic context, Bogart's trapped-animal seething could not help commanding attention. It is perhaps too much to say you couldn't take your eyes off him, but certainly there was little else worth looking at.

If *The Petrified Forest* did not quite do for Bogart what *The Public Enemy* had done for Cagney or *Little Caesar* had done for Robinson, since it was not as well made as those pictures and there was no need to provide him with a protagonist's sympathetic side, the studio could not help but notice the public noticing him. His roles in the next year and a half were many and mostly lengthy. Some of the programmers —*Bullets or Ballots, San Quentin, Marked Woman*—were solid melodramatic entertainments. And two of the pictures seemed important at the time. *Black Legion,* released early in 1937, was a cautionary social comment aimed at the Ku Klux Klan and other secret organizations enforcing their racial and religious prejudices violently as hooded mobs. In it Bogart plays a factory worker envious because he has been passed over for a promotion (the job he wanted was given to a Pole). Eventually he is indicted along with the rest of his group for a murder in which they all participated, but then he turns against them at the trial, thus regaining the respect of his wife and a measure of self-respect as well. The picture seems both too crude and too cautious now, but at the time it seemed to combine originality, dramatic bite, and unexceptionable sentiments.

Dead End, which Bogart made on loan-out to Goldwyn was, like *The Petrified Forest,* an adaptation of a Broadway hit widely believed to be distinguished. It is, in its way, as stage-bound as the earlier piece, but it is not quite as draggy, if only because it ranges over wider emotional territory as it anatomizes New York slum life, personified by characters operating at various levels in it. Bogart's role is not large; he plays a criminal who returns home for a visit and discovers that his sister has turned into a whore and that his mother despises him. The picture, of course, belongs to the Dead End Kids, a gang of streetwise boys who were to achieve ensemble stardom in a series of B pictures that stressed the comic side of their rough good nature, though here they were touched by a measure of pathos as the principal victims of society's indifference. Be that as it may, Bogart's discovery of mutual alienation between himself and the society that formed him hints at larger and more poignant isolations to come for his screen character.

But from this point until 1940, for reasons not entirely clear, his career seemed to stall. The studio kept him busy, and he appeared in more than a few films with strong budgets and good casts. But he was always in secondary roles, and clearly uncomfortable in them. He was, for example, notably edgy in the three films in which he worked with James Cagney—*Angels with Dirty Faces, The Oklahoma Kid,* and *The Roaring Twenties.* In them, Bogart's unredeemable badness was supposed to contrast with the vulnerable charm of Cagney's good-bad guys. But his hands always seemed too busy in these pictures, his eyes too shifty; in general, he was overplaying. Perhaps he was trying too hard to make an impression, but it seems likely that he simply could make no emotional connection with these supporting roles, could not find a way to inhabit them. He was bad in different ways in films like *The Amazing Dr. Clitterhouse,* in which he was supposed to play a more comical crook, and *Dark Victory,* in which, in his wildest miscasting he was a broody stablehand, a sort of half-realized Laurentian figure, who was briefly the vaguely menacing lover of Bette Davis's neurotically high-strung heiress. In nothing he did at this time was he able to assert anything of his singularity. In nothing was he able to achieve dominance even in a single scene. In nothing was he able to impart something to the public that it could take home and dream upon. He seemed in danger of slipping down into that large, almost anonymous stable of second leads and character men Warner Brothers, like all the studios of the time, maintained to keep its production schedule rolling along as smoothly as possible.

Looking back on this period, one sees just how ludicrous the imputation of even unconscious existentialist qualities to Bogart is. It is a central tenet of existentialism, for example, that all of us must remake ourselves every day in order to face the day. And many philosophers of this school have found in the actor the figure that most clearly exemplifies this necessity. But Bogart's problem at this moment was precisely that he did not know how to remake himself—not persuasively, at any rate. In the meantime, nothing that came his way offered him metaphors through which he could express some authentic aspect of himself.

One does not imagine that he could express his dilemma in those terms. But he was clearly aware that his personal life was at this time a misery. He and Mary Phillips had drifted apart—she found her work mainly in New York—and their marriage came to an end in 1937. He married Mayo Methot, or "Sluggy," as he called her, in 1938, and almost immediately they began joint construction on the legend of "the battling Bogarts," as the press soon began styling them. Officially their rows were understood as affection displayed with a sort of perverse humor. And the public was encouraged to think of them as living a kind of black screwball comedy. But it requires no great leap of the imagination to read between the lines of the yellowing clippings and see that theirs was the story of two alcoholics (she being by far the sicker of the two) locked in a punishing and dismal mutual dependency. Their screams at each other were, in effect, screams for help, which did not arrive for Bogart for six years and which never arrived for her.

Bogart, of course, never made any open complaint about her. To have done so would have been to violate his old-fashioned code of manners. Instead, his unhappiness leaked out in other ways. He was never a full-scale rebel against the exactions of the studio, as Cagney and Bette Davis were, but he was a constant complainer. "Bogie the beefer" is the way Raoul Walsh began thinking of him. He had directed Bogart in one of his early Fox films, and he was to be instrumental in his emergence as a star at Warner Brothers. He remembered the actor grousing continually about the long hours moviemaking required in contrast with the stage. And about the early-morning calls. And about the bad food on location. And, of course, about the roles. Walsh always claimed that the only way to lure Bogart out of his blackness was to remind him of how good the money was in the movies as opposed to any other line of endeavor he might reasonably have undertaken.

And indeed, the money was more than a mere consolation to Bogart in these frustrating years. Toward his career he adopted an air of detached professionalism. "I'm known as a guy who always squawks about roles, but never refuses to play one," he told a reporter once. "I've never forgotten a piece of advice Holbrook Blinn gave me when I was a young squirt and asked him how I could get a reputation as an actor. He said, 'Just keep working.' The idea is that if you're always busy, sometime someone is going to get the idea that you must be good." While he was waiting for that to happen, and as a defense against its never happening, he cultivated the air of a gentleman who either had known or could imagine better days. He mingled respect for the slightly raffish trade circumstances had forced him to follow, and a certain pride in the professionalism of the way he practiced it, with an aura of dismay that a man of his spirit and breeding should have to fit himself into other men's schemes and schedules.

The way of life he established in Hollywood in these days, and clung to even after true stardom was accorded him, puts one in mind of a type foreign to the American experience but made familiar to us by fiction. One thinks of the remittance men, the second sons of great English families, declassed by primogeniture or by scandal, seeking fortunes of their own in the more exotic outposts of empire, yet not entirely engaged in their work, drinking too much in order to dull the pain of separation from their more agreeable pasts, and amiably but perceptibly holding themselves aloof from their new societies. The only difference was that Bogart received no remittances. Rather the opposite, in fact; he sent them out.

Aside from his public brawls with his third wife, Bogart attempted to live quietly. He was never a free spender, and his home on Horn Avenue in West Hollywood was comfortable; but by Hollywood standards unimpressive. His only indulgence was sailing, but in those days, before he acquired his famous *Santana,* he owned only small boats, which he could handle alone, thereby gaining the silence and solitude he craved. When he was not working or sailing, he passed his days reading and working on chess problems; he had a reputation as an excellent amateur player.

But working or idle, when he was on land, he habitually ended his day at some fairly unpretentious restaurant since his taste was for booze and a certain unassuming, perhaps somewhat impersonal conviviality, not for great food or grand surroundings. Mike Romanoff's was a particular favorite. The host was a sort of living satire of Hollywood's social pretenses since he had styled himself a "prince," a descendant of the deposed Russian ruling family, and reveled in the fact that everyone knew his claim was fraudulent. Bogart's drinking companions rarely included actors or directors—Peter Lorre was an exception—and never executives. The majority of them were writers, but of a rather special type, which he had doubtless discovered in New York's speakeasy society of the 1920's. They generally had, or formerly had, a foot in journalism but had drifted toward the more profitable lines of work—writing humor or popular fiction or plays. Now they were connected in various ways with the still more profitable movies—some of them permanently, some of them only when their checking accounts needed a quick fix. His circle at various times included the likes of Mark Hellinger, Robert Benchley, John O'Hara, Lewis Bromfield, Nunnally Johnson, Quentin Reynolds, Dorothy Parker. Those directors who were permitted to join the circle—John Huston and Richard Brooks, for example—had similar popular journalistic backgrounds and were, indeed, *writer*-directors.

These people, and many of those who took their place in later years, were funny and intelligent, but not self-revealing. As writers they despised literary pretension. As movie colonists they were in the business, but never quite of it. And quite a few of them were quiet, mannerly, purposeful drinkers, uninterested in causing a disturbance unless they were themselves disturbed at their pastime by some loutish outsider. In this period it was typical of Bogart to find some of them on his way home from work and get an early start on the night's drinking. He would then continue on to his house, where he might rest a bit, change clothes, and possibly contemplate continuing his drinking in privacy. Sometimes he would. But more often, it seems, either marital discord or just inner restlessness would drive him back out into the night in search of his pals, from whom he did not part early. This pattern continued even after he had grown more successful and persisted in diminished degree even after his happy fourth marriage to Lauren Bacall. The difference was that he and she stayed home more and invited their friends to join them there for their quiet after-dinner revels. "I don't trust anyone who doesn't drink," Bogart often proclaimed, and there was more than bravado in that statement. It was a statement of principle, and he absorbed terrible physical punishment living up to it.

If Bogart's life-style was essentially immutable, his career was, like all others in show business, amenable to a change in luck. In 1940 he finished the second of the pictures Raoul Walsh directed him in at Warner Brothers. It was *They Drive by Night*, a fairly gritty portrayal of free-lance truckers fighting to keep their independence. In it he played a driver immobilized and embittered when he loses an arm in an accident. In its second half the picture spins entirely away from him into a rather stylized murder melodrama primarily involving its lead, George Raft. But given a chance to play a victim, and rather a self-pitying one at that, Bogart was hard yet sympathetic in a way he had not been since the latter portion of *Black Legion*. Now Walsh was set to do the adaptation of a novel by W. R. Burnett, one of the best, and still one of the least critically attended, of the hard-boiled crime writers (one of his novels formed the basis for *Little Caesar*). From the start of his work on the script Huston had insisted that there was a spirit in Burnett that most previous film versions of his novels had not caught. Take out "the strange sense of inevitability that comes with our deepening understanding of his characters and the forces that motivate them," he wrote in a memo to production chief Hal Wallis, "and only the conventional husk of a story remains. . . ." He would successfully strive to keep that shadow of fatefulness in his script, and the result was for the most part austere and affecting, the epitaph for the profitable gangster hero that the movies had been trying to write during the waning days of the 1930's—still romantic, of course, but wearier and bleaker than, say, *Angels with Dirty Faces* or *The Roaring Twenties*, which both copped more sentimental pleas for Cagney as he expired.

Walsh was the ideal director for a project like this, a man who at his best trusted the subtexts to speak for themselves, while he banged the action along efficiently, unsentimentally, contrapuntally. And the central role of the aging gangster growing vulnerable through the diminution of his formerly pure selfishness (he is undone by sentimental gestures toward a crippled girl and a winsome dog) was one any actor might have coveted—any actor, that is, but the ones the studio approached. Paul Muni turned it down because, he said, he didn't want to play another gangster, although in fact, he had only played one. George Raft, in Walsh's account, rejected it because he did not want to die in the end, although other accounts suggest Bogart slyly put that idea into his rival's egocentric head. In any event, Bogart, who was friends with everyone significantly involved in creating the picture (Hellinger, Huston, and Walsh), actively campaigned for the part, and the studio finally gave it to him—though he was forced to take second billing to his costar, Ida Lupino, to whom he was so unpleasant during shooting that she refused to work with him again.

The seriousness with which he took the part of Roy Earle is signaled by his haircut. Up to the crown it is virtually shaved, strictly prison barbershop work, which is realistically correct for a man who has been behind bars for eight years, and very un-Hollywood. As is his psychology, for Roy Earle finds himself suddenly free in a world in which he begins to see—as the result of a bungled robbery—that crime as he once practiced it is an anachronism, that he himself is an anachronism. That feeling was one Bogart knew something about. And the air of puzzled distaste for this new world was something the reluctant movie actor and citizen of Tinseltown could understand as well, for his own reasons, in his own way. There is about his Roy Earle the air of a man straining to pick out the melody in a new kind of music that grates harshly on his ears, an air, too, of a man who would just as soon die as try to adjust to a world that thinks this stuff is worth listening to. Bogart had not reached that point yet, never would reach it, but he could easily imagine it. As a result, for the first time in a movie he gave a full performance. And a touching one.

High Sierra was a hit. So was Bogart. Things moved so quickly at Warner Brothers that he had finished another quite forgettable picture before its success was clearly established. But when *The Wagons Roll at Night* was done, there was yet another picture and another Raft reject for him to help consolidate his new position. That was *The Maltese Falcon,* John Huston's adaptation of the Dashiell Hammett novel, which was also to be Huston's debut as a director. It is a film that depends more on the bold snap of its dialogue and the felicities of its casting than on showy directorial technique for its success. (In the event, Huston's taciturn *noir* manner is admirable, with his blocking of actors in the frame notably, and subtly, apt.) Still, at this stage of his career, Huston was understandably more confident of his skills as a writer, and as a judge of writing (many of the script's best lines are taken over directly from the book), than he was as a director, and the picture's confident air may derive more from his security with the script than with the camera. This was a point Howard Hawks always insisted he had made to Huston as he toiled for the wise older director on the script for *Sergeant York* and worried over what to select for his directorial debut. With sound basic material, Hawks said, all a director has to do is not screw up, as Huston definitely did not do.

The Maltese Falcon was also, and even more obviously, a wise choice for Bogart. It began the collaboration with Huston that would define, and continually refine, his stardom. More immediately it afforded him an opportunity to play another aspect of the radical self-sufficiency, and contempt for the conventional, that had distinguished his performance as Roy Earle. But with these differences: Where his hardness before had about it a softly burnished quality, here it gleamed brightly as he knifed through his scenes; where before his disgust with the world had rendered him nearly inarticulate, here it loosened his cynically quipping tongue; where before he had almost gratefully accepted his own death as atonement for his past sins, here he almost gratefully accepts the necessity of "sending over" the woman he says he loves to expiate her present sins. He's not the sort of man who ought to have any woman in his life permanently—we understand that. In his fine character sketch of Bogart, Alistair Cooke, who knew him at the end of his life, speaks of the puritan streak in the man. He also drew an interesting analogy between the modern private eye and his progenitor Sherlock Holmes, pointing out that they shared two important traits: a fondness for arcane knowledge and a tendency toward depression, which may account for their bachelor status.

In *The Maltese Falcon* it is, finally, Sam Spade's moral firmness that provides the mainspring of the story. In the end he has to establish the fact that though he may condone certain violations of the legal code as acceptably human frailties (thus encouraging the unobservant to miss his fundamental commitment to a larger morality), there are certain violations of his professional code (letting the murderer of his partner go free) and his personal code (pathological lying by someone who claims to love him and probably does after her fashion) that he cannot let anyone even mistakenly believe he can accept. Not and go on living with himself.

This, too, was something Bogart could understand, for it was an aspect of his own character, the motive for the sudden, if occasional, irate outbursts he let slip from behind his habitual mask of aloofness and indifference. This recognition seemed to energize Bogart. For the first time he was truly hypnotizing, and unambiguously attractive, on the screen, and the best critic of the day, Otis Ferguson, recognized it immediately: "He has a good part here, a steady outlet for that authority and decision and hard level talk of his ... he fills it without trying and you're with him." *Without trying.* Yes. At last. And the public now had what it required of all movie stars in those days, a reliable sense of a screen character, a feeling that they knew what they were bargaining for when they paid their money to see one of his pictures. And from this point onward, with his name fixed firmly above the title in the first-billing position he would never again be forced to relinquish, that is what he appeared in—Bogart pictures. He had become what a star had to be, a genre unto himself.

There was other, more routine business to conduct before finding his apotheosis in *Casablanca*. This included one more George Raft reject (would Bogart have become Bogart if Raft had not been so determinedly Raft, a crude and dim-witted egomaniac?). It was *All Through the Night,* about a Runyonesque group of mobsters called upon to unmask a Nazi spy ring in New York. Bogart was never comfortable in comedy and never comfortable attempting a lower-class accent. But the picture was amiable in its little way, and it did prefigure the main lines of his wartime work, in which he often played a man required to set aside his personal interests in order to serve the cause. He followed that with his last gangster film for Warner's, *The Big Shot,* and then teamed with Huston again for what we would nowadays call a spin-off, a picture that reassembled much of the cast of *Falcon* and attempted to re-create its mood. That was *Across the Pacific,* which is an agreeable entertainment but does not echo in memory as its predecessor does.

The film's somewhat hasty air doubtless reflects the fact that war having broken out, Huston was awaiting the call to take up his commission in the U.S. Army Signal Corps, for which he made three extraordinary documentaries—easily the best any of the Hollywood contingent made for the government during the hostilities. And in fact, having got Bogart into a situation from which it was logically impossible to extricate himself—imprisoned by Japanese spies intent on blowing up the Panama Canal—Huston was forced to leave it to Vincent Sherman, who finished the picture, to get the star out of his predicament. Be that as it may, *Across the Pacific* was the first, but not the last, film in which Bogart played a man declassed. He was an army officer who agreed to undergo a false court-martial and allow himself to be cashiered from the service in order to make him a plausible target for Japanese espionage agents to recruit.

Casablanca, of course, followed, and little more remains to be said about it as it affected Bogart's career, except, perhaps, to make this point: In *High Sierra* and *The Maltese Falcon* his romantic appeal had been couched in essentially masculine terms. Men and boys in those days were not encouraged to spill their guts; they might act out of clearly visible emotional motivations, but they were not supposed to discuss them analytically, even though women, as ever, wanted them to demonstrate their vulnerability. Now, in *Casablanca,* he was permitted to show his emotions, thus doubling his audience by showing himself to have previously unsuspected qualities to which women could readily respond. Obviously *Casablanca* would not have been made if there had not been a war on. But perhaps less obviously Bogart, most male movie stars would not have been given their many *Casablanca*-like opportunities to open up if there had not been a war on. It suddenly turned the movie hero into a blabbermouth.

In the typical American war movie men were daily faced with the possibility of making the supreme sacrifice in support of abstractions both righteous and dubious. That fascism could not be permitted sway in the world no right thinking person doubted; that its defeat would necessarily ensure the just, peaceful, progressive, rational, *Edenic* future movies stars were always promising as they spoke their epitaphs over the dead or prepared themselves (and the audience) for their own untimely extinctions was highly problematical. But not more so than the curious belief fostered by these films that ordinary citizens would calmly, routinely accept death in order to advance abstract, if uplifting, ideals. They were, in effect, offering cheap ideological answers to the enigma of heroism. Yet this was the prevailing convention of American movies during the war, and in the course of working themselves up to these noble moments actors like Bogart vented emotions, or what seemed like emotions, in a way that American movie heroes rarely had in the past.

In other words, Bogart had ample opportunities to exploit the opening *Casablanca* had provided him both during the war and in the immediate postwar years. He started slowly and discreetly, with two working-class figures, a merchant marine first officer who had risen from deckhand in *Action in the North Atlantic;* a professional soldier, a sergeant commanding a tank separated from its unit, in *Sahara*. In the former he very nicely underplayed his big scene, in which he was required to conduct a burial at sea of a group of sailors, killed in a raid, who represented every major American race, creed, and ethnic group. In the latter he had to hold together a smaller, but similarly mixed, crew (and assorted wayfarers they picked up) under assault from a Nazi horde and the desert climate. Here more Popular Front rhetoric was required of him (John Howard Lawson, truest of the true Communist believers among the Hollywood Ten, wrote both these films), but Bogart knew how to throw it away, make it sound almost naturalistic. And in both pictures he was spared—or perhaps insisted on sparing himself—from carrying the heaviest message.

The same was true in *Passage to Marseilles*. He had already been killed when his last letter to his son, overripe with hopes for the lad's future in a better world, was read out by Claude Rains. Long before that happened, however, the picture had collapsed from structural strain. Done entirely in flashback, it tries to make plausible the story of a group of convicts making a desperate escape from that infamous hellhole the French penal colony on Devil's Island, off the coast of

South America, in order to joint the Free French forces fighting the Nazis and their Vichy puppets. Today the film is interesting largely because it represents the longest fall Bogart's screen character was ever forced to take through the class structure. He was a prosperous liberal newspaper proprietor, jailed on trumped-up charges by rightist political enemies and degraded to the point of near madness—the condition in which the movie discovers him—by his servitude on Devil's Island.

That picture was released in 1944, and through 1948 he averaged a film a year in which he was radically declassed. In *Dead Reckoning,* for example, he is a decorated war hero and an officer, investigating the disappearance of his best wartime buddy. Before he solves the case, he is himself accused of murder and reduced to fugitive status and into a love affair with a near-psychopathic female. In *Dark Passage* he is a formerly well-to-do citizen, escaping from false imprisonment for the murder of his wife and seeking her real killers. He is on the run for the length of the movie, has to resort to plastic surgery and the kindness of a woman he encounters by chance in order to stay a half step ahead of his many pursuers. In *Key Largo,* his first postwar collaboration with John Huston, he is a man who has known better days, now seeking respite from the world (and the exactions of a liberal conscience) by making a visit to an isolated hotel in the Florida keys. His mission is to bring consolation to the widow (Lauren Bacall) and father (Lionel Barrymore) of his wartime friend, who was killed beside him in the Italian campaign. He feels he has done his bit in the fight against fascism during the war and is uninterested in taking arms against the breed in its native form, as personified by Edward G. Robinson, playing a particularly brutal mobster who, with his entourage, is in residence in the hotel. Bogart's fall here is less a social one than it is a descent from that special state of grace that moral rigor in the face of vulgar materialism is supposed to impart. Still, as *Casablanca* had led everyone to believe he always would, he eventually mobilizes himself and rids this little world of its oppressors just as he had previously helped rid the larger one of its dictators.

By this time one can imagine Bogart being a trifle tired of this narrative and emotional range, even if his audience was not. But while Huston was away at war, another great director, Howard Hawks, had taken a hand in Bogart's career (and, by accident, in his personal life), providing him with a brighter variation on his screen character and with the opportunity to meet and fall in love with the woman whose presence would, at long last, brighten (and stabilize) his private life as well.

She was, of course, Lauren Bacall. The picture was, of course, *To Have and Have Not.* Hawks had acquired his friend Ernest Hemingway's novel partly to help him out financially, partly to prove his contention that he could make a decent movie out of his "worst" work. He permitted his writers, Jules Furthman and William Faulkner, to keep the broad narrative outline of the Hemingway story. Its hero, Harry Morgan, is a fishing boat captain who does some smuggling on the side and reluctantly puts aside his interest in personal gain in order to place his criminal skills in the service of Free France's good cause (the setting is wartime Martinique) and comes to a tragic end as a result. In short, he admirably suited Bogart's type.

But Hawks hated doomy portents and downbeat endings in his stories. He also saw a chance to make a sort of anti-*Casablanca,* another story about a disillusioned rogue re-upping in the fight for democracy —but without the fine feelings and romantic sentiment. (Later he did something similar with *Rio Bravo,* which is *High Noon* with its sub-textual pleas for communitarian action blanched out and even satirized.) Besides, the director had detected in the offscreen Bogart a quality he had never seen on screen. He called it "insolence," and he wanted to feature that quality humorously. So the screenplay turned into a straight genre piece, an adventure tale told in the comic-romantic manner, with a female figure looming longer in Hawks's scheme than in Hemingway's. As Hawks later told the story of the filming, his largest effort so far as Bogart was concerned was to direct him to smile. He had always been afraid to do so before the cameras because he thought his scarred lip (which had also suffered nerve damage and was partly frozen) made the expression appear grotesque. This was the sort of small, sly manipulation in which Hawks specialized. He liked to unsettle actors by forcing them out of their tested mannerisms; it enlivened their performances, naturally, but it also rendered them insecure and thus more amenable to his powerful will.

There was no problem in making Bacall insecure. She was only nineteen, had virtually no training or experience as an actress, and had been discovered by Hawks's wife on the cover of *Harper's Bazaar.* He had signed her to a personal contract and begun working with her, in her own words, "inventing" her. It is well known that he had her read aloud, in her throatiest tones, in order to deepen her voice (she read *The Robe* sitting in her parked car on Mulholland Drive, with Los Angeles spread out below her). But more important to him was giving her confidence and flexibility before the camera, out of which would come an insolence to answer Bogart's. The tricks played on her were many, but after four months he deemed her ready for the lead in the Hemingway story, and in it she became, par excellence, the so-called Hawksian woman—that is to say, a woman who is knowingly humorous in her dealings with men, tolerant of their foibles, always willing to go along uncomplainingly on their foolish adventures, and, above all, direct and uncomplicated in her sexual exchanges with them.

It is hard to think of a screen newcomer who ever made a more forceful first impression than Bacall did in this role. But long before she captured the public's attention, she had captured Bogart's, much to Hawks's dismay. (He may have been jealous; he may merely have been concerned about his investment in her.) But taught to smile by the director and taught to love by Bacall, he responded with the most unshadowed performance of his career. His cynicism here was all on the surface, a manner of speaking as it were, not the sign of some deep disappointment or world sickness. And in his scenes with Bacall there was an unguarded quality he had never demonstrated before in his screen dealings with women—not even with Bergman in *Casablanca*.

Hawks's word on all this, many years later, was: "Bogie fell in love with the character she played, so she had to keep playing it the rest of her life." There is a certain shrewdness in that remark, if not, perhaps, the whole story.

Certainly their mutual attraction was instant, powerful, and forthright. She may have been inexperienced with men, but she responded to Bogart as any Hawks script would have had her do: honestly and without counting the consequences. He felt the same way, perhaps more powerfully so, given his dismal prior experiences with love. Some years later John Huston asked a group of dinner guests if there was a period of their lives they would live over if they could. Most of them shrugged noncommittally, but Bogart replied, "Yes, when I was courting Betty" (Bacall's real name). Yet for all his desire to break out of character, he could not fully do so. In her autobiography Bacall recounts an affair that seemed to consist largely of soulful hand holding in parked cars on the way home from work, hours snatched here or there in inconvenient circumstances, and many an after-midnight phone call from Bogart, as he wandered nighttown, drinking his conflict into temporary remission. For though he had clearly come to loathe the farce he had been playing with Methot, he was aware that her drinking had reduced her to a pathetic state, and now she was promising to make one last attempt to cure her addiction. A decent man could not leave her at such a moment, and, Bacall implies he implied, should she recover, he would not have a valid excuse to leave her. Not being an existential hero in real life, any more than he was on-screen, he could not make up a new self to match these new circumstances cheerily. He remained what he was, a sad and solitary sort of man, imprisoned by his code of traditional values.

And yet he had smiled on the screen. And the picture, and Bacall, were hits. Maybe there was a chance. After the first previews the studio asked Hawks to make another picture with the same stars, in the same vein, as quickly as possible. This was perhaps the worst period in Bogart's romance with Bacall, as he thrashed back and forth between her and his wife. But *The Big Sleep* went well. According to Bacall, Jack Warner sent a memo to the set: "Word has reached me that you are having fun on the set. This must stop." The plot, unslavishly derived from Raymond Chandler's novel, was wildly improbable, not to say incomprehensible, almost a parody of the typical detective story structurally. But Hawks pushed hard for outrageousness in the dialogue, encouraged the sexual electricity between his stars, put a comic twist even on routine expositional scenes as he made what was in effect a satire on the whole film noir vein—but without sacrifice of suspense or mood and without giving offense to that portion of the audience that just wanted to see a good detective story and would have greeted a more obvious satire of beloved conventions dubiously. In effect, Hawks and his writers provided Bogart a chance to send up his own screen self subtly—always an important thing for a star actor with a highly defined screen character to do. (It preempts other, less affectionate parodists and humanizes him for his public by showing him as a regular fellow capable of laughing at himself.) But they did not push him to travesty, which can be mistaken for self-contempt, as well as contempt for the audience's affections. In short, *The Big Sleep* represented an important step forward for Bogart, preparing the way for such later self-parodies as *The African Queen* and *Beat the Devil.*

In any event, when *The Big Sleep* was finished, it was clear to Bogart that he could not go on without Bacall. He freed himself at last from the constraints of a guilty conscience, and before the film went into its hugely successful release, he and Bacall were married. By every account the marriage was a good one. They accepted each other as they were. He did not attempt to remake her according to·some womanly ideal of his own—always a temptation when a man is a quarter of a century older than his wife. She did not object when he had to howl at the moon with his pals. But more and more they were quietly at home together, often in the company of other couples who appear to have been more a part of Hollywood mainstream than his older friends had been.

He developed what seems a telling habit in these years. Annually, on Christmas Eve, he would invite some friends over for a bibulous screening of *A Star Is Born,* which, according to reliable witnessess, usually ended with Bogart dissolved in sentimental tears. One has to think that in contemplating the sad fate of Norman Maine, the movie star who succumbs to alcoholism and suicide in that film, Bogart may have been contemplating his own good fortune in narrowly escaping a similarly miserable end. For certainly there were parallels in their stories that went far beyond their addiction to booze: The air they projected of being finer than their surroundings, their contempt for Hollywood manners and morals, their redemptive love for a young woman star in whose discovery they participated. The only difference was that Bogart's story came out happily—although, as things worked out, he, too, would die before his time, victim of the careless use to which he had long subjected his body.

For the moment, though, Bogart was entitled to his survivor's sentiments about the old movie. And to the other pleasures that were now his. For in his newfound calmness and security seemed to have a freeing effect on him as an actor. He began to take risks that many performers at his age and station in life cannot make themselves try. John Huston was obviously a major force in pushing him in new directions, one of which was paranoia. This was not a vein American movies may be said to have explored very often previously. And never before as unblinkingly, and with such scarifying wit, as Bogart brought to his portrayal of Fred C. Dobbs in 1947's *The Treasure of the Sierra Madre*. Walter Huston cackled an Oscar-winning counterpoint of sanity as he led greenhorn miners Bogart and Tim Holt to their El Dorado in the Mexican mountains, but he was, in the end, powerless to stop Bogart's character from cracking under the weight of sudden wealth. That, too, was a masterstroke of casting by his son, who won writing and directing Academy Awards for the picture. The elder Huston had been a worthy presence in the movies for years, a fine actor too often forced to stand on his dignity. No one was prepared for his toothless, jigging, goatish energy in this film. But no one was prepared for Bogart's performance either—braggadocio alternating with sniveling, with both emerging out of a steady mutter of demented suspicions and wild schemings. It is very bold work, acting that is clearly based on observation and imagination rather than on attractively polished aspects of his private self. And it is brave work, never once pausing to cop a sympathetic plea.

Bogart waited three years and made four other films before he found an opportunity as good—in a film that still has not achieved more than a cultish reputation: *In a Lonely Place*. It was made by an independent production company Bogart formed in 1949, and his portrayal of Dixon Steele, a screenwriter suspected of murder because everyone believes a man subject to his sudden fire storms of temper is surely capable of murder, represents Bogart's most complex exploration of his essential screen character, a summary of its development to date as well as an expansion into new territory.

The film depends more for its success on Andrew Solt's screenplay, with its unique understanding of the commercial writer's temperament and his Hollywood milieu, than it does on Nicholas Ray's direction, which serves the script unobtrusively, intelligently, flavorsomely, avoiding the mannered (and near-hysterical) fashion he sometimes embraced. For even though Dix Steele is a quintessential Ray figure, an

outsider, a failure, and mentally disturbed, what gives the film its powerful authenticity is the fact that this character inhabits the world that
Bogart himself knew so well in the years before his marriage to Bacall.
It is the Los Angeles world of quiet bars and restaurants, lacking chic,
where second-tier writers, small-time agents, minor character actors
foregather to exchange gossip and injustices and get soberly drunk.

Dix himself is not unlike Bogart. His WASPish name implies the
possibility of a solid background, as do his manners, dress, and literate
speech. To have ended up as a screenwriter is not what he expected,
any more than Bogart imagined ending up as a screen actor. Moreover,
Steele is now declassed in his profession as well. We understand that
in the fairly recent past he was employed adapting serious fiction—or
what Hollywood took to be serious fiction—to the screen and that he
had been well regarded for his skills. When we meet him, he is not
employed on much of anything—something to do with his personality.
But in the opening sequence his faithful, long-suffering agent tracks
him down in a bar, bearing a weighty tome, a trashy best seller. He
can get Steele the job adapting it if the writer can read the book
overnight and the next day give his slant on the project to the producer.
Grimly he agrees, then discovers the hatcheck girl in the restaurant
has read the thing and is agreeable to returning home with him to
synopsize the plot verbally. She does, proves flirtatious, and is sent
homeward by the writer in a cab. The next day we learn that she was
murdered and that the police suspect Steele, largely because of his
reputation for sudden and violent rages. A neighbor, Laurel Gray (very
well played by Gloria Grahame), provides Steele with an alibi, though
it is not airtight, and the possibility that he might actually have been
the killer lingers with both the police and the audience. In fact, it grows
as the film traces the course of the love affair that develops between
Dix and Laurel. For though she provides him with an emotional stability
that permits him to work well on his new assignment—despite his
troubles, he gets the adaptation job—the growing jealousy with which
he regards her and the rages that seem to come out of nowhere,
triggered by the most trivial of incidents, destroy her love for him and
enhance our suspicions of him right up to the bitterly ironic end
(another man confesses the murder, but Dix loses Laurel).

The plot is artfully braided, but it is the atmosphere in which it
proceeds, and the psychological portrait of its central figure, that make
the picture so haunting. The apartment house where Dix and Laurel
live is perfect, one of those low, vaguely Spanish affairs, built around
a courtyard, slightly shabby but still respectable, where, to this day,
people on the way up and people on the way down in the movies find
themselves. And Dix's digs are equally well realized. This is a true
writer's lair, dark, clean, but carelessly strewn with the detritus a preoc-

cupied man spreads in his wake. His favorite bar, the supporting players in his life, his social life with and without Laurel are done with equally restrained intelligence—no sordidness, but never a note of false glamour to amuse the fans either. Poignancy without sentimentality—that's the note the picture strikes.

Especially in the characterization of Steele. One type the movies never get right—the writer (for that matter, any creative person)—and another type they never touch—the angry man with no seeming motive for his anger—are efficiently struck off in a single figure by Solt and by Bogart. They do not necessarily have to connect, but they often do in life. Solt obviously knew writers of Steele's breed, and as we've seen, so did Bogart, who may have borrowed some of his personal style from them.* Men of literacy, wit, even a certain knowingness, some of whom had even made money from those qualities, they were never taken entirely seriously by the movie world with its traditional contempt for the writer or by the literary world who understood them as "sellouts." In time, of course, booze and lack of esteem turn their good qualities rancid. They cross the line into cynicism, which is, obviously, an isolating quality. And a lethal one when it is added to the solitude their craft imposes on them. Bogart's neatness of dress and precision of speech in this movie bespeak uncompromising attempts to compromise with convention, to signal his hope for understanding, while not obviously begging for favor. At the same time his manner is a defense of two kinds. He hopes that his calm, plainspoken contempt for the world in general, his business in particular, will rationalize his rages when they burst forth, allow them to be understood as the natural consequence of his quite sensible disgust with injustice and incompetence. Also, subjectively there is the hope that a reasonable expression of these feelings will vent the rage rolling inside him, prevent it from bursting forth in physical violence.

It is probably fair to call Dix Steele a paranoid schizophrenic and therefore akin to Fred C. Dobbs. But this is that form of mental distress presented as we more often encounter it in life, possessing a man of breeding, education, social grace, a man not from the fringe of society, but one who has been at one of its centers and is now falling away from it just because of this inexplicable thing that has taken possession of him. It is the glory of this script that it never introduces psychological testimony to this effect, never offers the conventional flashback-to-trauma to explain it. It is the glory of Bogart's performance that he never

---

*In his obituary column about Bogart drama critic John McClain, a drinking buddy, wrote: "He would much rather have made a more modest living as a writer, where he could have aired his frustrations in print. He was a guy that didn't open up much, but the people he always sought out were writers ... and they were the people for whom he had the most affection. In a funny way, he was almost one of them."

comments on his sickness either. No eye rolling, no hand wringing, not the slightest implication that he is aware of his condition. This was rare at a time when Hollywood had discovered mental illness as a topic and performers of every type were desperately seeking to enlist our sympathies in psychological tragedy. The picture's greatness lies in its straightforwardness, its trust in the audience to catch its understated drift. Bogart's performance, summarizing all his solitaries of the past decade, but draining them of all romance, referring to his work in *Treasure,* but draining it of its overt, often bleakly comic craziness, is great for the same reason: its control and restraint. He simply is.

In a sense Bogart completed his life's work here. In the six active years left to him after *In a Lonely Place* he added nothing essential to his screen character. Indeed, it is fair to say that many of the pictures he made in the fifties were unworthy of him. In this transitional decade some looked backward to studio routine and are best described by a term rapidly going out of date even then; movies like *The Enforcer, Sirocco, Battle Circus, Tokyo Joe, Chain Lightning* are essentially program features. Others like *Knock on Any Door* (also directed by Ray) embraced what the industry thought of as the new seriousness. In it he plays a prosecutor, himself risen from a slum neighborhood who tries but fails to reform a street punk (John Derek) before his troubles with the law reach a fatal stage. Like a lot of his films in this period, the picture was an exercise in liberal conscientiousness, with Bogart playing the spokesman for reformist values. (He has to make an endless courtroom speech at the conclusion in which social inequity is blamed for sending a good boy off in the wrong direction). These films, among which we might number *The Barefoot Contessa, The Left Hand of God,* and *The Harder They Fall,* imposed "thoughtful" themes on melodramatic and generic stories for the sober consideration of the middlebrow audience. But both the programmers and the pictures that provided him with lecture topics lacked the live-wire energy of Hollywood moviemaking when it was young and full of careless rapture.

Still, there were yet some good things for him to do, most notably the film that remains, next to *Casablanca,* his most widely beloved work, *The African Queen.* It is, of course, a joyful "fighting romance" (another old-fashioned Hollywood phrase) and the casting of Katharine Hepburn, spunky and full of her sweet arrogance as always, opposite Bogart, typically withdrawn and calculating, would have been inspired in any case. But his Charlie Allnut was a very able variation on his Fred C. Dobbs. They were at heart similar figures, drifters on civilization's farthest fringes. But Charlie's suspiciousness is well founded; a rational man confronting Hepburn's plans for escape from known perils by embracing the unknown ones of a river voyage aboard the eponymous rust bucket is entitled to his skepticism. Anyway, the thing was both funny and oddly touching under Huston's direction, and Bogart was sufficiently off-cast, and his service to Hollywood lengthy enough, to assure him of the 1952 Academy Award. If he had been better, perhaps, in other pictures, this one was big and splashy and popular and thus, by Hollywood standards, a suitable occasion to celebrate not just this performance but, by implication, his life's achievements.

After that there was *Deadline—U.S.A.*, writer-director Richard Brooks's newspaper yarn in which—again a gentleman in raffish waters—Bogart plays the editor of a newspaper the heirs to which wish to sell it to a chain, silencing its independent crusading voice. In the course of the picture he demonstrates his ability to speak many languages: that of a tough professional in a tough craft; that of the trusted servitor of the *grande dame* whose husband founded the sheet (she is played by Ethel Barrymore, and their scenes demonstrate Bogart's good breeding better than any he ever had); that of a conventional hero standing up to mob threats; that of a lover whose duties keep diverting him from romantic obligations. In other words, many of the basic elements of his screen character are on balanced and agreeable display in a sturdily made film.

On the whole, his next—and last—picture with Huston, *Beat the Devil,* is for sophisticated tastes more entertaining than *The African Queen,* though Bogart's role is straighter, more reactive—the still center of some truly divine lunacy. In terms of his overall career it is interesting largely because it is the last time he plays a gentleman fallen from social grace. Indeed, his Billy Dannreuther, trim in blazers and ascots, might well be Rick Blaine a decade later. An American expatriate of obviously good breeding, he has, until recently, lived well on the proceeds of various mysterious schemes—a great villa he once owned near Ravello, Italy (where the picture was shot), is shown; a grand car that was once his is displayed in the course of the story. Now, alas, down on his luck, he is reduced to helping an ill-assorted crowd of swindlers, led by Robert Morley (in a gorgeous display of pomp and menace), obtain mining concessions in "British East." He and his crowd have at least cornered the market in comically stated paranoia, and it is Bogart who here represents the reality principle, not only to them but to an Englishwoman (Jennifer Jones, in a blond wig and in the performance of her life), whose dottiness takes the form of compulsive lying and excessive romanticism. The picture apparently started out to be a straight melodrama, in the international intrigue genre; but it was entirely too routine in that form for Huston's taste, and Truman Capote was brought in to rewrite it with him. The result was a great shaggy dog story deliriously, but with marvelously straight face, sending up the conventions of the glamour-thriller. And a field day for a cast happily parodying themselves—except for Bogart, whose company produced the picture. He didn't particularly enjoy the joke or the cult that formed around the picture, and he especially did not enjoy its commercial fate; it was a box-office disaster.

But if *Beat the Devil* was too special in its appeal for mass-market success, Bogart was still on a good roll with his 1954 releases. It was followed into the theaters by *The Caine Mutiny.* With its worrying over the question of duty in a democracy, it was a middlebrow movie par excellence, but Bogart was excellent as the paranoiac Captain Queeg —Fred C. Dobbs and Dix Steele crammed into a professional naval officer's uniform. Looking at it now, one also sees a prefiguration of Richard Nixon with his tense rigidity masked by false good cheer in the film's early passages, the descent into lunacy as the pressures of command begin to reach his quaking soul in its later ones. In any event, Bogart's witness-stand breakdown is as good a scene as he ever played, and since he is playing (as the saying goes) a gentleman by act of Congress, and since the highly dubious moral of the Herman Wouk tale under adaptation is that gentlemanly dutifulness is the backbone of the Republic, the role provides him with the opportunity to offer a final gloss on his basic screen character.

A few months later Bogart appeared in *Sabrina,* this time, for the first time, playing a gentleman who is not the least bit declassed. As the responsible eldest son of a great family, a dour man in a black suit and a homburg, he soberly permits his raffish father and his playboy younger brother all the fun while he attends their vast holdings. He does, in the course of the film, permit himself to be declassed emotionally. For in trying to extricate his brother from an affair with their chauffeur's daughter (Audrey Hepburn) Bogart's character falls in love with her, and he extracts good humor from his belated efforts to loosen up and lighten up. In this picture, one imagines him imagining all those stage juveniles of his Broadway past—sobered up by thirty years of life, but given a chance to rediscover something of their lost youths.

His last five pictures are best left in near silence. He was the mouth-piece of Joseph Mankiewicz's incorrigible gliberalism in *The Barefoot Contessa,* a literate (and, of course, gentlemanly) film director commenting sardonically on the bad values of the business and of its allies in the international set; an escaped convict in a misbegotten comedy, *My Three Angels;* an overwrought gangster leading his mob into improbable refuge in a middle-class family's home (a reversion to his least successful type) in *The Desperate Hours;* a downed flier disguising himself as a priest to escape a Chinese warlord in *The Left Hand of God;* an out-of-work sportswriter—again a man of obvious breeding and better than his surroundings, of course—drawn into a scheme to promote an inept prizefighter to championship status in *The Harder They Fall,* his last movie. In this period he was saying, with considerable justification, "I'm a professional. I've done pretty well, don't you think? I've survived in a pretty rough business." He never spoke of art, which would have seemed pretentious, even grandiloquent to him, only of craft, according to Alistair Cooke.

He was, perhaps, astonished to be in a position to make this claim plausibly. To be sure, as we have seen, he had always believed that work breeds more work and recognition. But when he left the security of his Warner Brothers contract in 1948, he also left behind the necessity to make three or more pictures a year. And at his age, and with his reputation, there was no need to go on working at that pace. Yet he had done so—perhaps because he felt a need to provide for his young wife and the two children who were born in the first decade of their marriage, maybe because in producing many of his own films, and receiving percentages for his participation in others, he saw a chance to capitalize on his many years of less well-paid toil. But it would seem that he gained more satisfaction than he ever had from work. Indeed, as he lingered in his last illness, he kept insisting that if only he could return to work, he would return to health as well, such was the link he had made between well-being and gratifying employment.

On the night he won his Oscar for *The African Queen* his wife could not help reflecting that "Bogie had everything now—a happy marriage, a son, another child on the way, an ocean racing yawl [the legendary *Santana*], success, and the peak of recognition in his work." To put the matter simply, he had by that time far transcended the rewards one may reasonably expect from mere professionalism. Those modest satisfactions, in his line of work, come to character actors and to journeymen leading players who manage to hang on for more years than their gifts would normally permit them. Better still, he had achieved his legendary status in the most pleasing possible way. For he had transcended not by transforming himself, not by trying to be something he was not, but by finding within himself certain universal, or at least universally recognizable and appealing, traits. Which, after arduous apprenticeship, he learned to project without strain or self-consciousness. Perhaps he was lucky in finding these qualities and his mature performer's skill in presenting them at a moment, during the war, when the shadows of the film noir style began to steal across the face of the movie hero, symbolic representations of everyone's new awareness that idealism and masculine competence had to be shadowed by doubts and hesitations, by a new psychological self-awareness.

But he transcended this good luck just as he had transcended the bad luck of his earlier movie career, adding the blackness of Dobbs and Steele and Queeg to his repertory. They were in some sense logical—or should one say illogical?—extensions of his basic screen character, but since they were also clearly characters he could not create out of his entirely sane self, had to be made up out of observation and insight, they proved him at last to be an actor in the fullest sense of the word—something more than just a great movie star. Indeed, by the late fifties it was possible to argue that it was Humphrey Bogart, not Gable or Cooper or Cagney or even Grant, who had appeared in more films—close to a dozen of them—that are unarguably central to the history of the American cinema, whether it is regarded as an art form or a social force or both.

He had yet one more role to play—that of a brave man dying. When cancer (of the esophagus) struck him, he refused to admit it. Never once in the long months that he fought it off did he hint that his illness was more than a temporary thing. Though scarcely able to eat, he wasted away in a fashion terrible for his family and his friends to see. But he was stoic and gallant in a quiet way that has been remembered and admired as exemplary by everyone who witnessed his last year. Both John Huston and Alistair Cooke have, in fact, drawn unforgettable portraits of him in that time. It became the habit of his friends to drop in casually for brief visits at the end of the day. Bogart would be shaved and dressed in gray flannels and a red smoking jacket in his upstairs bedroom, then placed in a wheelchair and transferred to a dumbwaiter, which carried him to the first floor. Then he would be transferred to another wheelchair and taken to his den, where, drink in hand and a cigarette glowing, he would await his callers, each of whom would stay for a half hour or so. Around eight, after they had all left, he would be returned to his room by the same painful route he had left it. As Huston put it when he eulogized him, "No one who sat in his presence during those final weeks will ever forget. It was a unique display of sheer animal courage. After the first visit—the visit was spent getting over the initial shock—one quickened to the grandeur of it, expanded and felt strangely elated, proud to be there ... the friend of such a brave man. ..."

It was, of course, acting. Bravery always is. But it was acting of the special kind on which his fame had rested and his legend would continue to rest. He was dying as a gentleman must. With dignity. Without complaint. With his emotions under control and with thoughts spared for the feelings of his friends and loved ones. Even at the end he was in touch with his essence, clinging to it, believing in it, as he had, perhaps no less desperately, in an earlier time, when no one else had recognized it. Now, of course, everyone had gathered some sense of what he stood for, however incompletely they understood it. He would not let them down. Or himself. He died in his sleep on January 14, 1957.

MARLON BRANDO
A HERO OF OUR TIMES

*W*e began worrying about Marlon Brando almost immediately—not a half dozen years after he went to Hollywood and made his first movie. His great run of films—great at least in the sense that they permitted him to impress himself indelibly on a generation's consciousness—was perhaps the most exciting thing about the movies in the first years of the fifties. From *The Men* in 1950 through the film version of his stage masterpiece, *A Streetcar Named Desire,* to his one public brush with Shakespeare in *Julius Caesar,* to his disparate rebels in *Viva Zapata!* and *The Wild One* (one with a cause, the other without), and on to the Oscar-winning culmination of this first phase, *On the Waterfront,* he had laid out his credentials, and by 1954 they had finally been accepted by nearly everyone (witness the Academy Award) as genuine. Moreover, he had done it his way. He had worn his blue jeans in Bel Air (long before it became fashionable; indeed, he probably established the fashion); he had insulted Louella O. Parsons; he had picked his nose in public and said terrible things about mighty people. He was the star as antistar. But now, as the Chianti went 'round in the lofts and railroad flats of lower Manhattan, the discussions of "Marlon"—emotionally everyone was on a first-name basis with him—grew hot with anxiety, cool with gloom. Why was he staying so long on the Far Coast? When would he return home to his roots, enter again upon that temple of truth the theater? Was it possible—darkest of all possibilities—that he, of all people, was now in danger of "selling out"? Was it possible, perhaps, that the deal had already been struck? *Desirée* did not encourage.

Something quite astonishing, quite without historical antecedents in our culture, was going on here. Some three decades earlier D. W. Griffith, the man who had pioneered (with limited success) the radical notion that a moviemaker might be taken seriously as an artist, cast his eye wistfully over the history of American heroism, noting that in his time the military leader had been replaced as the repository of our highest admiration by the inventor and the entrepreneur. Now, in the 1920's, he wondered if sometime in the not too distant future the artist might, in his turn, replace these figures as "the one who expresses in the highest degree the achievement the people of the nation would like to achieve individually." At last, in postwar America the moment he, among others, had dreamed of was at hand. For the first time the mass media, the mass public indeed began to see certain figures in all the arts in a heroic light. We had now the time, the money, and the communications technology to attend, on a more intimate basis than ever before, the great drama of creation; we could now share immediately in the thrill of the artist's victories over his own demons and the indifference of the crass world, to suffer with him the agonies of his defeats. It was Brando's fortune (and misfortune) to be the new young actor, representing what seemed to be a radically new approach to his art, on which this unprecedented attention was focused.

He thus became the first actor to be burdened not just with the weight of conducting a significant and interesting career but with what seemed to be an obligation to transcending our customary expectations of the performer. His selections of roles, his actions offstage—these had symbolic implications, cultural consequences in the eyes of many of his beholders. Nor was that the end of his responsibilities as others defined them. He had, it seemed, a duty to the past—to redeem certain promises an older generation of theatrical idealists had made to themselves—and to the future—to lead what amounted to a revolution of rising expectations, passionately believed in by a younger crowd of idealists.

These were huge responsibilities. Moreover, they were responsibilities he had not sought. Brando, I now think, instinctively recognized what was going on. And just as instinctively he recognized that he was wrong for the part in which people, most of them strangers, some of them users, were trying to cast him. That was the source of the enigmatic behavior that was so worrisome to people at this early stage of his career. But his instincts were right. His best interviews through the years reveal a man with a wild sense of the world's pompous absurdities, a nice self-deprecating sense of humor, a desperate fear of seeming to take himself too seriously—or of allowing anyone else to do so—and an authentic desire for privacy that went far beyond the usual star protestations on that subject. If he was a great observer of people (by all reports, he was an acute, hilarious, quick-study mimic of anyone who crossed his path), he was no intellectual, so he was never comfortable generalizing and pronouncing on big topics. And he was certainly not a born leader of any cause or movement. If anything, he was a natural anarchist. He kept telling Truman Capote, who profiled him for the *New Yorker* in 1957, not to believe more than 40 percent of what he said. He also said that his attention span was never longer than seven minutes. One can see in retrospect that he was trying to warn people that the role of drum major in an aesthetic revolution was not within his neutral range.

Those of us who participated in the concern over him and his future course, young show folk and hangers-on like me, who had come to New York in part because the theater still had some vital connection with our lives thirty-odd years ago, did not realize how unprecedented our anxiety was. We were aware that our interest in Brando was of quite a different, more passionate order than the hushed respect we accorded the great knighted English actors then regularly visiting us, quite different, too, from the uncomplicated affection for certain movie stars that we had carried over from childhood. Certainly we understood that there was something generational in our regard for him, some sense that he spoke for those of us coming of age in the postwar years—or was trying to in his inarticulate way—and against many of the bourgeois assumptions and expectations about theatrical performance that older people frequently expressed to us when we squabbled with them about his work.

But we were truly unaware of the full burden that we were participating in pressing down upon him. Made conscious by the liberal and intellectual press that the 1950's were, in general, a period of extraordinary political, social, and artistic blandness, we were yet unaware that ironically, both the theater and the movies had reached a point where they required—or seemed to some people prominent within those fields to require—a symbolic figure around which a revolution or, at any rate, a long-dreamed-of reformation could coalesce. Certainly we were unaware that our youthful and quite innocent enthusiasm for the force and singularity of Brando's work was the source of that star power the reformers believed might be harnessed to their own reconstructive enterprises.

But if the reformers had misjudged this man, they had not misjudged this moment. If ever the time was right for basic changes in the way show business did business, this was it. Indeed, reforms of a sort were already beginning to occur. For it seemed that the corrupt old institutions of show business—vulgar, commercial Hollywood; vulgar, commercial Broadway—could not long endure in their present states. Hollywood's faltering condition was widely reported in the press of the time and remains widely known to readers of its history. The start of television networking in 1948 quickly undermined the movies' prosperity. In a few years the weekly audience for films had shrunk by two thirds. At the same time a consent decree in a long-fought antitrust suit forced the studios to divest themselves of their profitable, stabilizing theater chains. With no need to fulfill their former obligation to supply a weekly change of program to their theaters, and with hard times reducing their numbers, the need for a large number of productions and large numbers of stars to appear in them declined. The long-term contract binding stars to studios disappeared with the need for their regular services. As for Broadway, for a long time the only live theater that counted in this country, the source of new playwrights, new actors, and the font from which what was left of the theatrical road emanated, it seemed to shrink a little every year—fewer theaters, fewer new shows opening, fewer profitable long runs.

The doom of these monolithic institutions, which theatrical visionaries of the 1930's had predicted and had worked for, was not quite at hand; only the deeply radical hinted at that possibility. But if no one expected the old Hollywood and the old Broadway to disappear entirely, it was obvious that a profound process of change had been set in motion by the economic and social forces of the moment. And it began to seem that gifted and serious artists might now begin to work in both theater and film with far greater autonomy than they had ever known before, freely choosing their vehicles and enjoying greater control over their final shape.

At one end of the scale, in New York, the off-Broadway theater underwent a renaissance. Curious new voices, many of them from abroad, began to be heard there, and new performers were beginning their careers in these little theaters side by side with older performers who were expanding their range. There was, at last, or so it seemed at the time, a permanent place for the venturesome to repair. At the other end of the scale—and the country—that comparative handful of movie stars who remained in demand discovered that their rewards were now larger than ever. They could now get more for a single picture than they might have received for a year or two's work under their old contracts, and receive many other rewards as well. They could function as their own producers if they wished, bringing stories, directors, costars, whatever they felt they needed to the studios for financing. This gave them a far larger measure of creative control than they had ever known previously. Even if they did not want all that direct responsibility, they could insist on approval of the crucial elements in a project when they signed on for it and receive a percentage of the profits—sometimes the gross—for their efforts. Beyond that they were now free of the personal constraints that the old long-term contracts had imposed on them. They could live as they pleased, go where they wanted, do what they would, and, in an era that grew ever more tolerant in the realm of personal behavior—morals, if you will—suffer no consequences. Indeed, people quickly became eager to hear any confession any prominent person cared to make about any aspect of his life—and pay good money for the privilege.

Nor did performers have to set themselves adrift on these strange new seas without an ideological compass to guide them. On the contrary, they (especially the younger ones like Brando) had something wonderful to guide and comfort them. Narrowly defined, it was nothing more than a technique to help them in the perfection of their craft and in the presentation of themselves theatrically. But no one narrowly defined the Method. (No, let's put that another way: *the Method*). For in this period there quickly agglomerated around it a mystique and a politique that implicitly promised not just professional reward for its devotees but perhaps personal salvation as well. It was inevitable that something as passionately believed in as this system was by many of its converts should seem to offer redemptive possibilities for the entire theatrical enterprise, too.

Indeed, those possibilities had been implicit in it from the moment it was introduced to the United States, with the visit of Konstantin Stanislavsky's Moscow Art Theater in 1923 and 1924. It continued to gain adherents (notably Lee Strasberg) at the American Laboratory Theater, founded by two of the Russian's disciples in New York and, after that, in the Group Theater, which Strasberg cofounded with Harold Clurman and Cheryl Crawford in 1931. There Stanislavsky's techniques, which had been developed before the Russian Revolution, were married, as ultimately they had been in the Soviet Union, with a powerful leftist political orientation. This was committed theater of a kind that had never taken root before in the United States. Almost all of the Group's productions were of didactic, inspirational, socially conscious plays, many of which were developed and polished in its own workshops. And while playwrights like Clifford Odets were writing for this communally organized company, Strasberg, who was in charge of training its actors, was schooling them in Stanislavskian technique—more "realistic," psychologically, or at any rate more inward-looking, than the classical manner.

It was a distinctly odd hybrid, this blend of a kind of Marxist thought and a kind of Freudian thought; but it did bring a breath of modernism to the theater, and for a time the Group was unquestionably the most important center of theatrical innovation and controversy in the United States, perhaps the world. For a few years it was possible to believe that it might just accomplish what was clearly its ultimate objective: full-scale theatrical reconstruction, with the superficialities of bourgeois

comedy and parlor melodrama banished, a more profound engagement with the realities of everyday life and the political and social
issues of the day embraced.

In this it failed, the victim of harsh theatrical economics, perhaps
of changing times, certainly of its own successes, for many of its best
people were lured away into commercial theater and the movies. But
the idealistic spirit of the Group did live on, carried in the sometimes
guilty hearts of its former members as their careers developed. In the
decade after the Group disbanded, some of its members, like Clurman
and Elia Kazan, became important directors. Strasberg was beginning
to be heard from as a theoretician and teacher of acting. By the late
forties and early fifties the beginnings of legendary status started to be
conferred on them and on the organization that had informed them
as younger men.

For the rest of the nation the Fervent Years (as Clurman named
them in his memoir of the Group) were well past by this time, and in
fact, the people of the theater had stopped waiting for lefty, politically,
that is. But if the old socially conscious spirit of the Group could not
be revived in postwar America, the times had never been more pro-
pitious for the other, equally important aspect of its ideals, a new, more
psychologically truthful approach to performance. By this time the
metaphors of psychology had ceased to be the exclusive property of
the advanced intellectual class. The movies, popular fiction, and theater
were full of them, and an acting technique like the Method (as the
general public was now learning to call it), which broadly speaking
did for the actor what psychoanalysis did for the ordinarily bedeviled
citizen—permitted him to plunge creatively, redemptively into the
abyss of himself, his buried past, his hidden thoughts—was bound to
be alluring. The exercises and disciplines of the Method made it possible, or so it seemed, for the performer to present himself not merely
as an entertainer but as an artist engaged in an endeavor every bit as
serious, as morally testing, as brave as that of the great writers and
thinkers.

Slickness, superficiality, the merely elocutionary, or the merely
mnemonic were not good enough now. One must use the character
as a metaphor through which deep and universal behavioral truths
could be illuminated by the serious and striving actor. It seems obvious
that the best actors, throughout human history, must have devised ways
of making this connection between self and fiction. But never before
had these techniques been codified so that they were generally teach-
able, not just (after 1948) at the Method's temple, the Actors Studio in
New York, but wherever an adept could find loft space and some
aspiring disciples.

Implicit in the hope that the craft of acting could be reformed was

249

another, larger hope, the old hope that had animated the Group Theater. It supposed that if a sufficient number of performers could be sent forth, cleansed and purified, into a profession now confused and weakened as it attempted to grapple with its own changed economic conditions, they might, by their presences (and their refusals), cleanse and purify the ancient corruptions of show biz. The idea was not as farfetched as it may now seem, especially since the new breed of performers was being trained to a new subjectivity of style that seemed to suit the new subjectivity of an apolitical audience rather morose in its materialism, slightly guilty about its self-absorption. All the other revolutions promised by the 1930's had turned rancid with delay. But perhaps this one, also too long denied, might at long last have its moment.

All revolutions, we know, begin in the yearning hearts of a few courageous individuals. Those there were aplenty in the 1950's—actors and actresses by the score whose youthful idealism had been fired, as their skills had been tempered, not merely by "Lee," but by "Herbert" and "Uta" and "Sandy" and "Stella" and all the other legendary teachers whose first names rolled so trippingly off so many tongues on so many unemployment lines in New York in that decade. They wanted what young actors had always wanted—work!—but there was a special agony for many of them when they got a TV job or their first small part in a Broadway show because they thought they were selling out before they even got going (a roommate of mine contrived to lose the lead in a bit of Lindsay and Crouse commercialism less than a week after rehearsals started). In fact, they seemed to worry more about selling out than getting jobs, so much so that when I hear people talking about the bland and unprincipled materialism of the fifties, I think of my contemporaries in the theater and how little they suited that image. I think, too, of how the blacklists and graylists imposed on show business by McCarthyism helped staff the New York acting schools' faculties with gifted unemployables who added their bit to the antiestablishment fervor that one soaked up there.

If this was a conspiracy, it was, I hasten to say, an entirely unorganized one. No plot was afoot—just a shared set of attitudes based on a set of shared experiences among the older generation, a shared set of values eagerly embraced by the younger crowd. But both groups had come to agreement, through no conscious consensual process I could discern, on Brando as their hero and exemplar, the man on whose fate as an artist they had staked their largest hopes for change. If he could succeed in imposing his style and values on the world of mass entertainment, if he could use his new stardom to become something more than a mere star, if he could use it to become a moral and intellectual force (and be recognized for those qualities, not just within the profession but by the public at large), then there was hope that others might follow. If he failed, they would doubtless continue their assault on the citadels of show biz power (and the public consciousness, of course), but in grimmer mood, with a martyr in mind.

Looking back on it, we can see how easily Brando's career could have been made into a heroic epic—if only he had wanted to cast his life in that form. Joseph Campbell, the great contemporary scholar of myth, discerned in the heroic legends of all societies, Eastern and Western, what he termed a Monomyth, in which an exemplary figure acts out, each in his way, a version of the same archetypal three-part story. In the first act there is the drama of separation and departure from the community that nurtured him; in the next there comes a series of initiatory trials, leading to a victory of some sort; finally, there are the triumphant return and reintegration with the society from which he uprooted himself originally. It is interesting, and profitable, to set Brando's career to that music and to observe the discordancies he insisted on writing into the score.

Act One. It is important to understand how close Brando's ties to the Group Theater tradition were when he was a young actor. It is also important to remember that everyone who knew him as a young man remembers him as extraordinarily polite and respectful toward his elders. It is true that his Broadway debut was in a bourgeois heart-warmer, *I Remember Mama,* adapted from a family memoir by John Van Druten and presented by Rodgers and Hammerstein, no less; you can't get more mainstream than that. It is also true that a couple of years later he managed to offend many a traditionalist with his "work" (the word of choice for acting among the Method-minded) as the poet Marchbanks opposite Katherine Cornell in her Great-Lady-of-the-Theater production of *Candida.* But in these years he was studying with Stella Adler, who, with her brother, Luther, had been a Group stalwart and who was also then the wife of Harold Clurman. Between the productions just named, the latter cast him in a small role in a Maxwell Anderson flop, *Truckline Cafe,* in which, according to the reports of the few who saw this play, Brando was electrifying—and for the first time the Brando we all later came to know. This play, in turn, was copro-duced by Elia Kazan, who had been what might be termed an apprentice with the Group, who remembered Brando when another Group alum-nus, John Garfield, made such impossible demands that he could not be signed for *A Streetcar Named Desire* in 1947. Subsequently Brando did intermittently attend classes at the newly founded Actors Studio, where, naturally, he encountered Strasberg, though he always resented the latter's claims to have been a major influence on him. That, however, is of small consequence. It was a tradition—not any single individual

—that could lay claim to Brando, and that tradition was, without question, the Group Theater tradition.

It had produced successful actors before, including (to name only some stars) the problematical Franchot Tone, the tormented Garfield, and, just before Brando's emergence, Montgomery Clift (who was the student of Bobby Lewis, another Group graduate, and Mira Rostova, a Stanislavskian, but not a Strasbergian). But the fact remains that it was Brando's performance in the central role of a self-evidently significant, and possibly great, play that finally, belatedly brought that tradition to the center of theatrical consciousness. And controversy. The man had found his moment; the moment had found its man.

The curious thing was that many who saw him as Stanley Kowalski in *A Streetcar Named Desire,* which opened in December 1947, believed they were present at the creation of something new. They did not understand that actually the opposite was true, that they were witnessing the culmination of a movement, a dream, that could trace its history back over a decade and a half, longer than that if you date the beginnings of the Stanislavskian ideal in this country to that visit of the Moscow Art Theater in the 1920's. As a result of this ignorance, certain confusions developed. Brando's virtues, the Method's virtues, his limits, its limits became inextricably mixed in the public's mind. One has to believe that a certain resentment must have been created in him, a sense that he was not being given sufficient credit for the individuality of what he had created. Perhaps with it was born a desire to distance himself from those who wished to claim a share in that achievement.

For it was a remarkable one. Brando's performance, of course, is preserved on film—perhaps even enhanced by film, with its opportunities for intimate observation. It is breathtaking still, the more so in that Brando disliked the character. "Kowalski was always right, and never afraid. He never wondered, he never doubted.... And he had the kind of brutal aggressiveness I hate. I'm afraid of it. I detest the character."

The performance's greatness is born of that detestation. Brando in those days was an utterly beautiful young man. His chunky body was sculpted almost like a weight lifter's; there was a dark and enigmatic depth in his eyes, something noble about his brow and nose. The contrast between this (by stage and movie standards) unconventional handsomeness and the literally cocksure qualities of the character he was playing (not to mention the brilliant vocal manner he concocted, the very voice of modern mass man) made us understand how the genteel Stella fell under his sexual thrall: He may have been a brute, but he was a beautiful one. More than that, one sensed in his characterization unspoken dimensions, dimensions that were no more than shadows in the writing. For Tennessee Williams, one senses, it would have been sufficient had Stanley been no more than a brute force, crushing the fragile and poetic flowers of dreaming southern womanhood. But Brando gave him something more—an instinctive intelligence, a satiric (not to say satanic) humor, and, most important, a yearning quality that lent a tinge of sympathetic color to his thrashing bafflement with Blanche and the airs that she put on. Somewhere under his cheap knowingness, his confident sexuality, his sadistic humor (which perhaps no other actor could have made us laugh at so genuinely) Brando suggested a sensitivity so buried that Kowalski himself could not recognize it, even a vulnerability that, long ago perhaps, Stanley saw as weakness and hid under every kind of male denial.

This untutored, unspoken sensitivity informed most of Brando's early roles, and the suspense in all of them (other than *Streetcar* and, of course, *Julius Caesar*) revolved around whether or not he would acknowledge his best self, articulate his aspirations and his pain. In all of them he eventually did. In *The Men,* made after his Broadway run in *Streetcar* but before its filming, it was rage that rendered him inarticulate. He was a paraplegic, deeply resentful over his crippling in the war, deeply anxious over whether he could perform adequately as a husband should he marry his faithful fiancée. In *Viva Zapata!* (also directed by Kazan, from a John Steinbeck script) it was ignorance that had to be overcome. The title character is an illiterate peasant who becomes a revolutionary hero, then is brought to a more sophisticated political understanding as he sees the pure ideals that had motivated him betrayed by his colleagues when they come to power. (The piece can, and should, be read metaphorically as an anti-Stalinist tract particularly since Kazan was then under fire from American Stalinists for giving the names of sometime Communist colleagues to the House Un-American Activities Committee.) In *The Wild One* Brando's Johnny, leader of a motorcycle gang terrorizing an innocent small town, was a causeless rebel, perhaps the first such in popular entertainment. It was his lot to express the aimlessness and alienation that many young people claimed they felt at that moment, and so, though this was the poorest of Brando's early movies, and though his character turned out to be conventionally redeemable through romantic entanglement, it was a historically significant one. His black leather jacket, his "hawg," and the singular blend of contempt, befuddlement, and yearning that he brought to his role of an outsider challenging middle-class stability and titillating its secret desire to cut loose became emblems of the decade.

"Oh, Charlie, oh, Charlie ... You don't understand. I could have had class. I could have been somebody, instead of a bum—which is what I am." One could almost hear the national sigh of relief rising when, in 1954, in *On the Waterfront,* he uttered what turned out to be the most famous lines he ever spoke. Here at last was the articulation not only of what we took to be his own fears but of what we were sure were our own needs in a decade where, by common consent, no ambition was supposed to be vaulting. The film itself insisted that Terry Malloy, the ex-pug now living on the small change the waterfront mob scattered in his direction, find his best self in narrow and peculiar political action. Again Elia Kazan, this time abetted by the writer, Budd Schulberg, who had also cooperated with HUAC, was sending an obvious symbolic message, since Malloy's heroism consisted of being what they were accused of being—a stool pigeon—and then of suffering a terrible beating for (the poses of a pietà are employed to emphasize his martyrdom) his devotion to a higher good.

No matter. Or small matter. Official recognition of Brando's gift could no longer be denied. And the calumny he had suffered—the cruel parodies, the intellectual clucking over his lack of the classic actor's graces (which included the canard that he *always* mumbled), the fuming and fussing over his antisocial behavior—was if not entirely stilled, then muted. For no one, no matter how defensive of tradition, could deny the power of this performance. And if one was his contemporary and partisan, it was impossible not to draw analogies between his life and his role. There was heroism in his individuality, his resistance to the publicity mechanism (giving interviews, he later said, was "Navel picking—AND SMOKING IT"), his challenge to the tradition of the well-made actor.

It seemed to us, at this moment, that he had accomplished two significant things. He had redefined and expanded our notions of what constituted the heroic on stage and screen, so that it could include visible self-consciousness and visible self-doubting. The simple way of saying it is that he had brought the spirit of modernism over from literature and painting (where, increasingly, the subject of the work was the work itself) and applied it to performance. And as a public figure he had brought the same qualities to celebrity existence. We were involved, as we never had been before, in the actor's struggle to find and realize himself as an artist, and this experience was different—shall we say?—from our sympathetic enlistment in the cause of performers who made their personal troubles public, different from our worries, say, over Judy Garland's struggles with booze, pills, and victimization by her producers and managers.

For we actually knew very little of Brando's personal life. All his struggles were aesthetic. And by insisting on that metaphor, he changed the terms of the discussions his peers would have with their ostensible employers, the public. By implication he was asserting what was always implicit in the tradition that had formed him: that acting has a moral dimension, that at its best, honest work in this field can and should have strong and desirable social-political effects, and that the refusal to make this moral exertion was demeaning, perhaps unmanning to the actor.

Through *Waterfront* he had no problem living up to that code. His first half dozen films, however we may evaluate them now that a little history has intervened since their release, all were seriously meant and seriously taken. In associating himself with them, he had nothing to be ashamed of, though in the cases of *The Men* and *The Wild One* he had reason to be disappointed with recutting by the producers after he had finished his work. Thereafter, though, he entered upon what must have seemed to him the infinite second act of his adventure, an endless term of trial marked by miscalculation on his part, misuse by others and terrible disappointments that perhaps cannot be blamed on anything but the kind of mischief and mischance that endlessly afflict the movie game and people who think they can beat its odds.

Act Two. In effect Marlon Brando found himself pioneering a problem and then living with the ambiguous results of his—everyone's—failure to find a satisfactory solution to it, for most of the next two decades. Pauline Kael summarized this issue very well in 1975, when she wrote a long consideration of the actor who was Brando's apparent antithesis, Cary Grant (though, in fact, Brando recorded his admiration for this supremely gifted actor). Kael wrote:

> A young actor now generally feels that he is an artist only when he uses his technique for personal expression and something he believes in. And so he has a problem that [Grant] never faced.... They began to feel emasculated when they played formula roles that depended on technique only, and they had to fight themselves to retain their belief in the audience, which often preferred what they did when they sold out. They were up against all the temptations, corruptions, and conflicts that writers and composers and painters had long been wrestling with. Commerce is a bind for actors now....

Desirée. Yes. Within months of *Waterfront* came *Desirée*. Everything its predecessors had not been. Technicolor. CinemaScope. Brando as Napoleon in an adaptation of a trashy, best-selling historical romance. Studio-bound. Directed by a veteran contract craftsman whose career was based on reliability, not inspiration. A dinosaur he was forced to ride because he had backed off a similar mount he judged to be even worse (*The Egyptian*) and owed Fox a picture. And he had got into

255

this mess for the worst of reasons—money. He needed it for the cattle ranch he was trying to start. "Commerce is a bind. . . ."

No wonder people worried. Tone. Garfield. The Group had lost others to these starry temptations. Worse, these victims of the system had lost something of their best selves to it. What followed for Brando was never quite as stupefying as *Desirée,* but it was never near as exhilarating as *Streetcar* either. He next went into *Guys and Dolls,* for example, saying he thought an actor ought to try doing song and dance. It was not his fault that Joseph Mankiewicz, who had directed him in *Julius Caesar,* was no more experienced than he was with musicals. Or that Samuel Goldwyn as usual overproduced, squeezing the spontaneity out of the picture. It was "interesting" to see him in it—and something more than that when he acts more than he sings his big number, "Luck Be a Lady Tonight."

"Interesting." It was the word for everything he did through 1960. He crawled beneath heavy Oriental makeup to play Sakini, interpreter to the American occupation forces on Okinawa and a con man-cum-humanist, in *The Teahouse of the August Moon.* But if the performance was lovely, the role was queasy-patronizing. He crossed over to the other side of the color line for *Sayonara,* in which he plays a young American officer in the occupying army in Japan, giving up marriage to the general's daughter because he has fallen in love with a young Japanese woman. He insisted on playing the role with a southern accent, and the implication that he had come from a racist tradition made his love story the more poignant. For *The Young Lions* he died his hair blond to play the Nazi soldier whose fate is intertwined with those of American GIs in this adaptation of Irwin Shaw's novel. Again, he insisted on a development in the character that had not been in the original material or the early scripts. He wanted to play Christian Diestl as a man slowly coming to awareness of the horrors of the Nazism for which he fights. His invention was dramatically effective; it gave ironic force—even a pacifistic undertone—to his death at the end of the film, which occurs after his cause has become fully disgusting to him. As the decade turned, he was back on home ground, in *The Fugitive Kind,* an adaptation of Tennesee Williams's *Orpheus Descending.* The cast included his kind of performers, particularly Maureen Stapleton and Joanne Woodward; the director was Sidney Lumet, most notable, perhaps, as a director for whom many actors had done some of their best work; the film itself was black-and-white, small in scale. But he didn't like his costar, Anna Magnani, who was miscast opposite him, and his role was wrong for him. His sensitivity—he is, in effect, the Blanche DuBois of this film, a delicate soul set upon, ultimately martyred, by the cruel world—is established at the outset, and so the pleasure of seeing him come to consciousness is denied us and denied the actor as well. Brando has one strong scene at the beginning, a courtroom confessional in which the camera never leaves him, but the picture as a whole is lethargic, lugubrious, and lacking the poetic realism of Williams's best writing, the electricity a director like Kazan could bring to such projects.

All these films might be characterized as upper-routine. They were conscientiously produced, on substantial budgets, often with people who were regarded, at the time, as major figures writing, directing, costarring. All of them at least aspired to make serious, intelligent statements on their various themes. Many of them turned out to be commercially successful. It was certainly no disgrace for Brando to appear in any of them, and as we have observed, he tried very soberly to bring something singular to each of them. Yet, when all is said and done, these pictures were all too typical of the 1950's, which is without question the dullest decade in American film history. They were finally cautious and slow, entirely lacking the energy and eccentricity that marked Hollywood's best (and often its worst, but most entertaining) work in previous periods. They were like great, soft pillows, absorbing the force of Brando's explosive power, muffling the unique tone of his voice. He was in danger of becoming just another movie star—a major one to be sure, but not really different from, say, Kirk Douglas or Burt Lancaster in what he was doing.

As always with movie stars, there was a seepage between his public persona and his screen roles, and around this time one began to detect on the screen glimpses of the star profession's essence—its insecurities, its endless, quiet-bubbling contempt for the people they work for (which includes the audience), and, above all, the nagging, peculiarly American fear that acting may not be suitable work for a grown-up, heterosexual male. ("Why does anybody care about what any movie star has to say? A movie star is nothing important. Freud, Gandhi, Marx. These people are important. But movie acting is just dull, boring, childish work.")

He made a major effort to take large responsibility for his own destiny, to abandon the passive role, which is the lot of most actors, waiting by the phone for their agents to call, and to take on an active, manly role, proposing and disposing about the movies he made. It is clear that he was attempting to do precisely what his older theatrical mentors had always wanted to do and had been implicitly urging their children to do: seize what looked to be a revolutionary or prerevolutionary moment and thereby seize control of (dare one use the phrase?) the means of production. He was actually late in claiming this reward of revised show business practice. Older established movie stars had preceded him by some years in independent production. But he would have his own company, and even before he went into *The*

Fugitive Kind, he put into work the western project that was eventually known as *One-Eyed Jacks.* God alone knows how many concepts were outlined, how many scripts were written, before it went before the cameras. It is known that Stanley Kubrick was, for a time, going to direct it until he and the star had a falling-out and Brando took over. It is also known that his perfectionist ways caused a cost overrun of more than four million dollars (huge for those days) and that the rough cut he delivered to the studio was perhaps four hours long. It was slashed by other hands, and Brando pretty much disavowed the version that went into release in 1961 and failed to return its costs to the studio.

He went directly from disappointment to disaster. That was the remake of *Mutiny on the Bounty.* He initially turned down Clark Gable's old role as Fletcher Christian but then saw a chance to make a statement he valued. He said he would do the picture if the story could continue beyond the mutiny itself and take up the story of the mutineers after they took refuge on Pitcairn's Island, tried to build a new civilization for themselves, and self-destructed in the process. He spoke of an eternal theme to be found in this aspect of the story: "the struggle of black versus white, of the urge to create and the urge to destroy. If man cannot find happiness on an island paradise, where can he find it?" The film began to spin out of control long before it got to this point, with disputes about the humanizing of the Captain Bligh character and the complicating of the Christian character by Brando. Their set, a working replica of the *Bounty,* was late arriving in the South Seas; the weather was bad; writers were appearing and disappearing, unable to make a satisfactory script under forced draft, especially when no one was sure what was wanted in the first place. Carol Reed, the original director, quit, and his replacement, Lewis Milestone, was too old and ill to handle the project. The cost overruns far exceeded those of Brando's previous film, and though the movie grossed well enough when it limped to the box office more than a year late, it probably did not recoup its inflated costs.

The fault was by no means all Brando's, but he took a terrible beating in the press for both these failures (and got mainly uncomprehending critical notices for his *Bounty* performance, too). Paramount had financed *Jacks;* MGM was *Bounty*'s producer, and like all the majors in those days, they were clinging desperately to the old ways of doing business. They did what Hollywood had always done with wayward stars: They decided to punish Brando for his rebellious and costly behavior. They would whip him back into line by means of publicity—negative publicity. Outraged and outrageous anecdotes were fed to pliable newsmen, who were encouraged to write nastily about him in connection with these movies. This much power the studios still had, circa 1961 and 1962. The ugliest and most telling of the hack attacks came in the *Saturday Evening Post,* from a writer specializing in show biz sleaze (he seemed to think Brando was the thespic equivalent of Jimmy Hoffa). All this damaged Brando's reputation with other producers, who saw him as a potential troublemaker, likely to send them overbudget and equally likely to taint their product when it went into release by giving out interviews about how it did not measure up to his standards of purity. Moreover, the public, especially its older segment, which had always been suspicious of Brando, believed what it read. Good work became increasingly difficult for him to find in the years ahead. And financing for his own productions dried up completely; he never again functioned as his own producer.

Yet viewed objectively, both these "controversial" films were, in their ways and for their moment, quite remarkable. *One-Eyed Jacks* was, even in truncated form, obviously an ambitious attempt to reimagine the western form. It is a tale of betrayal and revenge covering many years in which, as in so many of his films, Brando plays a man coming to a higher consciousness of his humanity and his social obligations and enduring terrible punishment in payment for this knowledge (in this case, a vicious public flogging). It is also an assault on middle-class hypocrisy that is occasionally quite funny. And its imagery is both spacious and original (its last half is set along the Pacific shore and the beauty of horses and riders against the surf is breathtaking). *Mutiny* is a less striking film, but Brando's performance may be among the most daring he ever gave. For his Fletcher Christian is anything but a conventionally stalwart hero. He is introduced as an upper-class fop, with a lisping accent and a handkerchief tucked up his sleeve, and the development of this unpromising figure's disgust with the cruelties of nineteenth-century British naval life in general, the erratic sadism of Bligh in particular, imparts a dramatic interest to this film far beyond anything the foursquare Gable had brought to the role.

What Brando was quite consciously doing in these films was to bring the new conception of the film hero—self-aware, self-doubting, even morally flawed—that he had personified in his earlier pictures, which had been more suitably tailored to that effort, over into more conventional kinds of movies, genre films at heart, despite their epic proportions. It was a brave and foolish idea, more daring than any of the other star-producers attempted. The outraged response to his excessive care in the first instance, his excessive meddling in the second, and the commercial and critical failure of both films apparently wearied and embittered him. He would not, in the future, make such protean attempts to assert his artistic will in alien surroundings. His rebelliousness was to turn into public cynicism about acting in general, accompanied by much self-deprecation and increasing difficulty on his sets. These, indeed, were, for the rest of the sixties, much less grand, often actually marginal, than they had formerly been. For his box-office power declined along with his self-confidence.

Or perhaps he was grateful to give up a fight for which he had never had much heart. There is a strong possibility that we misunderstood him. And there is a possibility that he had earlier been misled about himself. He is a shy—and, in later years, even reclusive—man. If, at first, we thought he was of that breed of actors who go onstage because it offers unparalleled opportunities to show off, it is obvious that we were wrong. He appears actually to be of the second type, which is composed of people who are mimics and impersonators, people who like to assert themselves without actually revealing much of their insecure and often unformed selves in public. "Actors have to observe, and I enjoy that part of it," Brando once said. "They have to know how much spit you have in your mouth, and where the weight of your elbows is. I could sit all day in the Optimo Cigar Store telephone booth on 42nd Street and just watch the people pass by." Besides, he said, an actor, if he is working well and truly, has to "upset" himself, to dive down deep within himself and examine the junk and offal buried there, and the supreme effort of will that those explorations required grew increasingly difficult for him. "There comes a time in one's life when you don't want to do it anymore. You know a scene is coming where you'll have to cry or scream and all those things, and it's always bothering you, always eating away at you. . . ."

Here was irony! The man whom everyone expected to lead the heroic modern thespians' expedition to the heart of our twentieth-century darkness, the route to which perforce lay through his own soul, finally had no spirit for the job. If he could have stayed on the surface, achieved his effects technically, could have been, actually, a movie star of the old-fashioned stripe, he would have been happier. That was, he said, "a perfectly reasonable way to make a living. You're not stealing money, and you're entertaining people." But on this point he was speaking more out of envy than out of experience. For the ironic fact is that there is more self-exposure in being Cary Grant or Gary Cooper or any other long-lived star you care to name than there was in most of Brando's roles after *On the Waterfront*. For a star's screen persona must be based on some true aspect of his personality—not all of it, surely, but some part that is authentic and can thus stand the test of repeated examination. And that Brando did not wish to present to the world.

It now begins to seem obvious that from *Waterfront* onward, and always excepting the heroic efforts to establish himself as a new kind of genre hero in *One-Eyed Jacks* and *Mutiny*, he hid out in what amounted to a succession of character leads for almost two decades. To the roles we have already named that required odd makeups or for which he supplied curious accents he now added new eccentricities. He attempted light romantic comedy (*Bedtime Story*), played a double agent with yet another German accent (*The Saboteur: Code Name Morituri*), a glum southern sheriff (*The Chase*), a phony guru (*Candy*), a homosexual shuffling off his repressions, representing, perhaps, his best work in this period (*Reflections in a Golden Eye*), yet another nineteenth-century English officer-aristocrat in a hot tropical spot (*Burn!*).

The last two films were for directors he had reason to respect (John Huston and Gillo Pontecorvo) and he also worked disastrously for another filmmaker he greatly admired, Charles Chaplin (*A Countess from Hong Kong*). But even when the directors were not strong, one could almost always see some shadow of a reason why the actor took these parts. For in almost all his performances there was a teasing moment (or two or three) in which he took your breath away with some bit of acutely observed behavior by which he revealed some simple truth about his character—perhaps about himself—that no conventionally disciplined movie actor would ever have aired. And quite a few of them attempted some political or moral statement in which he full-heartedly believed, however badly the enterprise turned out in the end. Finally, though, he was playing an enigmatically menacing chauffeur in a kidnap drama, an Irish gamekeeper who likes to tie up the governess when his lordship leaves them alone in the great house in a "prequel" to Henry James's *The Turn of the Screw*. And in these pictures he seemed to be flaunting his contempt for his medium and his public and expressing no small amount of self-contempt as well.

He seemed to be trying to hide in plain sight, a purloined letter somehow mixed in with all the special delivery parcels of stardom. And in retrospect the range of the portrait gallery he created is remarkable, larger, bolder, braver than that created by any other movie star one can think of, however misbegotten most of their contents in this period. One ventures the thought that this gallery may seem still more remarkable as time goes on.

But so kindly a judgment was not then available to him. His old supporters felt betrayed. Where were the classic roles they had yearned to see him test himself in? If not those, then where were the deeply serious, unambiguously ambitious new works that would permit his voyage inward—to his soul depths? And ours. His old enemies felt justified. They could claim now that they were the first to see that his promise had been a false one, that he was just another broody hunk of actorish sound and fury, signifying nothing very much. Those who did not think of him as a joke now saw him as a tragic figure. Considering him in 1966, Kael quoted Emerson to the effect that the American artist "must pass for a fool and a churl for a long season." She added: "We used to think that the season meant only youth, before the artist could prove his talent, make his place, achieve something. Now it is clear that for screen artists, youth is, relatively speaking, the short season; the long one is the degradation *after* success."

His response to this was ever-deepening self-contempt. And insecurity. He was now saying that he had spent much of his adult life trying to make up his mind what he should really be doing—as if acting had always been but a way station for him on his way to some higher, or anyway more useful, calling. One thought: Perhaps he really is lost—forever. At which point, more dramatically than anyone in his line of work ever had, he found his way again. And, it seemed, his best self.

Act Three. The year of his redemption and reintegration was 1972. There was *The Godfather,* of course, the culmination of his career as a character actor. His Don Corleone was old and sweet and deadly—cunning in both senses of the word. He deserved the second Oscar he was awarded for the performance, and show biz deserved the fake Indian princess he sent to pick it up for him. In that same year, however, there was also *Last Tango in Paris.* Pauline Kael may now regret announcing that the date it premiered at the New York Film Festival, October 14, 1972, "should become a landmark in movie history comparable to May 29, 1913—the night *Le Sacre du Printemps* was first performed—in music history." Only a decade later *Tango* seems more a curiosity than a precursor to anything very much. But as a date in the history of modern celebrity, why, yes, it has a certain resonance. Bernardo Bertolucci, who both wrote and directed the film, said at the time that he liked to create characters based "on what the actors are in themselves," instead of asking them "to interpret something preexistent." This, after his years in the wilderness, was something Brando needed, and something his reputation needed, too. Time—long past time—to go pearl diving again.

Seeing the movie again, years later, one sees, as one did not amid the hoopla attendant on its initial release, that its sole significant business, the place where its vitality now resides almost exclusively, lies in this opportunity it provided Brando. *Le Sacre du Printemps,* indeed! The thing is the star vehicle to end all star vehicles. Yes, it aspires to something more, to some pure and daring statement about the relationship between man and woman. But no, on that level, its intellectuality is strictly soft-core.

The story has a nameless man and a nameless woman (she is played by Maria Schneider) meet in an apartment both are thinking of renting. Having checked it out, he falls upon her, and she, in the modern manner, accepts him as a quick, brutal fuck. Thereafter they meet for increasingly vivid fornications (the classic porn structure is followed with the domineering male and the submissive female isolated and thus freed from all restraint, which permits escalation in the intensity and daring of their sexual feats). Outside the apartment we see that she is involved with a young filmmaker, who is recording their affair (he will eventually propose marriage) and her biography for a documentary. He wishes to impose the spurious order of art on life. The Brando character's wife, it is revealed, has just committed suicide, and that has summoned both reminiscence and remorse on his part— along with the need for the affectless sanctuary the apartment and the girl afford. Eventually, and banally, there is a role reversal. He proposes a conventional living arrangement to her, just as she decides that she has got all the good she can out of the degradation (in slavery there is freedom, as the cliché goes) he has imposed on her. He follows her to the home she shares with her parents (Father is an army officer, no less), and when he violates that bourgeois sanctuary with his importunate presence, she kills him with her father's revolver.

But all this—whatever it started out to be in Bertolucci's original conception—serves Brando, and only Brando. Maybe originally it was supposed to be a duet, but it plays as an aria, with Schneider (a newcomer, who brought no resonances with her) serving as an accompanist (in a modern film we can tell who the star is not by who has the most lines but by who has to take off the fewest clothes, and she is the most exposed here). Be that as it may, the apartment is an existentialist symbol as well as a pornographic device—a central void in the universe, to be filled in the absence of God (or whatever) as we do these days with sex and autobiography. It is value-free, history-free, future-free, and Paul and Jeanne (as they are finally labeled) furnish it only with a bed, a plain table and chairs, lust, and memory.

The sex, as Norman Mailer pointed out in his memorable essay on the film, is faked—well faked, to be sure, but nevertheless visibly faked—and it is, as a result, in this context, strangely disappointing. As Mailer wrote, "Brando's cock up Schneider's real vagina would have brought the history of the cinema one huge march closer to the ultimate experience it has promised since its inception (which is to embody life)." The reason for our disappointment with this material lies precisely in the contrast between the filmed sex and the filmed talk. There, we feel, no niceties have been allowed to intervene; Brando, in particular, gives the impression that he has been allowed to say anything that comes into his head or anything that came into it during rehearsals and was saved for the takes.

This material is of two distinct characters. The first is pure autobiography, a rehearsal of the character's history from childhood to the present. It is full of snips and snaps and puppy dogs' tails that remind us of things we vaguely seem to remember hearing about the actor as well as oblique references to his film roles—an exquisite blending of private and public history. Here, then, we witness Kowalski-Malloy-Brando arrived at the mid-life crisis, the concluding unscientific post-script, as we were led to think, to the life in which we had taken such an avid interest these two decades, this life we thought we had shared. The authentic air of this dialogue is further reinforced by Brando's behavior throughout. As an actor he had by this time become—notoriously—a motherfucker to handle, a man rendered quickly bored and restless by repetitive rehearsal, by the stock conventions of his trade, yet also hating to appear bald-faced in roles where the public might mistake what it is seeing for his true self and where other actors hide out behind technique and their self-protecting mannerisms. That is why there is so much makeup, so many accents in his history. Here Bertolucci makes capital of Brando's frantic borrowings to escape his own skin. If the actor wants to drop into an English accent or adopt the mannerisms of a bouncy adolescent, he lets him. Brando can mumble his lines or stumble on them; he can strike poses or he can sulk. Best of all, he can indulge his free-associational humor, which leads him inevitably toward the sexual and scatological. And the more he tries not to be Brando, the more he is Brando. For the essence of his art has always derived from the tension between his impulse to truth and his instinct to hide.

And so autobiography and behavior combine to guarantee—or seem to guarantee—the truth of the second major portion of his dialogue, the sexual fantasies, which up to a point his partner must act out for him. And if, whether fantasized or acted out, these disgust or appall, so be it. All right, he seems to say, you wanted the truth about me. Well, here it is, go gag on it. When Brando buggers Schneider's chic, saucy, *cultured* little bourgeois ass, he is buggering all and everything that has bugged him. And when he forces her to explore his own fundament, the while describing his fancy of her copulation with a dying pig, he is saying something about the fate he has reserved for all who have tried to probe him for his secrets these many years. In these moments we are all Blanches to his time-warped Stanley, allowing ourselves to be reamed breathless by his contempt.

Mailer: "The crowd's joy is that a national celebrity is being obscene on screen. To measure the media magnetism of such an act, ask yourself how many hundreds of miles you might drive to hear Richard Nixon speak a line like: 'We're just taking a flying fuck at a rolling doughnut' or 'I went to the University of Congo; studied whale pronging.' Only liberal unregenerates would be so progressive as to say they would not drive a mile. No, one could start mass migrations. . . ."

It is surreal, says Mailer, but he adds, surrealism has become the objective correlative of our time. "A private glimpse of the great becomes the alchemy of the media, the fool's gold of the century of communication. In the age of television we know everything about the great but how they fart—the ass wind is, ergo, our trade wind. It is part of Brando's genius to recognize that the real interest of audiences is not in having him portray sex between a man and a woman, it is rather to be given a glimpse of his kinks. His kinks offer sympathetic vibration to their kinks."

But—and this is a crucial point Mailer did not explore—we do not certainly know that these kinks are really his kinks. For all we actually know, Brando may prefer the missionary position—in the dark with his pajamas on. In 1972, when the lights in the theater went up, the possibility of a splendid duplicity lingered. Let us posit, for the moment, that the scatological is not his bag. Let us propose, instead, that he was speaking in the tongues of metaphor, that Bertolucci had presented him, in this film, with the long-dreamed-of opportunity for apotheosis, and finally, that he intended to use it not for the minor and dubious "bravery" of confirming the gossipists' speculations about private life, that he was not some Shelley Winters naming the names of good and bad lays in her autobiography. We can see, as well, that he was not making, herewith, some simpleminded statement of political belief or social protest. If he wasn't Shelley Winters, he wasn't Jane Fonda either. No, he was finally doing what he was supposed to have been doing: speaking from his depths.

But these were now polluted depths. What was once a pure and authentic spirit—that of an idealistic artist, as he perhaps saw it, certainly an uncorrupted individualist—now carried the poisons of fame in his system. It was this bile that he would spew here, under the not entirely erroneous assumption that we, the audience, were as much responsible for its creation as he was and deserved a sample of its bitter taste. And so what we had was the first (and so far only) performance in which the *fact* of the star's stardom—not just the idea of stardom, which we sometimes get in movies about movies and the theater—was the subject of the starring role. Brando had taken all of it—his conceptions and misconceptions of himself, our conceptions and misconceptions about the same subject—and made a role out of the mess. And we are not talking here about just a few scribbled rewrites on the set, designed to match image and skills more closely to the demand of the writer's blueprint. No, we are talking about an organic symbiosis, something that does not, I think, exist in nature but can perhaps be used as a term of description in the unnatural world of celebrity. Brando, especially toward the end of the film, when he puts on his fallen angel mask, begs for a tragic interpretation of all this, and one feels like conceding it to him in gratitude for the high-grade farce that went before. And our gratitude, as well, for the Bronx cheer (or was it authentically a fart?) he sent in the direction of his critics and the volunteer keepers of his conscience.

Somehow, his old, good instincts had been made to function once again, and he had shown us where the demand for subjectivity, for "truth," unguarded, unshaped by psychological distancing and stylization, is bound to take us in the age of celebrity—that is, toward a confusion between personality and product that can never be art, must inevitably end up in publicity. He had better reason to know this than anyone, for self and statement are inextricably bound together for the performer, with his power to command his own fate being utterly dependent on his fame. In the age of celebrity the only truly heroic act an artist can perform is to protect his vision and his virtue by cloaking them in a modesty that is near to the secretive. And that, as a practical matter, amounts to taking a vow of poverty—especially for actors. Brando's *Last Tango* whirled us to the center of his knowledge. His final act of heroism lay in his despairing acknowledgment not of his "kinks"—that was just sleight of hand—but of the terrible confusions that had brought him low and by which he would then, at least briefly, restore himself.

Briefly indeed. It was as if *The Godfather* and *Last Tango* had exhausted Brando. The epilogue for any myth involving the hero with a thousand faces is always brief. In legend he returns home from his courageous wanderings and at last finds both honor and contentment in the contemplation of the great task successfully accomplished, the admiration of his old hometown. But the actor with a hundred faces lives on in our messed-up world, with a leftover life to kill in a culture that offers no home, no rest, only the cold comfort of empty celebrity. After 1972 there was only silliness and money to occupy Brando—*The Missouri Breaks, Superman, Apocalypse Now, The Formula.*

The disgust with the public, with himself for paying attention to that public, endemic in all performers, especially as they age, was now in full heat. His final disguise was as a fat man too lazy to learn his lines, pasting them on the camera, on his fellow performers' foreheads for the close-ups. After which there was only silence and rumors.

His self-loathing had a scale about it that might, perhaps, be termed heroic. And his end might, perhaps, be termed tragic. But we must also ask if the flaw that brought him down was really in him. His hubris, after all, had only a short season, and his only consistent fault was its opposite—a desire to evade conscription as leader of a cultural revolution, to serve it in some more modest capacity, possibly as a sort of guerrilla or partisan, operating daringly, individually behind the lines. Maybe the flaw lay in the rest of us—in the mentors who tried to impose their alien dream on him, in his 1950's contemporaries, who somehow believed he could, and should, articulate for us our silent generation sensitivities, our longings and outrages and confusions. His accomplishments—fewer than they might have been and always hinting at a larger promise he never fulfilled—assure his place in the history of performance and among the legends of lost. In the end, though, it may be that we will honor him most not for his intermittent accomplishments but for his steadfast refusals, which include, finally and most important, the refusal ever to explain himself coherently.

V
UNITED ARTIST

WOODY ALLEN
THE COHERENT LIFE

*W*oody Allen is the only major American filmmaker who leads a life that is comprehensible to me and, I suspect, to most people who try to engage critically with contemporary movies. By contrast, his peers—if, indeed, he actually has any—all seem to have gone overbudget, emotionally speaking. Their reality, like their real estate, is not something one can comfortably contemplate; their concerns, like their motor vehicles, are too exotic for any response but distant envy. However modest and reassuring they sound in their interviews, the attempt to divine a recognizable humanity always seems to end in either moralism or indulgence. Woody, though, I get—ethically, intellectually, and, to a degree, emotionally—in a direct and sympathetic way.

I don't mean to imply that I have discovered the hidden wound or childhood trauma that, like the revelation flashback in some "psychological" movie of the 1940's, explains the hitherto enigmatic behavior of our hero. It is merely that I can find points of reference—unavailable to me when I try to engage with most other film artists—between his life, my life, and the lives of people well known to me. I know instinctively where he's coming from, and equally instinctively I have some sense of where he's going. I do not feel quite the same way about anyone else in the performing arts or, for that matter, anywhere in our public life.

This sense of intimacy with what he is doing is very basically generational: Woody is just a couple of years younger than I am, and though he was born a Brooklyn Jew and I was born a middle western WASP, those distinctions are of less significance to us, to everyone of our age-group and from our aspiring middle-class social group, than they are

271

to any previous generation. We were the first Americans to be less significantly formed as individuals by religious, ethnic, and geographical factors than we were by mass media, mass education, and (latterly) mass prosperity. No matter where we were born, no matter what creeds and prejudices were pumped into us by our parents in our impressionable years, they were overridden first by powerful, glamorous, and fantastic popular imagery, then by what was, in effect, the first mass marketing of ideas through near-universal higher education. To put the matter concretely, figures like Bogart, Grant, and Astaire got into our heads early and stayed late, to be joined, as we grew a little older, by the likes of Freud, Dostoyevsky, Camus, Orwell, among many others who, as we came of age in the fifties, became both heroes and conversational commonplaces to a larger "audience" than writers and thinkers had ever before gathered in the United States. Living inside this very curious, even mildly dislocating mental landscape is what set us apart from everyone who preceded us.

What sets us apart from everyone who came later is the fact that although the media were a pervasive influence in our lives, they were not yet *all*-pervasive. Television, which reordered the sensory balance and all the other priorities of everyone who came later, appeared when we were adolescents, after our sensibilities were pretty well formed, and anyway, it was not, in its primitive days, the domineering force it was so soon to become. There was still plenty of time for us both to flick out and to pursue our supplementary reading. And there was silence enough to indulge ourselves in all the self-examination we required, which was a great deal.

It was one of our number, Renata Adler, who observed, some two decades ago, that even those of us who did not actually become writers were rather writerly in our values. The primacy of the word—especially as opposed to "mere" imagery—was almost sacred, entirely unquestioned by all of us. We implicitly understood—or were led to understand, more likely—that writing was the only medium subtle and supple enough to have some hope of rendering accurately our newly complicated reality and our responses to it. Moreover, like the professional writer, this generation tended to know at least a little about a lot of things and to pride itself on its eclecticism. (Adler defined our range as stretching from *The Green Hornet* to Joseph Conrad.) This age-group was like the typical writer in other ways, too: We tended to work obsessively, and rather joylessly, while at the same time standing "at a certain humorous remove from our experiences"; to view with irony and skepticism organized religion, organized politics, mass movements, and ideologies of all kinds; to revere individual as opposed to group creativity; to worry endlessly about "selling out," since it was more obvious to us than to our predecessors, and more worrisome to us than our more casually acceptant successors, that in the new age of mass media literary values had, when only slightly corrupted, a market value that was rising all the time; and, for some reason (the new technologies of mass slaughter perhaps?), to think overmuch about mortality. (What is writing, after all, but an attempt to erect a pathetic paper bulwark against death?)

From the start Woody asserted these concerns and values more clearly than any of our contemporaries in the popular arts, and through the years his work has provided an accurate barometer of our shifting interests. All the while he was maintaining a standard of integrity in the conduct of his career that continued to match our youthful ideals even as the rest of us were failing them.

At the very outset of his career, when he was doing stand-up comedy in Greenwich Village nightclubs, he was speaking our language—hilariously. A typical Allen gag in those days might be: "Not only is God dead, but try getting a plumber on weekends." Or, "There is no question that there is an unseen world. The problem is how far is it from midtown and how late is it open?" These jokes seemed to me then, and still seem to me now, perfect little summaries of a generational attitude. They are, to begin with, neatly polished and admirably balanced—obviously worked over by a craftsman's careful hand. More important, though, is the way he interrupts his yearning lurch toward metaphysical speculation with practical considerations. Our generation longed to think big thoughts—what use was all that expensive education if we didn't?—but knew we were supposed to make lives and livings in a hard world—what use was our parents' experience of the Depression and their continuing insistence on the work ethic if we didn't? In any case, one did not dare go too far, become too abstract or too literary. That would have been "pretentious," of all sins the one most abhorrent to us.

Woody worked his other metaphors in the same spirit. Sex was always—famously—on his mind in those days, and his comic persona was built around the awkwardness and frustration of his relationships with women. But his basic joke on this subject was like his basic metaphysical joke. He—we—had all this information, drawn from every level of the culture (from Freud to Kinsey to Pat Boone) at our disposal, but applying it in the real, practical world always turned out to be impossibly difficult. Here was a case where knowledge, far from being power, actually increased one's sense of powerlessness. And anxiety.

Woody's relationship with literature—another great topic in those years—was less openly anxious. The parodies that began appearing in the *New Yorker* in the late sixties, like the movie parodies that always formed a significant part of his collagelike early films, were expert, assured, and gorgeously funny—by far his highest attainments of these years, in my opinion. The range of his subjects (his first collection of pieces, 1971's *Getting Even,* includes send-ups of Albert Speer's memoirs, Kafka scholarship, Dostoyevsky, Hemingway, college catalog writing, Latin American leftists, hard-boiled detective fiction and even a parody of the master parodist S. J. Perelman) bespoke admirable knowledge, and his perfect imitation of many voices implied considerable art. But if parody at this level is sometimes the highest form of flattery and sometimes one of the higher forms of criticism, it is also a signal of ambition repressed. Simultaneously it says, "Look, I can do it," and, "Just kidding, folks." No one was going to accuse him of "pretentiousness." That, as it turned out, would come later.

There are two views of Woody's work in these years. There are simple fans and complicated critics like Pauline Kael who insist that the early comedies are his best. Kael, for instance, has deplored the loss of "vulgar vitality" in the later pictures and has found in them signs of—yes—pretentiousness. Woody is painfully aware of this opinion—hence the fans in *Stardust Memories* who keep telling Sandy Bates, a character who has to be read as Woody's alter ego, they like his "funny" movies best and keep wondering when he's going to go back to making them. In recent years Woody has himself raced out ahead of this disagreeable tide, issuing curt retrospective dismissals of his early pictures more devastating than any his critics have offered—"infantile" is one word he has publicly applied to them.

Everybody is wrong, of course. There was lovely and highly original work in the early movies. (In particular I admire his assaults on the revolutionary political illusions of middle-class youth in the sixties, the nationalist delusions of their parents, and, the very thing Woody decries, the free-narrative form of these movies, which was not unlike the free-associational form of his stand-up routines—or, if you want to find a tradition for it, the structure of a pre-MGM Marx Brothers movie or a good W. C. Fields comedy.) There was, without question, more work of quality to follow, work that was—is—thematically consistent with the first films but at its best is more fully developed and sustained, with access to an expanded tonal range. The problem lies in the application of inappropriate standards to Woody's achievements by both parties. His critics do not seem to understand the imperatives driving him; Woody is entirely too unforgiving in applying them to his work.

When *Hannah and Her Sisters* appeared in 1986, Vincent Canby stated very simply something that had needed saying for some time: "There's nobody else in American film who comes anywhere near him in originality and interest." To that thought he appended another: "One has to go back to Chaplin and Buster Keaton, people who were totally responsible for their own movies, to find anyone comparable to him."

It is an equally accurate observation, but it does not go quite far enough in its search for comparisons. It seems to me the truly relevant analogies are to be found not in film at all but in literature. Someone like John Updike, who approximates Woody in age, steady productivity, and consistency of quality, comes to mind. He is not exactly Robert Ludlum or Danielle Steel when it comes to the best-seller charts. But viewed narrowly, purely commercially, he is a viable proposition. His books make the occasional brief appearance on the charts and sell to the reprinters and book clubs. Doubtless he earns out his advances. He is thus free to go about his exemplary business quietly, not forced to submit an outline or a first draft of a project before getting financing, to show his work to nervous executives as it proceeds, or to perform prodigies of publicity in order to help it along in the marketplace when it is finished.

This is not yet completely remarkable in the literary world, though we are obviously living in a time when large numbers of American writers have decided to conduct their literary lives under show biz rules. But for someone to use this model as a guide to managing a career in the movies, where just about everyone really is Danielle Steel (no matter what directors claim about the singularity of their "auteurship"), that is astonishing. And since it is virtually without precedent in American moviemaking, it represents, in and of itself, a brilliant act of creative and moral imagination.

From the start Woody naturally wanted what all moviemakers want: as much creative autonomy as he could obtain from an industrialized and bureaucratized system. This he quite quickly got and has tenaciously defended. But he seemed to understand at an equally early point that some of the worst threats to artistic freedom in this field arise from within the artist himself. The unchecked desire to assert one's ego by making high-budget, high-risk movies is one of them since there is nothing like a cost overrun or a box-office failure with one of these enterprises to make ever-anxious executives insist on reasserting control over a director next time out. Unchecked greed is another. If you measure your achievements by the purely monetary aspects of your deals or by the size of the mortgage on your Bel Air acreage, you will sooner or later have to give up something to service these debts. The price may not be final cut—not at first anyway—but it may be a string of pictures with higher and higher Roman numerals trailing their titles. Reformist zeal is perhaps the most dangerous of all the success's temptations. Sometimes good and sober people attempt to use the astonishing rewards one or two hugely profitable movies can bring to incorporate—quite literally—idealistic alternatives to the usual Hollywood methods of doing business and a few years later find themselves, like Francis Coppola, auctioning off the company's furniture. Finally, though, the temptation to passivity may be more dangerous than the call to activism: increasing isolation in one or more far-flung retreats; longer and longer silences between pictures; the acquisition of legendary status, with the ego satisfied by offering the hungering public only a few teasing glimpses on well-controlled occasions. This is particularly appealing to performer-directors for obvious reasons.

These are, so far as I can see, the principal modes of success available to individuals whose imaginations are limited to the models offered by the motion picture business itself. None of them is strikingly attractive, particularly when they are contrasted with the life and career Woody has constructed by looking beyond the conventions of his profession for a model.

He has actually achieved the most nearly perfect autonomy of anyone making movies in America today. So long as his budget remains under a certain figure (said to be in the ten-million-dollar range), he has to submit no script or outline to Orion Pictures in order to go to work, to show nothing he has made to its executives before he wants to, to make no changes they think might be helpful when he does finally present them with his finished work. On the other hand, his schedules and budgets permit him time to reshoot entire sequences if he determines that something is not working properly once he has assembled his rough cut. This is a form of control over his finished work that no other director I know of has. And again, the model is literary; when he reshoots, he is in the position of a writer calmly revising his first draft before sending it off to his publisher, not that of the typical director desperately trying to oblige his second thoughts (and, often enough, his employers' whims), yet confined to his editing room, frantically searching his trims and outtakes, looking for a miracle, because no one would think to give him the money to do the job properly by retakes.

Woody's power over the fate of his work extends even beyond this remarkable point. He also has near-total control over the advertising, promotion, and marketing of his movies, including the right to keep them off television unless they are shown uncut and uninterrupted by commercials. Not only is this a better deal than any other filmmaker has, but it is actually—allowing for a difference in the marketing issues that confront him—a better deal than all but a few highly regarded novelists have with their publishers.

These long-standing arrangements have other, less obvious advantages that no other filmmaker knows, but which at least a few favored writers enjoy (and all the rest of us envy). The one I would judge to be most important to Woody is the ability to move straight on from one film to the next, without having to waste months (or even years) selling his next project and setting up the deal for it. He is a man who must keep working uninterruptedly and for whom that dread concern of younger generations—"burnout"—is meaningless. This ability to stay more or less steadily at work is also permitting him to do what the studio contract did for directors in the 1930's and 1940's, when they were required to make two or three pictures a year and what the Grub Street publishing contracts of the nineteenth century forced writers to do, which is to build up a large body of work. If you have the constitution to stay this rigorous course, it has advantages often unremarked. For one thing it relieves the anxious pressure that can build up around a single work that requires years to complete and that must, as a result, bear a disproportionate share of the artist's hopes for recognition and economic reward. At the same time it frees him from the temptation to go for the momentary sensation, in our publicity-mad world perhaps the worst trap of them all.

As a result of his singular habits of work Woody has in two decades made eighteen films for which he can claim sole authorship, far more than any other American director has produced in that period. They constitute a body of work that is already substantial enough to make an impress on posterity by weight alone. More important, this body of work is coherent, undistorted by any discernible compromises, commercial or otherwise, and it is one in which one can clearly trace a recognizable sensibility growing, changing, retreating, rallying, making no mistakes that are unforgivable, achieving no triumphs that appear to be merely lucky.

Another way of putting this point is: The typical American moviemaker is the prisoner of commercially dictated cycles; either he fits into what the industry judges for the moment to be the prevailing box-office trends or he doesn't work or works in veins unsuited to him. Woody, by contrast, works within cycles of his own creation. As a result, he is the only currently active American filmmaker whose work is roughly divisible into chronological "periods," marking off coherent stages of development in his interests and his talent, and he is the only one whose films can also be thematically grouped. In this sense, again, the logical comparison inevitably must be to writers patiently working through (and circling back on) their obsessions.

All this being so, why does Woody compete with his critics in saying terrible things about his accomplishments? For he not only decries the purely comic early movies but excoriates himself for his subsequent failures to make a "great" film, by which he means something on the order of *Bicycle Thief* or *Grand Illusion*. That's partly generational, too. We were taught—to borrow the minatory phrases of childhood—not to rest on our laurels or to toot our own horns. And—to borrow the word Woody once thought of using as the title for *Annie Hall*—that anhedonia, the inability to relax and enjoy ourselves, is a destiny not entirely to be deplored.

But there is something more individual at work here as well. Woody's intelligence is, in large measure, a critical and reactive one, as his predilections for parody and for social commentary indicate. It is not unusual for minds of that turn to regard their own workings as somehow inferior to those that function in a more "purely" creative fashion. Perhaps Woody's denigration of comedy as somehow less worthy of respect than more self-evidently serious work encompasses this feeling.

It is also possible that his excesses of modesty may have some roots in autodidacticism. People who are largely self-educated, as Woody is, tend to impute to formally trained thinkers and creators a consciousness in designing their effects and a moral rigor in the conduct of their professions that are not entirely realistic. It is dubious, for example, that Da Sica or Renoir believed before the fact or during production that either of the films Woody cites were going to turn out to be exemplary works. The process of creation is at once too all-absorbing and too harum-scarum to permit more than a passing hope in that direction. But since Woody reveres the outcome of their efforts and, given his preoccupation with the subject, must envy the immortality they appear to have achieved through these universally admired films, he is obliged to think that if only he works a little harder, takes himself a little more seriously, he can emulate them.

Or it may simply be that Woody is suspicious of the facility with which comic ideas occur to him. He has testified in many interviews about the ease with which he writes humor or can improvise a joke or a piece of business in order to solve a problem when he is shooting. Strange—the belief that hard work is necessarily an earnest of high intent, that inspiration compares unfavorably to perspiration in its contributions to the creative process. But characteristic, certainly, of our joyless generation. Sometimes, when he is confronting the higher reaches of our cultural heritage, Woody reminds me of a bedazzled graduate student who, because he can deduce high purpose in a major work, believes it unquestionably must have arrived there through a painfully conscious inductive process on the part of the auteur.

Still, if this represents a flaw in Woody's perception of reality, it is on the whole an endearing one—better, certainly, than the rampant egotism and megalomania more characteristic of successful movie people. Of all current moviemakers, he is the one perhaps most entitled to the proprietary "A Film by ..." credit, which, of course, he never takes. Moreover, though he occasionally speaks out on issues that directly concern him, like the colorization of old black-and-white movies for television and the creative rights of directors, and in 1988 surprised everyone with a statement criticizing Israel on its treatment of the Palestinian settlers, he is admirably reserved with his opinions on most public matters.

Indeed, this avoidance of public forums, his refusal to trade on his fame, is an important source of that comprehensibility that I spoke of at the outset of this essay as well as of the coherence with which his vision has developed through the years. On several occasions he has refused to borrow the good opinion of others to enhance his own fortunes by vetoing ads for his films quoting the reviewers. And his explanation for not attending the Academy Awards ceremonies when he has been nominated for Oscars has always struck me as definitive. If you are willing to accept the praise of others—by which he means the Hollywood whose life-styles and mind-sets he has rejected—then you have to be equally willing to accept their criticism. In short, the reserve and integrity with which Woody conducts his public life are to my mind exemplary and, these days, virtually without parallel.

I am speaking here with a certain familiarity. For by chance, for something like a quarter of a century, we kept running into each other as we made our professional rounds in New York. The first time I saw him was when I was working as a book reviewer on a Sunday afternoon culture klatsch on television and he appeared as a guest doing what I recall as a rather dim monologue worked up for an occasion I can no longer remember (was it possibly Mother's Day?). A little later I went to the Bitter End in the Village to hear some folksinger friends and discovered him on the bill. There was nothing dim about him here. His singularity was suddenly, and brilliantly, apparent; he was the first comedian I had ever heard who drew for his material on the social, sexual, and intellectual insecurities that I—or any contemporary of his—could recognize as common property. It was not only that we had been shaped by the same childhood trash but that we had earnestly pursued the same reading lists and, so it seemed, the same women. Here, it seemed, was someone worth reckoning with.

Thereafter our careers and lives kept touching. I became a movie reviewer around the same time he became a moviemaker, so inevitably I wrote about his work—generally enthusiastically. In 1973 *The New York Times Magazine* asked me to write what turned out to be a highly subjective piece about his appeal to people of my age, and I did it mainly by quotation from his published writing and without interviewing him, which I gathered he appreciated. In that same year he came to a party for a television series I did on movie directors of the 1930's and 1940's, and I enjoyed introducing him to Howard Hawks, Raoul Walsh, and Bill Wellman, whose professional respect for him seemed to startle Woody. I think he thought these older men could not possibly

279

have noticed what he was doing, since this was in the early seventies, when he was still more cult figure than celebrity.

I continued to encounter him casually as the years wore on. For a long time we lived in the same neighborhood, so I would see him on the street from time to time. Or at a movie screening. Or emerging from the old Regency Theater, which was the best film revival house in New York. Or, for a time, at New York Knicks basketball games. Once he spotted me in the audience at Michael's Pub, where the Dixieland jazz band in which he plays clarinet performs every Monday, and surprised me by joining my table at the break, even though there were strangers present, one of whom became embarrassingly unhinged in Woody's presence. In 1979 I wrote the *Time* cover story on *Manhattan,* and we talked a little bit about the film. (Again I did not interview him in the formal sense; by this time it seemed to me something of an intrusion on our agreeably distanced acquaintance.) On New Year's Eve of that year, when he gave his famous party welcoming the new decade, I was among the several hundred New Yorkers he invited to the only thoroughly pleasant function of that size I have ever attended.

We did not become friends as a result of these glancing contacts, but there was something heartening in the immutability Woody demonstrated over the years. When, for example, my television series had been broadcast, Woody dropped me a note in which he said that he had liked the show on King Vidor best. It made sense to me: Of all my subjects, King was the most self-consciously intellectual and forthrightly idealistic, and he was the one who, like Woody, had taken the largest risks in addressing subjects that were not self-evidently popular. Subsequently, when we have discussed movies, I never heard Woody praise the work of any filmmaker who did not demonstrate those qualities. Indeed, no matter what we happened to talk about, his manner was always the same: sober; thoughtful; earnestly intent on what others had to say. He is a very composed man, as far away in manner from his nervously stammering, desperately articulate screen character as it is possible to get. Over the years I have never heard him say anything hilarious in private conversation. Perceptive, yes. Intelligent, yes. But funny, no.

In his habitual attire—a plaid sport shirt, corduroy or chino slacks, sneakers, perhaps a large, disguising hat, and a fatigue jacket or windbreaker if you happened to encounter in the street—going about his habitual rounds, seeing his handful of very close friends of very long standing, eating in the few restaurants where he feels comfortable, he is the picture of stability. And of course, it is well known that he has been involved since the start of his career with the same firm of manager-producers, has made his films for distribution by the same team, following them from one company to another when their fortunes shifted. It is true that he has been lengthily involved with several women; but several over a lengthening lifetime is no longer a sign of instability, and now at last he and Mia Farrow, whose gift as an actress has flourished in the stable environment his stock company of players provides, have had a son. To put the matter simply, he dresses, eats, works, lives in a manner enigmatic to show folks and striven for by writers who know that the key to productivity is a well-regulated life. Another way of saying that is that he seems to conceive of himself as a man whose job is anonymously to observe his chosen landscape, not to turn it into a stage for a celebrity drama.

What I particularly appreciated was the fact that he accepted me as a natural part of that landscape, too. I am still a movie reviewer, and there is inevitably a constraint in such contacts as I have had with the people whose work I write about. Some of them are falsely flattering. Most are falsely polite. Almost all are in conflict: They want my good opinion and dislike themselves for wanting it. Everyone is ill at ease. Including me.

But not when I'm talking to Woody. I particularly recall one occasion when having heard that I had moved to Los Angeles, he expressed delight at seeing me and hearing that my removal there had been merely temporary. He made me feel that any defection from the city-scape as he is accustomed to it, even from its periphery, diminishes him. The implication of his attitude then, and on other occasions, was that critics are not just to be tolerated but are perhaps even to be treasured for their contributions to the play of ideas and opinions, that general sense of intellectual stimulation and opportunity that is the main reason a sensible person goes on living in inconvenient late-twentieth-century Manhattan. To put it mildly, this is not an attitude one finds very often in show business, which basically defines the reviewer as nothing more than an omnipresent threat to everyone's profit participation.

In any event, I was not the only representative of my trade present at that New Year's party. It seemed to me that the standard he applied to us in issuing invitations was the same that he applies in granting interviews: The colleagues I saw there were not the ones who had universally endorsed his work but those who had attempted to com-prehend it—and movies in general—seriously. The people from other professions I recognized there were not necessarily great stars or mem-bers of the social elite; they were instead people who pursued their work with care as well as flair, a microcosmic representation of the urban ideal sensibly defined.

Manifestly Woody has been working on various aspects of this def-inition since 1977, when *Annie Hall* offered its twin portraits of the old Heavenly City (New York, nervously resisting decline) and the emergent one (Los Angeles, smugly demonstrating that it will never have anything to decline from). Almost all the films since then have been to greater or lesser degree occupied with urban imagery—romantic (*Manhattan*), malevolent (*Stardust Memories*), and somewhere in between (*Broadway Danny Rose* and *Hannah and Her Sisters*). I would argue, in fact, that the three movies I regard as Woody's best—*Zelig, The Purple Rose of Cairo,* and *Radio Days,* which are among the most delicate and imaginative fantasies ever created by an American moviemaker—are not at all the exercises in false or irrelevant nostalgia that some people took them to be. Each is, in different ways, an evocation of some aspect of the great dream of urbanity that New York's image (and its imagery, diffused through popular culture) sustained for all of us up until the most recent historical moment. It seems to me that if one had to name a single element that informs in equal measure the conduct of his life and the content of his art, it is the desire to keep alive this turn-of-the-century notion that the modern city, then coming into full flower, might represent a new and higher form of civilization.

That city, of course, was meant to have been—and for a time came close to being—a marvel of convenience, freeing one's time and mind for the play of ideas and of wit. It was as well the site for high-technological manifestations, like the early skyscrapers, with their inspiring aesthetic dimension that, in the past, awakened no moral qualms. It was also meant to have been—and for a time was—a marvel of cosmopolitanism. It was a place where all the arts and professions could freely mingle and cross-pollinate, where an elite of the talented and the ambitious could rise unencumbered by the pettiness and provinciality of rural and small-town life. And where, as a result, unlikely romance could flourish and the possibilities of bestartlement and bedazzlement were everyday hopes. The knowledge that one acquires strolling about such a city, Henri Bergson once observed, is akin to the knowledge one acquires intuitively, rather than through conscious study. He implied, as well, that knowledge of the former kind was the higher kind and that anything that encourages it at the expense of the purely rational is to be treasured.

I had happened across that bit from the great modernist philosopher just before I saw Woody a month or so after *Hannah and Her Sisters* opened in 1986 and mentioned it to him. He agreed with it happily. "I reach for the urbanity of the city," he said. "I've always walked the streets. In every crisis of my life, the way I've responded is that I immediately put on my coat and walk the streets endlessly. There are places that are meaningful to me because they were part of one of these crises—a park bench, maybe, or a coffee shop where I stopped for a piece of pie and coffee."

This encounter with Woody was, for a change, not accidental. I had sought him out for the formal interview to which I had never before wanted to subject either of us. (Gentlemen of our age have, by recently fashionable definition, "an intimacy problem," for except in a very few carefully chosen instances, our favorite distance from most people is, as it were, at some distance. And more power to us!) I feared, as well, a betrayal of another, related principle. I believe that the direct, seemingly objective question is the bluntest possible instrument for investigating the mysteries of creation. The only way to get at a work of art is indirectly, by examining your own responses to it. But ... I hadn't talked with Woody in a while. ... I had convinced myself that I could conduct our meeting more as a casual chat than as an interrogation (my editors in far-off London—I was supposed to be writing a profile for one of the Sundays—had indicated they would be satisfied with just enough "quotes" to prove I had fulfilled the pro forma requirements of celebrity journalism, the face-to-face encounter). ... Besides, to adapt one of Woody's most famous punch lines, "we needed the eggs."

Thus it was that on a blustery Saturday afternoon in March I reported to Woody's apartment, a penthouse atop a fine old building on Fifth Avenue. The spectacular views from its terrace, across Central Park to the West Side, he shared with audiences in the opening montage of *Manhattan*. The interior contains good but not overwhelming art of this century and clean-lined American antique furniture. The living room coffee table, across which we talk, is piled high with books, and there are perhaps a hundred more stacked underneath it. Woody's life may not be a riot of material self-indulgence, but he has obviously been rewarded—justly so—for his unrelenting work.

We spent some time mourning the demise of the old Trans-Lux movie theater at Eighty-fifth and Madison and the marvelous luncheonette that abutted it. Both had been built in the thirties. The theater had incised murals depicting archetypal newsreel scenes, for it had originally been designed to show those and other short subjects on hourlong programs; the restaurant had featured Formica-topped tables and Leatherette banquettes which commanded huge windows from which you could comfortably observe the ever-changing life of the street outside. From one of those booths I once saw Jackie Kennedy round on a paparazzo who had been hounding her and slug him with her pocketbook. "One day I stood there," Woody said. "The buildings were gone. The lot was completely empty, and the sun shining down on it made it seem even more desolate. And I kept thinking how I used to sit there in the dark, with an entire exotic world engulfing me. Life up there on the screen was so vivid and so real. You couldn't believe that one day it wouldn't exist." He paused for a moment. "It's occurred to me that I'm in on the tail end of something. That someday they're going to invent a wonderful high-resolution television screen and kids are going to grow up without having the experience of going to a well-appointed theater, that they won't know what it's like to go to a *movie*."

I think that we have already reached something very close to that point. The abandonment of the cities by the middle class has, of course, been a major demographic trend in postwar America, but culturally the suburban population has perhaps reached critical mass only in the last decade or so. At the same time, and in part because of this group's desertion of the metropolitan core, the city has become a much more menacing place in fact and—especially—in fantasy. Movies set there now mostly cater to the idea that it is typically the scene of rapacious terror, not the setting for moments of high romantic grace. As our vision of the city has shrunk, so has the context in which the movies project it. The images we see on the tiny screens in the tiny theaters in a shopping mall multiplex affect us more like television images than like old-fashioned movie images. Psychologically the experience of seeing any movie, but especially one of the rare ones that seek to evoke the romantically generous spirit and scale of former times, in one of these cramped and purely functional rooms is a diminishing one.

Aside from his regret over the passing of the gracious and civilized venues in which movies were formerly seen, and aside from some impersonal and generalized comments he has made to interviewers about American popular culture's becoming "a kind of junk food," Woody seems to have arrived at a calm acceptance of the fact that in the United States his work, except when a lucky accident strikes, is doomed to elitist status. The issues he takes up, he said to me, are in effect luxuries. "If you don't have enough to eat, that cancels everything out, or if you're worrying about a farm foreclosure. It's only after you've got things like that taken care of that the others can come to the others—like thinking about what it means to get old or die." As for the young mass movie audience, he shrugs. They know, standing outside a theater where one of his pictures is playing, that what's being offered "is not a quick pop at *Porky's*." They are not, as he put it, "cross-referencing," meaning their pleasure is not in tracing themes and patterns and overall developments. In his work. In anybody's. Shrug. "They want their car chases and shoot-outs and naked girls."

No arguing with that. But the sociology of moviegoing as it has developed over the past two or three decades has had interesting and complex effects on the composition of Woody's audience. To put the matter simply, the prime customers for the majority of his movies are now regularly drawn from only a very narrow band of his fellow countrymen. The larger number of his loyalists are Europeans. It is only rarely—say, every fourth or fifth picture—that he achieves substantial financial success at home as well as abroad. It is, indeed, the coincidence of one of these rare domestic hits with the expectation that it will perform up to recent expectations in Europe that has caused my London employers to order up this piece.

There is a note of ironized wonder in Woody's voice as he announces that *Hannah and Her Sisters* "is performing just like a regular picture" at the North American box office, by which he means its grosses are living up to general industry standards for a well-received film released by a major organization rather than down to Woody's customary expectations (eventually *Hannah* will gross around forty million dollars in the United States and Canada and more than fulfill everyone's high hopes for it in the foreign and ancillary markets). Later he will tell another interviewer that this was all a terrible mistake, that the picture's popularity was a result of its coming out "more up and optimistic than I had intended," and that this optimism occurred "in the sections I failed."

One does wonder sometimes: Does he have to see every success as evidence of moral failure? How far can you go with anhedonia? He really ought to be able to relax, for surely he understands that commercial hits are nowadays rare enough for him so that no one could possibly accuse him of "selling out" when he has one. He might even look at the discomfort they cause him as the price he must necessarily pay to keep working. Or it may be that he has reached a point where strong domestic grosses represent more threat than promise to him. After all, it is not difficult to analyze the elements that are common to all of Woody's late American successes—his presence playing some not-too-radical variant on his established screen character in a contemporary romance—and to repeat them. Europe, on the other hand, is nowhere near as narrow in its demands. It respects and rewards him, it seems, for his total artistic personality, not merely his on-screen one, and since, as he told me, his foreign receipts have grown to the point where they assure him of his artistic independence, he may feel it best to avoid the temptations his home market presents. In any case, for a man of his temperament the presence of an ocean between himself and his most enthusiastic supporters must be comforting. At that distance there is no danger of their intruding on his privacy or turning his head.

At one level the slow, somewhat erratic, but finally undeniable breaking up of his American audience is mysterious and disturbing. In our mythology things are not supposed to work out that way. An artist whose work—whatever its occasional flaws—essentially grows richer and deeper is supposed to find his audience growing as the years go on: Melville's career is really the American anomaly, not the American paradigm. The problem, of course, is that Woody is an artist working in a popular medium, and success there is typically dependent on repetition, not innovation. Or if there is innovation, it must be very subtle—variations on a well-established theme, not a rapid succession of self-evidently new ones. In a relatively brief film career—only two decades as a completely independent creator—Woody has already passed through five distinct phases.

The first, of course, encompassed the "funny" movies. The comic persona Woody established in his twenties, in the clubs, on records and TV, and, as he turned thirty, with his work on and in two movies he (correctly) deplored, *What's New, Pussycat?* and *Casino Royale.* This character he developed to magnificent fullness in the first movies he cowrote (with Mickey Rose), directed, and starred in (*Take the Money and Run* in 1969 and *Bananas* in 1971). There were fairly easy sells to a profitable public. I was hardly his only contemporary to hear my own inner voice issuing from his lips. No one cared if these movies were narratively thin and patchy. Indeed, that may have helped them; they played like monologues with a few simple production values added. But not so many that they distracted from the pleasure of renewing our one-on-one relationship with his familiar, indeed beloved creation—coward, ambitious (but failure-prone) womanizer, and Freud/death/God-haunted Hamlet manqué. His adaptation of his own Broadway success, *Play It Again, Sam,* directed by Herbert Ross, but featuring Woody as a sexually inept film scholar receiving advice for the lovelorn from Humphrey Bogart's shade, and *Everything You Always Wanted to Know About Sex,* more a response to than an adaptation of a best-selling book of sexual advice, both in 1972, brought this phase of his career to a climax.

Both before and since *Play It Again, Sam* Woody has permitted his characters fantasy lives which he made visible on the screen, often as movie parodies. But not until much later, in *The Purple Rose of Cairo,* did one of his narratives so basically depend on the relationship between a character and a figment of, in the latter case, *her* imagination. This film therefore represented a significant development for him. *Everything You Always Wanted to Know About Sex* represented either a purification of what he had been doing or a regression all the way back to the point where his comedy had no narrative obligations whatsoever. It all depends on how you evaluate the film, which is simply an anthology of sketches, most of which featured Woody dealing with various sexual contretemps, all of which parodied some movie form. The latter varied wildly in quality from piece to piece, but some of them (like an Antonioni parody and another in which Gene Wilder, playing a veterinarian, falls hopelessly in love with a sheep) were very sharp and more lengthily sustained than the hit-and-run bits of the previous pictures. In any case, both pictures were substantial commercial hits, and a less conscientious or ambitious individual might have viewed them as marking off the parameters of his career, the boundaries behind which he could safely and profitably work.

But now, only four years after directing his first movie, Woody entered a new phase—anyway a demiphase—with *Sleeper* (1973) and *Love and Death* (1975), both written without a collaborator. The former projected his screen character forward into an Orwellian future while permitting him to pay tribute (these were true *homages,* not parodies) to the tradition of silent-screen clowning (he was often a Harold Lloyd figure in Buster Keaton situations). In the latter he reeled backward in time to Napoleonic Russia. It seems to me his anachronistic gags work less comfortably in the past than they do in the future, and it seems, too, that there was more of a "Jewish" tinge to them here than there had been in his other films. Still, he confronted the deadly lunacies of nationalism and ideology more firmly than he had before, and he stopped contemplating mortality in order to envision it on film: He put his own character to death at the end, in an artfully antic fashion. I think *Sleeper* is Woody's most perfectly realized pure comedy; *Love and Death* is somewhat more problematical. But no matter, really. Both represent great leaps forward narratively and in sophistication of film technique. These are movies in the full sense of the word. There is scope to the action and a range of visual humor that begins to match the undiminished play of his verbal gags.

But the films were not wildly successful at the box office. Maybe the displacement of Woody's character into other times and places bothered his fans without appealing to strangers. Maybe they felt the earlier pictures, which certainly contained more—and more obvious —jokes per linear foot of film than these did gave them more for their money. Maybe they felt—correctly—that Woody was trying to slip away from that old one-on-one relationship with them, to speak to them less directly, through the ventriloquisms of art. Maybe in these first signs of Woody's maturation they saw the beginnings of their own and were not happy to receive the information. Whatever. But around this time the movie business, shrewdly reading economic signs, abandoned all hope of an Allen blockbuster. His pictures played well only in the most sophisticated urban centers, and they had a top limit economically, it was said, of around twenty million dollars in domestic grosses. Since foreign receipts were in those days negligible, that meant he had to cut thin to win.

This phase was brief and transitional. The next one was also brief but unquestionably major. *Annie Hall* (1977) and *Manhattan* (1979) —with the austerely mannered *Interiors* between, a necessary film for Woody to make, but an impossible one for the rest of us to take to heart—were written with Marshall Brickman, and they reimagined Woody's comic persona while reinserting it back into contemporary life. Now Alvy Singer and Isaac Davis (Woody's fictional names in these movies), despite their self-doubts, were much more confident sexually and professionally than they had ever been before and more aggressive verbally in the defense of their emotional turf. The issues before them were the issues before all of Woody's contemporaries as they entered their forties: accepting and sustaining success in their work, sustaining and accepting losses in their personal lives (both figures are divorced), and maintaining the nerve and energy to transcend both, a process which in the first film involves coming to terms with the past—all those surreal flashbacks to Alvy's childhood—and in the second, coming to terms with the future's very ambiguously presented possibilities—Isaac quitting his job to write, the relationship he forms with a very young girl.

Commercially *Annie Hall,* helped first by the good nature with which it took up an issue then much on everyone's mind, the relationship between a "new" man and "new" woman (though as Woody was at pains to show, it was more styles of self-presentation than substance that were new in them), and then by its Academy Awards, broke the recently proclaimed limits on the rewards Woody could expect at the box office. *Manhattan,* which is a much darker and more ambitious film, did all right but did not, as they say in the trade, "break out" domestically.

Yet it, more than its predecessor, for all the affection and awards it gathered to it, is the turning point in Woody's career. For one thing *Manhattan* was the last movie until *Hannah and Her Sisters* in which the character Woody played was still clearly linked to his original comic persona. In the films he appeared in between them—all of which, not incidentally, were commercial failures in the United States—he was never quite himself. That is to say, he was never quite the familiar fiction people had come to believe was himself. More important, setting aside *Interiors,* the first of his films in which he did not appear at all, this was Woody's first attempt to show the character he played engaging in a whole set of relationships instead of just a single romantic one. As a result, *Manhattan* becomes a sort of group portrait of the class that sets the city's tone, its relentlessly articulate media-oriented intellectuals.

In this movie everyone, not just the Woody figure, is hugely verbal. And much more dangerous than any cast of characters he previously assembled. Their chat is brittle, often contemptuous of people, ideas, emotions we know Woody values, and the laughter they evoke is, for the first time in his work, double-edged. Eventually he means us to see these people, including his own character, as shallow and treacherous, betrayers of his ideal of urban civility.

There is something else about them that is new in his work. They all are engaged in quite desperate efforts to find sexual fulfillment, and whatever jokes are strewn along their path, there is ultimately nothing funny about these pursuits. Isaac himself takes up with an adolescent girl, Tracy (Mariel Hemingway), whose innocent joy in their very straight and straightforward relationship is meant to serve as a contrast with everyone else's complexities. Isaac's former wife embraces lesbianism and writes a tell-all book about their marriage. His mistress, Mary (Diane Keaton), is a dark Annie Hall, hiding her insecurities, and a rather unpleasant critical spirit, beneath a dizzy and falsely naive surface. Ultimately she will betray Isaac with his best friend, a scholar who cannot finish his magnum opus.

These are not—shall we say?—inherently funny (or romantic) folks. If we have seen their like before in a Woody Allen movie, it was in *Interiors*. But they are both more entertainingly and, I think, more intricately and ambiguously studied here. They all are people knowingly in pursuit of inappropriate and ultimately self-destructive loves yet unable to stop themselves. This "victimization by one's own emotions" is particularly a vice of the urban middle and upper classes, Woody thinks. "I know that passion, I see it all the time—the unfathomableness of desire," he said to me, the subject having arisen because *Hannah and Her Sisters* so forcefully reverts to this theme seven years later. "The smartest men and women are trapped by it. They think they can control situations like this, but they can't."

Why this so fascinates him it is impossible to say—even famous people have secret lives, real or imaginary—but Woody quite openly identifies this subject as his major preoccupation, the one he believes he will never escape. "You go to see a Bergman film, and you know you will be dealing with God's silence. Whenever you see a Scorsese film, you know there is going to be a sociopath in it. With me, it's this thing. It's there over and over again. You can't help it—you need to deal with it in order to live." The switch into the objectifying second person is too late; it cannot disguise the passion of his concern with passion's victims.

He cooled it more artfully in the film itself, by locating these tormented souls against an idealized background, the city itself revisioned through Gordon Willis's ravishing black-and-white cinematography. It deliberately recalls 1930's Hollywood's vision of New York as the capital of a more genial romantic sophistication than these people will ever know, and the score, entirely adapted from Gershwin, reinforces this point. The contrast between these aspiring spires, cool and poised, and these obsessed people, trying hard to match their environment, but steaming and frantic inwardly, is one of the great visual conceits of recent American film. More than that, this contrast wordlessly carries the moral of the picture: This is what we are capable of; this is what we are. At the time *Manhattan*'s "photography" was widely commented upon for its novelty and its nostalgic resonance—an odd, indeed contradictory coupling—but very few caught its full implications for the design of the film. Fewer still saw that the simplicity and originality of his imagery were an annunciation of Woody's arrival, after a decade of steadily growing, mostly unremarked, felicity with his camera and in the editing room, at complete mastery of the movie medium. (The typical movie critic may perhaps be characterized as a man or woman of modest literary bent who is incapable of comparable development. Most start out viewing all movies as literary constructs, matters of plot, dialogue, and characters they either "like" or "dislike" and never learn to respond to them as systems of visual signs.) But the achievement of this fluent literacy in a language foreign to most highly verbal people may be, in fact, the most remarkable accomplishment of a man whose basic bent is literary. Certainly it is one that from this point onward will be an evident delight in all of his work.

There is one more factor that makes *Manhattan* a crucial event in Woody's career. It was, Woody says, the beginning of his breakthrough in Europe, the film that helped him begin to gather the audience that would replace the defectors here. It is not entirely surprising. For one thing, Woody could license his films to state-owned, commercial-free television there, helping build his audience. (The rise of free cable and the VCR here has helped mitigate the effect of declining theatrical revenues.) But the main thing is, of course, that moviegoing remains an adult recreation on the Continent, where, in any case, the economic organization of the motion picture industry has from its beginnings revolved less around stars and genres, more around strong and singular authorial figures. Moreover, almost all the great ideas of what constitutes a desirable urban culture are European in origin. (Even now, Americans remain infected by Jeffersonian contempt for the city and tend to focus their nostalgic impulses on the innocence that was lost when we abandoned our formerly agrarian ways.) Then, too, the sophistication of the sexual arrangements examined in *Manhattan* and the cool manner of their presentation—no visible signs of shock, implicit rather than explicit moralism—were much more in their tradition than ours. Woody was becoming—thematically, stylistically, methodologically—a European filmmaker. And audiences here and abroad were picking up on that development and responding to it predictably.

He would require the kind of authorial tolerance Europeans habitually grant favored filmmakers. *Manhattan* had been both summarizing and predictive, an orchestration in a single film of Woody's largest gifts and preoccupations, and now he seemed to want to press on beyond it. But he did not do so confidently. The transitional passage to come was the most problematical he endured.

I admire *Stardust Memories* (1980) morally. It takes enormous courage for a well-known man to take up the subject of celebrity as a consequential social issue instead of as a personal nuisance. The more so since he chose to employ his own public persona, one that large numbers of people are convinced is a fairly straightforward projection of his private self, in the lead role. By playing a filmmaker whose comedies have been successful, but who finds his view of the world darkening, he obviously increased the risk that he would elicit precisely the kind of reaction he got: What's he complaining about? He's rich and famous, isn't he?

That's an awfully vulgar reading of the film. The response of Sandy Bates (Woody's character) to his predicament is much more complex and in some respects more touching than that. The movie's portrayal of a New York as malevolent as it was enticing in *Manhattan* is vividly done, and the portrayal of the all-too-archetypal weekend film seminar, offering a Sandy Bates retrospective, is marvelously mordant—the earnest idiocy of the higher movie fandom has never before been recognized fictionally, and it is hard to imagine anyone improving on Woody's surreal representation of it. But the ravenous movie moguls and functionaries who periodically appear to gnaw at Sandy's vitals are pop cultural clichés, borrowed from a thousand other tales of movie madness. And the appeal of at least one of the objects of Sandy's "unfathomable desires," Dorrie (Charlotte Rampling), is highly problematical. She is such an emotional mess, and she is presented so dispassionately, that she sours the center of the film irredeemably. Finally, Woody cannot seem to find a way to place an affectionate satirical edge on his *hommage* here. He imitates the Fellini manner expertly but seems unable to bring any authentic response of his own to it. Nor can he, as an actor, touch his Sandy with the humanity with which Marcello Mastroianni redeemed *8 ½*'s equally impossible Guido.

But if *Stardust Memories* is a failure, it is a more honorable and questing one than people allowed at the time. The next picture, *A Midsummer Night's Sex Comedy,* is something else again—the only entirely negligible movie Woody ever made. More "unfathomable desires," of course, and an expertly rendered Bergman mise-en-scène (taken over from *Smiles of a Summer Night*). But Woody's comedy is restrained and pallid; the setting, a turn-of-the-century country house party, is unsuited to his natural rhythms and subjects; and he does not want to risk too obviously anachronistic material in these surroundings. Finally, the obsessions which power his best work are muted in an antique mannerliness that Woody may admire, but which he does not fully comprehend. If the movie proves anything, it is that Woody requires the grounding of one or the other of his chosen milieus—the physical one of the city (it is their absence from it, not their presence in it, that agitates some of these characters) or the imaginative one of the movies (Woody's character here is an inventor experimenting with a vision-producing device, but imagistic hardware does not have the same stirring effect on his creator's imagination that imagistic software does).

The swing from the boldness of the previous picture to the timidity of this one was worrisome; one felt something had gone awry with Woody's previously steady inner compass. Perhaps understandably. As a man approaching his fifties he had to find a way of keeping his feet firmly planted on emotionally essential ground; whatever their current state in reality ("I'm not a big fan of reality," Woody murmured at one point in our talk), the *idea* of the movies as gracefully glamorous resort, the *idea* of the city as a gracefully civilized venue for people like himself had to be kept alive in his work. Direct assaults on their current ills had not worked for him in *Stardust Memories;* ignoring both topics had not worked for him in *A Midsummer Night's Sex Comedy.* Certainly at this late date he could not return to the kind of direct and abrasively comic confrontations with himself (more properly, the fictionalized version of himself) which had energized his earliest work. Nor was the parody-*hommage* really an option anymore. He had done all that as well as he or anyone else was likely to do it.

The answer as it turned out lay in intensification. Between 1983 and 1987 he produced a group of three films (interspersed with two others somewhat less strong)—*Zelig, The Purple Rose of Cairo,* and *Radio Days*—that are fictions in the highest sense of the word—that is to say, they are the imaginative projections based on a highly selective and compressed recall of the past. We are not in the realm of nostalgia here, which is the usual movie mode when addressing the immediate past. For nostalgia is a form of generalization, in which highly familiar objects—a *Casablanca* poster, say, the Betty Grable pinup, and a recording of "In the Mood"—are used to summon up a historical moment some of us really shared and a lot of others are beginning to think they shared thanks to the easy availability of pop cultural icons from every era. This stuff can put us in a pleasantly relaxed mood. But it does not deeply stir us because it does not evoke authentic memories, which are highly personal and highly specific. In other words, no one is going to glance at an old Lucky Strike ad and start writing his or her *Remembrance of Things Past.*

One suspects, however, that these three movies of Woody's were triggered initially by some profoundly personal encounter with the past, that they are true memory plays, in which pleasing fictions are authenticated by a recollection so pungent that it need not even be mentioned in order for it to do its work. Of the three, *Zelig* is the most intricate and resonant construct. It is, of course, a parody documentary, composed of real and brilliantly faked newsreel clips blended seamlessly together, to which the other kinds of antique visual material (also faked) we are used to encountering in compilation films—stills, home movies, newspaper headlines, even scientific footage, and clips from a fictionalized B movie biopic alleged to have been made about the eponymous subject—have been added. This odd lot is held together by a blandly informative, never insightful, voice-over narration, and occasionally contemporary intellectuals (Saul Bellow, Susan Sontag, Bruno Bettelheim) give their analyses of the peculiar life and times of Leonard Zelig.

At its simplest level the film functions as a parody of the most traditional kind of documentary, the sort of clunky cultural-historical journalism that still finds a regular place on the PBS schedule. But parody is not an end in itself here; it is a means to an end. Nor is technique an end in itself, though, in fact, this may be the most brilliant special-effects picture ever made, precisely because it employs the same vast range of optical trickery to create its imaginary world that the creators of *Star Wars* used to create its, but does so without calling attention to itself. Woody and his colleagues, notably Gordon Willis and Susan E. Morse, the very gifted editor who has been with him since *Manhattan,* are trying to paper over completely the line that usually separates illusion from reality in movies, a line that at some level we never forget no matter how deeply we are absorbed by the action on the screen.

Zelig is a paradigmatic figure of our century, a man without talent by any traditional definition, who seeks fame for its own sake and ultimately achieves it, a man without character in any traditional sense who ultimately achieves at least the status of a "character." He is a sort of human chameleon, who, precisely because he is so psychologically featureless, can intrude himself in the public life of his times with impunity—and eventually achieve notoriety because of these stunts. Here he is with Eugene O'Neill, here he is with Calvin Coolidge—and so on through the roster of 1920's and 1930's celebrityhood. What a rich figure he is. The ultimate fan, of course, the Everyman who believes proximity with the accomplished and the notorious may grant him magical powers. The ultimate actor, perhaps, endlessly trying out for a role in the biggest movie of them all—twentieth-century life. The ultimate victim, very likely, of the information explosion, which has placed so many role models before us that anyone lacking a powerful sense of vocation, a magnificent obsession, as it were, is bound to try on in fantasy as many different roles as *People* magazine can propose. At any rate, in *Zelig* Woody faces the whole issue of celebrity with the indirection that art requires and that he could not find through the direct confrontation he attempted in *Stardust Memories*.

And the source of this triumph is memory. The newsreels and the newspaper halftones of our childhoods, Woody's and mine, offered us many Zeligs, public figures that grown-ups seemed to understand but whose functions were mysterious to us—Bernard Baruch, Elsa Maxwell, Grover Whelan, that crowd. We were innocently correct about them: They had no real function except to help fill journalistic time and space. Some of us grew up to understand that and grew up to understand as well that they were paradigms for the more extensive celebrity system to come, in which, even if fame originally derives from authentic achievement, it ultimately detaches from its source to become a kind of self-fulfilling prophecy. Somewhere in the workaholism of the man who made *Zelig* and a critic who admires it inordinately, there abides the fear that if we relax, let down our guard, the Zelig inside us will out.

The Purple Rose of Cairo (1985) is an equally original conceit. It is the story of Cecilia, a socially and sexually downcast movie fan (brilliantly played by Farrow), who is trapped in a brutal marriage and an awful job. One day one of her dreamboats comes down off the screen where he is appearing in the eponymously titled movie-within-the-movie. He wishes to romance her in real life, then takes her back up on the screen for a taste of reel life. Her existence, though it is photographed in softly glowing color by Willis, reminds one of the early passages of an old Joan Crawford movie, something like the 1931 *Possessed,* in which her home is a shack, her job (in a cardboard box factory) is a sweaty nightmare, and her first costume is a housedress. In that film she is spotted by a swell, lounging on the observation platform of a rich man's private railroad car and invited to join the party around the white pianos of the New York penthouse set. In other words, a fantasy is presented as a realistic, if farfetched, option. Structurally Woody's film imitates the old one, whether consciously and specifically I cannot say (there were many such movies a half century ago). For the movie life Cecilia is invited to enter is a parody version of that life which Crawford took up (at the price of her virtue) so long ago in the second half of *Possessed.* People in evening dress shake up pitchers of martinis, go to smart clubs, exchange seemingly sophisticated badinage, and have not a care in the world; they lark off to the Middle East in search of madcap adventure, quipping all the way. They are, in short, citizens of, symbols in, that old urban dream of Woody's, everybody's.

There is, however, one salient difference between Woody's film and its models. Here (in contrast with *Zelig*) the moral is to be found not in blurring the line between fantasy and reality but in rigidly maintaining it. He may not be "a big fan" of reality, but he knows that madness is, by definition, losing your grip on it. He will permit his heroine to be inspired by the dreamworld, but not to surrender to it. In other words, she is Zelig's exact opposite. If *The Purple Rose of Cairo* reflects, once again, the intensity of Woody's own relationship with the movies—the thralldom in which they have held him since childhood and his grown-up sense of the dangers inherent in the power they exercise over some of us—the point is put with great subtlety and enormous charm. It is a wonderfully playful movie, especially when Cecilia's dream lover (played with disarmingly boyish egotism by Jeff Daniels) attempts to apply heroic movie solutions to real-life issues. Again, the parodic elements in this film are not an end in themselves,—indeed, the references to one film form, the Joan Crawford "woman's" picture, are completely hidden—and the movie-within-the-movie finally functions less as a parody of a specific genre than as an example of the all-encompassing movie composed of our memories of hundreds of actual productions that each of us cuts together, plays on a loop in our minds, and, yes, acts in all of our lives.

Remembered fantasy is also the subject of *Radio Days* (1987). Structurally it appears at first glance to be much simpler than the other films in this trilogy. Voice-over Woody recalls some archetypal radio shows of his childhood and demonstrates how the dreams they beamed into everyone's home caused a certain amount of goofy emulative behavior in a little boy who is apparently a fictional version of himself and among various of his relatives, neighbors, and friends. These programs are hilariously visualized as the mind's eye of a long-ago listener might have imagined them. There is a certain poignancy in the proximity of the film's radio fans to the source of their enchantment. They are residents of Brooklyn; the broadcasts they tune in emanate mainly from Manhattan, just across the river: so near and yet so far.

That proximity lends credibility to one more element in the film, gossipy tales and speculation about the real lives of the radio stars fed to listeners via the radio fan magazines and newspaper columns. In the case of this film's characters these stories were supplemented by first- or at least secondhand information brought back from the magic place across the river by commuting Brooklynites, who in those days habitually referred to it as "the city." These stars unquestionably lent *Manhattan* some of its glamour for outlanders, especially since radio personalities were among the most mysterious, therefore fascinating, celebrities we have ever known—or, rather, not known. Their voices were as familiar to us as the faces of the movie stars—perhaps more so, since we were in touch with them every week, sometimes every day, instead of three or four times a year, and in the privacy of our own homes at that. Yet they were at the same time remote and even godlike creatures, for we did not, could not know what they looked like, might pass one of them on the street and never know it. We were thus encouraged to very free, quite awed imaginative reconstruction of their selves and lives, using as building materials a curious mixture of hard gossip and soft fantasies. In *Radio Days,* when broadcasters are shown away from their microphones, it is in these oddly mixed terms, and it grants the film its singular air, innocent and yearning.

There were two other qualities about radio that set it apart from the other media. The first was that unlike the movies, it had the capacity to communicate reality along with fantasy. Indeed, the ease with which this new and unprecedented medium could get a man with a microphone to a place where news was happening, and get his reports on the air was often very disturbing. No one then was practiced in handling the ability of an electronic medium to shrink the geographical and emotional distance between event and audience. Moreover, since there were no pictures to help tie these reports to recognizable reality, they had a roiling power on our imaginations that was unprecedented and remains unduplicated. Woody gets at this point very powerfully late in the movie, when radio takes up its watch as rescuers attempt to save a child trapped in a cave-in. This is a medium of happy endings, of dreams fulfilled; the listeners expect, almost as a right, a comfortable, comforting conclusion. When the rescue fails and the child dies, the shock is profound. In the film it plays almost as if, out of nowhere, the topic of original sin had been raised, insisted upon. Woody touches very lightly on that point, passes on quickly, but of his many meditations on mortality and on the confusions between reality and fantasy created by the modern media, none is more powerful than this one.

The other astonishing thing about radio is the way it evanesced. Yes, of course, it is still with us, but as an accompaniment to our lives, a sort of existential wallpaper we live with every day without really noticing. But as a compelling force, something we took account of in planning our days, something we really took in emotionally, its days were brutally brief. And this is a point Woody puts very forcefully. To that little boy listening in, radio is an institution he can no more imagine disappearing than he can the other crucial institution in his life, his family. His attitude regarding the medium is matched by the prospering, privileged people he shows us working in it. They are last glimpsed confidently welcoming in a 1940's New Year on a Manhattan hotel rooftop, the lights of the magical city, also seemingly impervious to change, glowing all about them. But the narrator, looking back, knows: Radio, as he then knew it, has only a few historical moments still to live; the great city that nurtured it is soon to enter upon its decline; and mortality and happenstance will simultaneously begin to erode the family's circle. The film's last shot is of the radio people turning back down the steps to reenter the hotel, beginning a descent not to hell but to reality, ordinariness. Once again memory has been used not for nostalgic purposes but to light our way, to propose a meditation on how "all that is solid melts into air"—which is, of course, the most basic of modernist themes.

The two films that intersperse this trilogy strike me as far less resonant. *Broadway Danny Rose* (1984) is also a memory piece. A group of Borscht Belt comics sit around a table in the Carnegie Deli, recalling the amazing career the title character, a small-time Broadway agent, ferociously loyal to the grotesquely inept acts he books for parties, small clubs, and Catskill resorts, who falls in love with a mob moll (another remarkable performance by Farrow) and somehow survives it all on gall, energy, and bravura articulateness. The film, shot in black-and-white, is oddly timeless. The clothing and decor are now; the attitudes are then—that is, more common to the first New York Woody ever encountered as a grown-up. He was very much the little Brooklyn boy of *Radio Days* now free to explore "the city" on his own recognizance for the first time.

When he talked about *Danny Rose* to me, he recalled his first Manhattan visit. "My father first brought me to the city in 1941, and I remember getting out of the subway at Forty-second Street and seeing for the first time thirty theaters standing in a row. To this day I always have a Runyonesque feeling when I'm in the streets. Cole Porter's New York I'm always trying to find." And in fact, much of his young manhood was tied up with this nervously juking and jiving "main stem." It was to Broadway columnists that as a teenager he sold jokes which they put in the mouths of celebrities; it was along these neon-lit streets that as a young writer for television shows like Sid Caesar's and Garry Moore's he achieved his first recognition; it was characters from this world, like Neil Simon's older brother, whose name perhaps not uncoincidentally is Danny, who taught him the basics of the gag writer's craft. This picture is a tribute to the New York of his professional beginnings and, as it happens, mine, too. I arrived from the prairies carrying the same imagistic baggage he brought from equally remote Brooklyn. I found that as a young journalist I could afford to eat in the "old" Lindy's when I arrived in the fifties, and most of the institutions that had been landmarks of legendary Broadway—Jack Dempsey's with its great clam bar, the Optimo cigar store with its wall of phone booths allowing young actors to make their calls and study the passing parade—were still in place and functioning. The district was raffish but not trashy—and not dangerous. And the evocation of emotions attending our discovery of this territory in *Broadway Danny Rose* is touching to me.

Especially as it is all gone now. Runyon's New York has faded at the same pace as Porter's; both are the merest shadows of their former selves. But Woody's evocation of the first glamorous world he was permitted to know intimately is of a different quality from his evocations of the world he was permitted only to imagine. His attitudes toward it are more ambivalent; he once told a critic that his recollections of his days as a TV gag writer were mostly of "an infernal noise" as he and his colleagues competed to get their gags and skits accepted. And precisely because this was a very small and specialized society, the source of fewer thinner fantasies for the rest of us, its resonances are not as profound as those of high society New York. Its energy—talk about "vulgar vitality"—is compelling, and there is authentic affection for the brash characters who set the tone of Woody's first and only trade school. But there are limits on this material. Finally, it resists full imaginative transformation.

Hannah and Her Sisters, despite its profitable, accidental connection with the emerging—and perhaps already submerging—yuppie zeitgeist of the mid-1980's, also reverberates less strongly for me than most of Woody's other work in this decade. Pauline Kael sneeringly dismissed it as "a romance of gentrification," which is much too harsh a judgment. Woody brings to this story authentic emotion—and novelty—in two of its crucial aspects. Quite simply the relationship between female siblings fascinates him. It was a principal subject of *Interiors,* of course, and he told me he traces this concern back to childhood. His mother was one of seven sisters, most of whom produced girl children when they married. He was brought up surrounded by "their expression of emotions for one another." Then, coincidentally, some of the significant women of his adult years—Janet Margolin, Diane Keaton, and now Mia Farrow (who plays Hannah)—all had more than one sister. "I don't know, could you get at the same sort of family emotions through brothers?" Woody asks. "I don't think so. All that manly reserve." I think he might have gone even further in examining their jealousies and affections, but I must also admit that few American films have gone any distance at all in anatomizing family ties in a thoughtful, unmelodramatic way.

Then there is the interesting romantic enigma at *Hannah*'s dramatic center. It is stated through an affair that develops between Hannah's husband, Elliot (played by Michael Caine), and her youngest and most vulnerable sister, Lee (Barbara Hershey). This is potentially slippery ground—hard to tread while satisfying both dramatic imperative and good taste. Yet it is, for Woody, inescapable ground, another example of desire's unfathomability, and he is at pains to make Elliot's behavior less explicable than anything similar in his earlier movies: The man has every reason to be happy with Hannah, no reasonable excuse for cheating on her with anyone, let alone with her sister. Nor does Lee have any grievances with Hannah, though Lee does have the consequences of her own former unfathomableness to try to escape—a marriage to the most chillingly bloodless, intellectual (Max Von Sydow) Woody has ever written. He seems to be saying that it is precisely the near incestuousness of the Elliot-Lee relationship that makes it irresistible, and that is a coolly daring, and true, point to make.

Still, when all is said and done, *Hannah* obviously represents a reversion to and an updating of *Manhattan*'s material. It is not a step forward of the kind he made in the fantasy trilogy. Woody himself is back in it in something like his old guise, as Mickey Sachs, a TV comedy producer whose career is frantic with meaningless activity and who must submit to and await the results of a battery of tests that will tell him if he has a fatal illness. Once again, he is trying to joke death away, and in yuppie America, where everyone is trying to distract the grim reaper with jogging, dieting, and other healthful strenuosities, this has become perhaps a more generally riveting subject than it formerly was. Taken together with Woody's return to type as an actor, it may help explain some of the film's popularity. So, too, may cinematographer Carlos De Palma's glowing realizations of New York—less stylized, a deceptive touch more realistic than Willis's in *Manhattan*—which play on the devotion of this new class to preserving, protecting, and admiring the urban environment. But frankly, *Hannah* does not have the originality or the symbolic power of the earlier work. And what is true of the imagery must be said of the film as a whole. We have, in essence, met these relentlessly articulate people in restless pursuit of libidinal outrages before. If there are curiosities and originalities in their characterizations, the fact remains that they do not strike us with the force of the new that their *Manhattan* predecessors did in 1979.

One thinks: When you reach a certain age, it becomes more and more difficult to confront reality directly. Especially contemporary reality. In my own fifties I find myself drawn to movies—to art in general—that are highly stylized or use the past or the future as a metaphor by which to examine not so much current conditions as that which is—dare one use the pompous word?—universal in them. One craves, finally, visionary and transforming representations of life, not the real thing. Of those, at a certain point in our lives, we all have had quite enough. It seems to me that Woody's spirit congeals somewhat when, dutifully, because it seems the moral and striving thing to do, he tries to confront the psychopathology of everyday middle-class life. (Whose does not?) It is that shrinking—it is like a slight, involuntary flinch—that one perceives in his spirit, not the deliberate lack of humor that makes something like *Interiors* or *September* so chilly. The latter is, however, distinguished by a subtle elegance with the camera, and by Sam Waterston's interesting sketch of a writer blocked by lack of conviction (one wonders if something of Woody's mood as he wrote this script didn't seep into this figure). Moreover, since it deals soberly with what is for Allen the central issue bedeviling the leisure of the theory class, its inability to make emotional connections, it very clearly prefigures his next film, *Another Woman,* which is, despite its generally dim critical reception, quite the best of his "serious" films, precisely because it has a wit that his other work in this vein lacks.

No, I did not say jokes. I said wit, which is integral to the structure of the movie. The nature and situation of Marion, its protagonist, whose disassociations from her emotions (and her own personal history) are very subtly and bravely portrayed by the great Gena Rowlands, are without precedent in American movies. She plays a philosopher on sabbatical to write a book. To further that enterprise she sublets an apartment, where she can find both solitude and what she hopes will be a slight, stimulating change in her routines. She gets rather more than she bargained for, because a quirk of architecture permits her to overhear conversations in the flat next door. Since it is a psychiatrist's office, she is soon privy to high emotions of the kind she has steadfastly ruled out of her own life. And though she tries to resist the temptation to eavesdrop, she cannot. Particularly when a young woman (Farrow), great with child and great with all sorts of inchoate feelings, is on the couch.

This is, as I said when I reviewed the film, a premise another filmmaker—even the young Woody Allen—might have used as the basis for farce or romantic comedy. But no, Marion senses this woman, whose name is not accidentally Hope, as a sort of double—someone not unlike herself who has embraced rather than shunned life's emotional risks (she is, for example, carrying a child; Marion, we learn, chose abortion the only time she was pregnant). This is, obviously, a variation on the theme Bergman developed in his masterpiece, *Persona,* but though Woody even has Sven Nyquist, Bergman's cameraman, with him here, *Another Woman* is not an *hommage* in the usual sense. It is a much subtler acknowledgment by one artist of another's influence on him. In any event, Marion is soon following her double in the street, finally even encountering her and engaging her in conversation. These strayings from her well-worn path lead to other encounters, both real and in dreams and reveries, with figures from her past (her emotionally devastated father and brother, a friend and lovers she betrayed), and finally to a confrontation with the emptiness of her present life. (Lunching with Hope she sees her husband and one of their best friends sharing a meal, and by their attitudes understands they are having an affair.) The film becomes, in the last analysis, an exploration of that moment in midlife at which we are all called upon to count the cost not of our incautions, but our cautions, and as such it makes a firmer connection, I think, with a near-universal preoccupation than Woody's other "serious" films do. It is, God help us, "relevant" in ways that they are not.

And, beyond the wit and originality of the story it tells, it offers another form of wit that the films akin to it in tone do not. This is a very restrained, even duplicitous, verbal wit. Marion narrates her own story in a language of great formality, dry and cliché-laden, exactly what you might expect from a philosopher trying—and failing—to find the words she needs to express not ideas but events and emotions. These words, by the way, are spoken by Rowlands in an extremely flat manner, as if she were trying to objectify them still further, turn her life, in its recounting, into a kind of case history. The writing and the playing both strike me as highly courageous and subtle renunciations. Yet many reviewers did not see this for what it was, a triumph of subtle obser-vation, but as a failure of imagination. It is such a simple point to see: self-irony, self-humor would have saved Marion, and it is precisely this attribute that her creators must deny her if she is to be a plausible, indeed exemplary, figure. But then, of course, in the busy reviewer's life, it is always easier to criticize a film for not being what you want it to be than it is to come to grips with what it is, and what it aspires to be.

Even admiring *Another Woman,* and thinking that Woody has achieved in it more of what he wants for himself (as opposed to what we want from him), I find it difficult to leave there—high and dry-minded, as it were. For in the last analysis it does not make any dif-ference how one judges any one film of Woody's or how one finally ranks it in the body of his work. It is, as he said to me of Ingmar Bergman's films: "It's almost irrelevant to say you like this one better than that one, to say I like *The Seventh Seal* better than I like *Shame.* They are all aspects of him." They are all, in fact, aspects of a com-mitment that is ultimately and consciously resistant to trends, fads, shifts in critical fashion, that stakes everything on creating an edifice large enough and sturdy enough to resist time's passage and to submit itself to posterity's judgment.

It is a commitment of this order that Woody Allen—alone of Amer-ican filmmakers—has made. The result is a capacious, continuously growing group of films that will unquestionably define our times as they were experienced by the most significant segment of our society—that which passed for an elite—for future times better than any body of screen work made in this country in this era. "I don't want to gain immortality in my works," Woody has famously cracked. "I want to gain it by not dying." Too bad, he is going to have to settle for the former—no matter what he thinks of his achievement when the dark mood is on him. And live with the fact that he has not had to die—or to refrain from making jokes—in order to gain the considered respect of at least some of his not entirely frivolous countrymen.

INDEX

INDEX

INDEX

INDEX

INDEX

INDEX

INDEX

INDEX

INDEX

311

INDEX